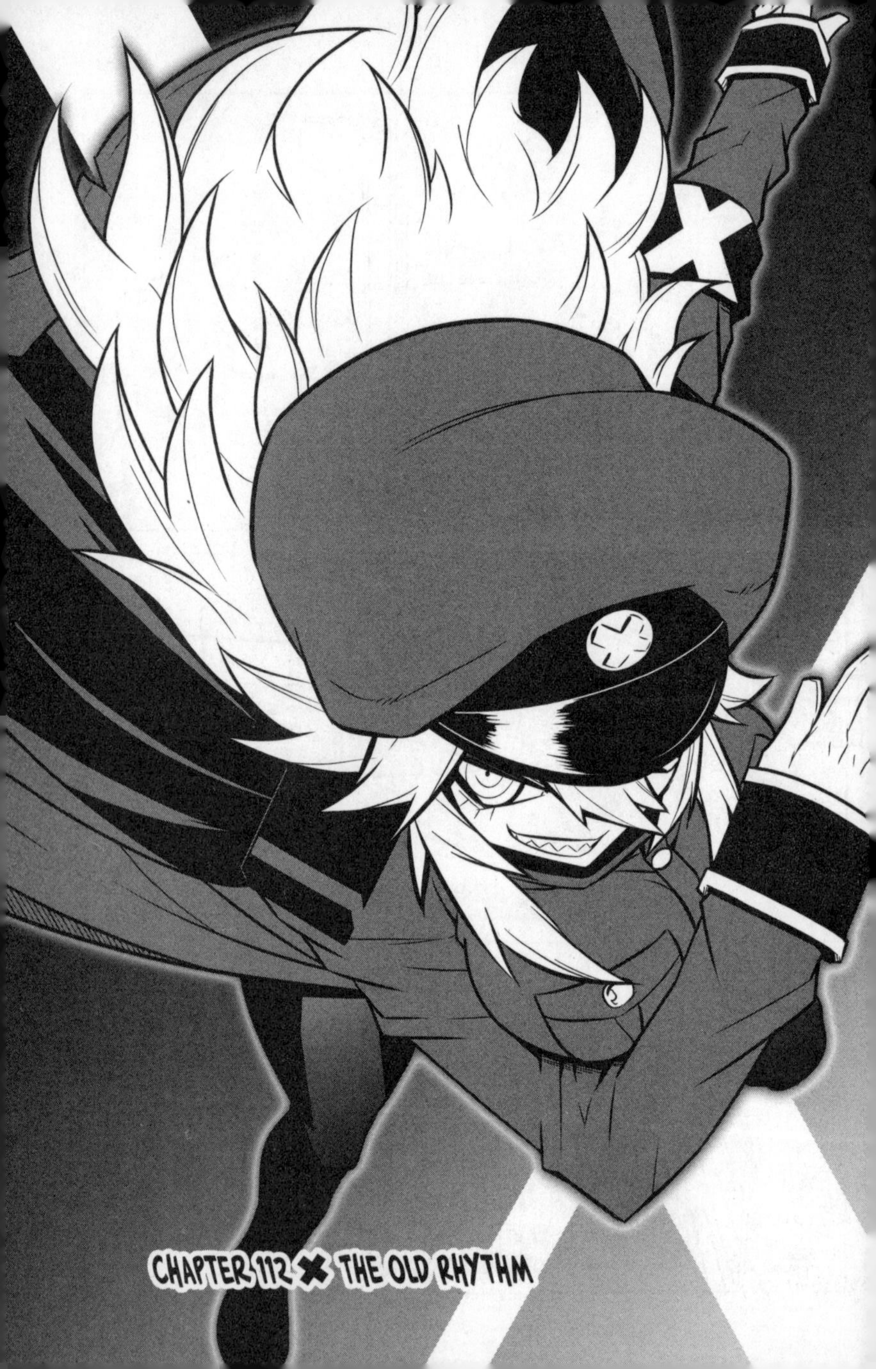
CHAPTER 112 ✖ THE OLD RHYTHM

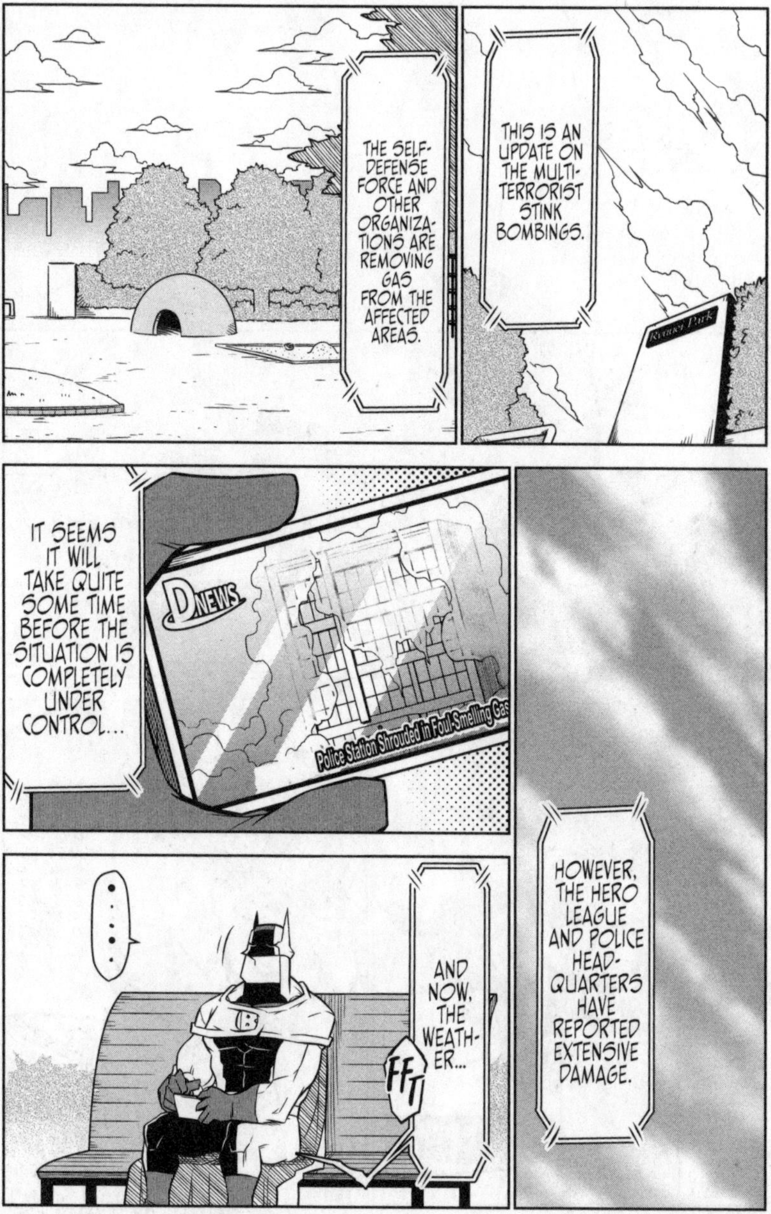
THIS IS AN UPDATE ON THE MULTI-TERRORIST STINK BOMBINGS.
THE SELF-DEFENSE FORCE AND OTHER ORGANIZATIONS ARE REMOVING GAS FROM THE AFFECTED AREAS.
HOWEVER, THE HERO LEAGUE AND POLICE HEAD-QUARTERS HAVE REPORTED EXTENSIVE DAMAGE.
IT SEEMS IT WILL TAKE QUITE SOME TIME BEFORE THE SITUATION IS COMPLETELY UNDER CONTROL...
DNEWS
Police Station Shrouded in Foul-Smelling Gas
AND NOW, THE WEATH-ER...
FFT
.....

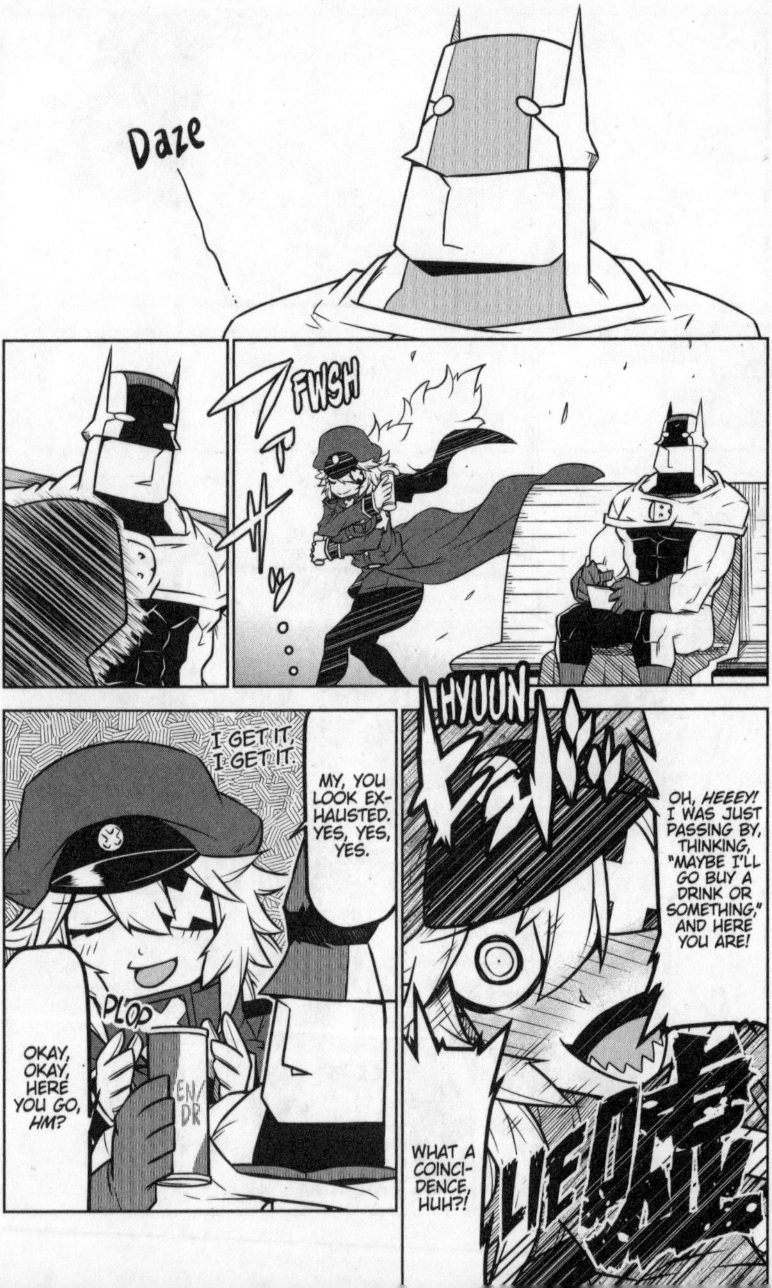
Daze
FWSH
HYUUN
OH, *HEEEY!* I WAS JUST PASSING BY, THINKING, "MAYBE I'LL GO BUY A DRINK OR SOMETHING," AND HERE YOU ARE!
WHAT A COINCI-DENCE, HUH?!
MY, YOU LOOK EX-HAUSTED. YES, YES, YES.
I GET IT, I GET IT.
PLOP
OKAY, OKAY, HERE YOU GO, *HM?*

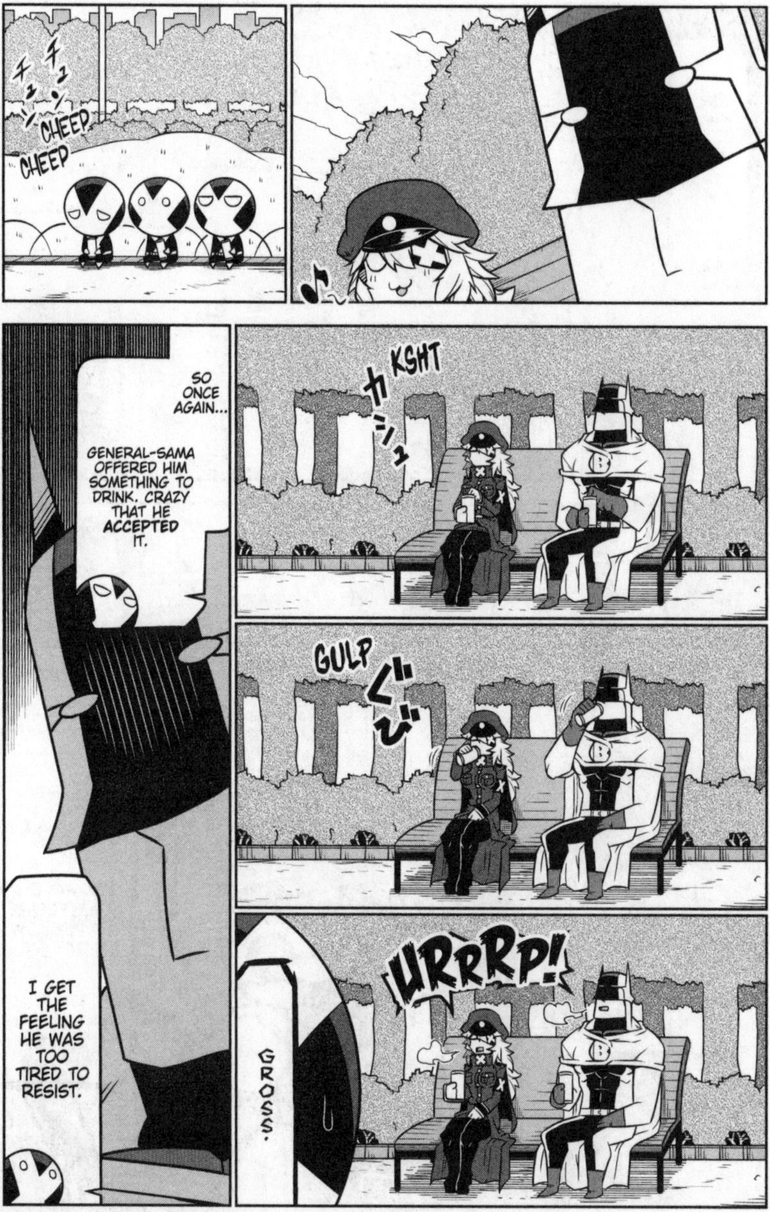
チュンチュン
CHEEP
CHEEP
KSHT
カシュ
GULP
ぐびび
URRRP!
GROSS.
SO ONCE AGAIN...
GENERAL-SAMA OFFERED HIM SOMETHING TO DRINK. CRAZY THAT HE ACCEPTED IT.
I GET THE FEELING HE WAS TOO TIRED TO RESIST.

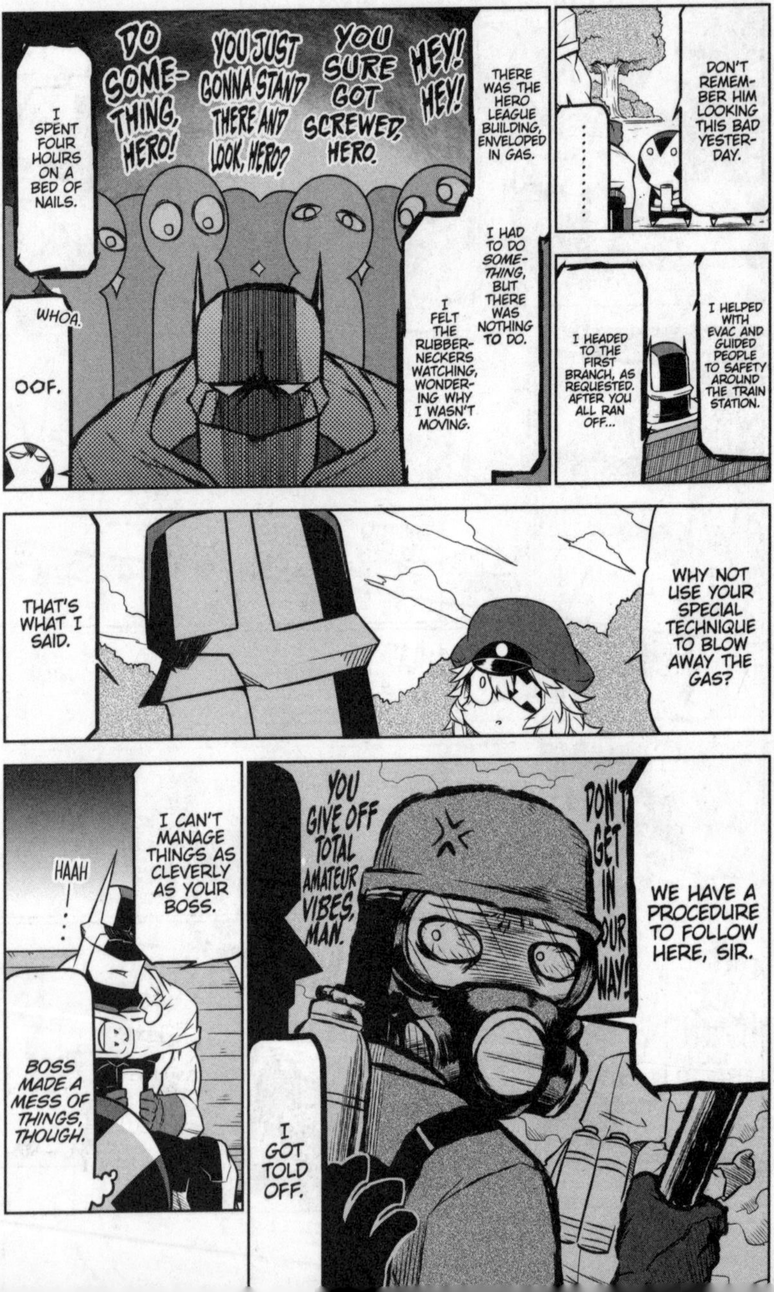
DON'T REMEMBER HIM LOOKING THIS BAD YESTERDAY.
......
I HELPED WITH EVAC AND GUIDED PEOPLE TO SAFETY AROUND THE TRAIN STATION.
I HEADED TO THE FIRST BRANCH, AS REQUESTED. AFTER YOU ALL RAN OFF...
THERE WAS THE HERO LEAGUE BUILDING, ENVELOPED IN GAS.
I HAD TO DO SOMETHING, BUT THERE WAS NOTHING TO DO.
I FELT THE RUBBERNECKERS WATCHING, WONDERING WHY I WASN'T MOVING.
HEY! HEY!
YOU SURE GOT SCREWED, HERO.
YOU JUST GONNA STAND THERE AND LOOK, HERO?
DO SOMETHING, HERO!
I SPENT FOUR HOURS ON A BED OF NAILS.
WHOA.
OOF.
WHY NOT USE YOUR SPECIAL TECHNIQUE TO BLOW AWAY THE GAS?
THAT'S WHAT I SAID.
WE HAVE A PROCEDURE TO FOLLOW HERE, SIR.
DON'T GET IN OUR WAY!
YOU GIVE OFF TOTAL AMATEUR VIBES, MAN.
I GOT TOLD OFF.
I CAN'T MANAGE THINGS AS CLEVERLY AS YOUR BOSS.
HAAH!...
BOSS MADE A MESS OF THINGS, THOUGH.

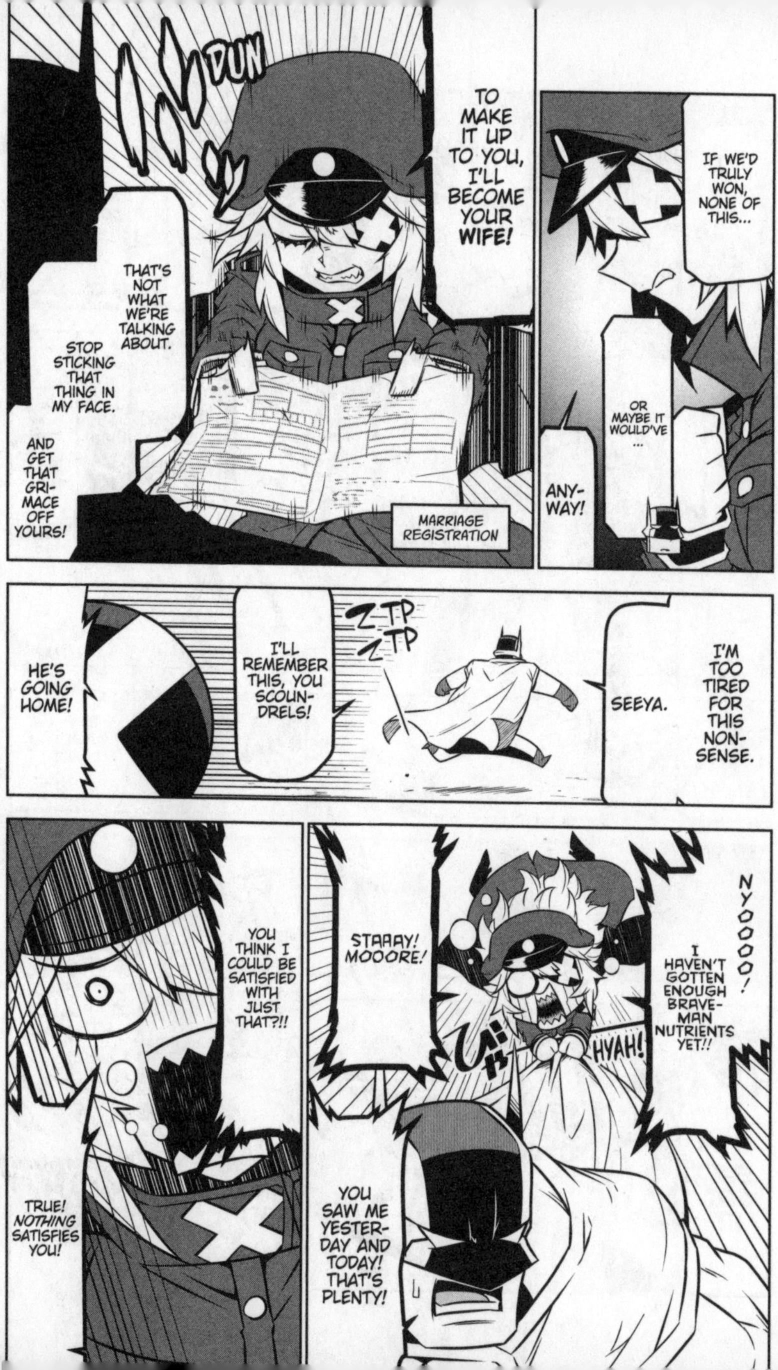
IF WE'D TRULY WON, NONE OF THIS...
OR MAYBE IT WOULD'VE ...
ANY-WAY!
TO MAKE IT UP TO YOU, I'LL BECOME YOUR WIFE!
DUN
THAT'S NOT WHAT WE'RE TALKING ABOUT.
STOP STICKING THAT THING IN MY FACE.
AND GET THAT GRI-MACE OFF YOURS!
MARRIAGE REGISTRATION
I'M TOO TIRED FOR THIS NON-SENSE.
SEEYA.
ZTP ZTP
I'LL REMEMBER THIS, YOU SCOUN-DRELS!
HE'S GOING HOME!
NYOOOOO!
I HAVEN'T GOTTEN ENOUGH BRAVE-MAN NUTRIENTS YET!!
HYAH!
STAAAY! MOOORE!
YOU SAW ME YESTER-DAY AND TODAY! THAT'S PLENTY!
YOU THINK I COULD BE SATISFIED WITH JUST THAT?!!
TRUE! NOTHING SATISFIES YOU!

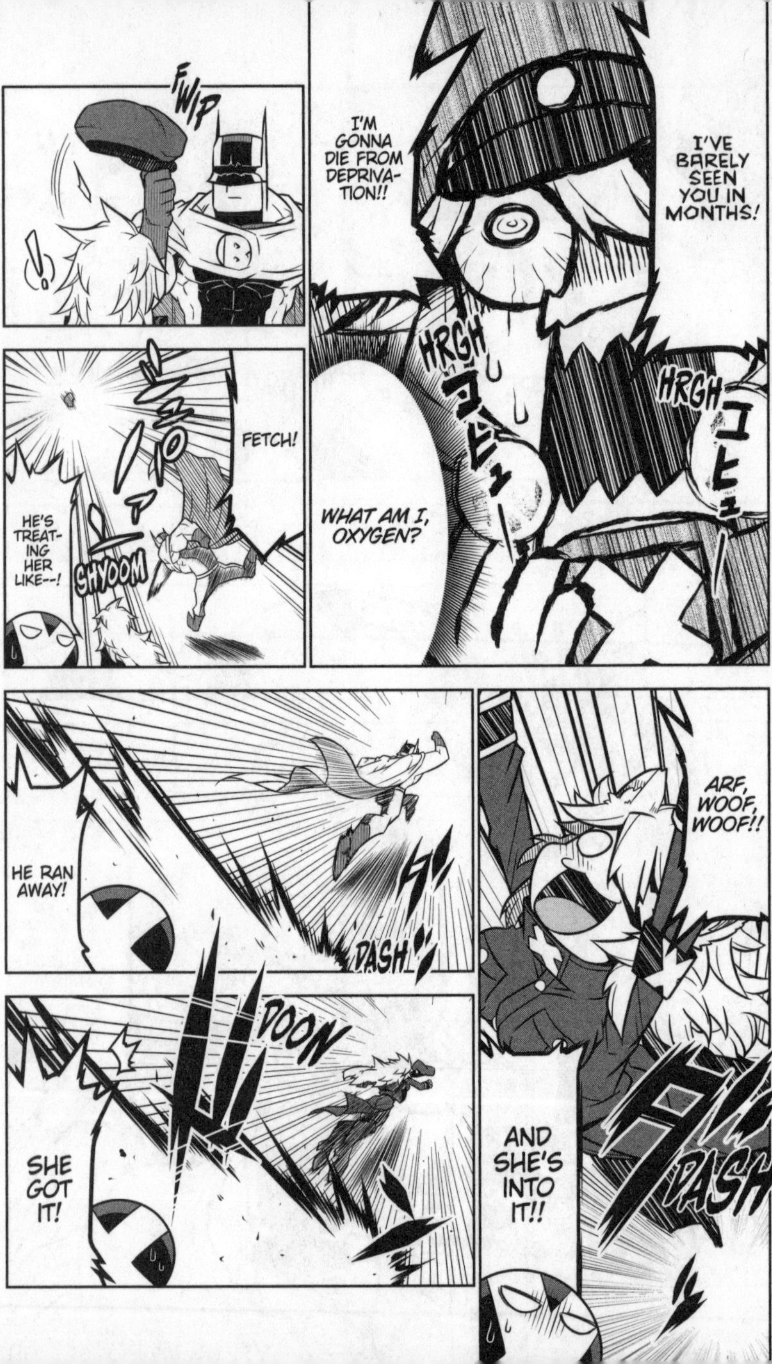

I'VE BARELY SEEN YOU IN MONTHS!
I'M GONNA DIE FROM DEPRIVATION!!
HRGH
HRGH
WHAT AM I, OXYGEN?
FWIP
FETCH!
HE'S TREATING HER LIKE--!
SHYOOM
ARF, WOOF, WOOF!!
DASH
AND SHE'S INTO IT!!
HE RAN AWAY!
DASH
DOON
SHE GOT IT!

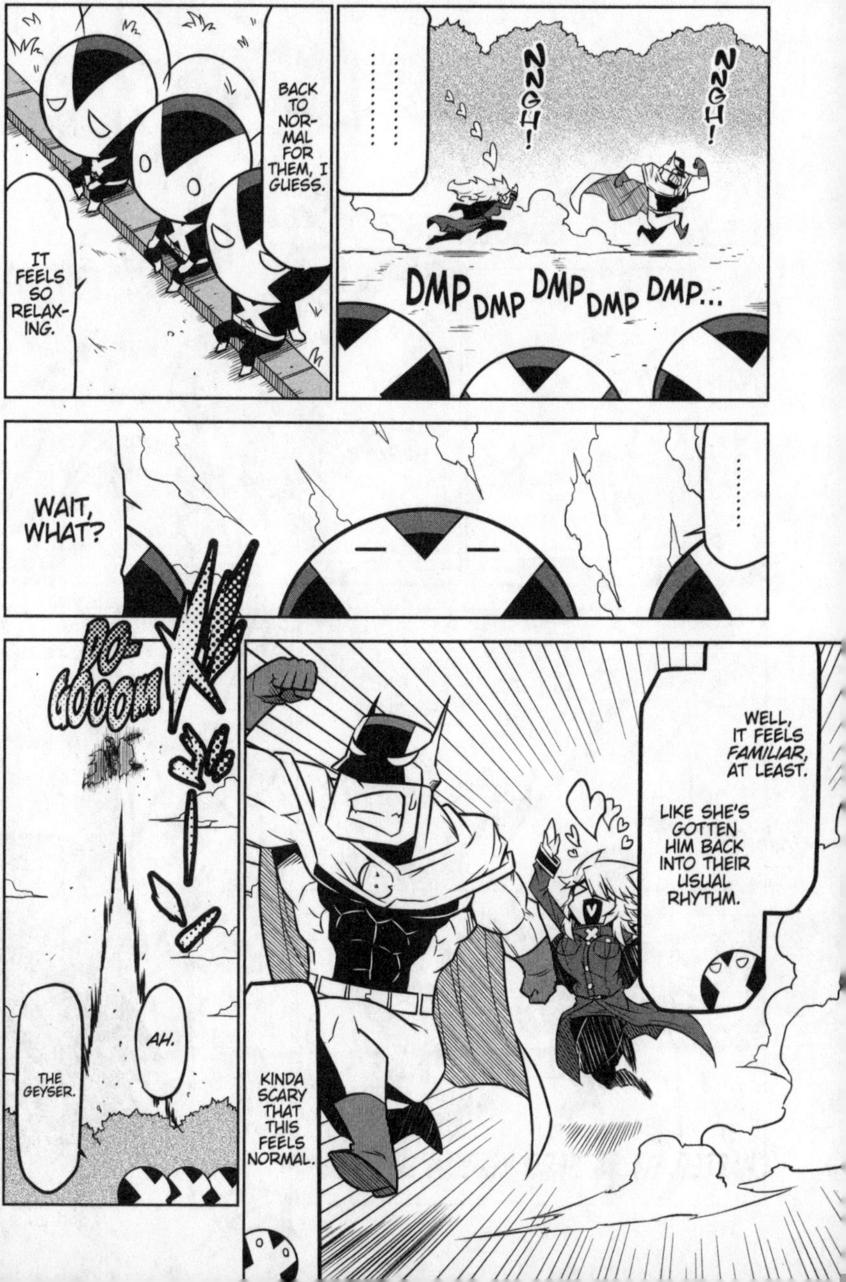
NNGH!
NNGH!
……
DMP DMP DMP DMP DMP…
BACK TO NORMAL FOR THEM, I GUESS.
IT FEELS SO RELAXING.
……
WAIT, WHAT?
WELL, IT FEELS *FAMILIAR*, AT LEAST.
LIKE SHE'S GOTTEN HIM BACK INTO THEIR USUAL RHYTHM.
KINDA SCARY THAT THIS FEELS NORMAL.
DO-GOOOM
AH.
THE GEYSER.

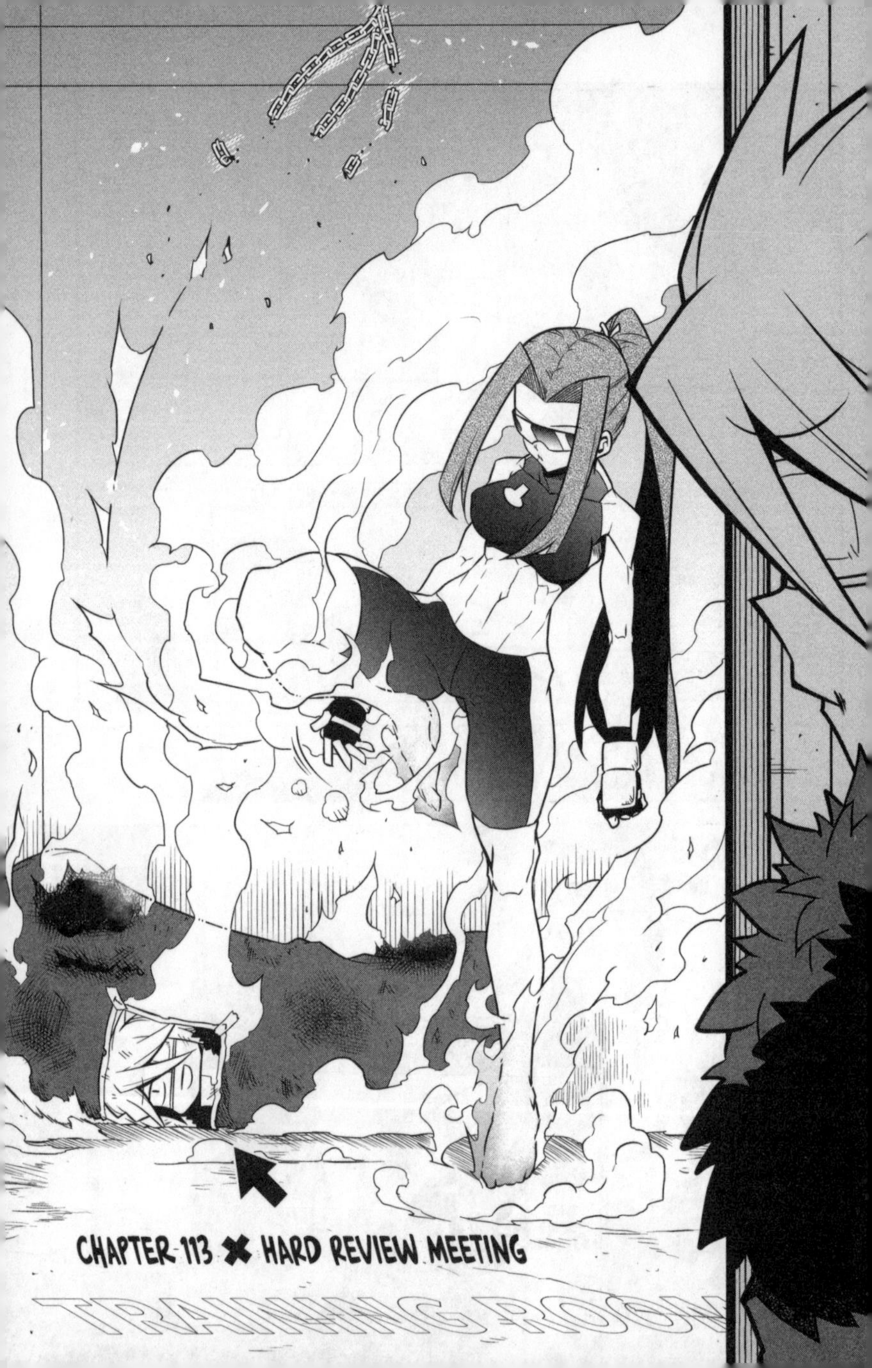

CHAPTER 113 ✖ HARD REVIEW MEETING
TRAINING ROOM

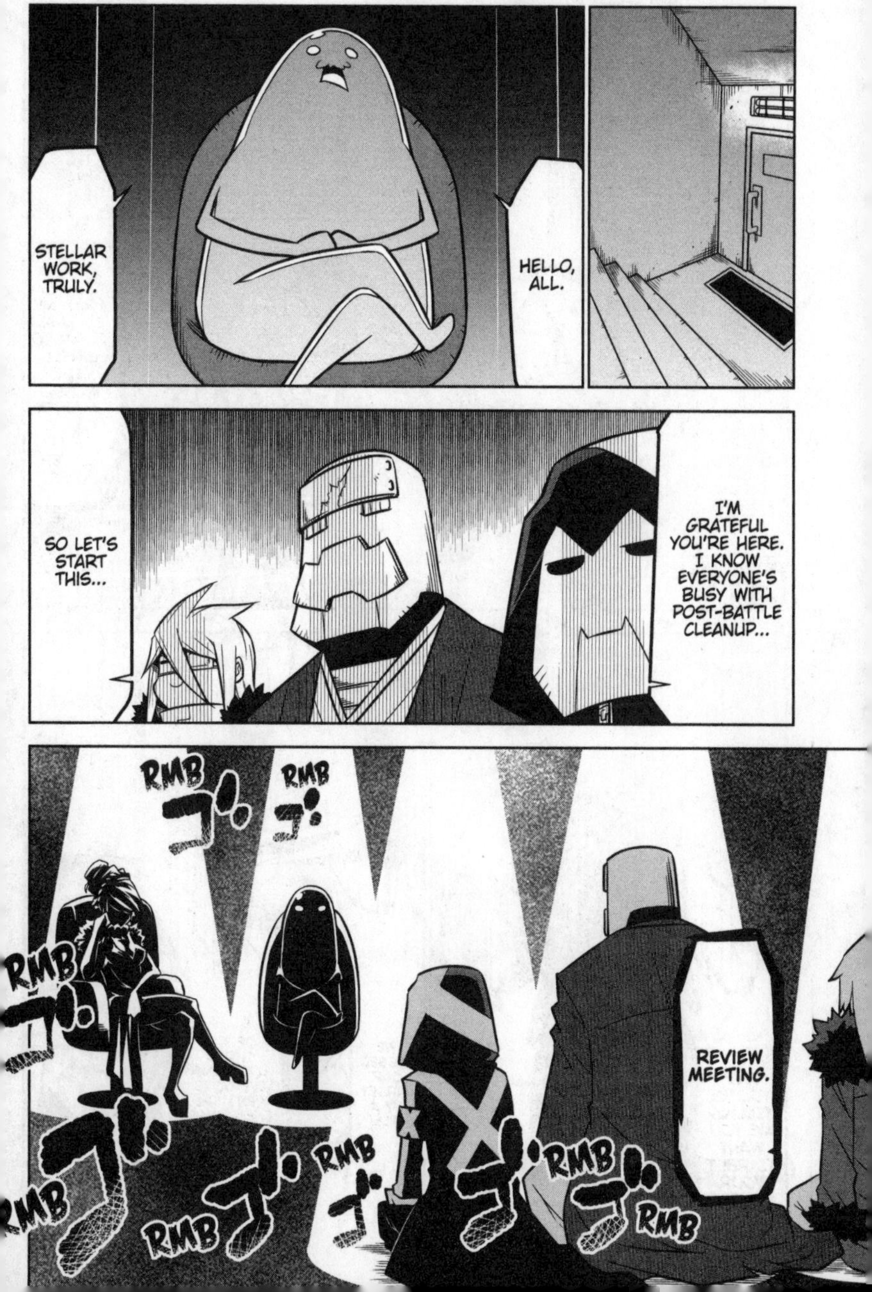
HELLO, ALL.
STELLAR WORK, TRULY.
I'M GRATEFUL YOU'RE HERE. I KNOW EVERYONE'S BUSY WITH POST-BATTLE CLEANUP...
SO LET'S START THIS...
RMB
RMB
RMB
REVIEW MEETING.
RMB
RMB
RMB
RMB
RMB
RMB

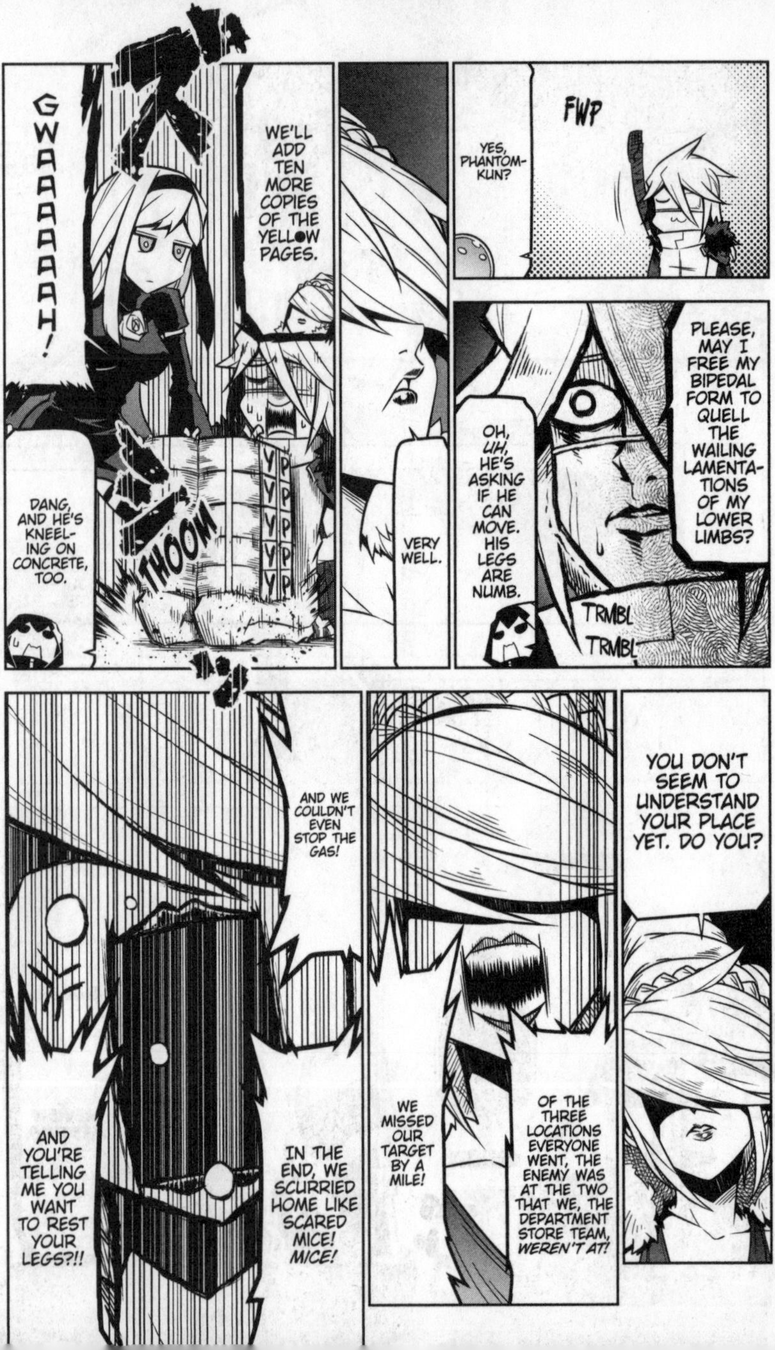
FWP
YES, PHANTOM-KUN?
PLEASE, MAY I FREE MY BIPEDAL FORM TO QUELL THE WAILING LAMENTATIONS OF MY LOWER LIMBS?
OH, *UH*, HE'S ASKING IF HE CAN MOVE. HIS LEGS ARE NUMB.
TRMBL
TRMBL
VERY WELL.
WE'LL ADD TEN MORE COPIES OF THE YELLOW PAGES.
GWAAAAAAAH!
THOOM
DANG, AND HE'S KNEEL-ING ON CONCRETE, TOO.
YOU DON'T SEEM TO UNDERSTAND YOUR PLACE YET. DO YOU?
OF THE THREE LOCATIONS EVERYONE WENT, THE ENEMY WAS AT THE TWO THAT WE, THE DEPARTMENT STORE TEAM, *WEREN'T* AT!
WE MISSED OUR TARGET BY A MILE!
AND WE COULDN'T EVEN STOP THE GAS!
IN THE END, WE SCURRIED HOME LIKE SCARED MICE! *MICE!*
AND YOU'RE TELLING ME YOU WANT TO REST YOUR LEGS?!!

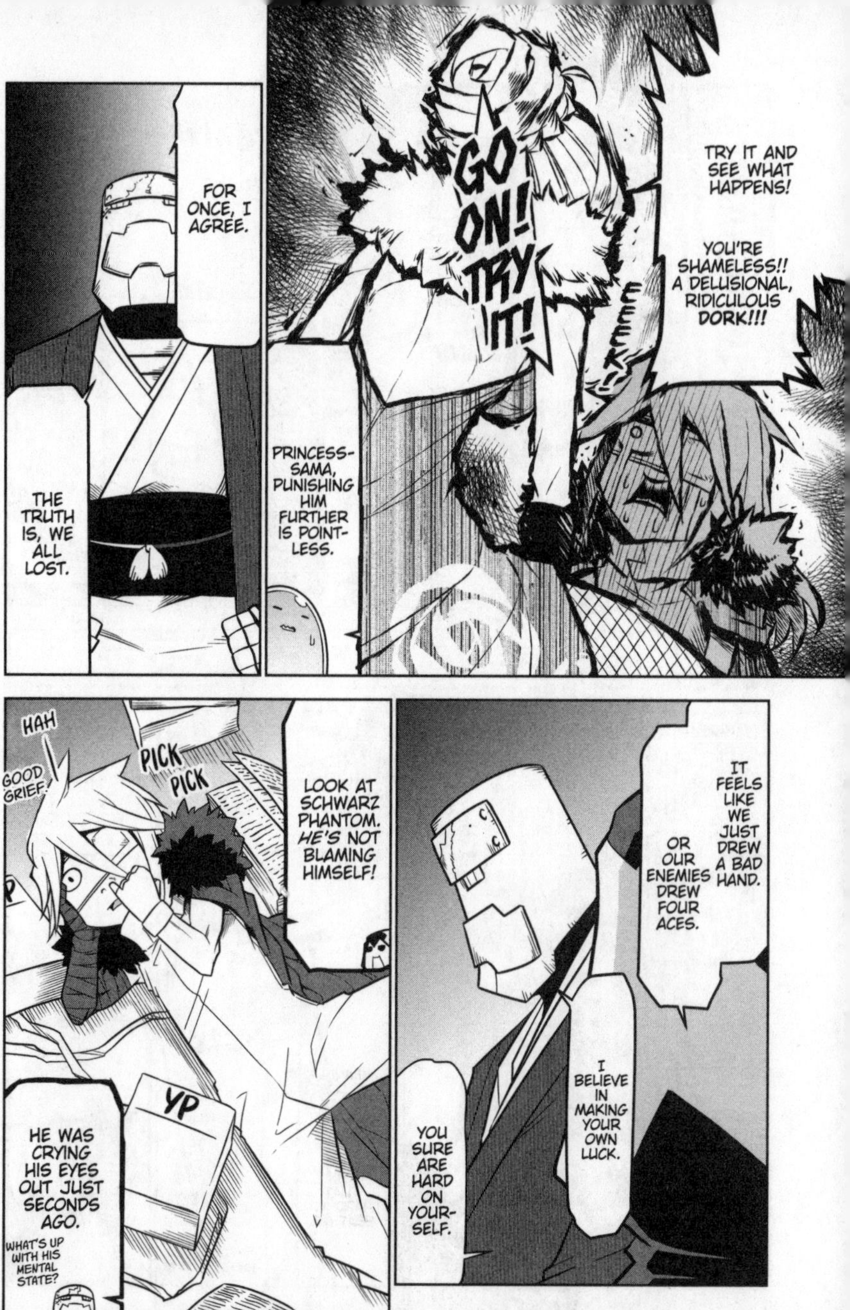
TRY IT AND SEE WHAT HAPPENS!
YOU'RE SHAMELESS!! A DELUSIONAL, RIDICULOUS DORK!!!
GO ON! TRY IT!
EEEEK!!
PRINCESS-SAMA, PUNISHING HIM FURTHER IS POINTLESS.
FOR ONCE, I AGREE.
THE TRUTH IS, WE ALL LOST.
IT FEELS LIKE WE JUST DREW A BAD HAND.
OR OUR ENEMIES DREW FOUR ACES.
I BELIEVE IN MAKING YOUR OWN LUCK.
YOU SURE ARE HARD ON YOURSELF.
LOOK AT SCHWARZ PHANTOM. *HE'S* NOT BLAMING HIMSELF!
PICK PICK
HAH
GOOD GRIEF.
YP
HE WAS CRYING HIS EYES OUT JUST SECONDS AGO.
WHAT'S UP WITH HIS MENTAL STATE?

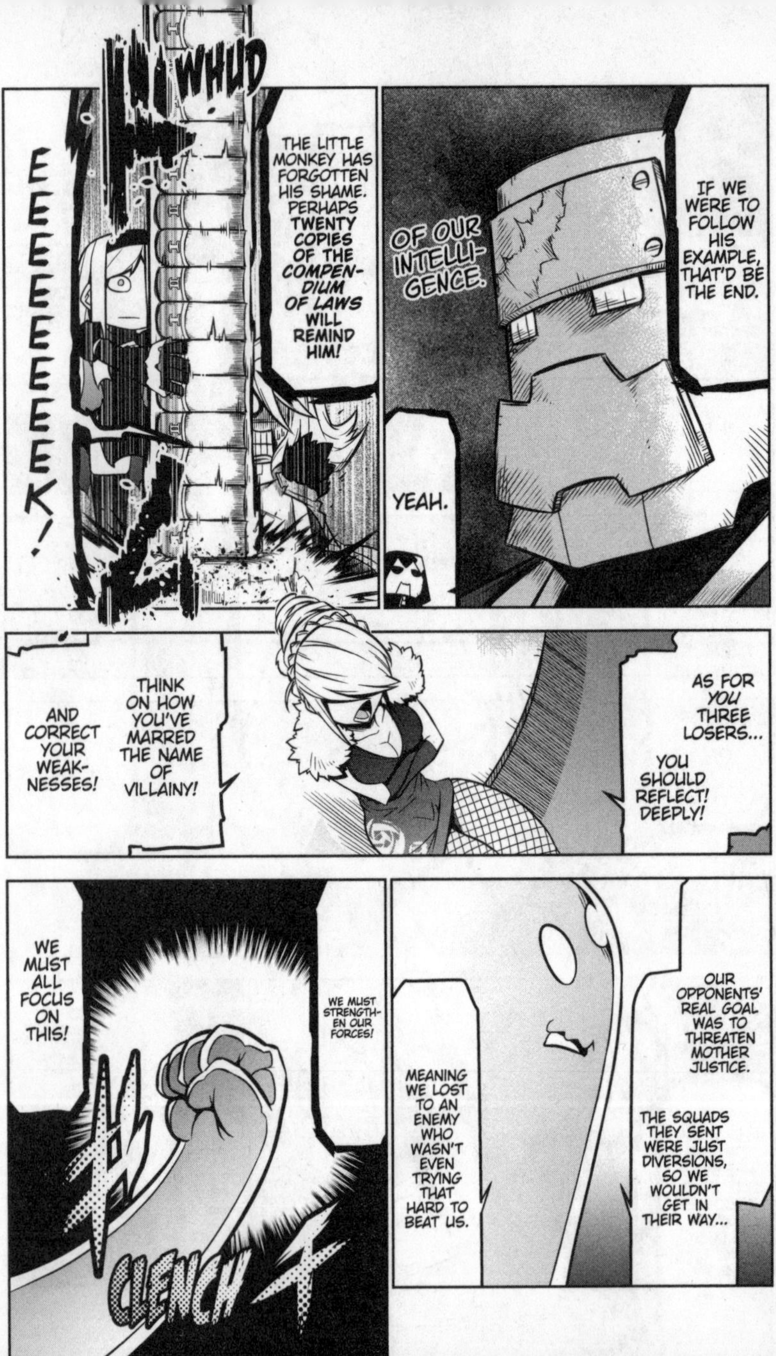

IF WE WERE TO FOLLOW HIS EXAMPLE, THAT'D BE THE END.
OF OUR INTELLIGENCE.
YEAH.
THE LITTLE MONKEY HAS FORGOTTEN HIS SHAME. PERHAPS TWENTY COPIES OF THE *COMPENDIUM OF LAWS* WILL REMIND HIM!
WHUD
EEEEEEEEEEEK!
AS FOR *YOU* THREE LOSERS...
YOU SHOULD REFLECT! DEEPLY!
THINK ON HOW YOU'VE MARRED THE NAME OF VILLAINY!
AND CORRECT YOUR WEAKNESSES!
OUR OPPONENTS' REAL GOAL WAS TO THREATEN MOTHER JUSTICE.
THE SQUADS THEY SENT WERE JUST DIVERSIONS, SO WE WOULDN'T GET IN THEIR WAY...
MEANING WE LOST TO AN ENEMY WHO WASN'T EVEN TRYING THAT HARD TO BEAT US.
WE MUST STRENGTHEN OUR FORCES!
WE MUST ALL FOCUS ON THIS!
CLENCH

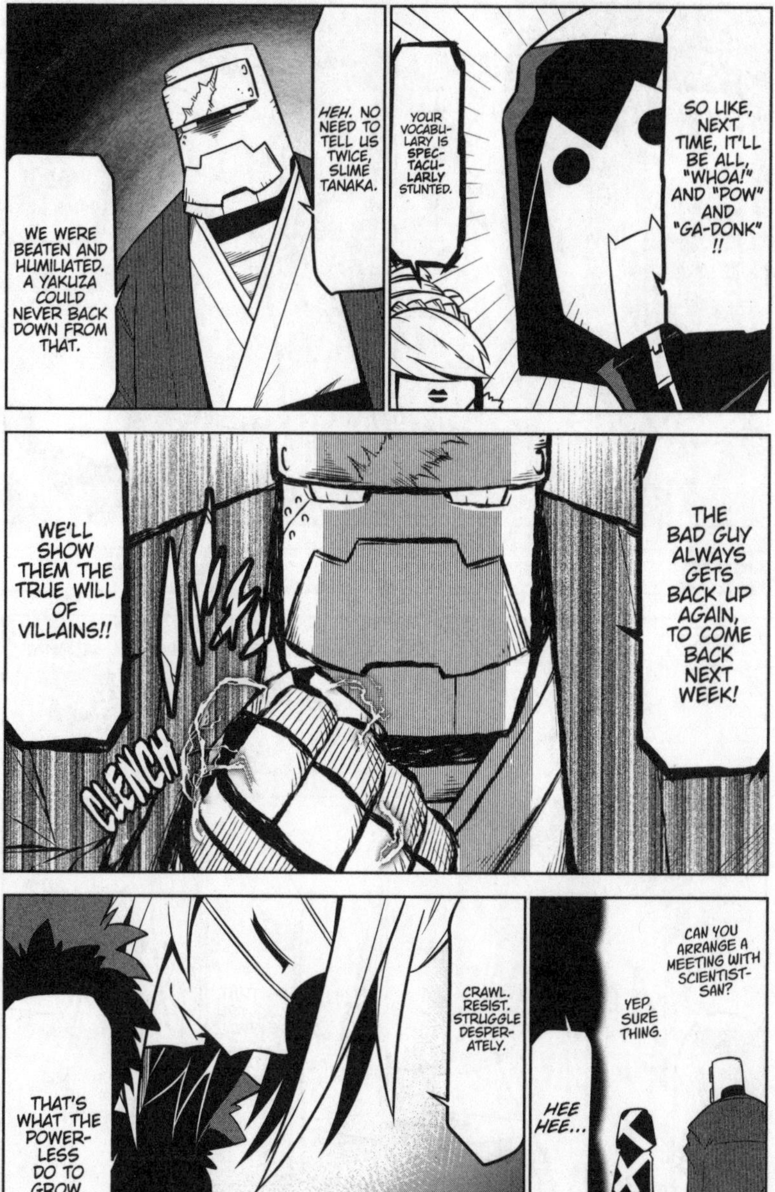
SO LIKE, NEXT TIME, IT'LL BE ALL, "WHOA!" AND "POW" AND "GA-DONK"!!
YOUR VOCABULARY IS SPECTACULARLY STUNTED.
HEH. NO NEED TO TELL US TWICE, SLIME TANAKA.
WE WERE BEATEN AND HUMILIATED. A YAKUZA COULD NEVER BACK DOWN FROM THAT.
THE BAD GUY ALWAYS GETS BACK UP AGAIN, TO COME BACK NEXT WEEK!
WE'LL SHOW THEM THE TRUE WILL OF VILLAINS!!
CLENCH
CAN YOU ARRANGE A MEETING WITH SCIENTIST-SAN?
YEP, SURE THING.
HEE HEE...
CRAWL. RESIST. STRUGGLE DESPERATELY.
THAT'S WHAT THE POWERLESS DO TO GROW.

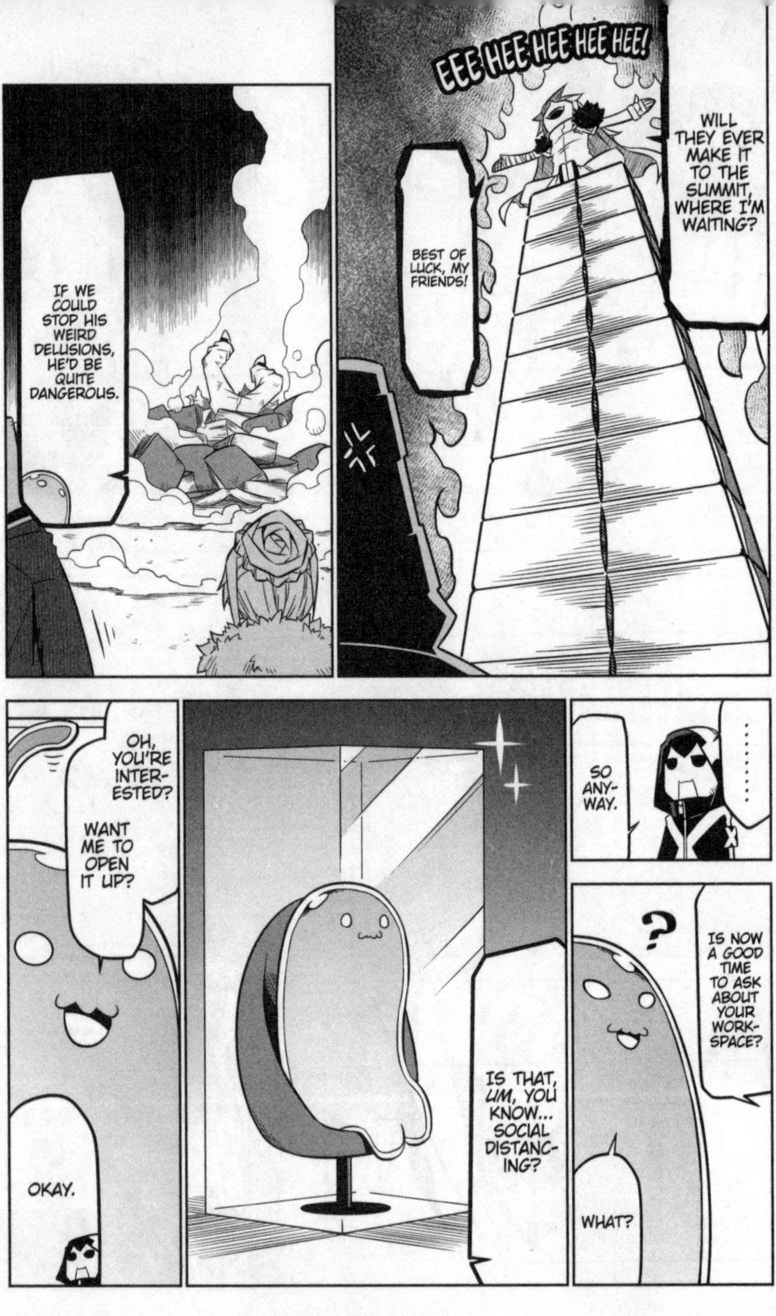
EEE HEE HEE HEE HEE!
WILL THEY EVER MAKE IT TO THE SUMMIT, WHERE I'M WAITING?
BEST OF LUCK, MY FRIENDS!
IF WE COULD STOP HIS WEIRD DELUSIONS, HE'D BE QUITE DANGEROUS.
......
SO ANY-WAY.
IS NOW A GOOD TIME TO ASK ABOUT YOUR WORK-SPACE?
WHAT?
IS THAT, UM, YOU KNOW... SOCIAL DISTANC-ING?
OH, YOU'RE INTER-ESTED?
WANT ME TO OPEN IT UP?
OKAY.

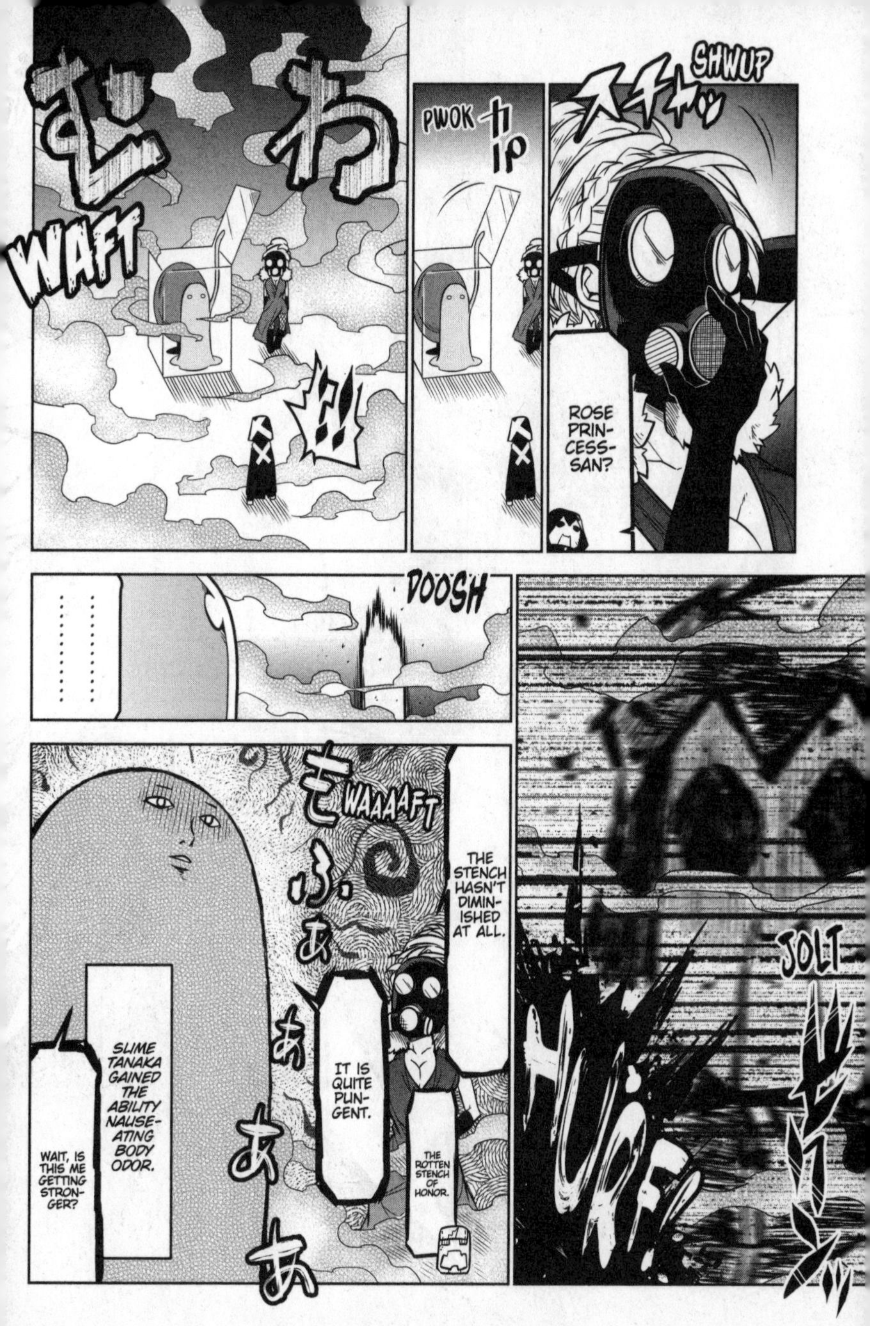
SHWUP
ROSE PRINCESS-SAN?
PWOK
WAFT
!?!!
JOLT
DOOSH
......
WAAAAFT
THE STENCH HASN'T DIMINISHED AT ALL.
IT IS QUITE PUNGENT.
THE ROTTEN STENCH OF HONOR.
SLIME TANAKA GAINED THE ABILITY NAUSEATING BODY ODOR.
WAIT, IS THIS ME GETTING STRONGER?

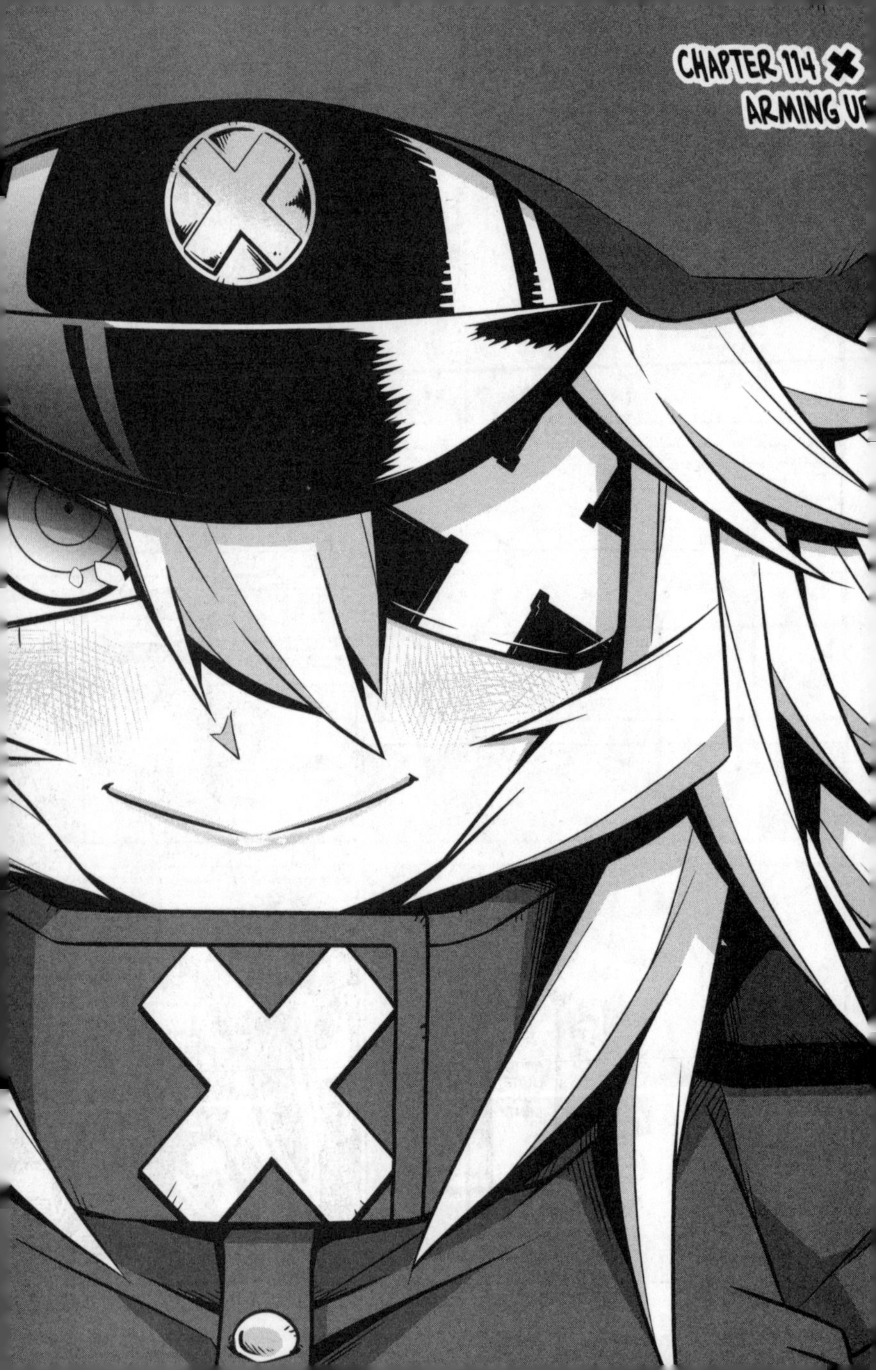
CHAPTER 114 ✖
ARMING UP

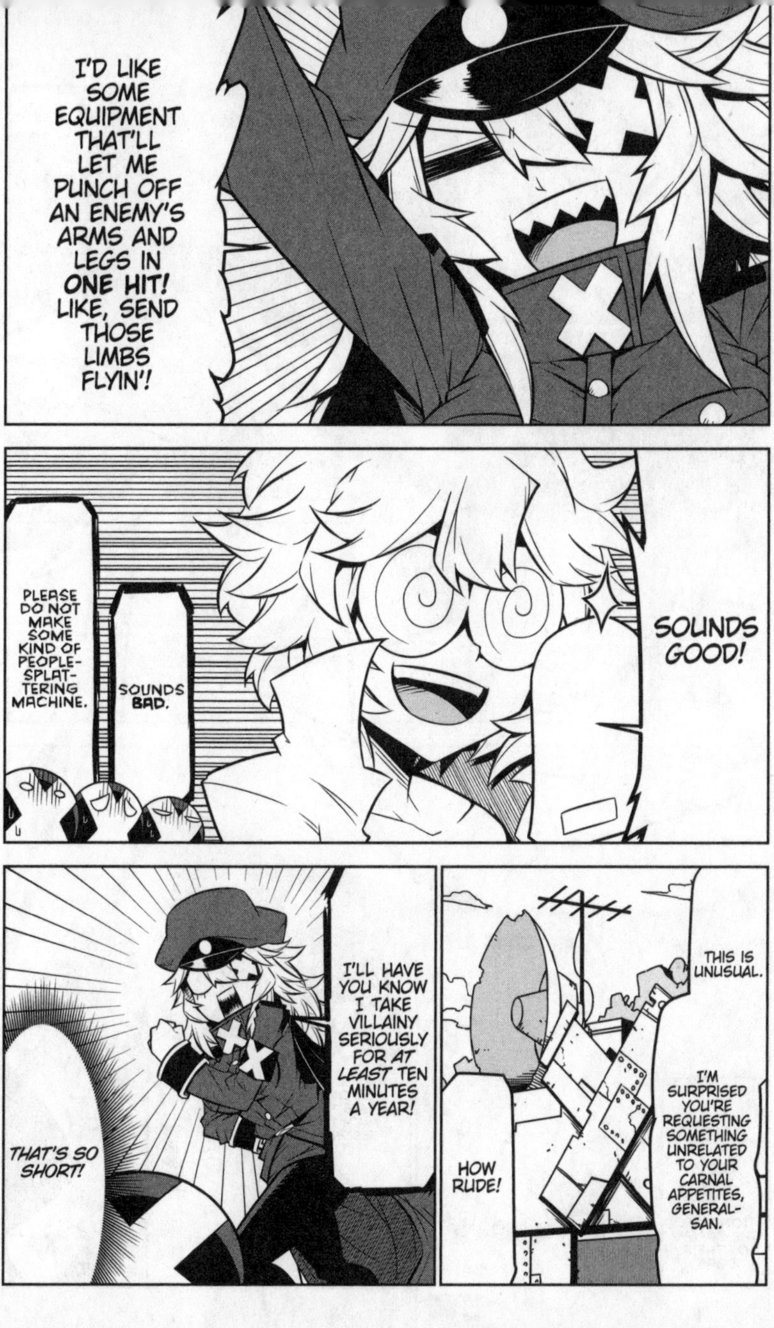
I'D LIKE SOME EQUIPMENT THAT'LL LET ME PUNCH OFF AN ENEMY'S ARMS AND LEGS IN ONE HIT! LIKE, SEND THOSE LIMBS FLYIN'!
SOUNDS GOOD!
SOUNDS BAD.
PLEASE DO NOT MAKE SOME KIND OF PEOPLE-SPLATTERING MACHINE.
THIS IS UNUSUAL.
I'M SURPRISED YOU'RE REQUESTING SOMETHING UNRELATED TO YOUR CARNAL APPETITES, GENERAL-SAN.
HOW RUDE!
I'LL HAVE YOU KNOW I TAKE VILLAINY SERIOUSLY FOR AT LEAST TEN MINUTES A YEAR!
THAT'S SO SHORT!

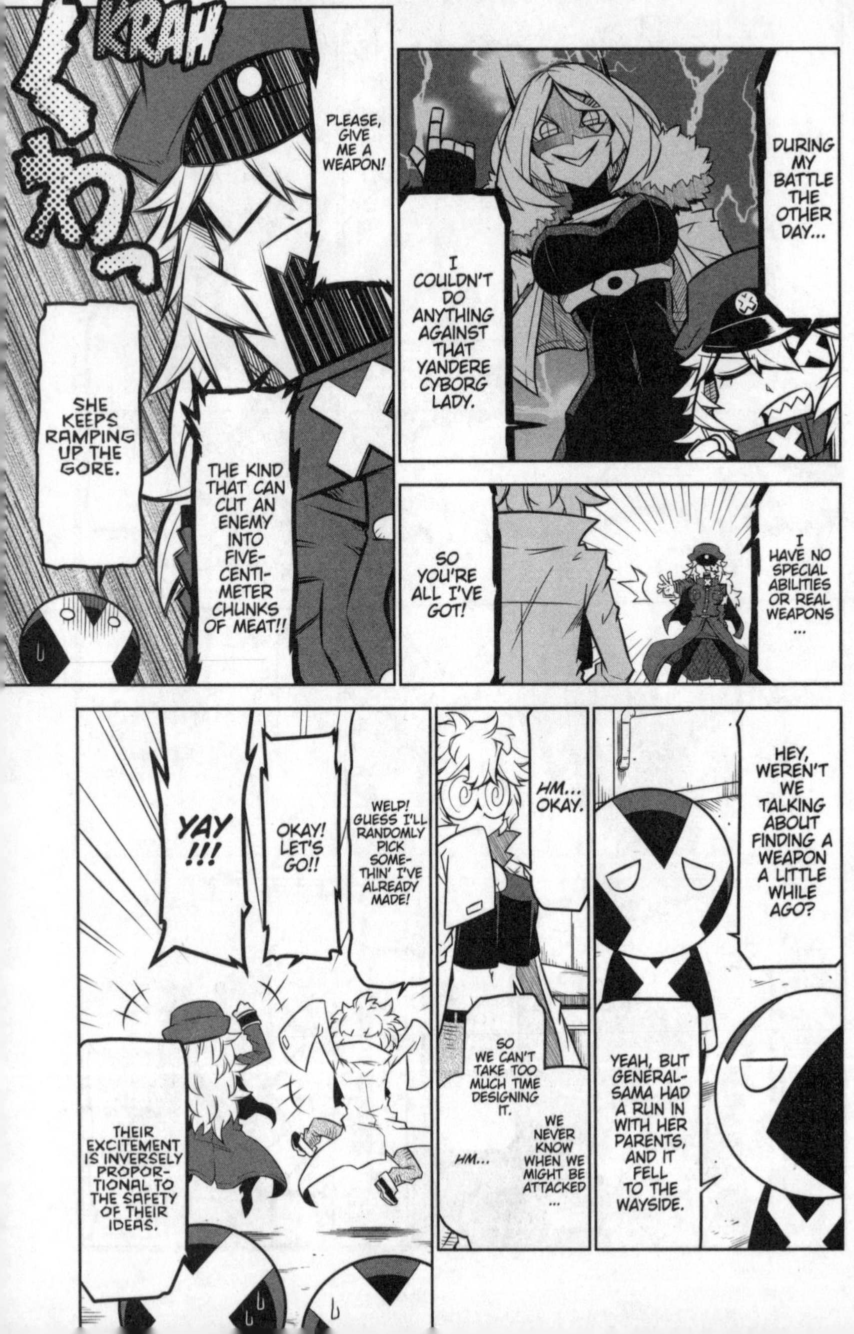
DURING MY BATTLE THE OTHER DAY...
I COULDN'T DO ANYTHING AGAINST THAT YANDERE CYBORG LADY.
I HAVE NO SPECIAL ABILITIES OR REAL WEAPONS...
SO YOU'RE ALL I'VE GOT!
KRAH
くわっ
PLEASE, GIVE ME A WEAPON!
THE KIND THAT CAN CUT AN ENEMY INTO FIVE-CENTIMETER CHUNKS OF MEAT!!
SHE KEEPS RAMPING UP THE GORE.
HEY, WEREN'T WE TALKING ABOUT FINDING A WEAPON A LITTLE WHILE AGO?
YEAH, BUT GENERAL-SAMA HAD A RUN IN WITH HER PARENTS, AND IT FELL TO THE WAYSIDE.
HM... OKAY.
SO WE CAN'T TAKE TOO MUCH TIME DESIGNING IT.
WE NEVER KNOW WHEN WE MIGHT BE ATTACKED...
HM...
WELP! GUESS I'LL RANDOMLY PICK SOMETHIN' I'VE ALREADY MADE!
OKAY! LET'S GO!!
YAY!!!
THEIR EXCITEMENT IS INVERSELY PROPORTIONAL TO THE SAFETY OF THEIR IDEAS.

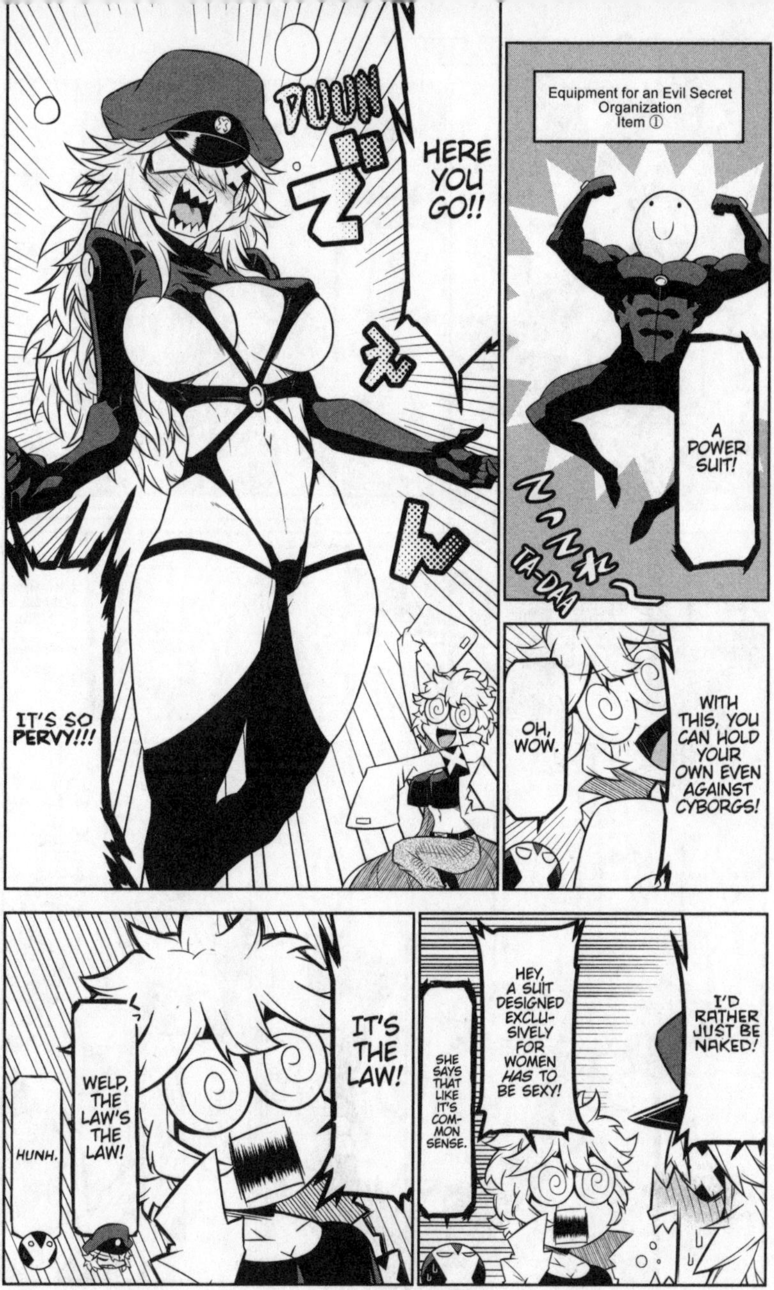
Equipment for an Evil Secret Organization Item ①
A POWER SUIT!
TA-DAA
WITH THIS, YOU CAN HOLD YOUR OWN EVEN AGAINST CYBORGS!
OH, WOW.
HERE YOU GO!!
DUUN
IT'S SO PERVY!!!
I'D RATHER JUST BE NAKED!
HEY, A SUIT DESIGNED EXCLUSIVELY FOR WOMEN *HAS* TO BE SEXY!
SHE SAYS THAT LIKE IT'S COMMON SENSE.
IT'S THE LAW!
WELP, THE LAW'S THE LAW!
HUNH.

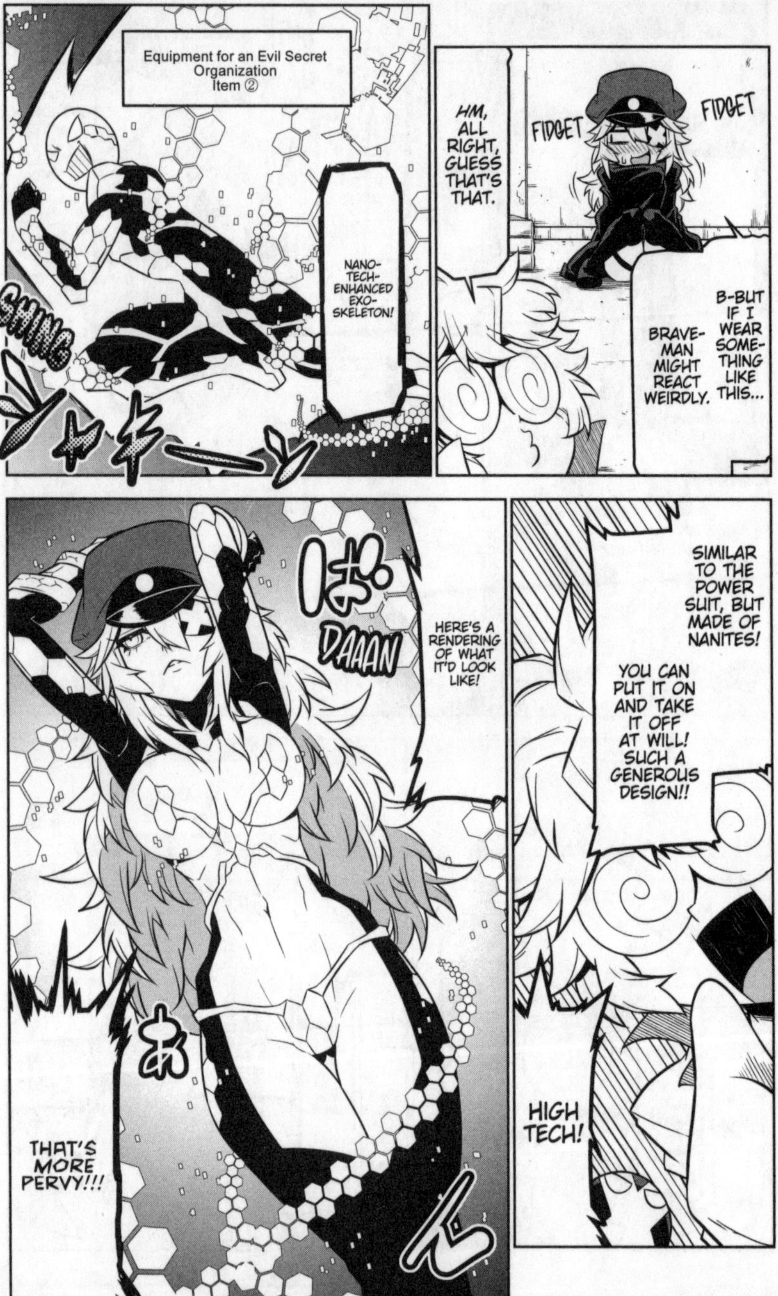
FIDGET
FIDGET
HM, ALL RIGHT, GUESS THAT'S THAT.
B-BUT IF I WEAR SOMETHING LIKE THIS... BRAVEMAN MIGHT REACT WEIRDLY.
Equipment for an Evil Secret Organization Item ②
NANO-TECH-ENHANCED EXO-SKELETON!
SHING
SIMILAR TO THE POWER SUIT, BUT MADE OF NANITES!
YOU CAN PUT IT ON AND TAKE IT OFF AT WILL! SUCH A GENEROUS DESIGN!!
HIGH TECH!
DAAAN
HERE'S A RENDERING OF WHAT IT'D LOOK LIKE!
THAT'S MORE PERVY!!!

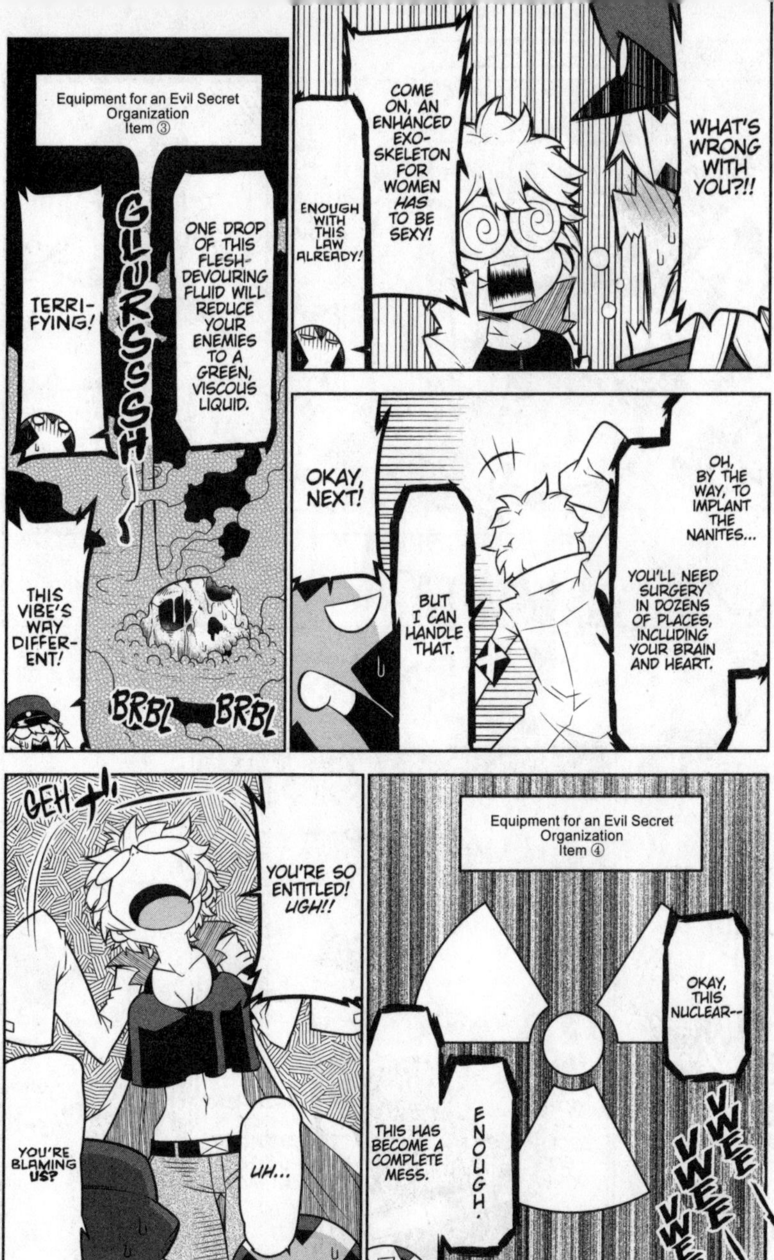
WHAT'S WRONG WITH YOU?!!
COME ON, AN ENHANCED EXO-SKELETON FOR WOMEN *HAS* TO BE SEXY!
ENOUGH WITH THIS LAW ALREADY!
OH, BY THE WAY, TO IMPLANT THE NANITES...
YOU'LL NEED SURGERY IN DOZENS OF PLACES, INCLUDING YOUR BRAIN AND HEART.
OKAY, NEXT!
BUT I CAN HANDLE THAT.
Equipment for an Evil Secret Organization Item ③
ONE DROP OF THIS FLESH-DEVOURING FLUID WILL REDUCE YOUR ENEMIES TO A GREEN, VISCOUS LIQUID.
GLURSSSH
TERRI-FYING!
THIS VIBE'S WAY DIFFER-ENT!
BRBL BRBL
Equipment for an Evil Secret Organization Item ④
OKAY, THIS NUCLEAR--
VWEE VWEE VWEE VWEE
ENOUGH.
THIS HAS BECOME A COMPLETE MESS.
GEH
YOU'RE SO ENTITLED! *UGH!!*
UH...
YOU'RE BLAMING **US**?

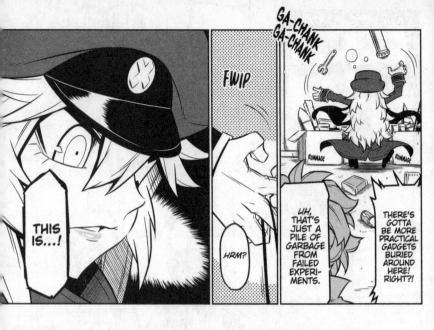

GA-CHANK
GA-CHANK
RUMMAGE
RUMMAGE
THERE'S GOTTA BE MORE PRACTICAL GADGETS BURIED AROUND HERE! RIGHT?!
UH, THAT'S JUST A PILE OF GARBAGE FROM FAILED EXPERI-MENTS.
FWIP
HRM?
THIS IS...!
THE NEXT DAY.
Ryuuei Park
ANOTHER DAY, ANOTHER GEYSER ATTACK.
WOW, HE LOOKS SO DONE.
HEE HEE HEE...
KNCH

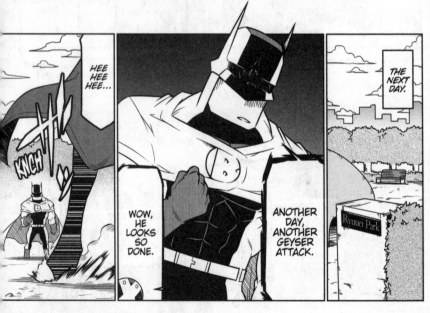

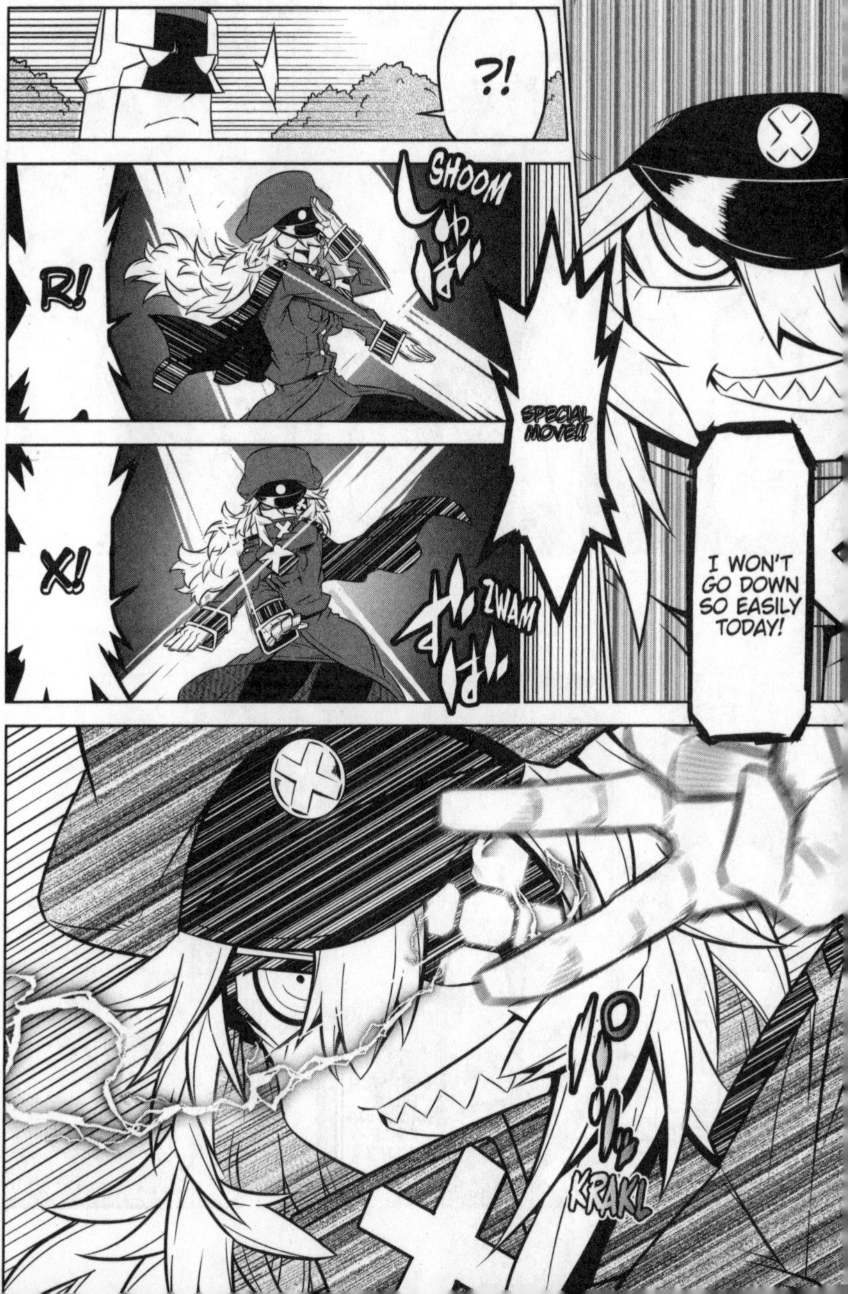
SPECIAL MOVE!!
I WON'T GO DOWN SO EASILY TODAY!
?!
SHOOM
R!
ZWAM
X!
KRAKL

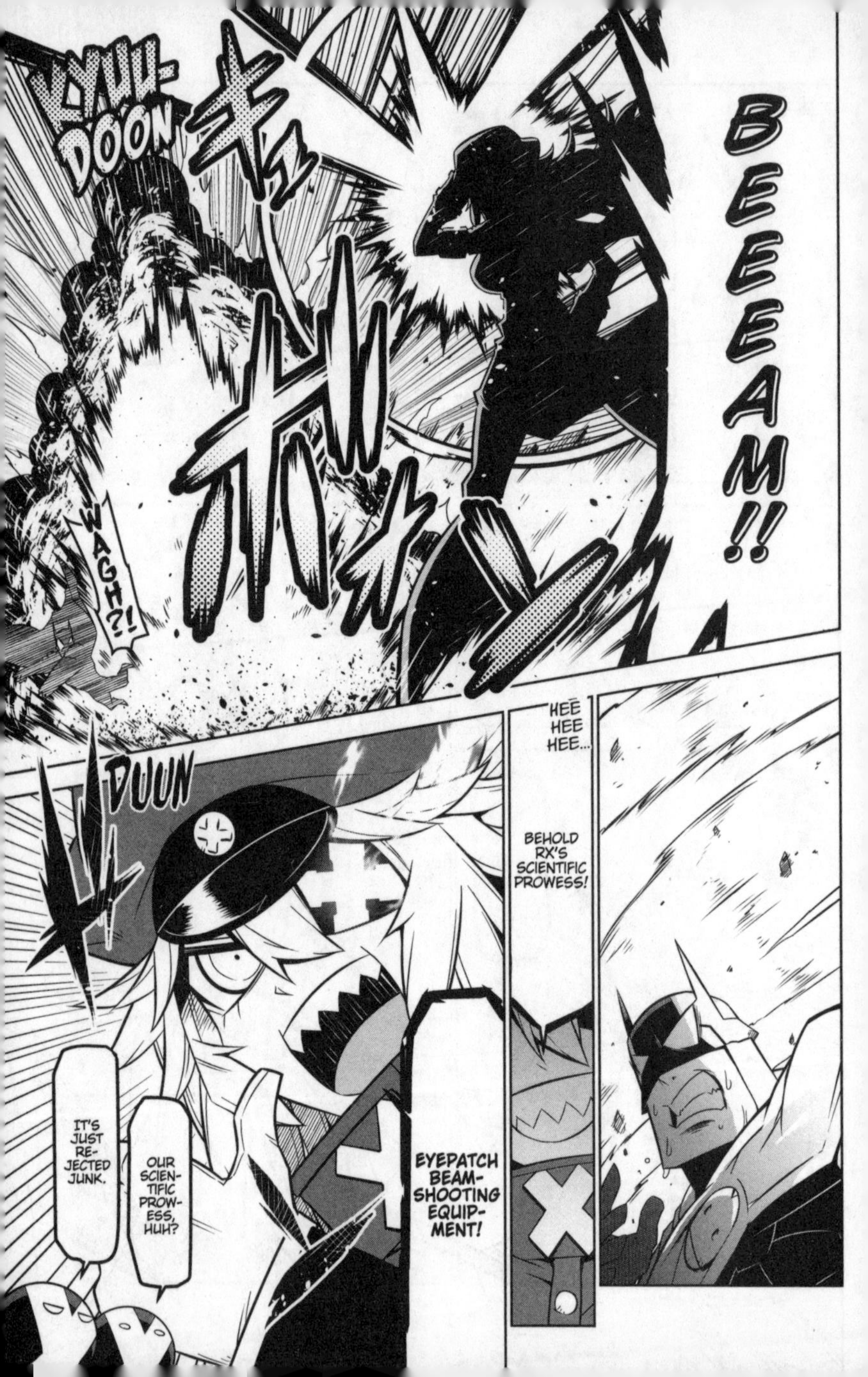
BEEEAM!!
KYUU-DOON
WAGH?!
HEE HEE HEE...
BEHOLD RX'S SCIENTIFIC PROWESS!
EYEPATCH BEAM-SHOOTING EQUIPMENT!
DUUN
OUR SCIENTIFIC PROWESS, HUH?
IT'S JUST REJECTED JUNK.

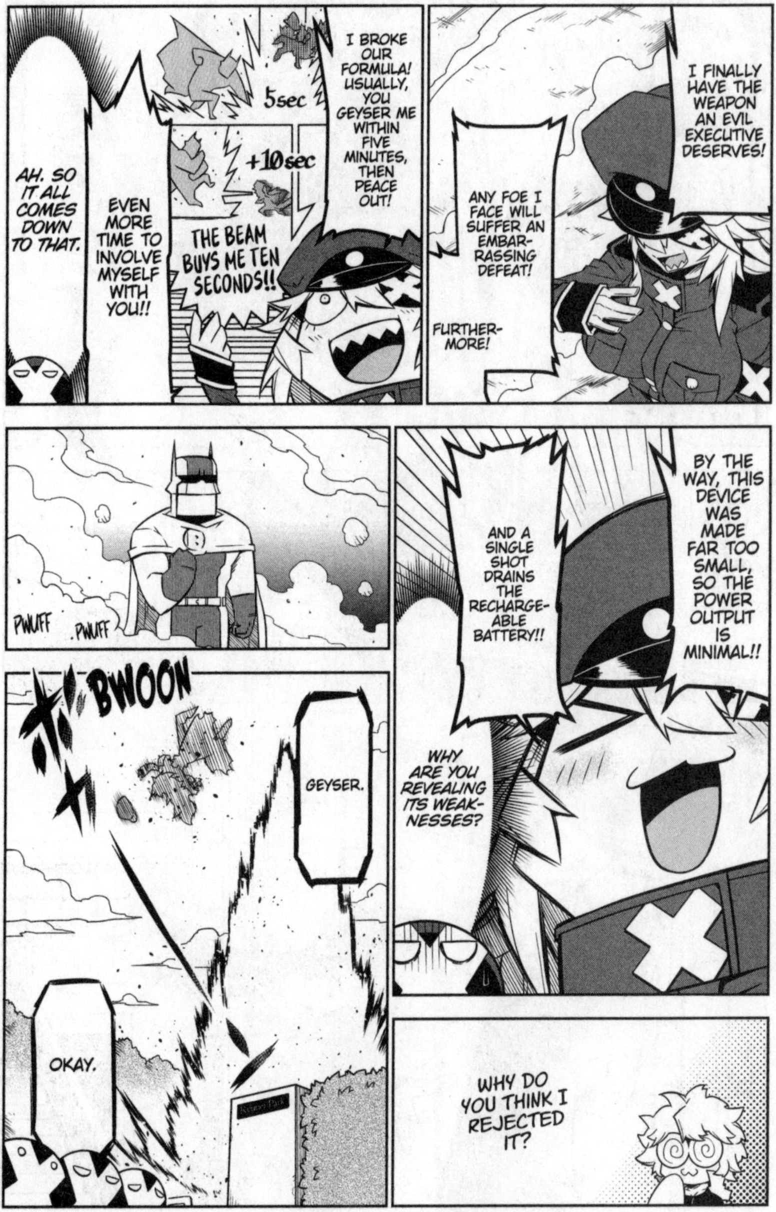
I FINALLY HAVE THE WEAPON AN EVIL EXECUTIVE DESERVES!
ANY FOE I FACE WILL SUFFER AN EMBARRASSING DEFEAT!
FURTHERMORE!
I BROKE OUR FORMULA! USUALLY, YOU GEYSER ME WITHIN FIVE MINUTES, THEN PEACE OUT!
5sec
+10sec
THE BEAM BUYS ME TEN SECONDS!!
EVEN MORE TIME TO INVOLVE MYSELF WITH YOU!!
AH. SO IT ALL COMES DOWN TO THAT.
BY THE WAY, THIS DEVICE WAS MADE FAR TOO SMALL, SO THE POWER OUTPUT IS MINIMAL!!
AND A SINGLE SHOT DRAINS THE RECHARGEABLE BATTERY!!
WHY ARE YOU REVEALING ITS WEAKNESSES?
WHY DO YOU THINK I REJECTED IT?
PWUFF
PWUFF
BWOON
GEYSER.
OKAY.

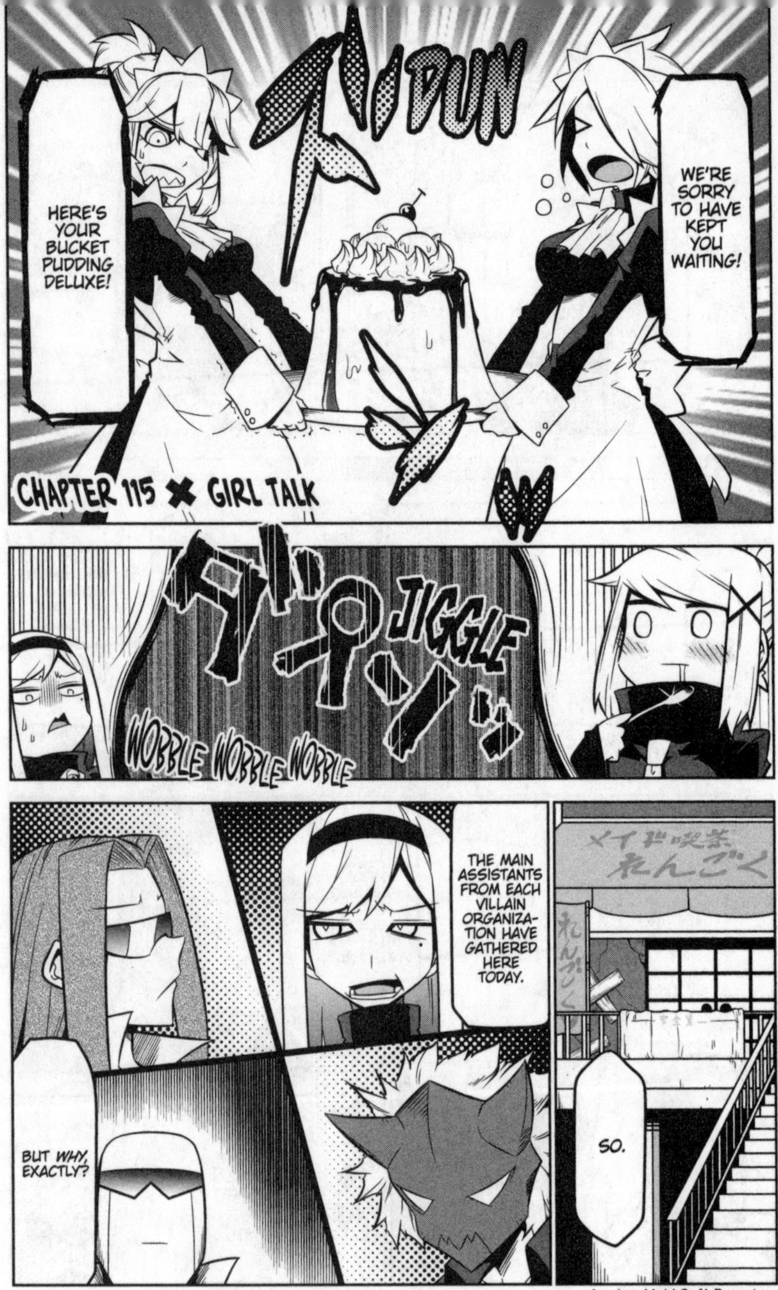
WE'RE SORRY TO HAVE KEPT YOU WAITING!
DUN
HERE'S YOUR BUCKET PUDDING DELUXE!
CHAPTER 115 ✖ GIRL TALK
JIGGLE
WOBBLE WOBBLE WOBBLE
メイド喫茶 れんごく
れんごく
SO.
THE MAIN ASSISTANTS FROM EACH VILLAIN ORGANIZATION HAVE GATHERED HERE TODAY.
BUT *WHY*, EXACTLY?

Awning: Maid Café Purgatory
Banner: Purgatory
Cloth: Safety first

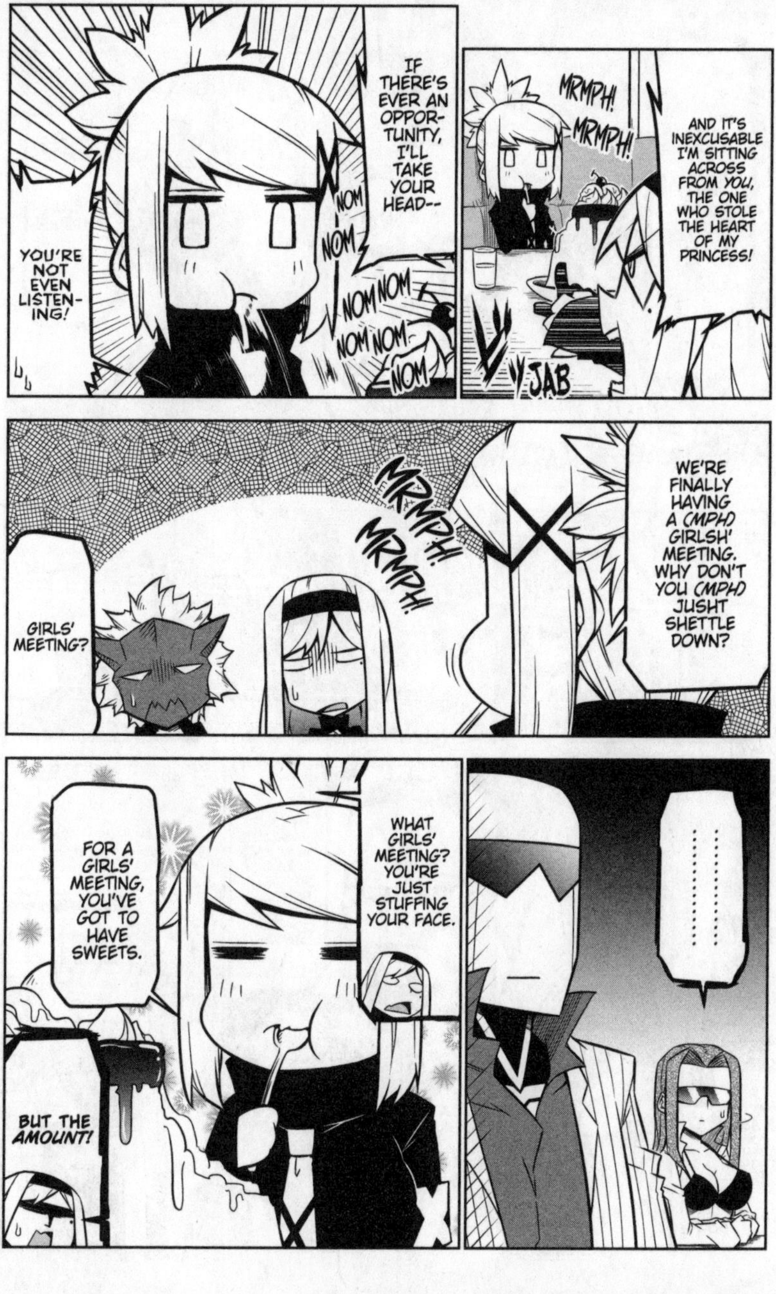
MRMPH!
MRMPH!
AND IT'S INEXCUSABLE I'M SITTING ACROSS FROM *YOU*, THE ONE WHO STOLE THE HEART OF MY PRINCESS!
JAB
IF THERE'S EVER AN OPPOR-TUNITY, I'LL TAKE YOUR HEAD--
NOM
NOM
NOM NOM
NOM NOM
NOM
YOU'RE NOT EVEN LISTEN-ING!
WE'RE FINALLY HAVING A *(MPH)* GIRLSH' MEETING. WHY DON'T YOU *(MPH)* JUSHT SHETTLE DOWN?
MRMPH!
MRMPH!
GIRLS' MEETING?
......
WHAT GIRLS' MEETING? YOU'RE JUST STUFFING YOUR FACE.
FOR A GIRLS' MEETING, YOU'VE GOT TO HAVE SWEETS.
BUT THE *AMOUNT!*

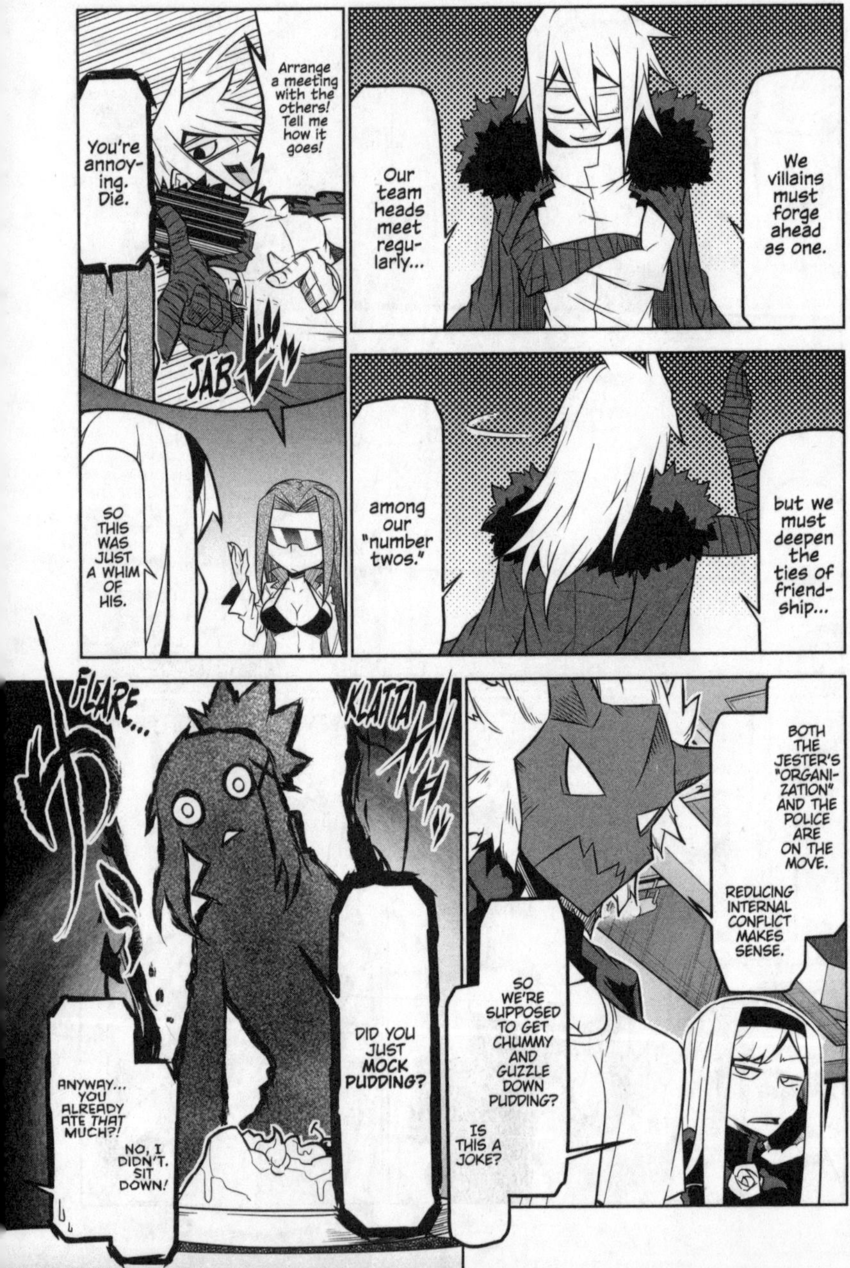
We villains must forge ahead as one.
Our team heads meet regularly...
Arrange a meeting with the others! Tell me how it goes!
You're annoying. Die.
JAB
but we must deepen the ties of friendship...
among our "number twos."
SO THIS WAS JUST A WHIM OF HIS.
BOTH THE JESTER'S "ORGANIZATION" AND THE POLICE ARE ON THE MOVE.
REDUCING INTERNAL CONFLICT MAKES SENSE.
SO WE'RE SUPPOSED TO GET CHUMMY AND GUZZLE DOWN PUDDING?
IS THIS A JOKE?
KLATTA
DID YOU JUST MOCK PUDDING?
FLARE...
ANYWAY... YOU ALREADY ATE THAT MUCH?!
NO, I DIDN'T. SIT DOWN!

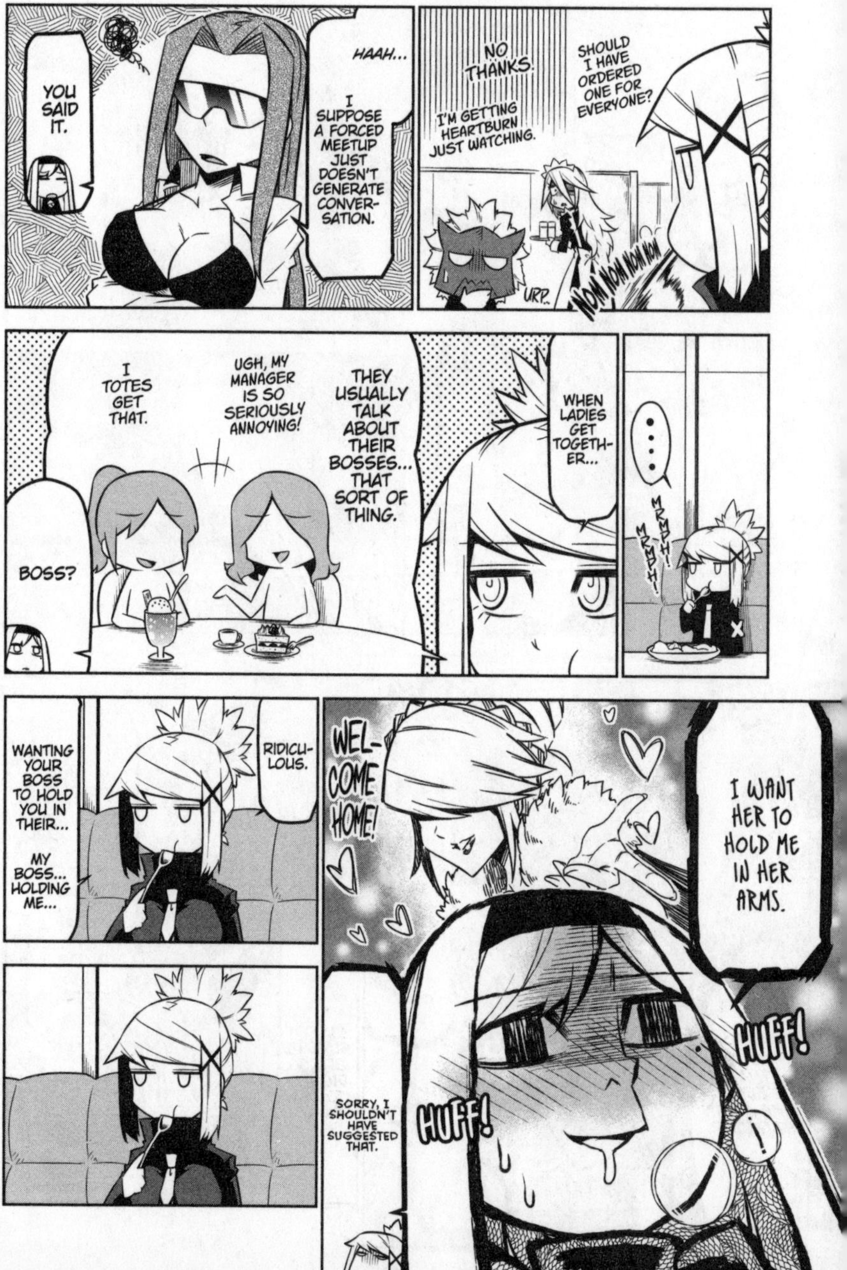
SHOULD I HAVE ORDERED ONE FOR EVERYONE?
NO THANKS.
I'M GETTING HEARTBURN JUST WATCHING.
URP..
NOM NOM NOM NOM
HAAH...
I SUPPOSE A FORCED MEETUP JUST DOESN'T GENERATE CONVER-SATION.
YOU SAID IT.
....
MRMPH! MRMPH!
WHEN LADIES GET TOGETH-ER...
THEY USUALLY TALK ABOUT THEIR BOSSES... THAT SORT OF THING.
UGH, MY MANAGER IS SO SERIOUSLY ANNOYING!
I TOTES GET THAT.
BOSS?
I WANT HER TO HOLD ME IN HER ARMS.
WEL-COME HOME!
HUFF!
HUFF!
!
SORRY, I SHOULDN'T HAVE SUGGESTED THAT.
RIDICU-LOUS.
WANTING YOUR BOSS TO HOLD YOU IN THEIR...
MY BOSS... HOLDING ME...

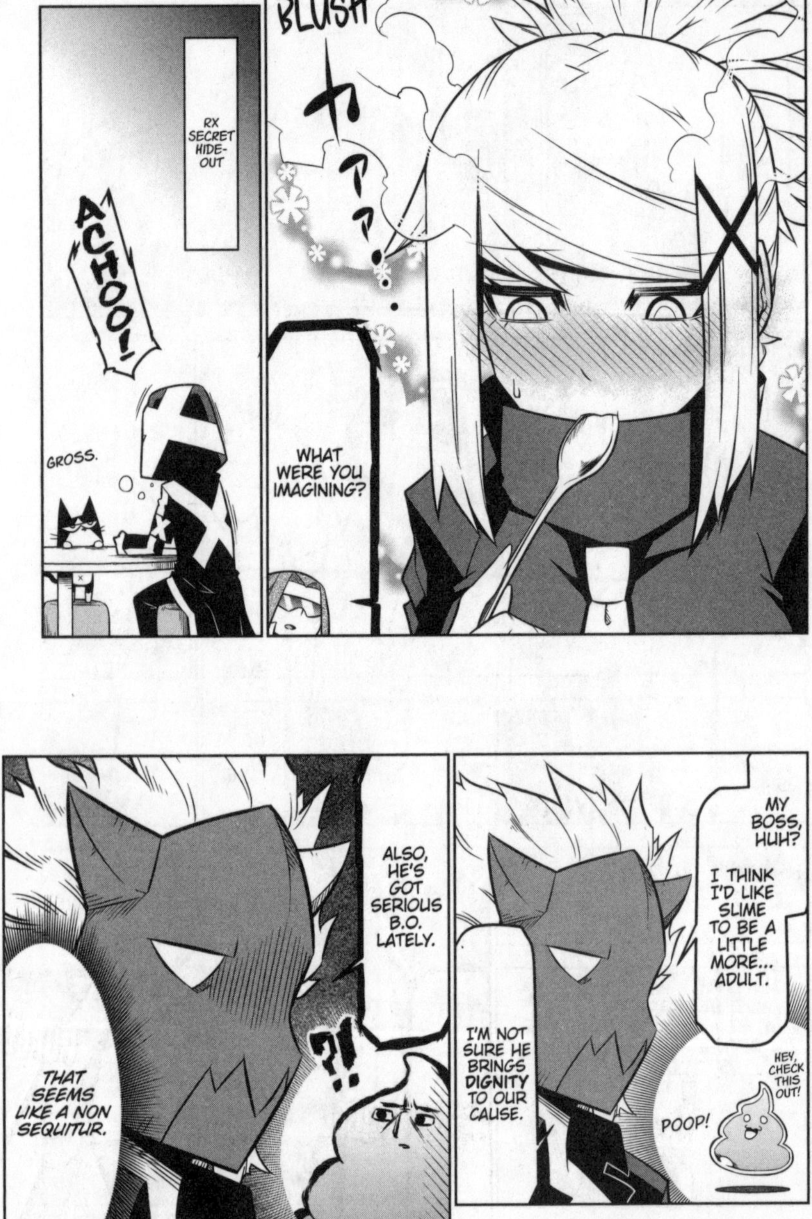
BLUSH
カァァ
WHAT WERE YOU IMAGINING?
RX SECRET HIDE-OUT
ACHOO!
GROSS.
MY BOSS, HUH?
I THINK I'D LIKE SLIME TO BE A LITTLE MORE... ADULT.
HEY, CHECK THIS OUT!
POOP!
I'M NOT SURE HE BRINGS DIGNITY TO OUR CAUSE.
ALSO, HE'S GOT SERIOUS B.O. LATELY.
?!!
THAT SEEMS LIKE A NON SEQUITUR.

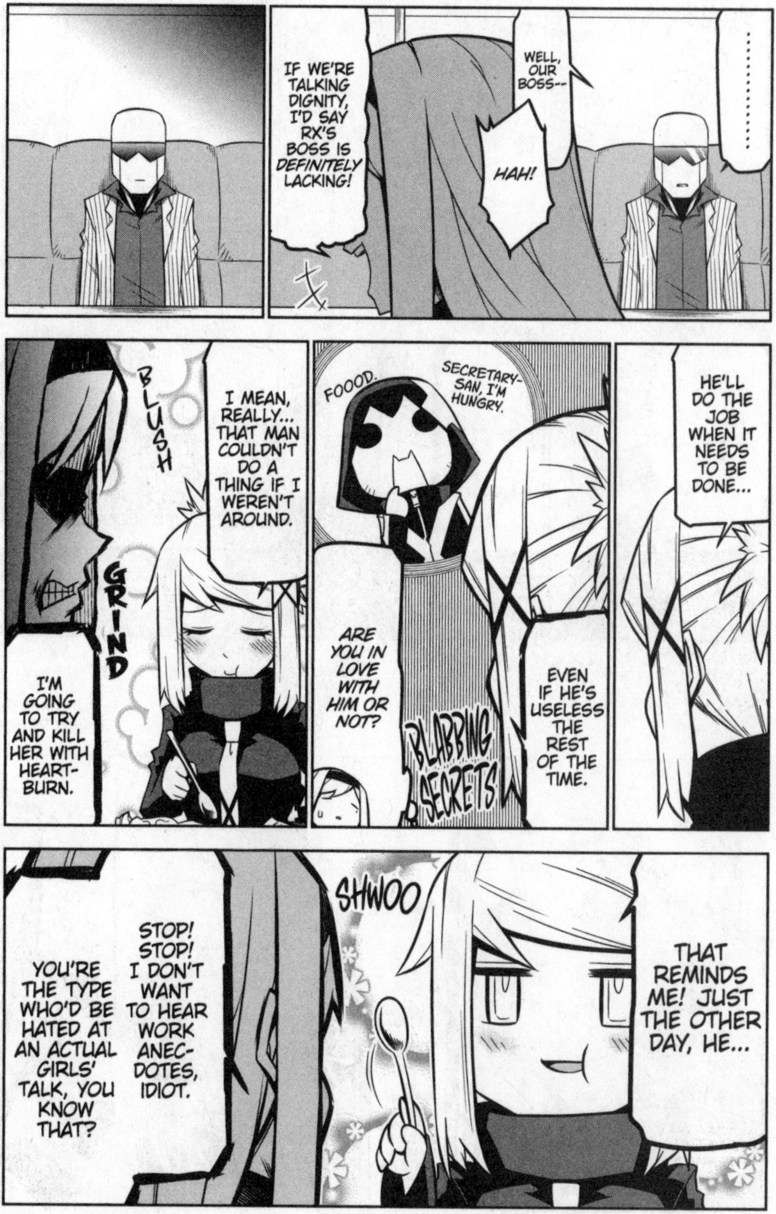
......
WELL, OUR BOSS--
HAH!
IF WE'RE TALKING DIGNITY, I'D SAY RX'S BOSS IS DEFINITELY LACKING!
HE'LL DO THE JOB WHEN IT NEEDS TO BE DONE...
EVEN IF HE'S USELESS THE REST OF THE TIME.
SECRETARY-SAN, I'M HUNGRY.
FOOOD.
ARE YOU IN LOVE WITH HIM OR NOT?
BLABBING SECRETS
BLUSH
I MEAN, REALLY... THAT MAN COULDN'T DO A THING IF I WEREN'T AROUND.
GRIND
I'M GOING TO TRY AND KILL HER WITH HEARTBURN.
THAT REMINDS ME! JUST THE OTHER DAY, HE...
SHWOO
STOP! STOP! I DON'T WANT TO HEAR WORK ANECDOTES, IDIOT.
YOU'RE THE TYPE WHO'D BE HATED AT AN ACTUAL GIRLS' TALK, YOU KNOW THAT?

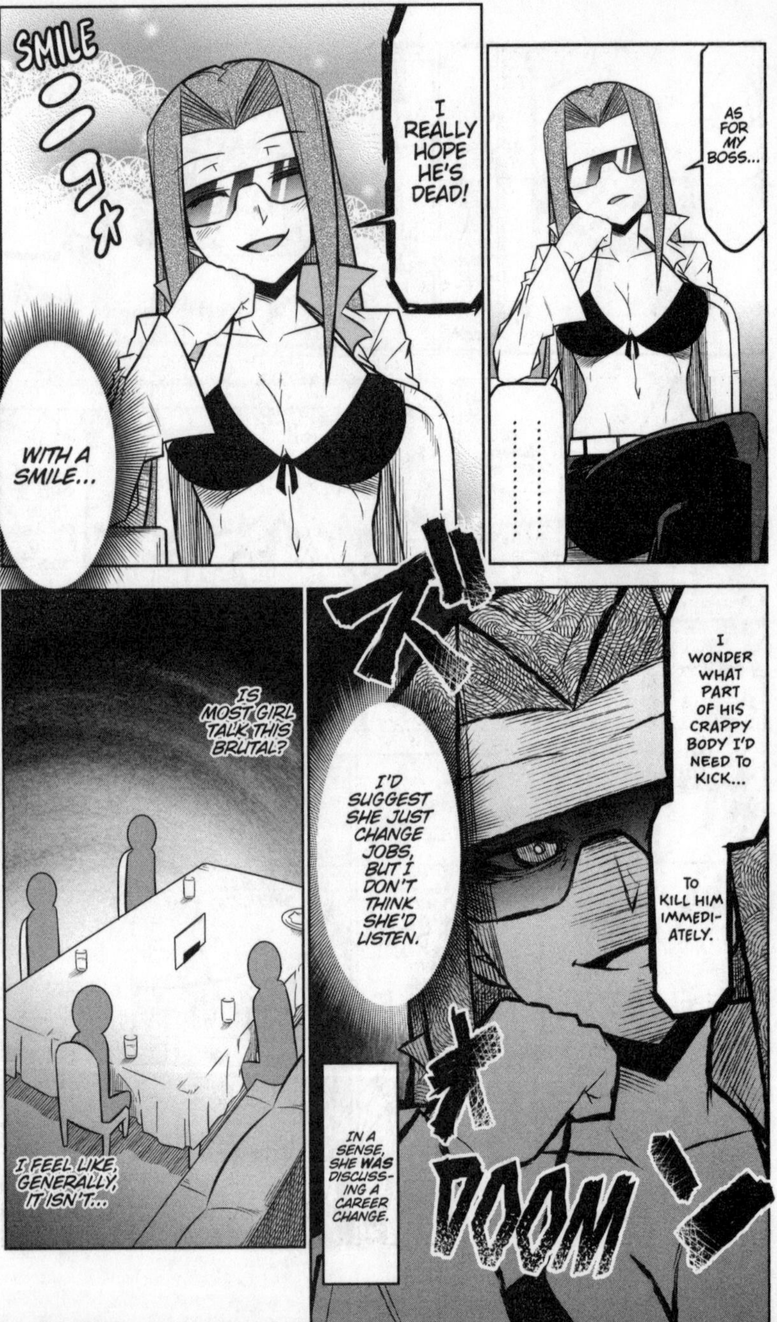
AS FOR MY BOSS...
......
I REALLY HOPE HE'S DEAD!
SMILE
WITH A SMILE...
I WONDER WHAT PART OF HIS CRAPPY BODY I'D NEED TO KICK...
TO KILL HIM IMMEDI-ATELY.
I'D SUGGEST SHE JUST CHANGE JOBS, BUT I DON'T THINK SHE'D LISTEN.
DOOM
IN A SENSE, SHE WAS DISCUSS-ING A CAREER CHANGE.
IS MOST GIRL TALK THIS BRUTAL?
I FEEL LIKE, GENERALLY, IT ISN'T...

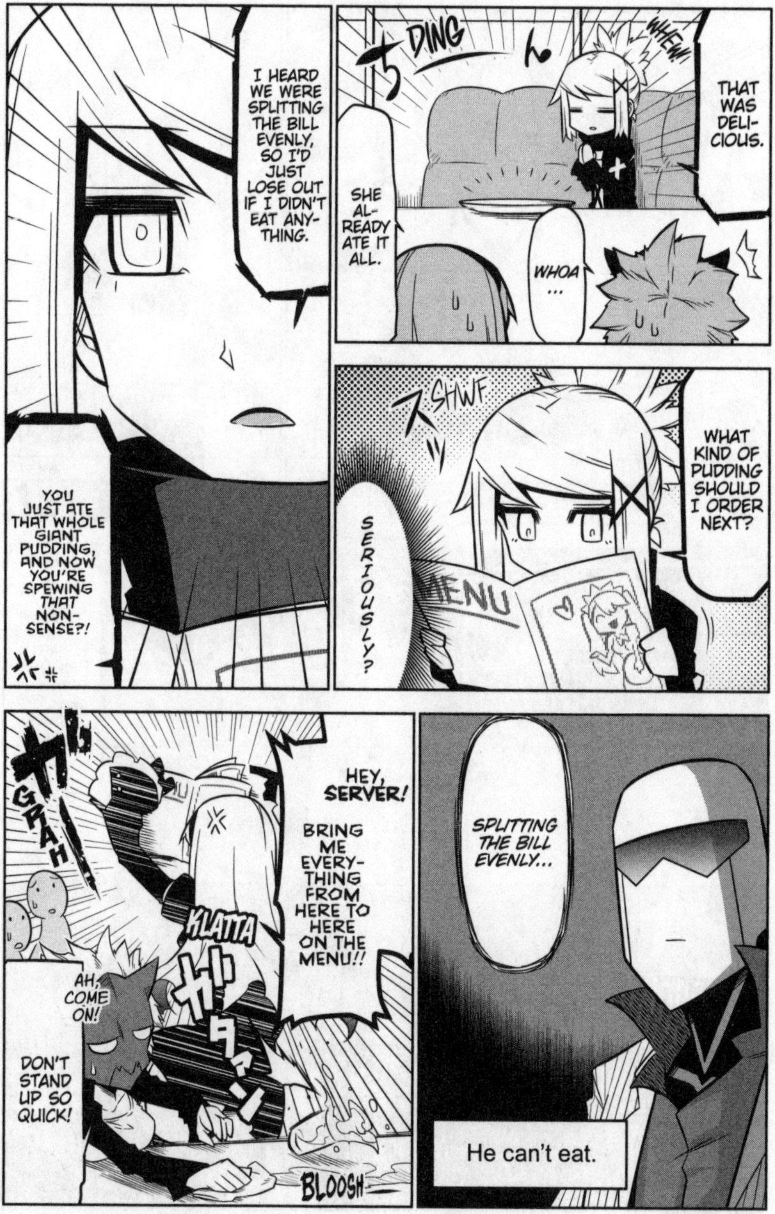

WHEW!
THAT WAS DELICIOUS.
DING
WHOA...
SHE ALREADY ATE IT ALL.
SHWF
WHAT KIND OF PUDDING SHOULD I ORDER NEXT?
SERIOUSLY?
I HEARD WE WERE SPLITTING THE BILL EVENLY, SO I'D JUST LOSE OUT IF I DIDN'T EAT ANYTHING.
YOU JUST ATE THAT WHOLE GIANT PUDDING, AND NOW YOU'RE SPEWING THAT NONSENSE?!
SPLITTING THE BILL EVENLY...
He can't eat.
HEY, SERVER!
BRING ME EVERYTHING FROM HERE TO HERE ON THE MENU!!
GRAH
KLATTA
AH, COME ON!
DON'T STAND UP SO QUICK!
BLOOSH

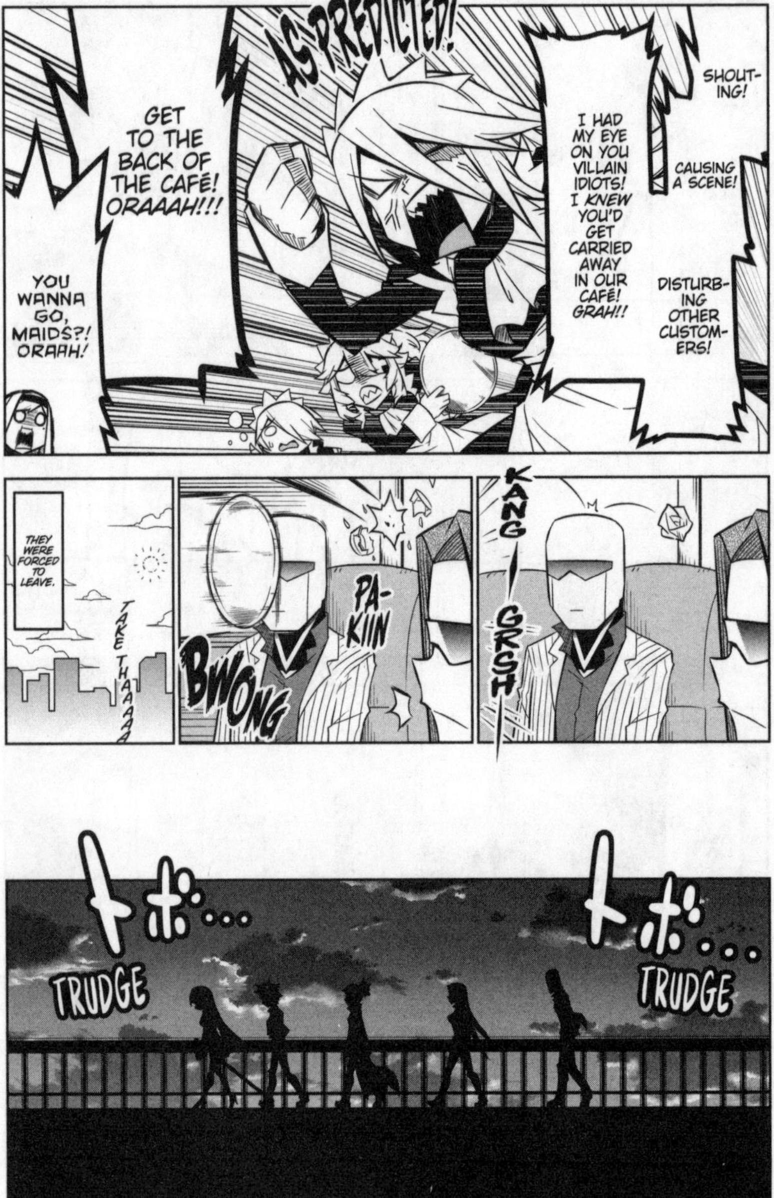
SHOUTING!
CAUSING A SCENE!
DISTURBING OTHER CUSTOMERS!
I HAD MY EYE ON YOU VILLAIN IDIOTS! I KNEW YOU'D GET CARRIED AWAY IN OUR CAFÉ! GRAH!!
AS PREDICTED!
GET TO THE BACK OF THE CAFÉ! ORAAAH!!!
YOU WANNA GO, MAIDS?! ORAAH!
KANG
GRSH
PA-KIIN
BWONG
THEY WERE FORCED TO LEAVE.
TAKE THAAAAA
トぼ…
TRUDGE
トぼ…
TRUDGE

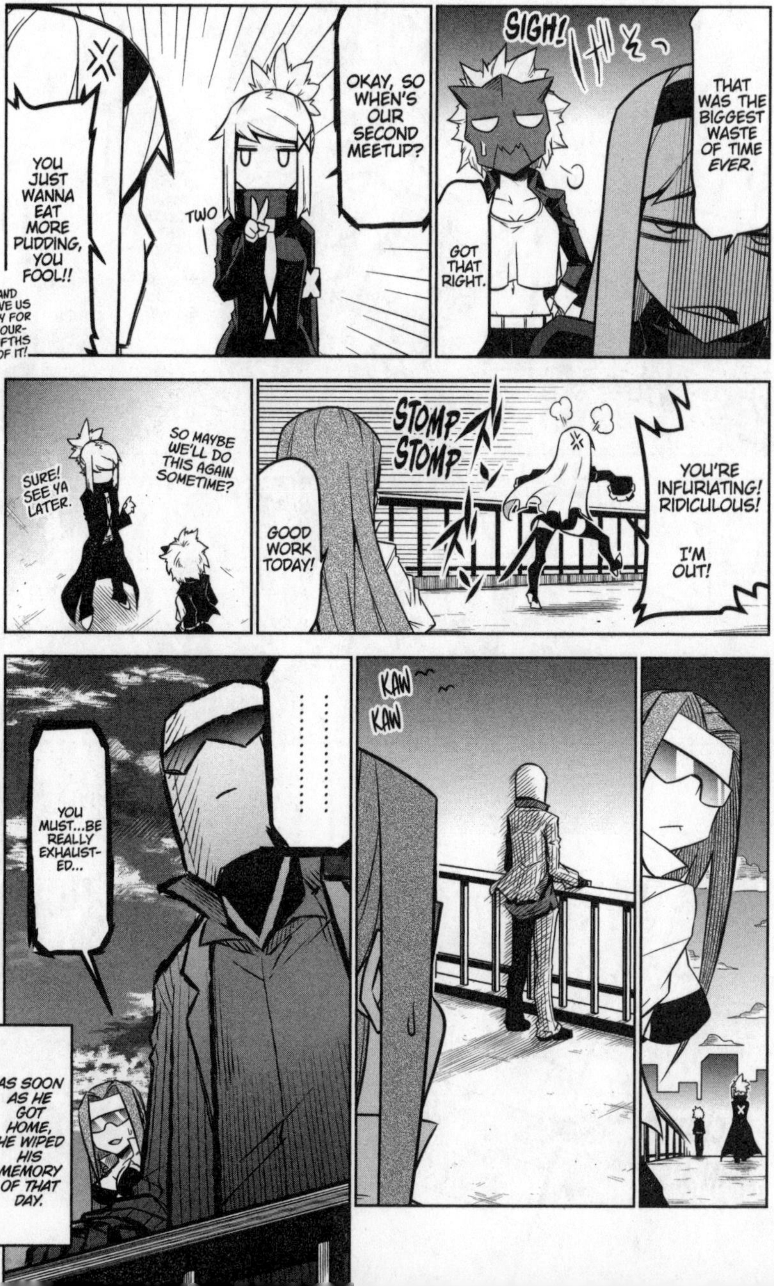
SIGH!
THAT WAS THE BIGGEST WASTE OF TIME EVER.
GOT THAT RIGHT.
OKAY, SO WHEN'S OUR SECOND MEETUP?
TWO
YOU JUST WANNA EAT MORE PUDDING, YOU FOOL!!
AND HAVE US PAY FOR FOUR-FIFTHS OF IT!
STOMP STOMP
YOU'RE INFURIATING! RIDICULOUS!
I'M OUT!
GOOD WORK TODAY!
SO MAYBE WE'LL DO THIS AGAIN SOMETIME?
SURE! SEE YA LATER.
KAW KAW
......
YOU MUST...BE REALLY EXHAUSTED...
AS SOON AS HE GOT HOME, HE WIPED HIS MEMORY OF THAT DAY.

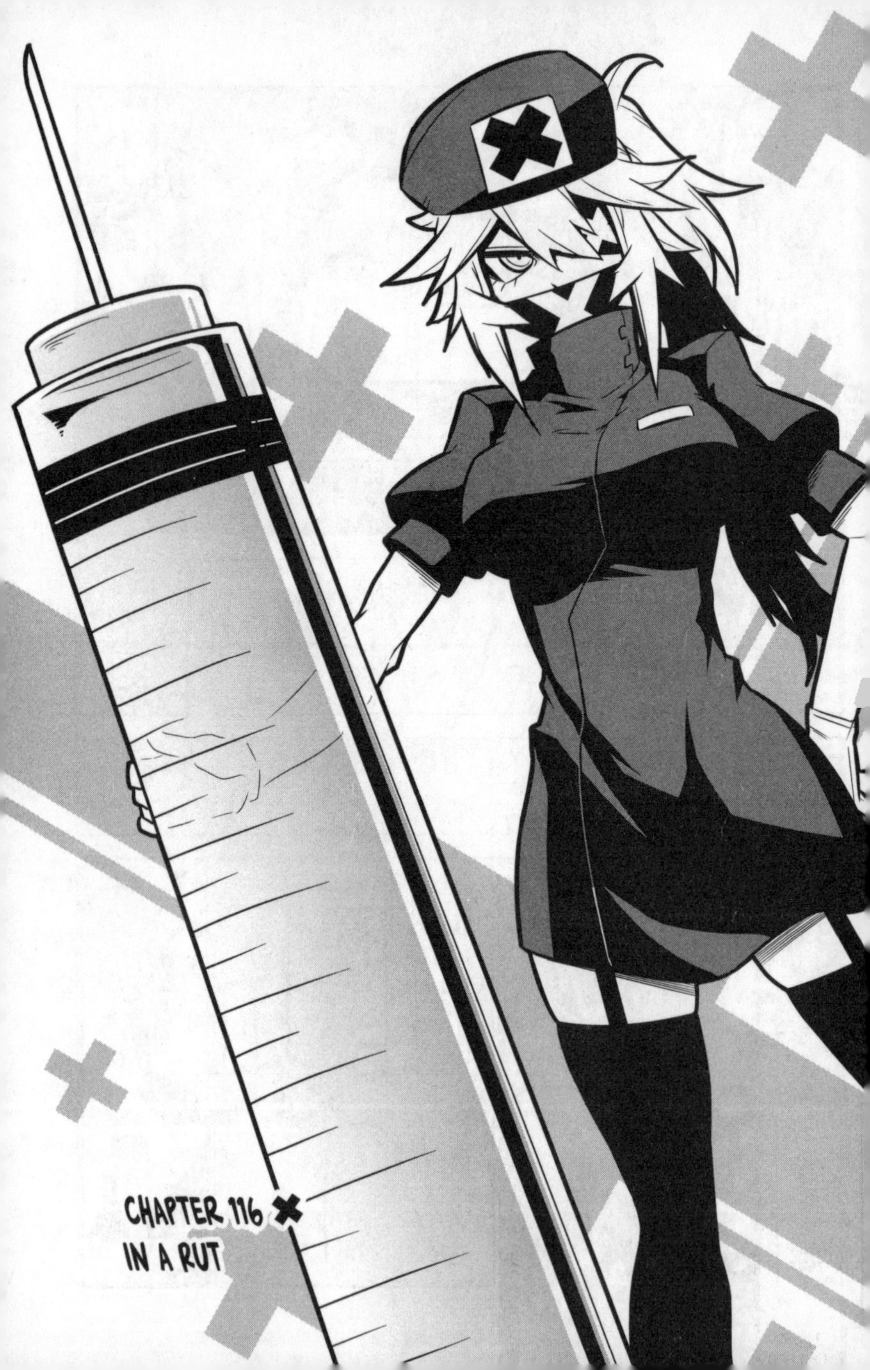
CHAPTER 116
IN A RUT

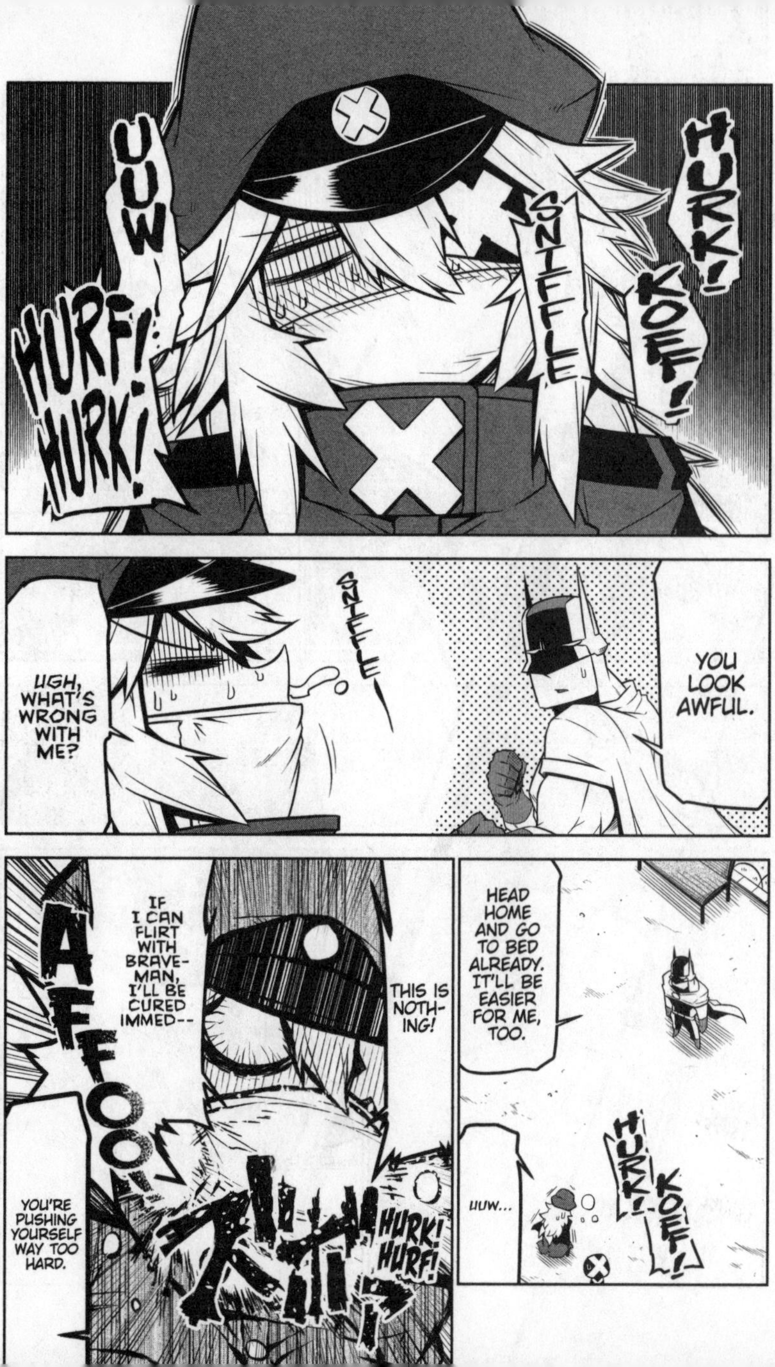
HURK! KOFF!
SNIFFLE
UUW
HURF! HURK! HURK!
YOU LOOK AWFUL.
SNIFFLE
UGH, WHAT'S WRONG WITH ME?
HEAD HOME AND GO TO BED ALREADY. IT'LL BE EASIER FOR ME, TOO.
HURK! KOFF!
UUW...
THIS IS NOTH-ING!
IF I CAN FLIRT WITH BRAVE-MAN, I'LL BE CURED IMMED--
AFFOO!!
HURK! HURF!
YOU'RE PUSHING YOURSELF WAY TOO HARD.

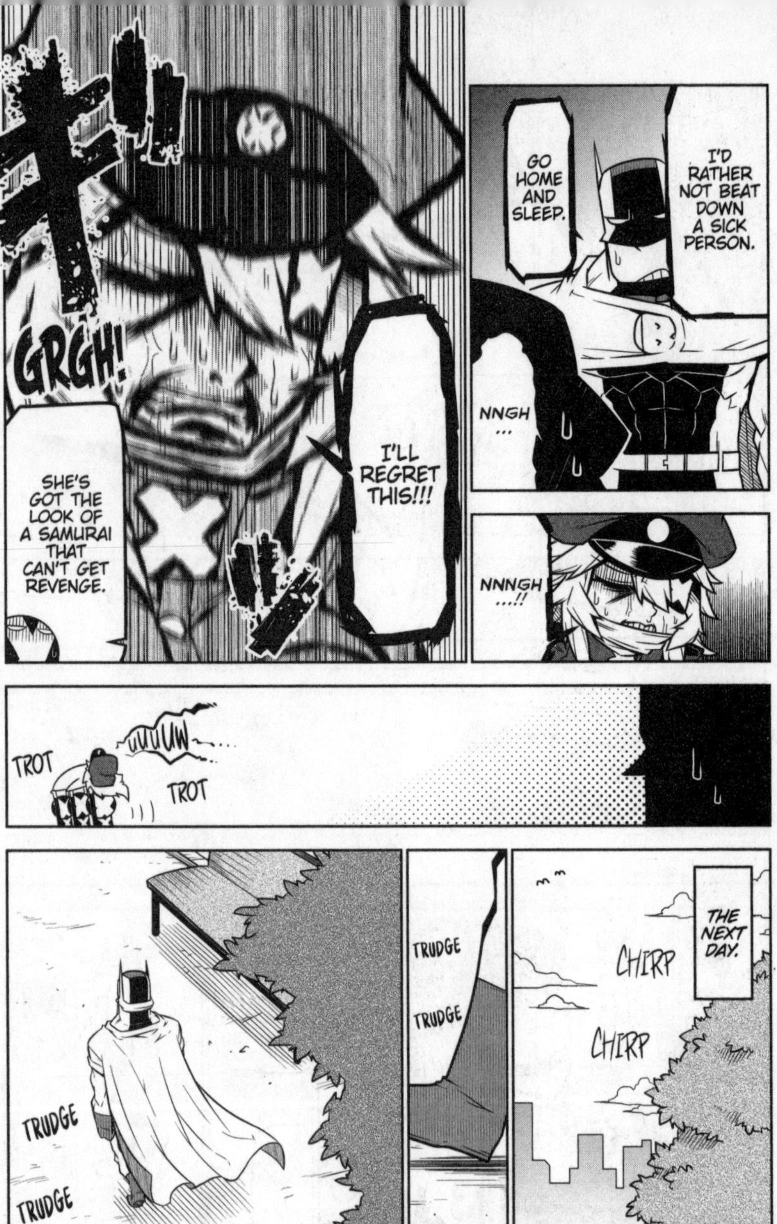
I'D RATHER NOT BEAT DOWN A SICK PERSON.
GO HOME AND SLEEP.
NNGH ...
NNNGH ...!!
I'LL REGRET THIS!!!
GRGH!
SHE'S GOT THE LOOK OF A SAMURAI THAT CAN'T GET REVENGE.
UUUUW
TROT
TROT
THE NEXT DAY.
CHIRP
CHIRP
TRUDGE
TRUDGE
TRUDGE
TRUDGE

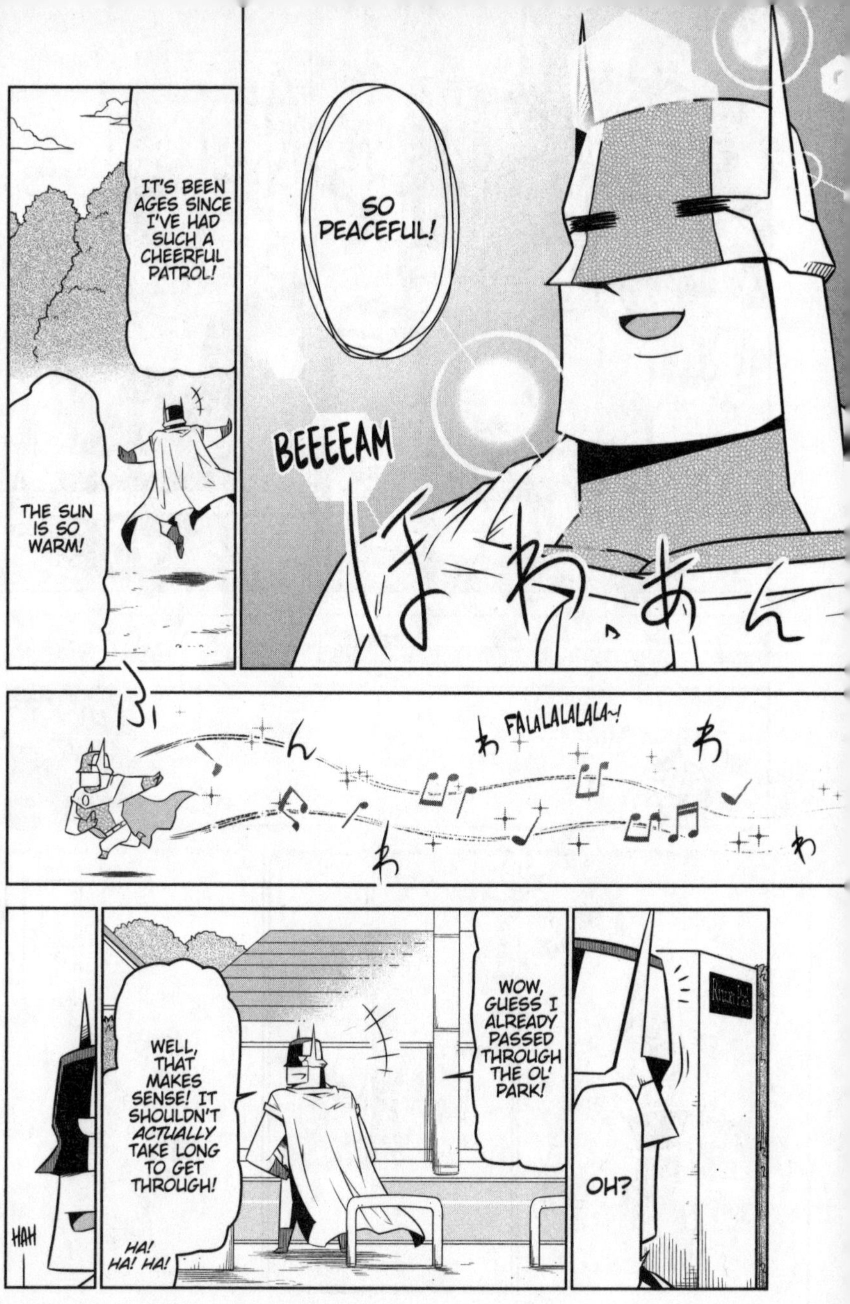
SO PEACEFUL!
BEEEEAM
IT'S BEEN AGES SINCE I'VE HAD SUCH A CHEERFUL PATROL!
THE SUN IS SO WARM!
FALALALALALA~!
OH?
WOW, GUESS I ALREADY PASSED THROUGH THE OL' PARK!
WELL, THAT MAKES SENSE! IT SHOULDN'T ACTUALLY TAKE LONG TO GET THROUGH!
HA! HA! HA!
HAH

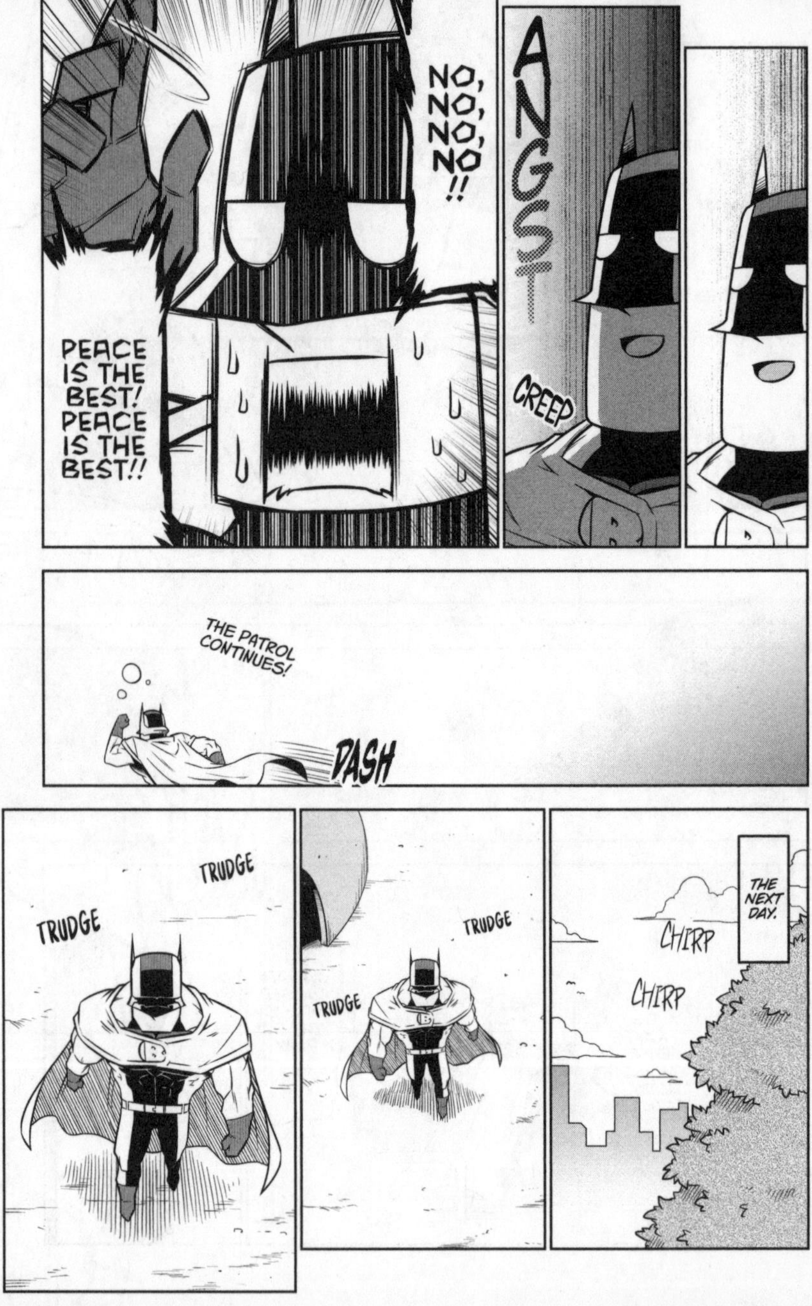
ANGST
CREEP
NO, NO, NO, NO!!
PEACE IS THE BEST! PEACE IS THE BEST!!
THE PATROL CONTINUES!
DASH
THE NEXT DAY.
CHIRP
CHIRP
TRUDGE
TRUDGE
TRUDGE
TRUDGE

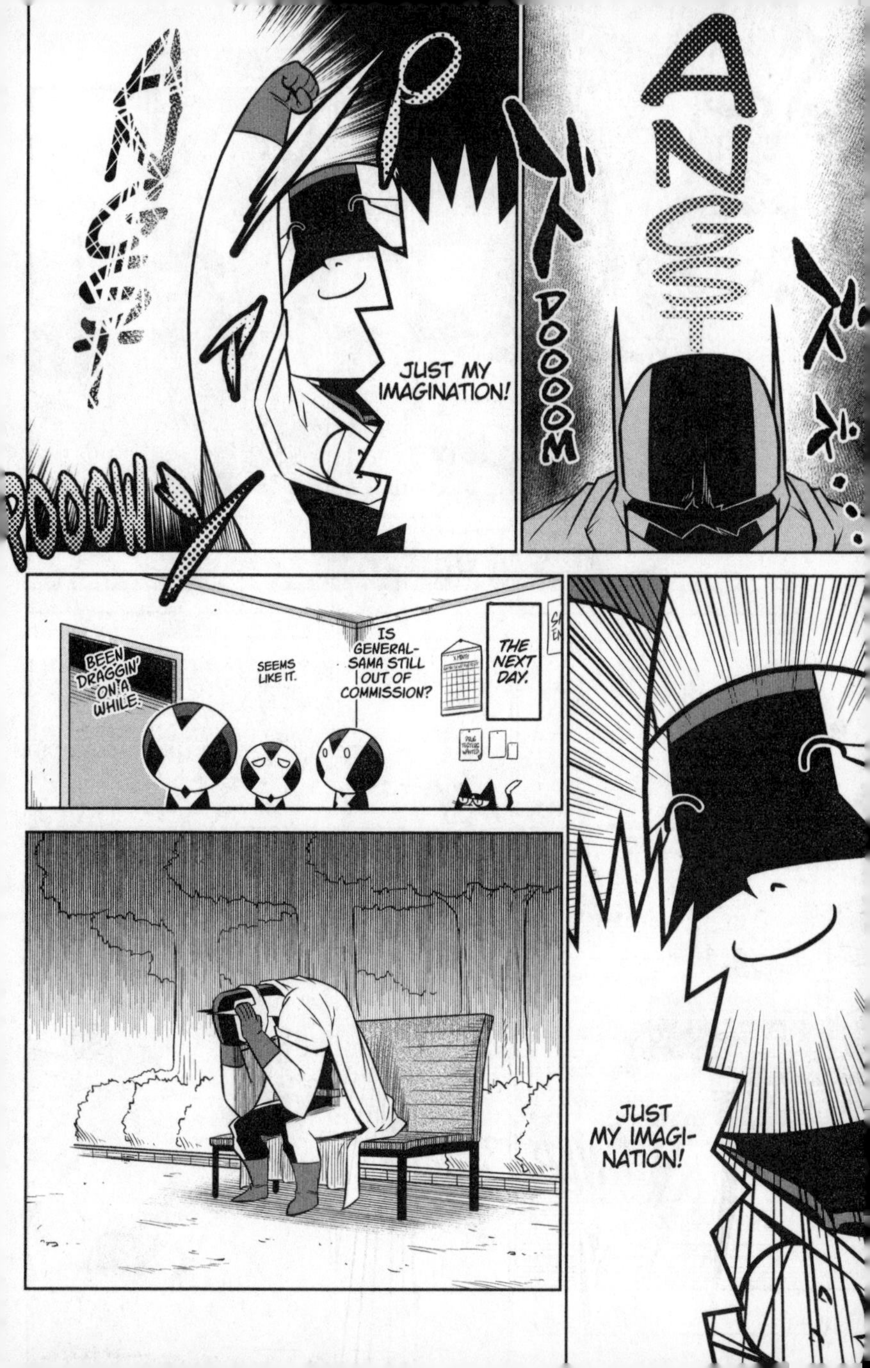
ANGST
DOOOOM
JUST MY IMAGINATION!
POOOW
JUST MY IMAGI-NATION!
THE NEXT DAY.
IS GENERAL-SAMA STILL OUT OF COMMISSION?
SEEMS LIKE IT.
BEEN DRAGGIN' ON A WHILE.

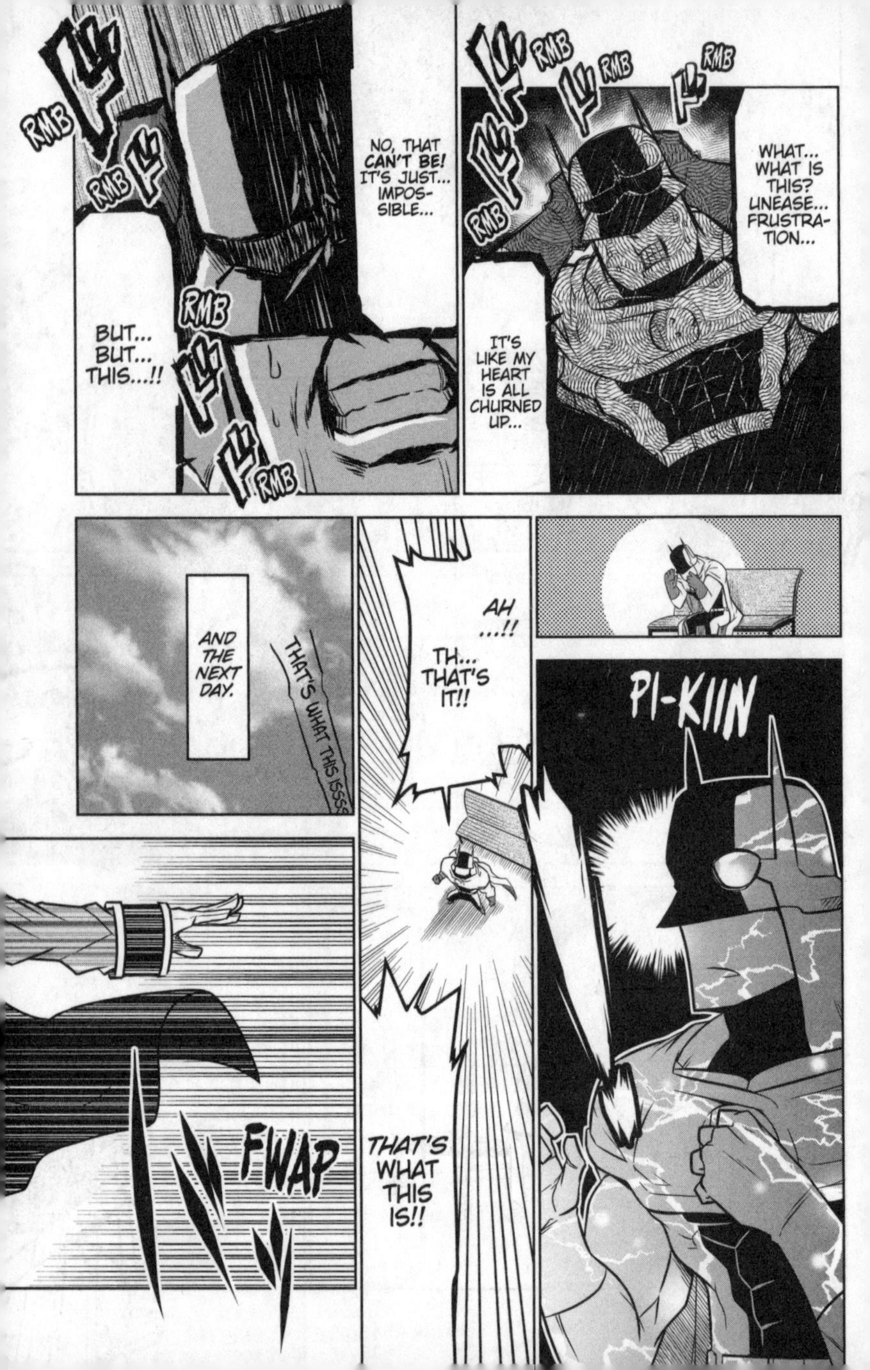
RMB
RMB
RMB
RMB
WHAT... WHAT IS THIS? UNEASE... FRUSTRATION...
IT'S LIKE MY HEART IS ALL CHURNED UP...
RMB
RMB
NO, THAT CAN'T BE! IT'S JUST... IMPOSSIBLE...
RMB
BUT... BUT... THIS...!!
RMB
PI-KIIN
AH ...!!
TH... THAT'S IT!!
THAT'S WHAT THIS IS!!
AND THE NEXT DAY.
THAT'S WHAT THIS ISSSS
FWAP

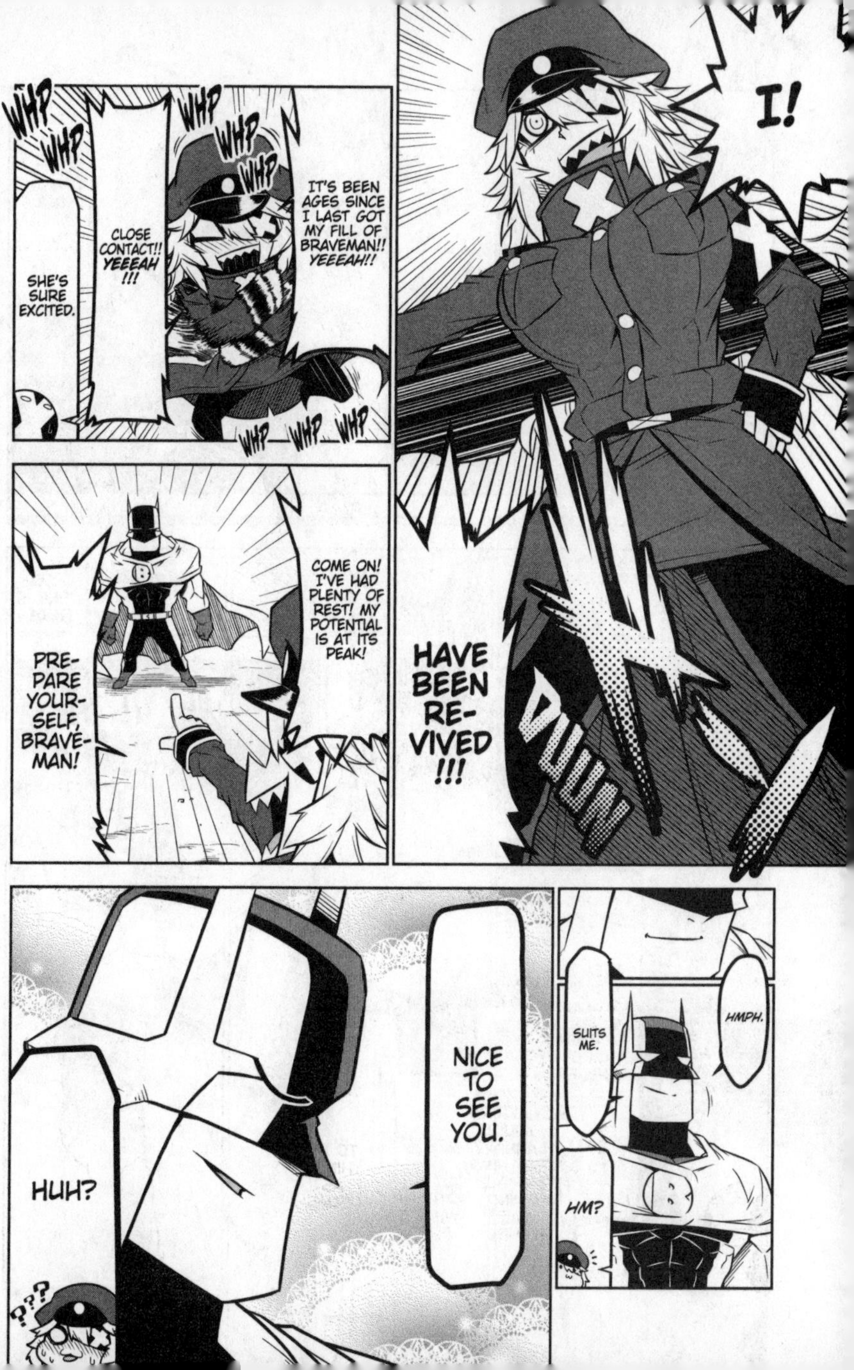

I!
HAVE BEEN RE-VIVED!!!
DUUN
WHP WHP WHP WHP WHP WHP
IT'S BEEN AGES SINCE I LAST GOT MY FILL OF BRAVEMAN!! YEEEAH!!
CLOSE CONTACT!! YEEEAH!!!
SHE'S SURE EXCITED.
WHP WHP WHP
COME ON! I'VE HAD PLENTY OF REST! MY POTENTIAL IS AT ITS PEAK!
PRE-PARE YOUR-SELF, BRAVE-MAN!
HMPH.
SUITS ME.
HM?
NICE TO SEE YOU.
HUH?
???

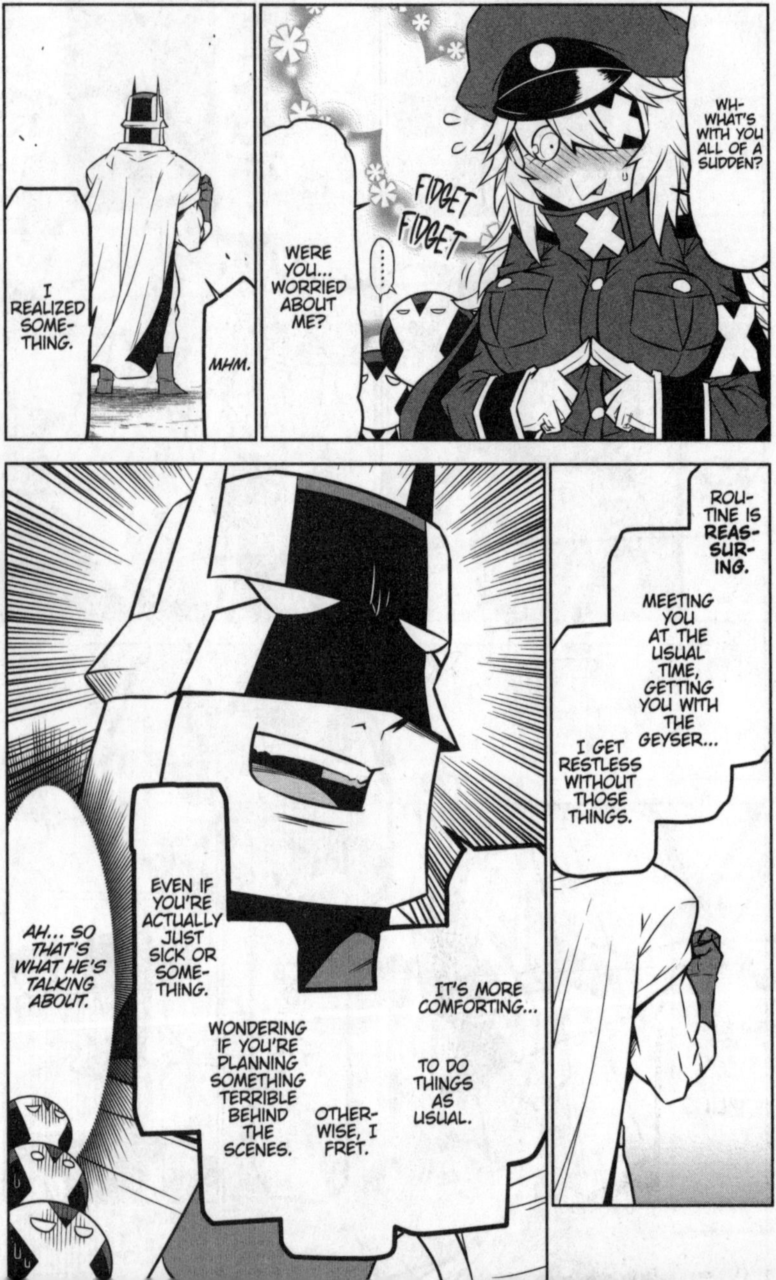
WH-WHAT'S WITH YOU ALL OF A SUDDEN?
FIDGET FIDGET
...
WERE YOU... WORRIED ABOUT ME?
MHM.
I REALIZED SOMETHING.
ROUTINE IS REASSURING.
MEETING YOU AT THE USUAL TIME, GETTING YOU WITH THE GEYSER...
I GET RESTLESS WITHOUT THOSE THINGS.
IT'S MORE COMFORTING...
TO DO THINGS AS USUAL.
OTHERWISE, I FRET.
WONDERING IF YOU'RE PLANNING SOMETHING TERRIBLE BEHIND THE SCENES.
EVEN IF YOU'RE ACTUALLY JUST SICK OR SOMETHING.
AH... SO THAT'S WHAT HE'S TALKING ABOUT.

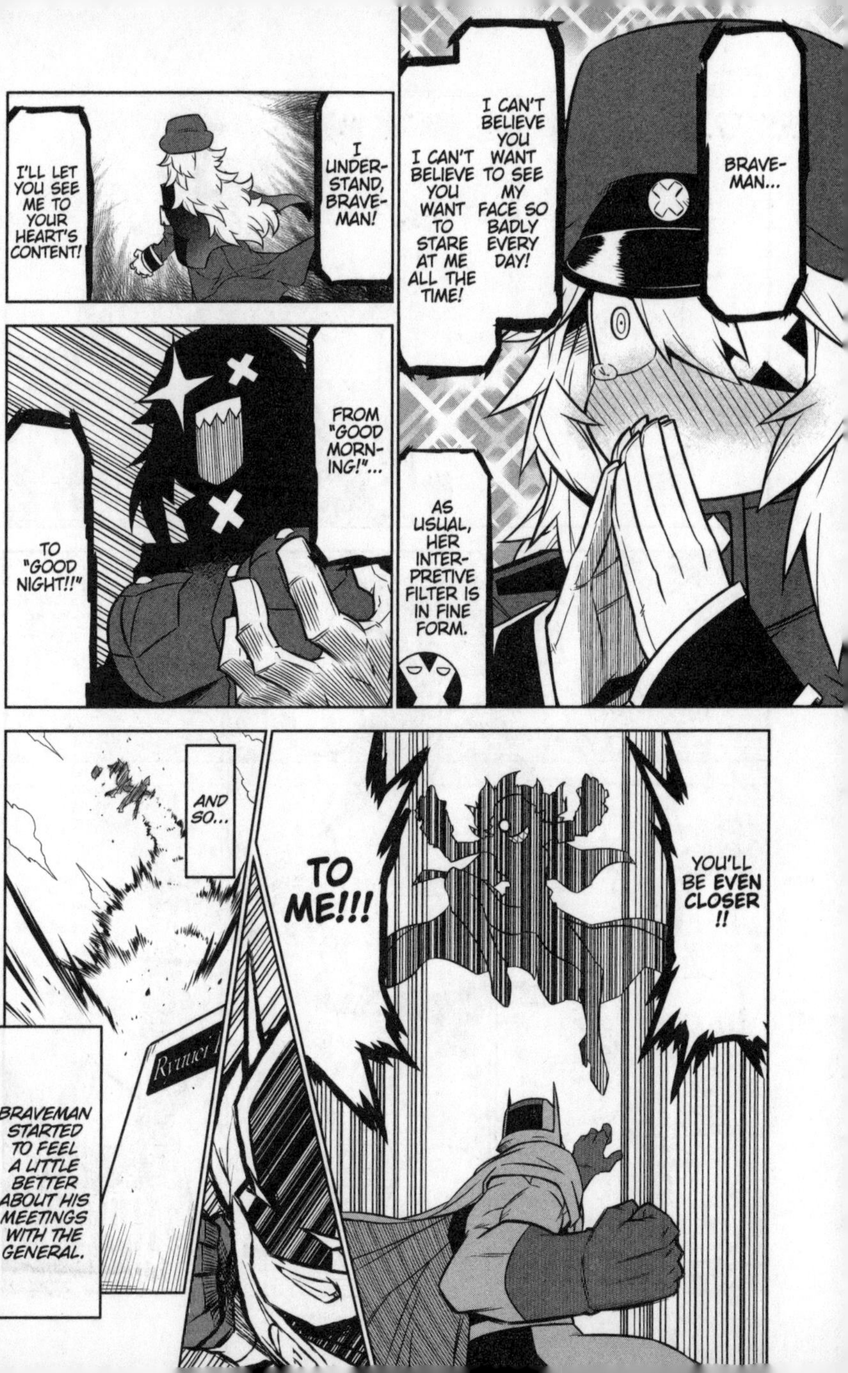
BRAVE-MAN...
I CAN'T BELIEVE YOU WANT TO SEE MY FACE SO BADLY EVERY DAY!
I CAN'T BELIEVE YOU WANT TO STARE AT ME ALL THE TIME!
AS USUAL, HER INTER-PRETIVE FILTER IS IN FINE FORM.
I UNDER-STAND, BRAVE-MAN!
I'LL LET YOU SEE ME TO YOUR HEART'S CONTENT!
FROM "GOOD MORN-ING!"...
TO "GOOD NIGHT!!"
YOU'LL BE EVEN CLOSER !!
TO ME!!!
AND SO...
BRAVEMAN STARTED TO FEEL A LITTLE BETTER ABOUT HIS MEETINGS WITH THE GENERAL.

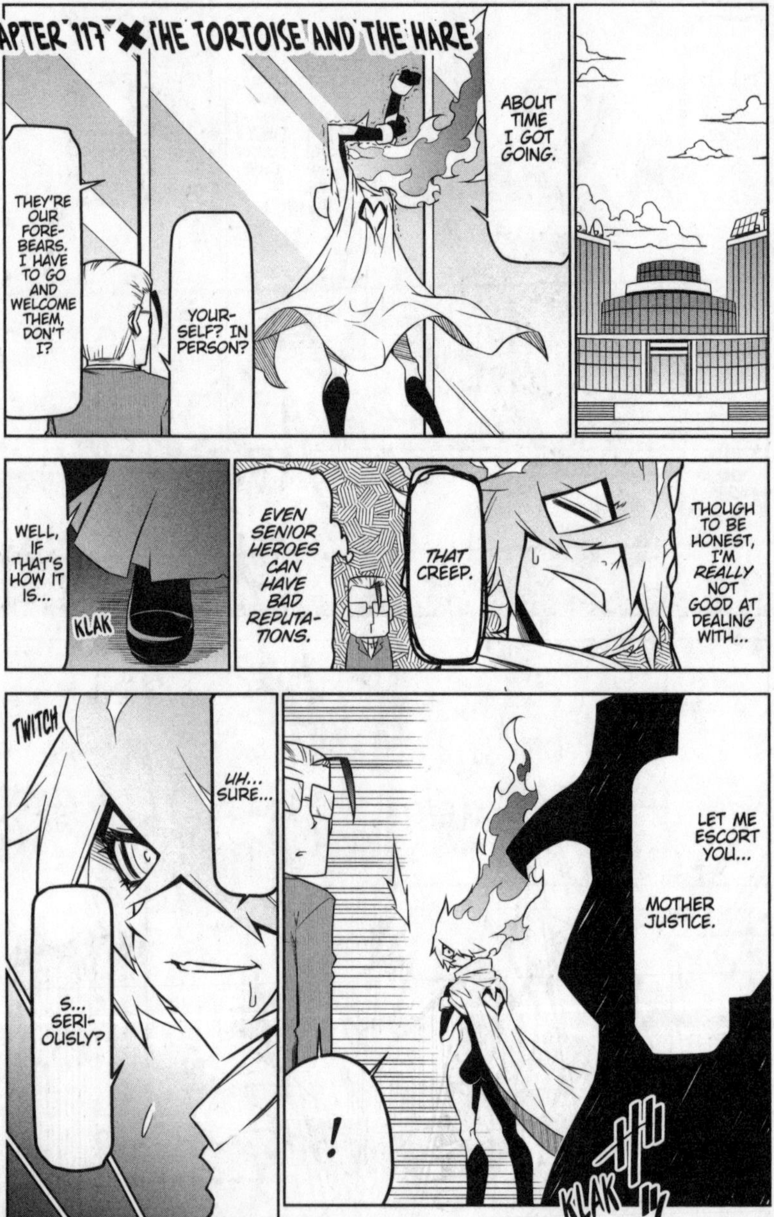
CHAPTER 117 ✖ THE TORTOISE AND THE HARE
ABOUT TIME I GOT GOING.
YOURSELF? IN PERSON?
THEY'RE OUR FOREBEARS. I HAVE TO GO AND WELCOME THEM, DON'T I?
THOUGH TO BE HONEST, I'M *REALLY* NOT GOOD AT DEALING WITH...
THAT CREEP.
EVEN SENIOR HEROES CAN HAVE BAD REPUTATIONS.
WELL, IF THAT'S HOW IT IS...
KLAK
LET ME ESCORT YOU...
MOTHER JUSTICE.
KLAK
!
TWITCH
UH... SURE...
S... SERIOUSLY?

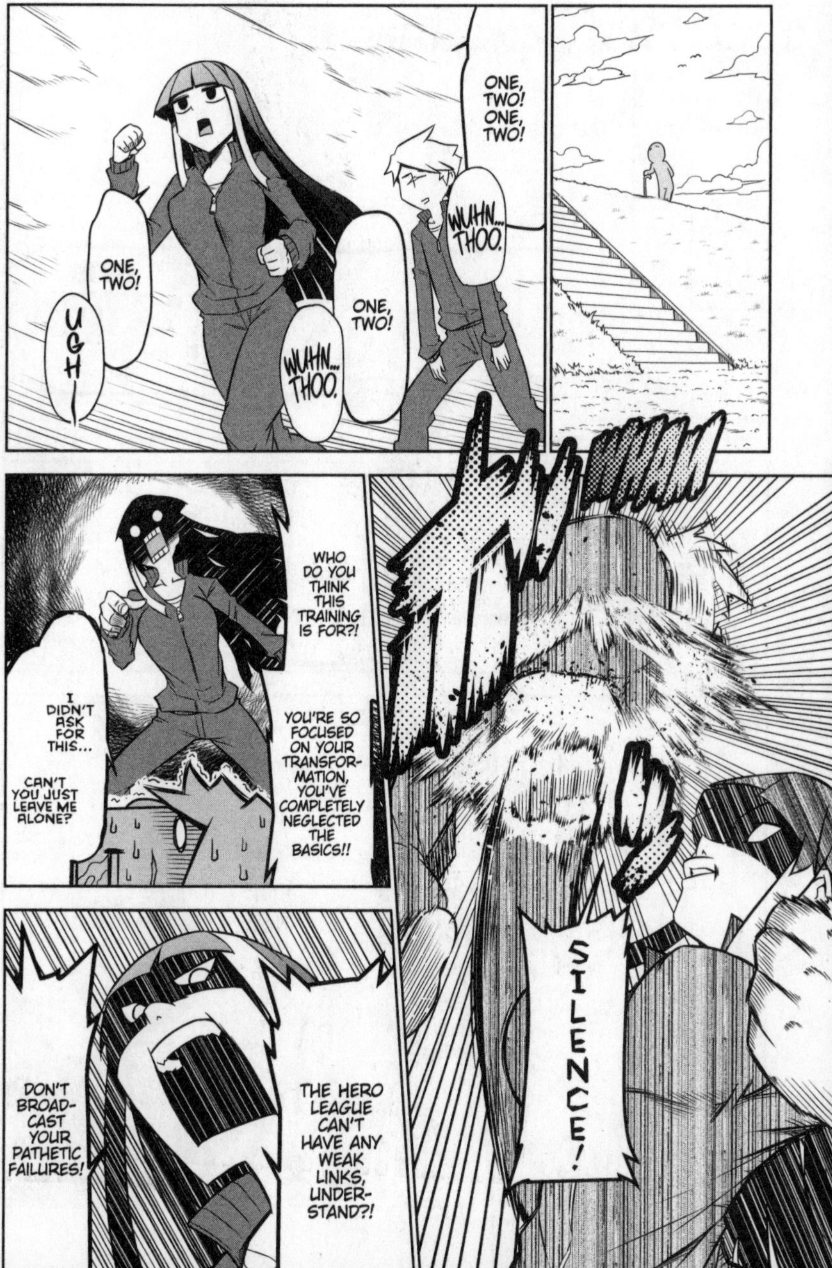
ONE, TWO! ONE, TWO!
WUHN... THOO.
ONE, TWO!
ONE, TWO!
WUHN... THOO.
WHAM
SILENCE!
WHO DO YOU THINK THIS TRAINING IS FOR?!
YOU'RE SO FOCUSED ON YOUR TRANSFORMATION, YOU'VE COMPLETELY NEGLECTED THE BASICS!!
I DIDN'T ASK FOR THIS...
CAN'T YOU JUST LEAVE ME ALONE?
THE HERO LEAGUE CAN'T HAVE ANY WEAK LINKS, UNDERSTAND?!
DON'T BROADCAST YOUR PATHETIC FAILURES!

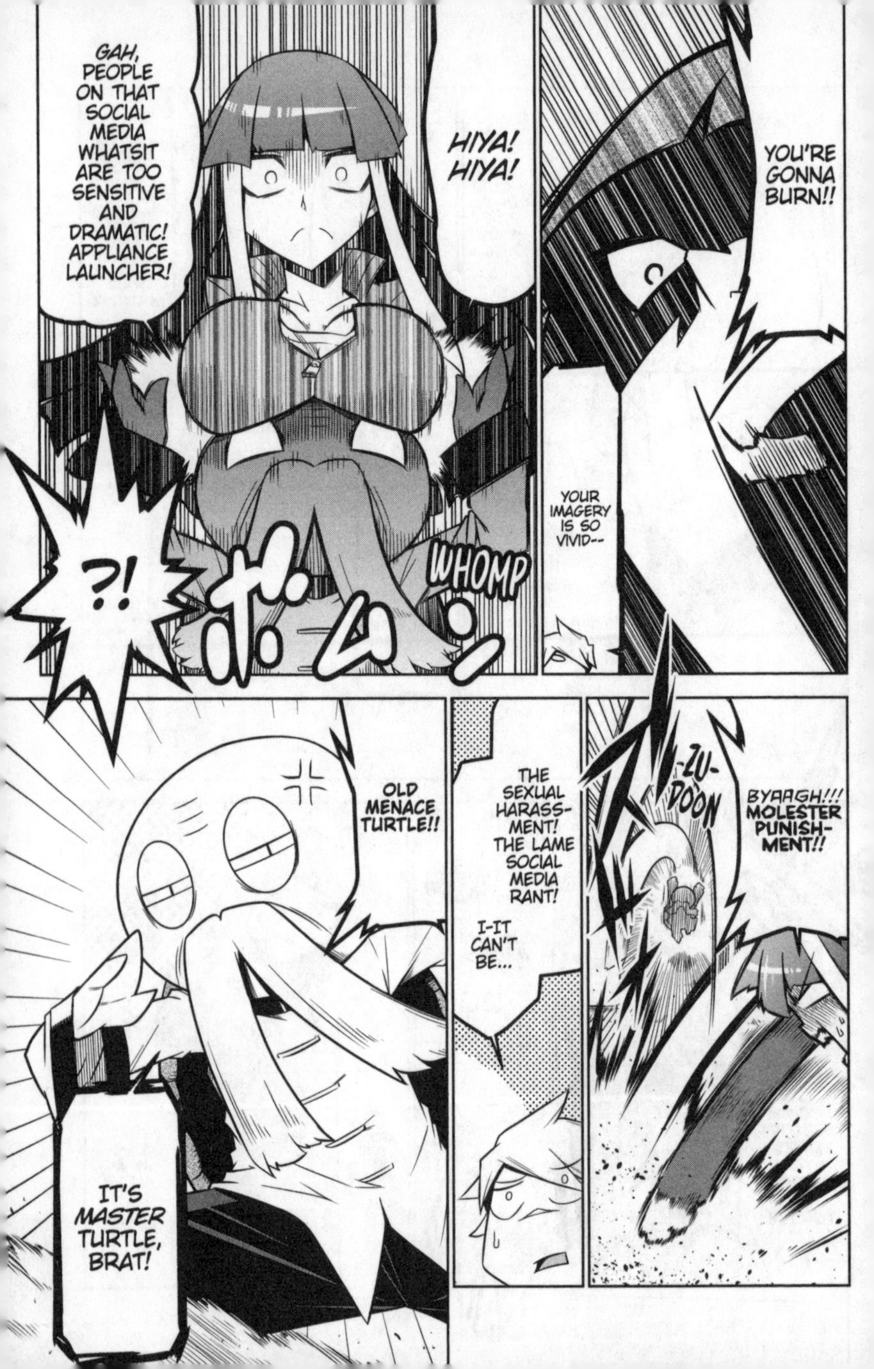
YOU'RE GONNA BURN!!
YOUR IMAGERY IS SO VIVID--
HIYA! HIYA!
GAH, PEOPLE ON THAT SOCIAL MEDIA WHATSIT ARE TOO SENSITIVE AND DRAMATIC! APPLIANCE LAUNCHER!
WHOMP
?!
-ZU-DOON
BYAAGH!!! MOLESTER PUNISHMENT!!
THE SEXUAL HARASSMENT! THE LAME SOCIAL MEDIA RANT!
I-IT CAN'T BE...
OLD MENACE TURTLE!!
IT'S MASTER TURTLE, BRAT!

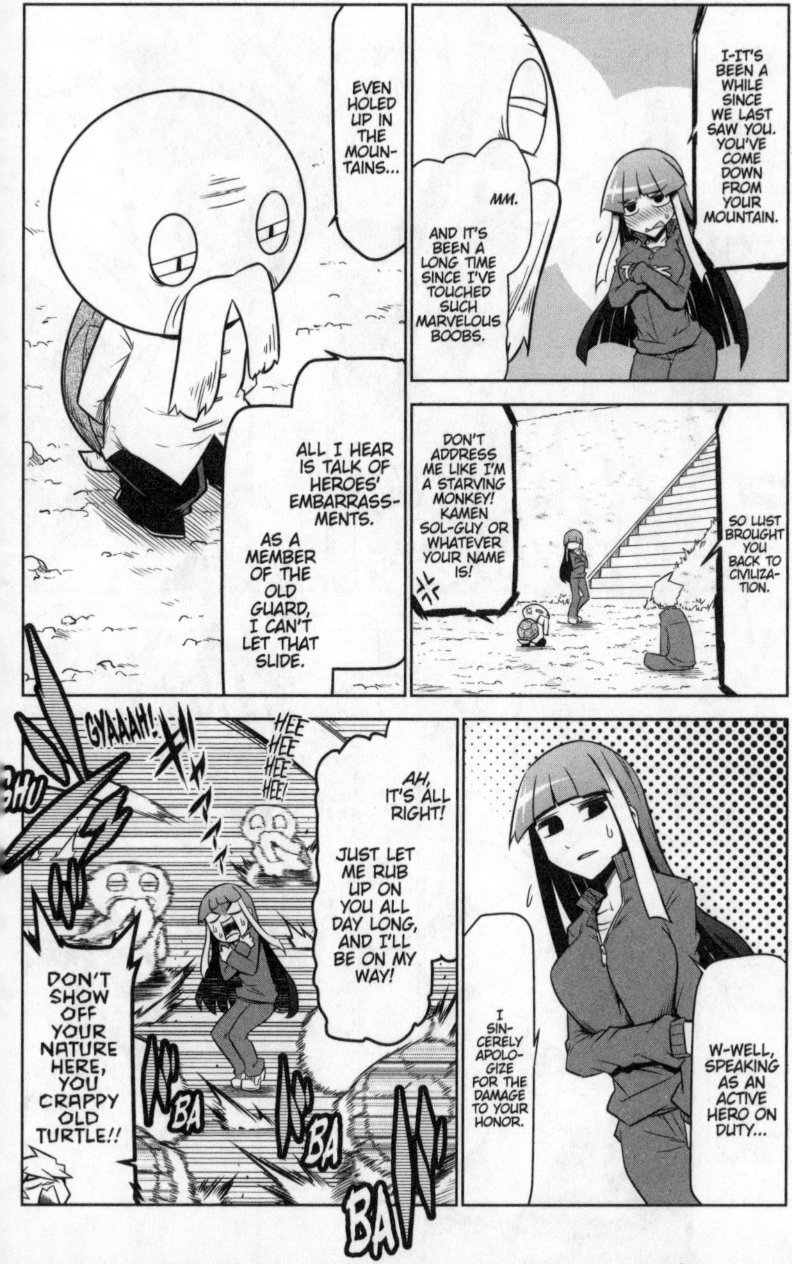
I-IT'S BEEN A WHILE SINCE WE LAST SAW YOU. YOU'VE COME DOWN FROM YOUR MOUNTAIN.
MM.
AND IT'S BEEN A LONG TIME SINCE I'VE TOUCHED SUCH MARVELOUS BOOBS.
SO LUST BROUGHT YOU BACK TO CIVILIZATION.
DON'T ADDRESS ME LIKE I'M A STARVING MONKEY! KAMEN SOL-GUY OR WHATEVER YOUR NAME IS!
EVEN HOLED UP IN THE MOUNTAINS...
ALL I HEAR IS TALK OF HEROES' EMBARRASSMENTS.
AS A MEMBER OF THE OLD GUARD, I CAN'T LET THAT SLIDE.
W-WELL, SPEAKING AS AN ACTIVE HERO ON DUTY...
I SINCERELY APOLOGIZE FOR THE DAMAGE TO YOUR HONOR.
AH, IT'S ALL RIGHT!
JUST LET ME RUB UP ON YOU ALL DAY LONG, AND I'LL BE ON MY WAY!
HEE HEE HEE HEE!
GYAAAH!
SHU
DON'T SHOW OFF YOUR NATURE HERE, YOU CRAPPY OLD TURTLE!!
BA
BA
BA

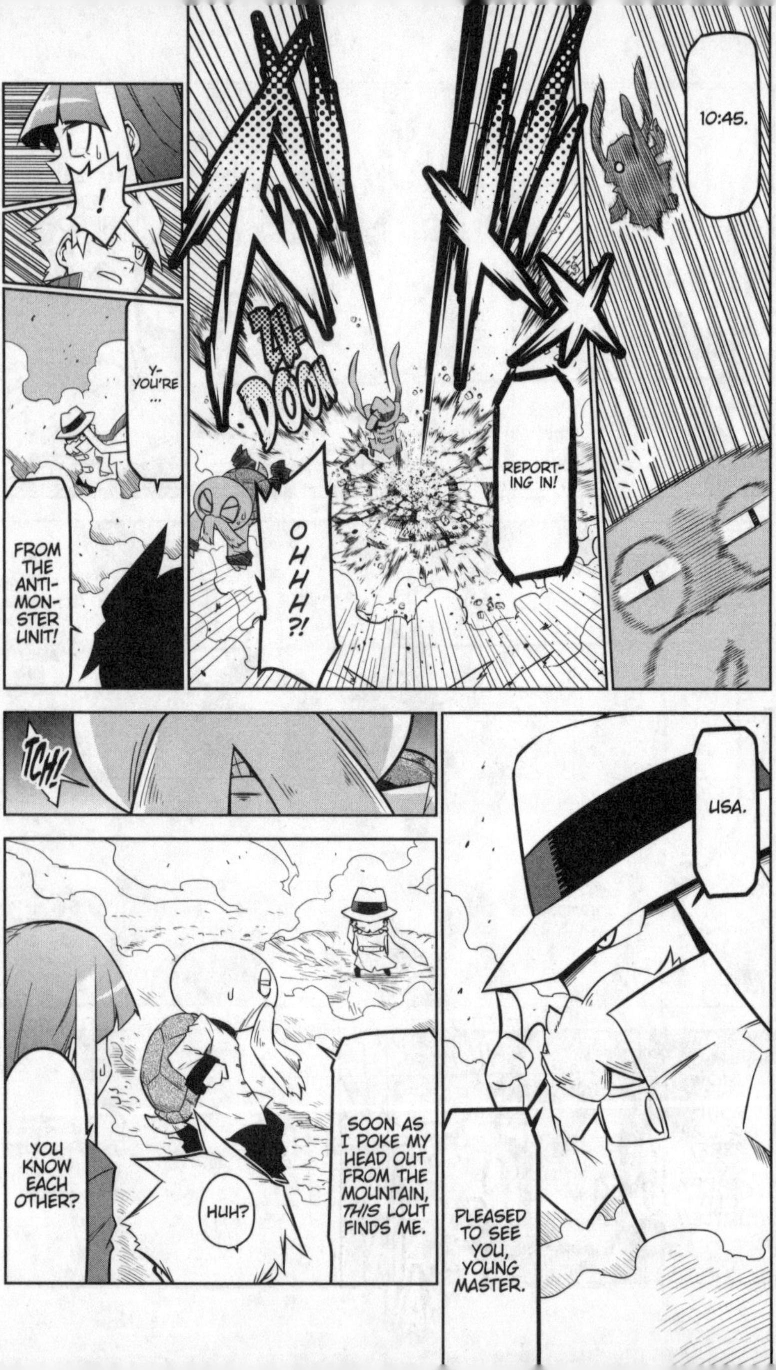
10:45.
REPORTING IN!
ZA-DOON
OHHHH?!
!
Y-YOU'RE ...
FROM THE ANTI-MONSTER UNIT!
USA.
PLEASED TO SEE YOU, YOUNG MASTER.
TCH!
SOON AS I POKE MY HEAD OUT FROM THE MOUNTAIN, *THIS* LOUT FINDS ME.
HUH?
YOU KNOW EACH OTHER?

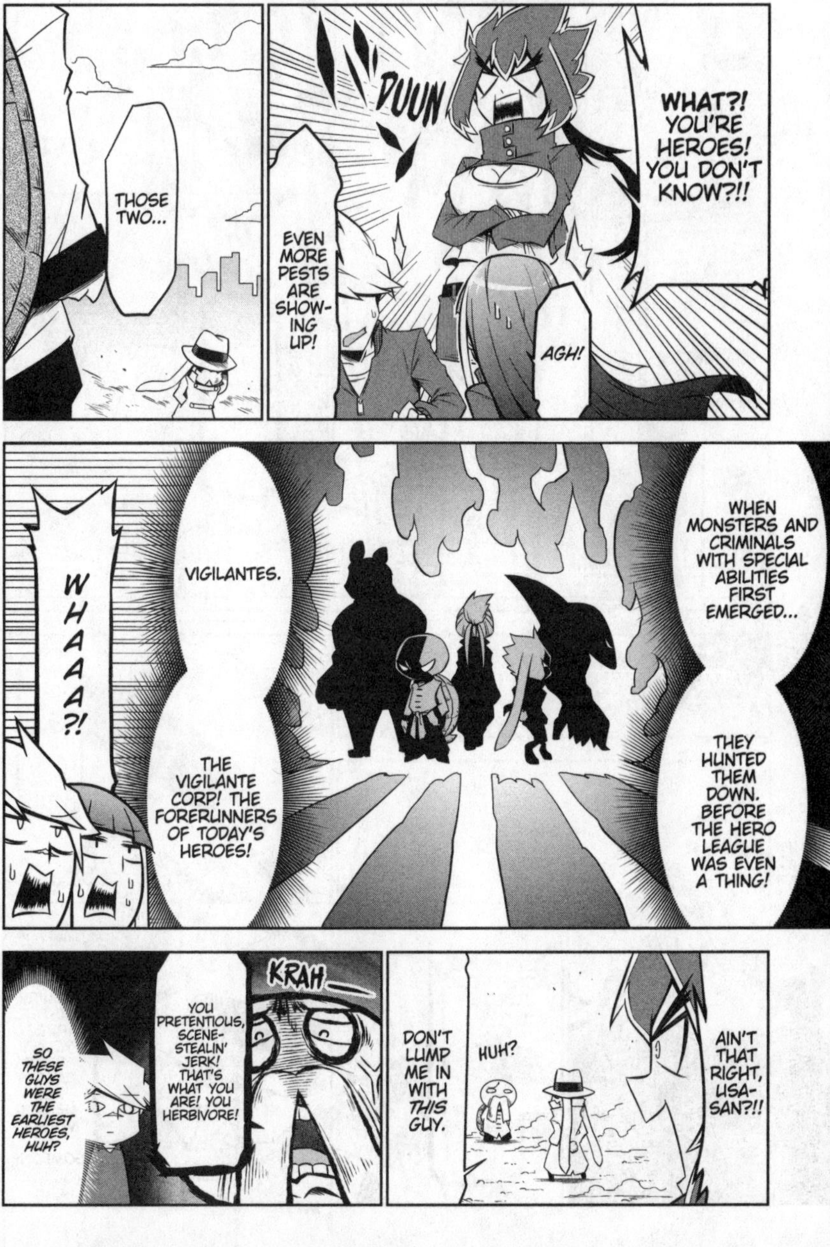
WHAT?! YOU'RE HEROES! YOU DON'T KNOW?!!
DUUN
EVEN MORE PESTS ARE SHOW-ING UP!
AGH!
THOSE TWO...
WHEN MONSTERS AND CRIMINALS WITH SPECIAL ABILITIES FIRST EMERGED...
THEY HUNTED THEM DOWN. BEFORE THE HERO LEAGUE WAS EVEN A THING!
VIGILANTES.
THE VIGILANTE CORP! THE FORERUNNERS OF TODAY'S HEROES!
WHAAAA?!
AIN'T THAT RIGHT, USA-SAN?!!
HUH?
DON'T LUMP ME IN WITH *THIS* GUY.
KRAH
YOU PRETENTIOUS, SCENE-STEALIN' JERK! THAT'S WHAT YOU ARE! YOU HERBIVORE!
SO THESE GUYS WERE THE EARLIEST HEROES, HUH?

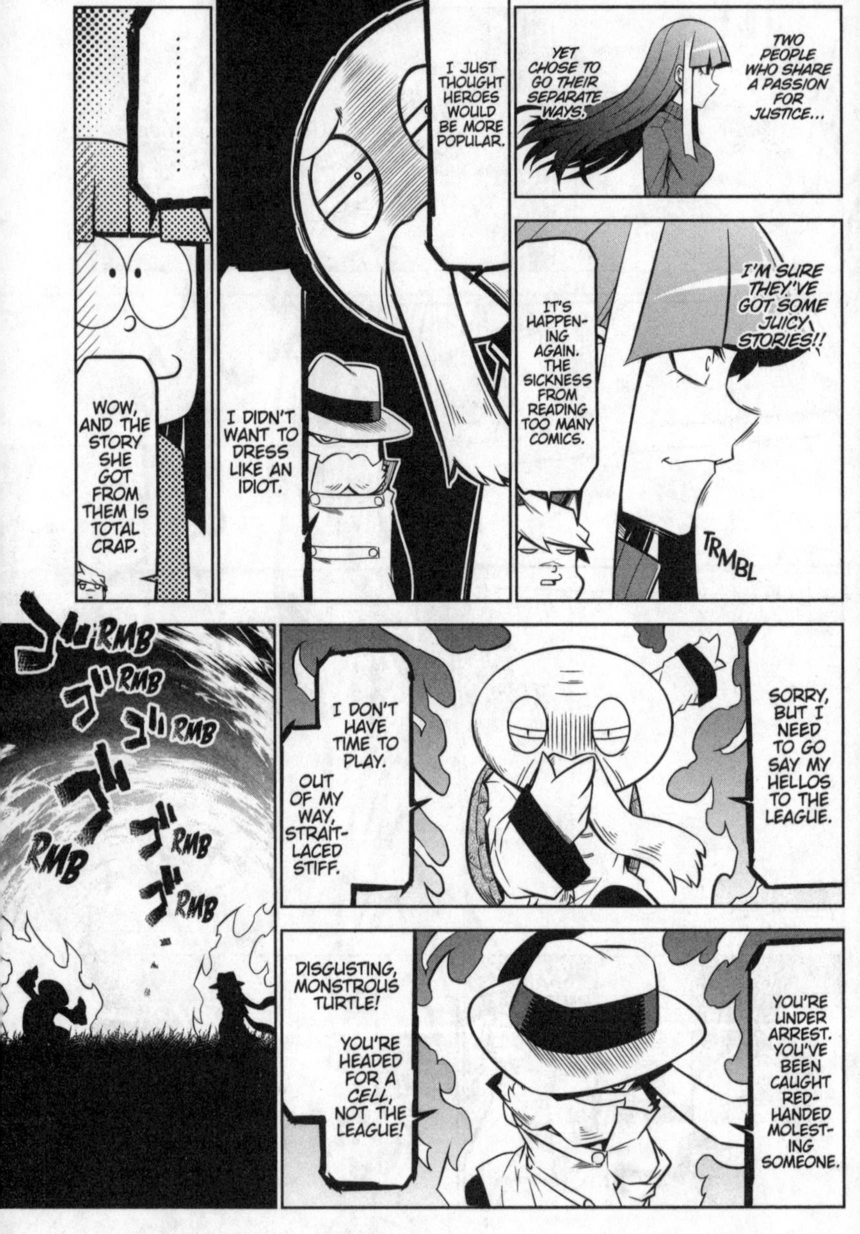
TWO PEOPLE WHO SHARE A PASSION FOR JUSTICE...
YET CHOSE TO GO THEIR SEPARATE WAYS.
I'M SURE THEY'VE GOT SOME JUICY STORIES!!
IT'S HAPPENING AGAIN. THE SICKNESS FROM READING TOO MANY COMICS.
TRMBL
I JUST THOUGHT HEROES WOULD BE MORE POPULAR.
I DIDN'T WANT TO DRESS LIKE AN IDIOT.
......
WOW, AND THE STORY SHE GOT FROM THEM IS TOTAL CRAP.
SORRY, BUT I NEED TO GO SAY MY HELLOS TO THE LEAGUE.
I DON'T HAVE TIME TO PLAY.
OUT OF MY WAY, STRAIT-LACED STIFF.
YOU'RE UNDER ARREST. YOU'VE BEEN CAUGHT RED-HANDED MOLEST-ING SOMEONE.
DISGUSTING, MONSTROUS TURTLE!
YOU'RE HEADED FOR A CELL, NOT THE LEAGUE!
RMB
RMB
RMB
RMB
RMB
RMB

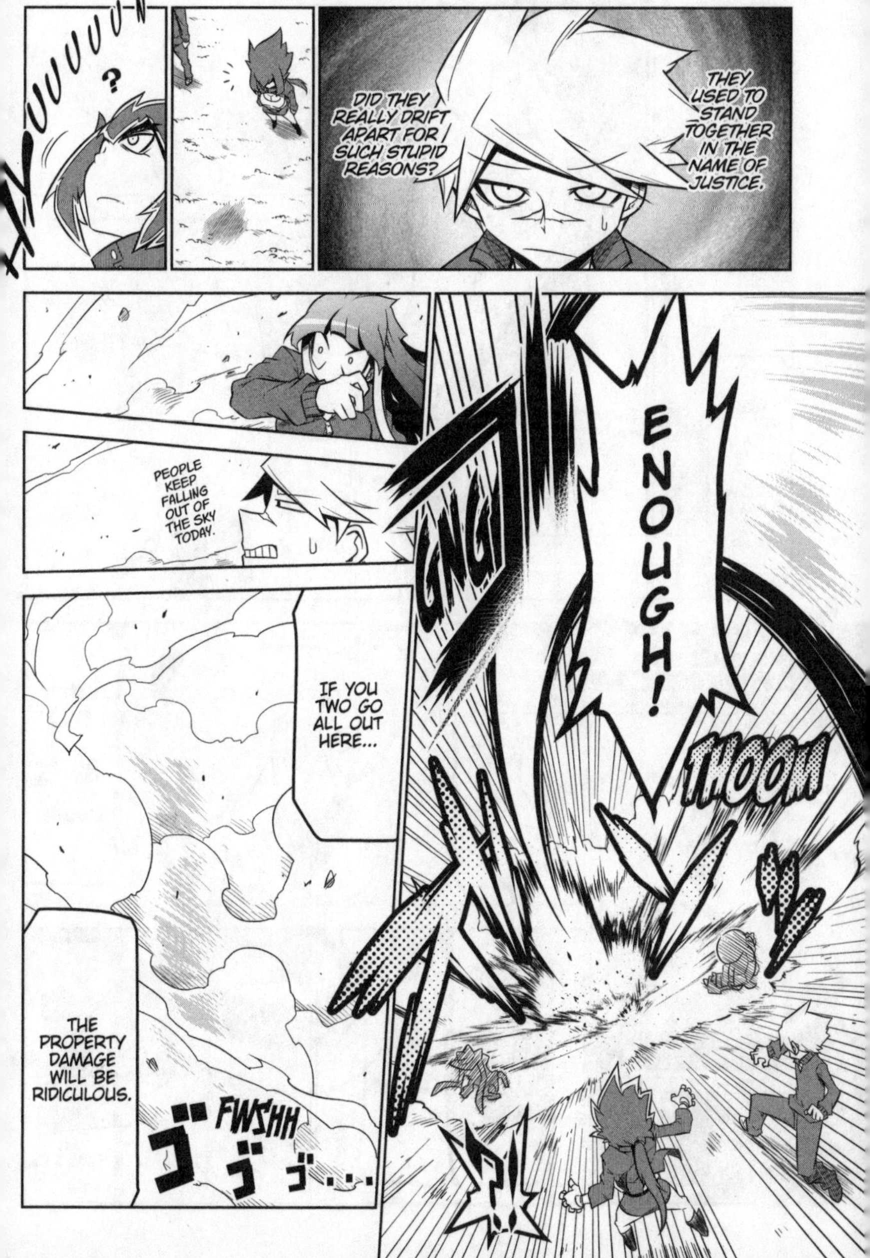
THEY USED TO STAND TOGETHER IN THE NAME OF JUSTICE.
DID THEY REALLY DRIFT APART FOR SUCH STUPID REASONS?
HYUUUUUUN
?
ENOUGH!
GNGH
THOOM
?!
PEOPLE KEEP FALLING OUT OF THE SKY TODAY.
IF YOU TWO GO ALL OUT HERE...
THE PROPERTY DAMAGE WILL BE RIDICULOUS.
FWSHH
ゴゴゴ...

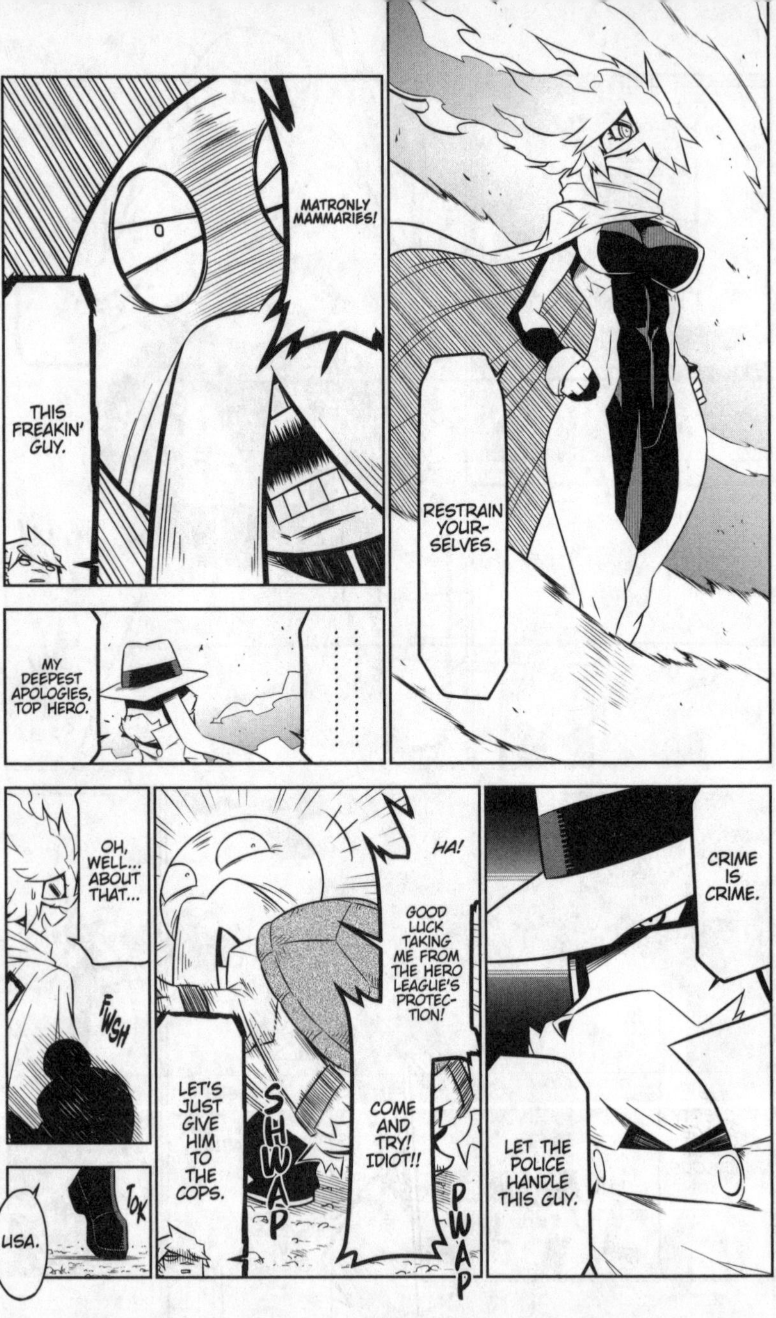
RESTRAIN YOURSELVES.
MATRONLY MAMMARIES!
THIS FREAKIN' GUY.
MY DEEPEST APOLOGIES, TOP HERO.
CRIME IS CRIME.
LET THE POLICE HANDLE THIS GUY.
HA!
GOOD LUCK TAKING ME FROM THE HERO LEAGUE'S PROTECTION!
COME AND TRY! IDIOT!!
PWAP
SHWAP
LET'S JUST GIVE HIM TO THE COPS.
OH, WELL... ABOUT THAT...
FWSH
TOK
USA.

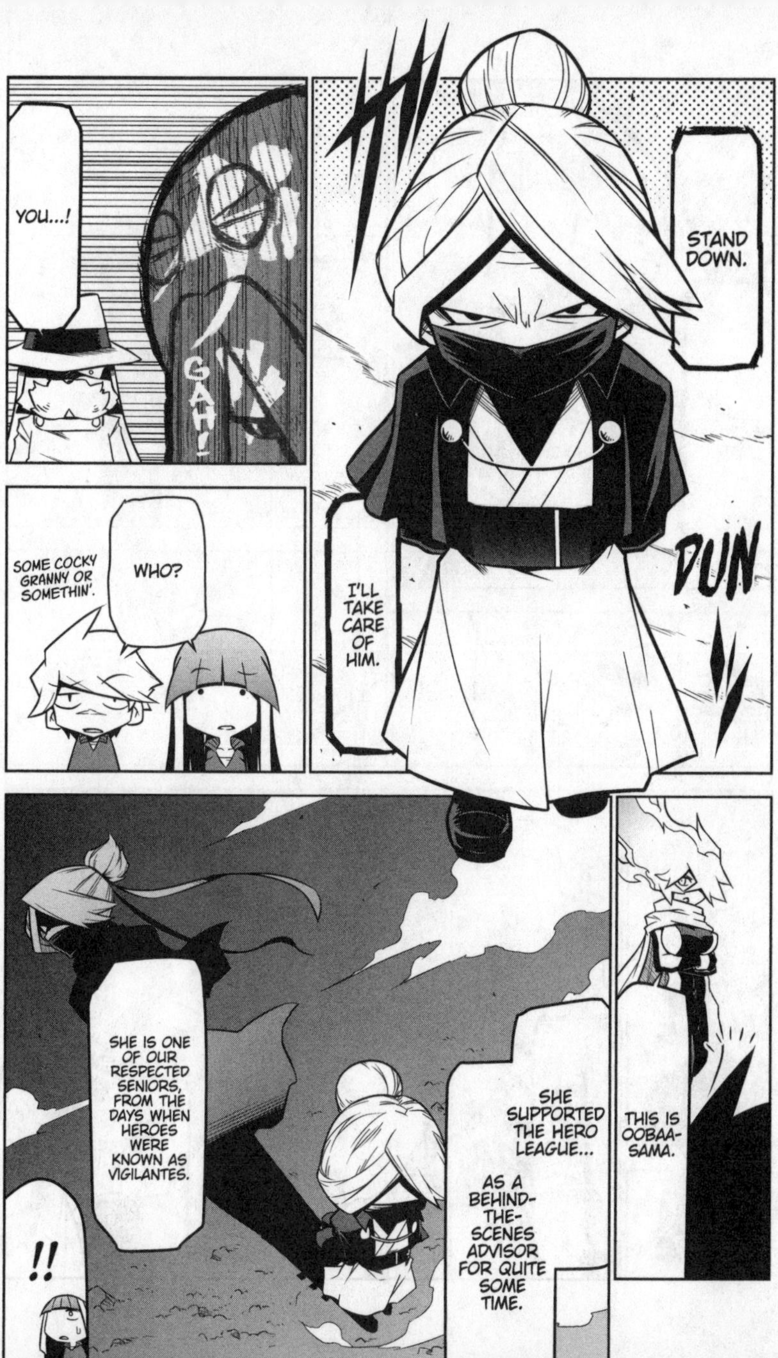
STAND DOWN.
I'LL TAKE CARE OF HIM.
DUN
YOU...!
GAH!
WHO?
SOME COCKY GRANNY OR SOMETHIN'.
THIS IS OOBAA-SAMA.
SHE SUPPORTED THE HERO LEAGUE...
AS A BEHIND-THE-SCENES ADVISOR FOR QUITE SOME TIME.
SHE IS ONE OF OUR RESPECTED SENIORS, FROM THE DAYS WHEN HEROES WERE KNOWN AS VIGILANTES.
!!

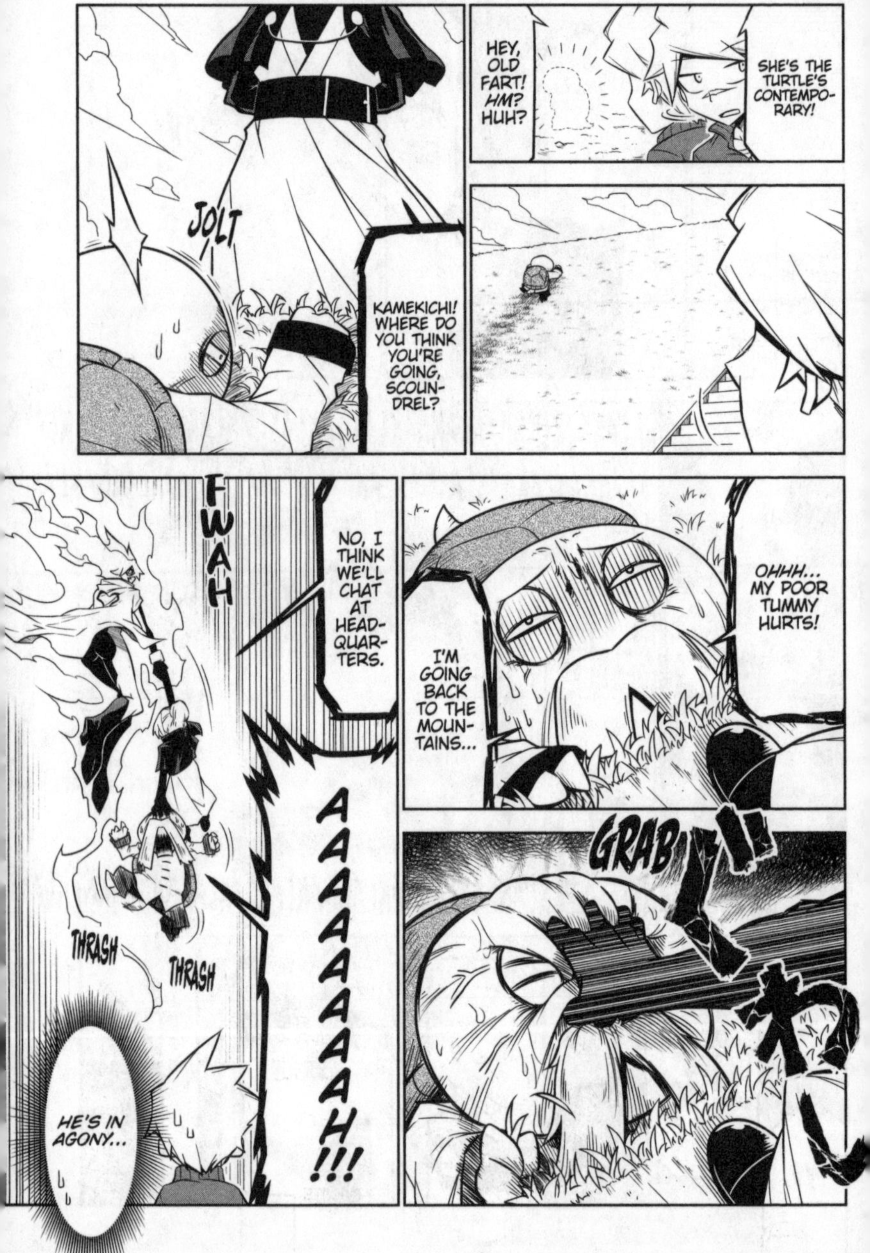
HEY, OLD FART!
HM? HUH?
SHE'S THE TURTLE'S CONTEMPORARY!
JOLT
KAMEKICHI! WHERE DO YOU THINK YOU'RE GOING, SCOUNDREL?
OHHH... MY POOR TUMMY HURTS!
I'M GOING BACK TO THE MOUNTAINS...
GRAB
NO, I THINK WE'LL CHAT AT HEADQUARTERS.
FWAH
AAAAAAAAAAAH!!!
THRASH
THRASH
HE'S IN AGONY...

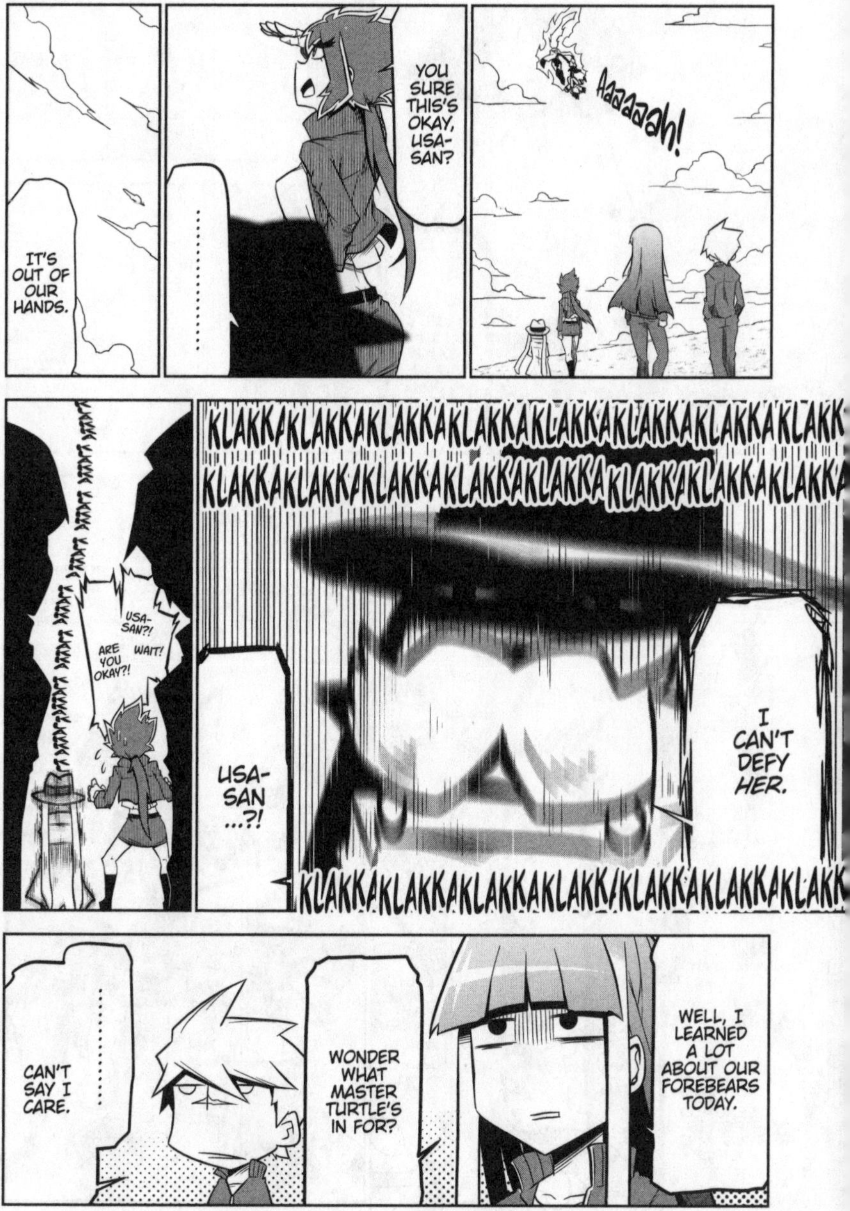
Aaaaaah!
YOU SURE THIS'S OKAY, USA-SAN?
......
IT'S OUT OF OUR HANDS.
KLAKKAKLAKKAKLAKKAKLAKKAKLAKKAKLAKKAKLAKKAKLAKK
KLAKKAKLAKKAKLAKKAKLAKKAKLAKKA KLAKKAKLAKKAKLAKKA
I CAN'T DEFY HER.
USA-SAN ...?!
KLAKKAKLAKKAKLAKKAKLAKK KLAKKAKLAKKAKLAKK
USA-SAN?!
WAIT!
ARE YOU OKAY?!
WELL, I LEARNED A LOT ABOUT OUR FOREBEARS TODAY.
WONDER WHAT MASTER TURTLE'S IN FOR?
......
CAN'T SAY I CARE.

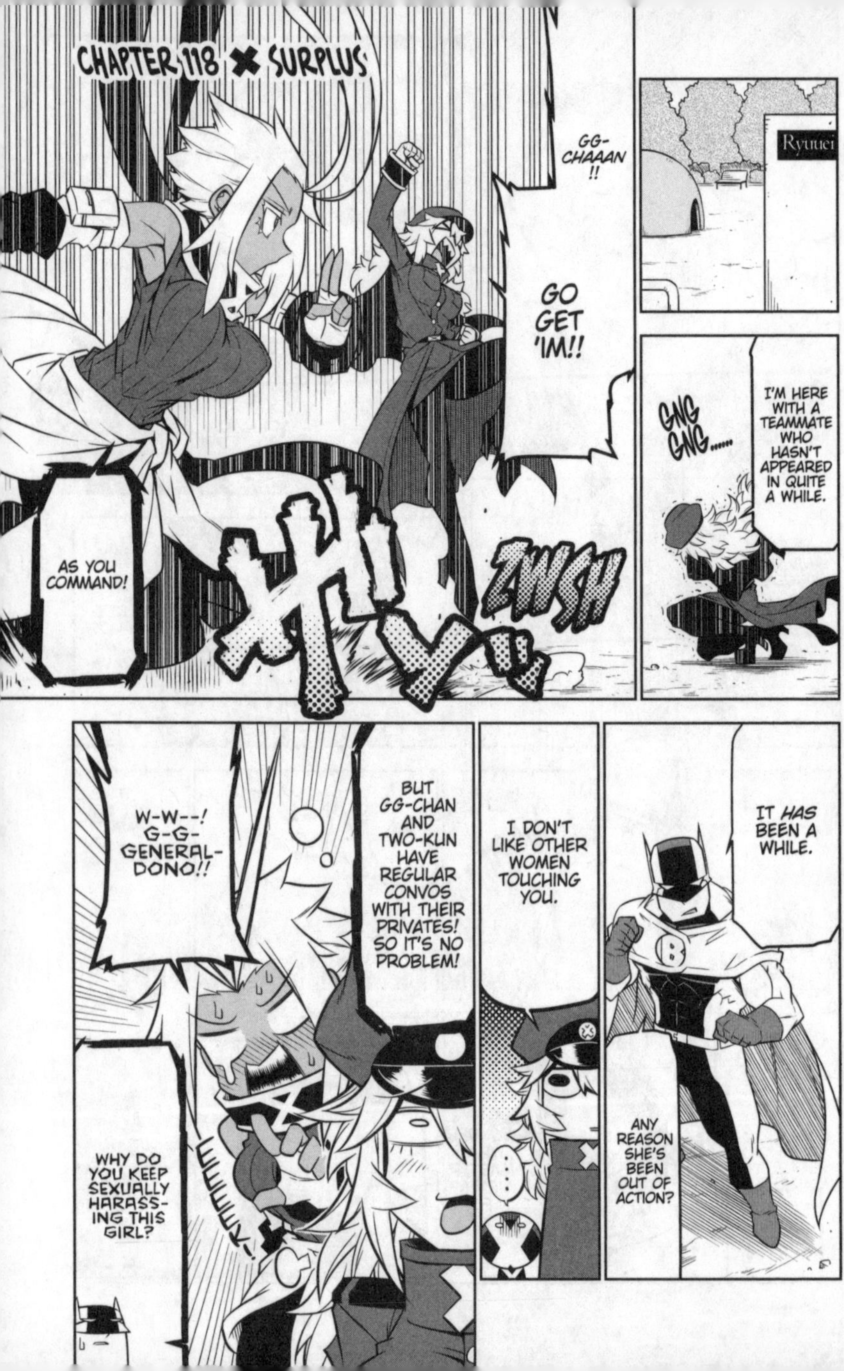
CHAPTER 118 ✖ SURPLUS
Ryuuei
GNG GNG......
I'M HERE WITH A TEAMMATE WHO HASN'T APPEARED IN QUITE A WHILE.
GG-CHAAAN!!
GO GET 'IM!!
AS YOU COMMAND!
ZWSH
IT HAS BEEN A WHILE.
ANY REASON SHE'S BEEN OUT OF ACTION?
I DON'T LIKE OTHER WOMEN TOUCHING YOU.
...
BUT GG-CHAN AND TWO-KUN HAVE REGULAR CONVOS WITH THEIR PRIVATES! SO IT'S NO PROBLEM!
W-W--! G-G-GENERAL-DONO!!
WHY DO YOU KEEP SEXUALLY HARASSING THIS GIRL?

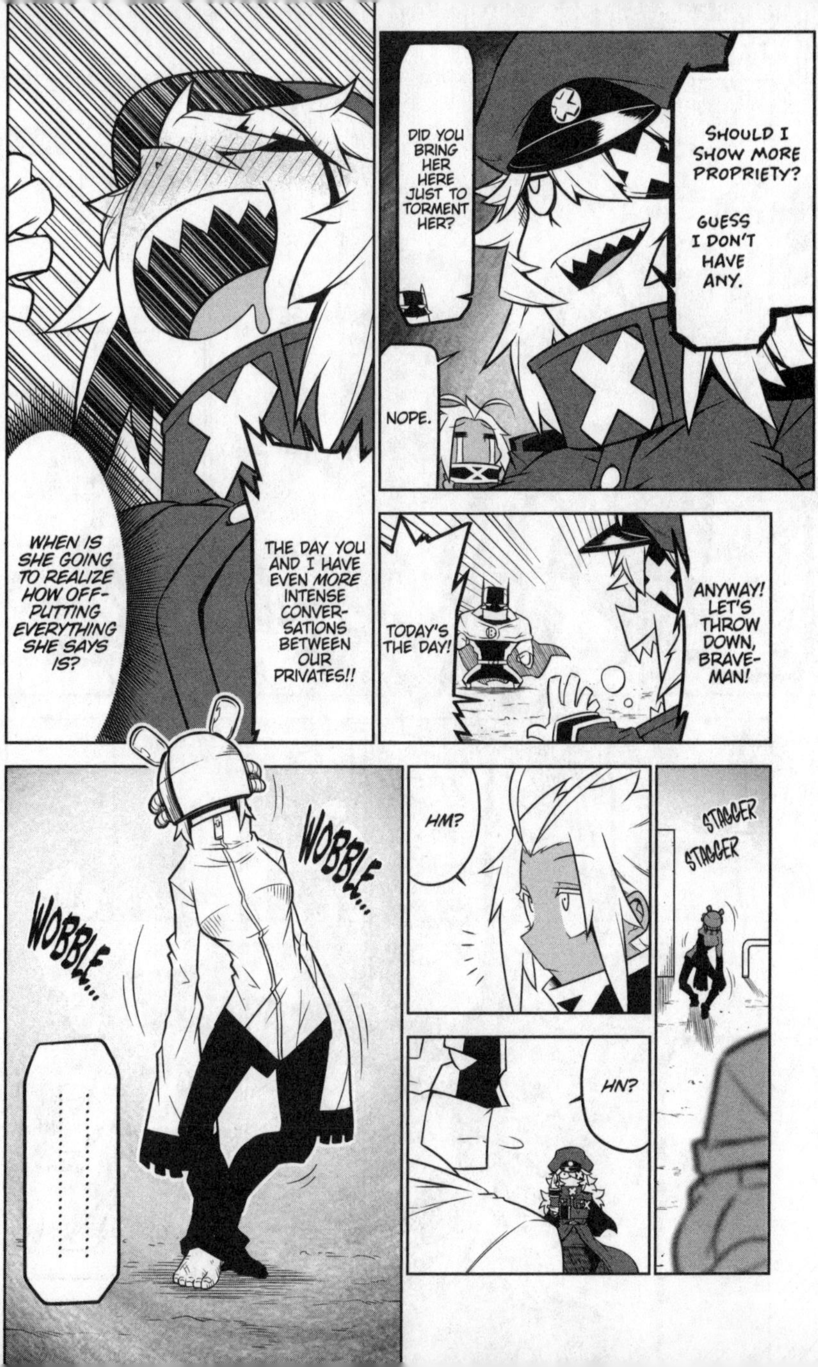
SHOULD I SHOW MORE PROPRIETY?
GUESS I DON'T HAVE ANY.
DID YOU BRING HER HERE JUST TO TORMENT HER?
NOPE.
WHEN IS SHE GOING TO REALIZE HOW OFF-PUTTING EVERYTHING SHE SAYS IS?
THE DAY YOU AND I HAVE EVEN MORE INTENSE CONVER-SATIONS BETWEEN OUR PRIVATES!!
TODAY'S THE DAY!
ANYWAY! LET'S THROW DOWN, BRAVE-MAN!
STAGGER
STAGGER
HM?
HN?
WOBBLE...
WOBBLE...
......

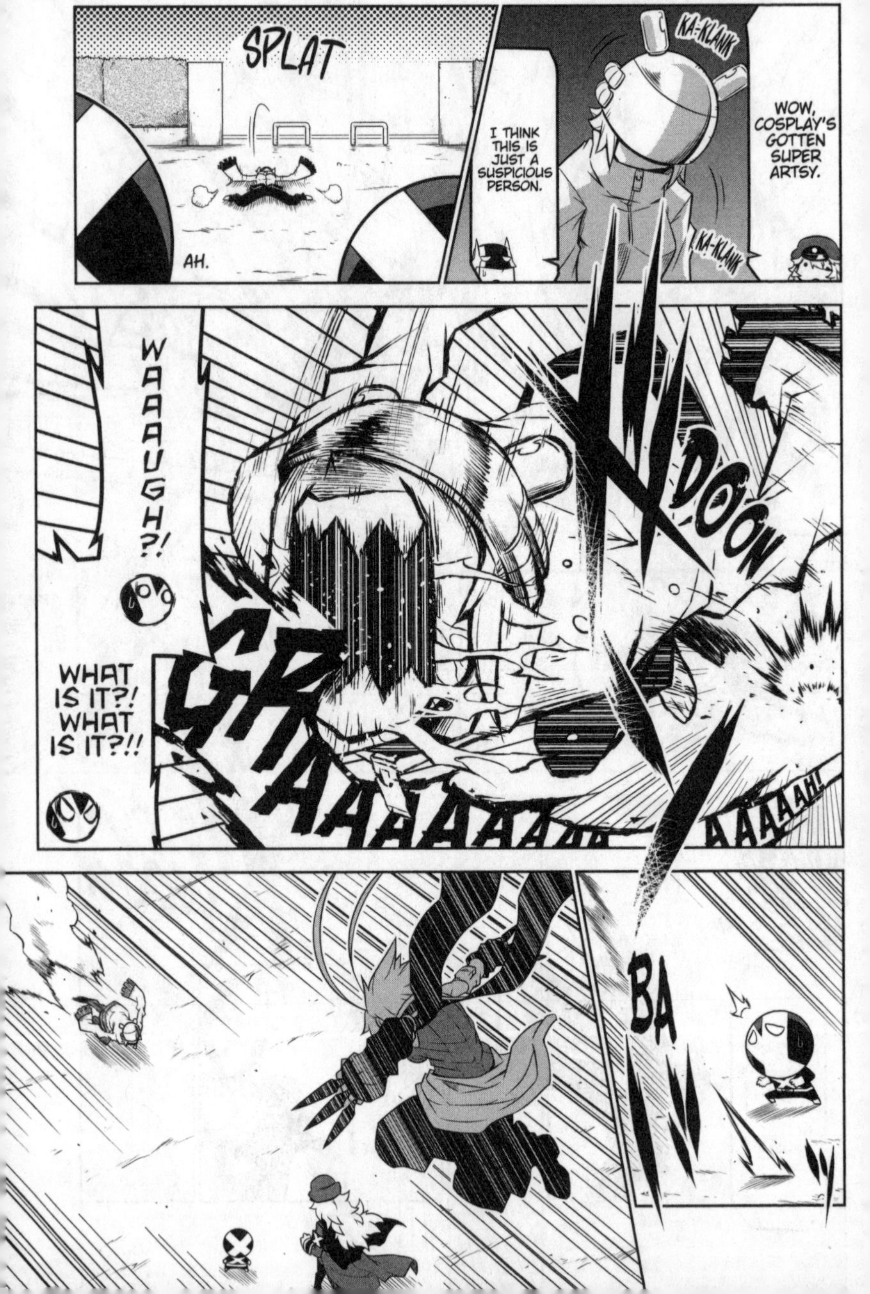
KA-KLANK
WOW, COSPLAY'S GOTTEN SUPER ARTSY.
I THINK THIS IS JUST A SUSPICIOUS PERSON.
KA-KLANK
SPLAT
AH.
DOOON
AAAAAH!
GRAAAAAAAAA
WAAAAUGH?!
WHAT IS IT?! WHAT IS IT?!!
BA

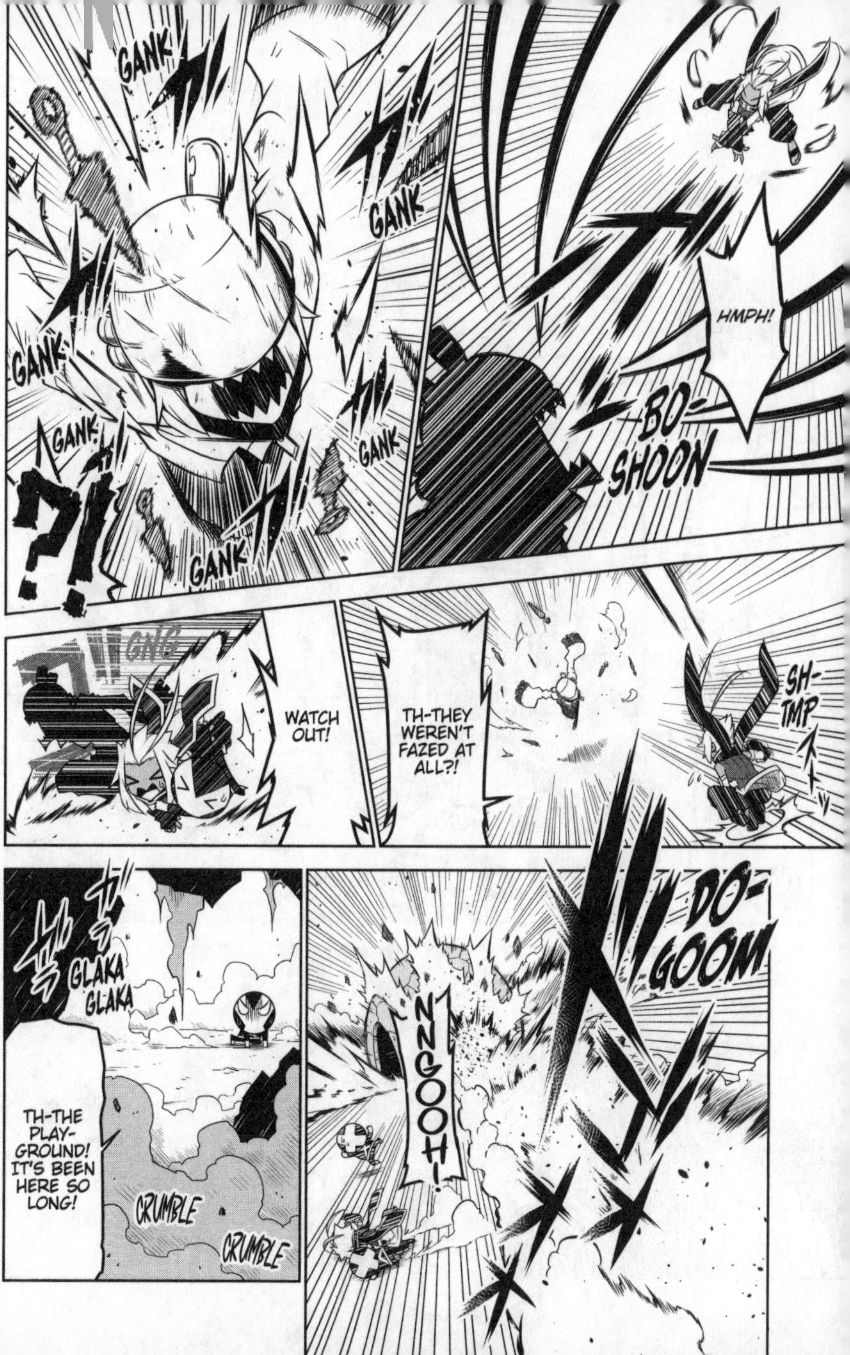
HMPH!
BO-SHOON
GANK
GANK
GANK
GANK
GANK
GANK
?!
SH-TMP
TH-THEY WEREN'T FAZED AT ALL?!
WATCH OUT!
GNG
DO-GOOM
NNGOOOH!
GLAKA GLAKA
TH-THE PLAY-GROUND! IT'S BEEN HERE SO LONG!
CRUMBLE
CRUMBLE

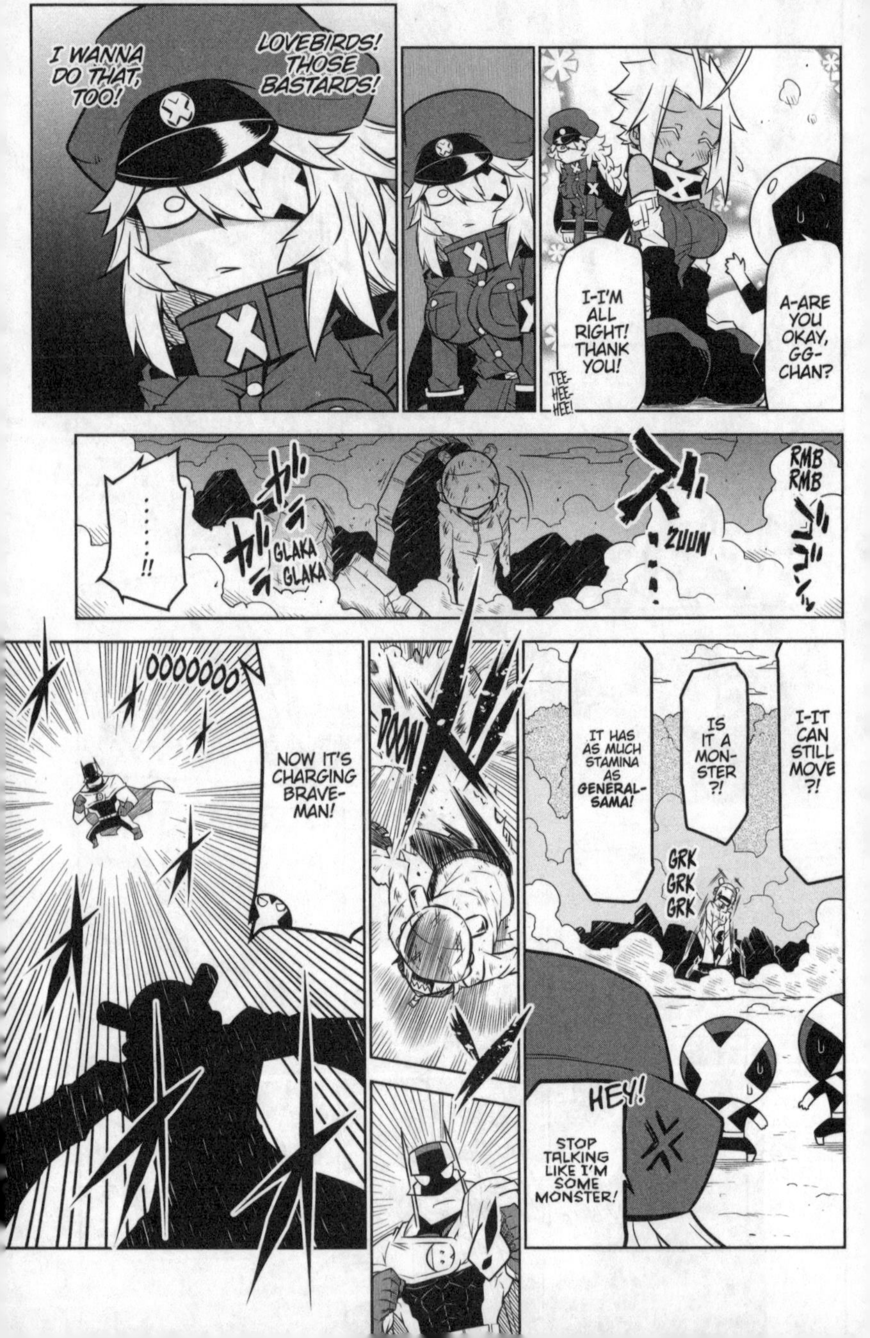
A-ARE YOU OKAY, GG-CHAN?
I-I'M ALL RIGHT! THANK YOU!
TEE-HEE-HEE!
LOVEBIRDS! THOSE BASTARDS!
I WANNA DO THAT, TOO!
RMB RMB
ZUUN
GLAKA GLAKA
......!!
I-IT CAN STILL MOVE?!
IS IT A MON-STER?!
IT HAS AS MUCH STAMINA AS GENERAL-SAMA!
GRK GRK GRK
HEY!
STOP TALKING LIKE I'M SOME MONSTER!
DOON
NOW IT'S CHARGING BRAVE-MAN!
OOOOOOO

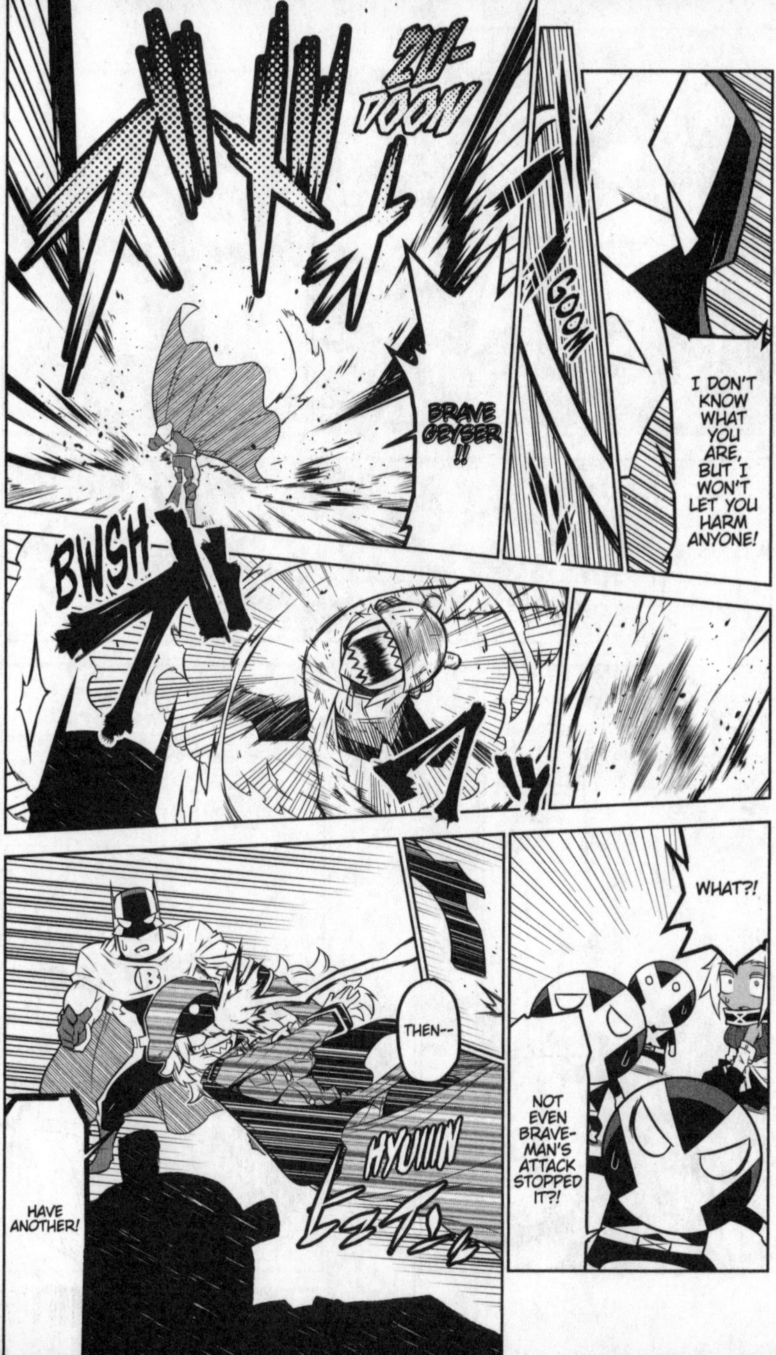
GOOM
I DON'T KNOW WHAT YOU ARE, BUT I WON'T LET YOU HARM ANYONE!
ZU-DOON
BRAVE GEYSER!!
BWSH
WHAT?!
NOT EVEN BRAVE-MAN'S ATTACK STOPPED IT?!
THEN--
HYUIIIN
HAVE ANOTHER!

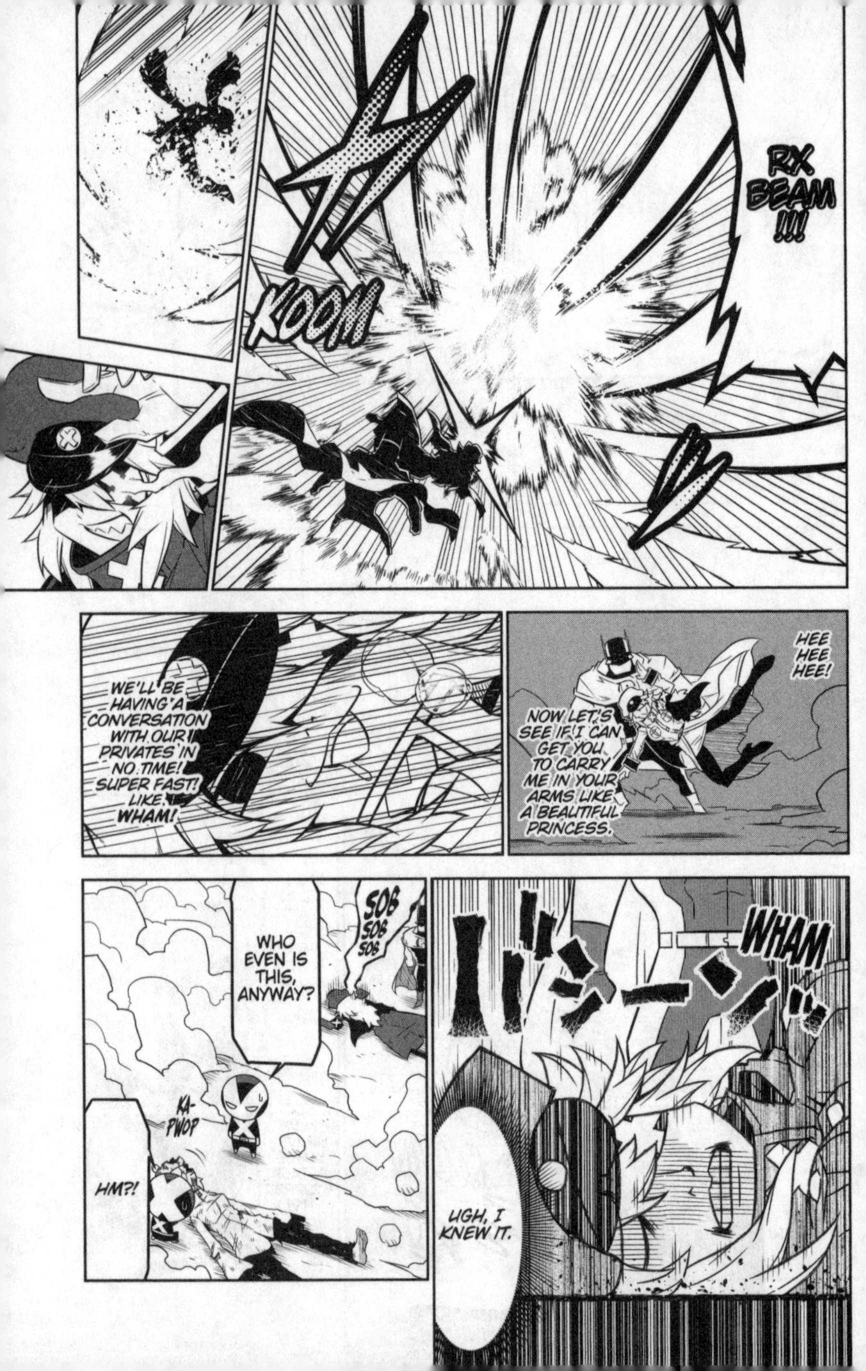
RX BEAM!!!
KOOM
HEE HEE HEE!
NOW LET'S SEE IF I CAN GET YOU TO CARRY ME IN YOUR ARMS LIKE A BEAUTIFUL PRINCESS.
WE'LL BE HAVING A CONVERSATION WITH OUR PRIVATES IN NO TIME! SUPER FAST! LIKE. WHAM!
WHAM
UGH, I KNEW IT.
SOB SOB SOB
WHO EVEN IS THIS, ANYWAY?
KA-PWOP
HM?!

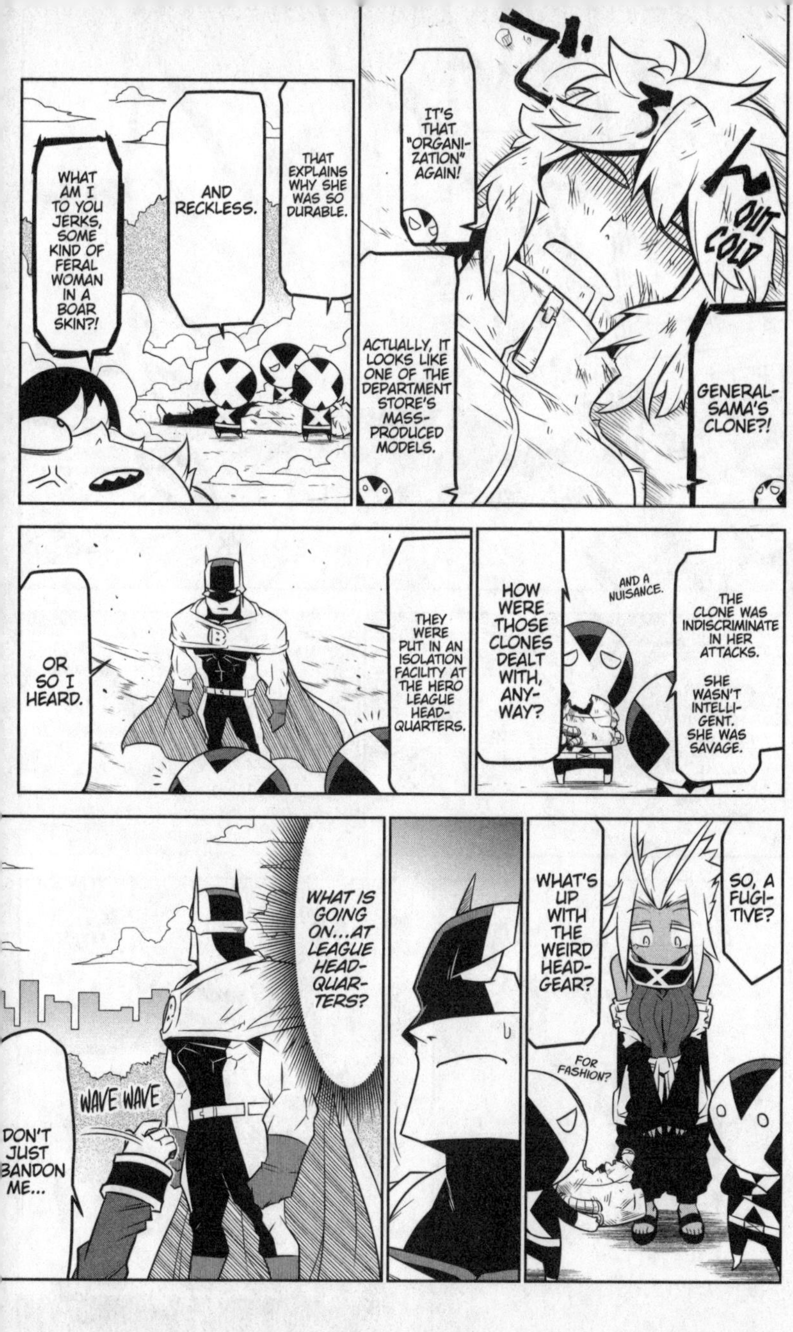

OUT COLD
GENERAL-SAMA'S CLONE?!
IT'S THAT "ORGANIZATION" AGAIN!
ACTUALLY, IT LOOKS LIKE ONE OF THE DEPARTMENT STORE'S MASS-PRODUCED MODELS.
THAT EXPLAINS WHY SHE WAS SO DURABLE.
AND RECKLESS.
WHAT AM I TO YOU JERKS, SOME KIND OF FERAL WOMAN IN A BOAR SKIN?!
THE CLONE WAS INDISCRIMINATE IN HER ATTACKS.
SHE WASN'T INTELLIGENT. SHE WAS SAVAGE.
AND A NUISANCE.
HOW WERE THOSE CLONES DEALT WITH, ANYWAY?
THEY WERE PUT IN AN ISOLATION FACILITY AT THE HERO LEAGUE HEADQUARTERS.
OR SO I HEARD.
SO, A FUGITIVE?
WHAT'S UP WITH THE WEIRD HEADGEAR?
FOR FASHION?
WHAT IS GOING ON...AT LEAGUE HEADQUARTERS?
WAVE WAVE
DON'T JUST BANDON ME...

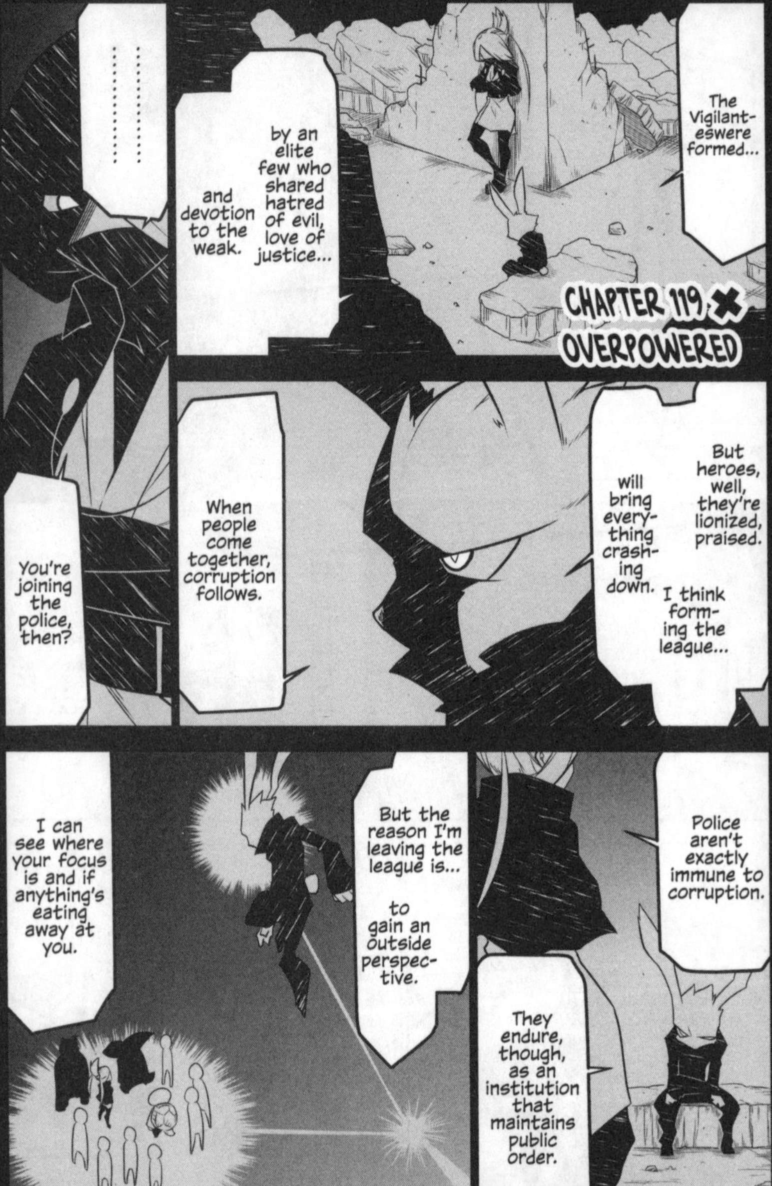
CHAPTER 119 ✖ OVERPOWERED
The Vigilant-eswere formed...
by an elite few who shared hatred of evil, love of justice...
and devotion to the weak.
But heroes, well, they're lionized, praised.
I think forming the league...
will bring everything crashing down.
When people come together, corruption follows.
......
You're joining the police, then?
Police aren't exactly immune to corruption.
They endure, though, as an institution that maintains public order.
But the reason I'm leaving the league is...
to gain an outside perspective.
I can see where your focus is and if anything's eating away at you.

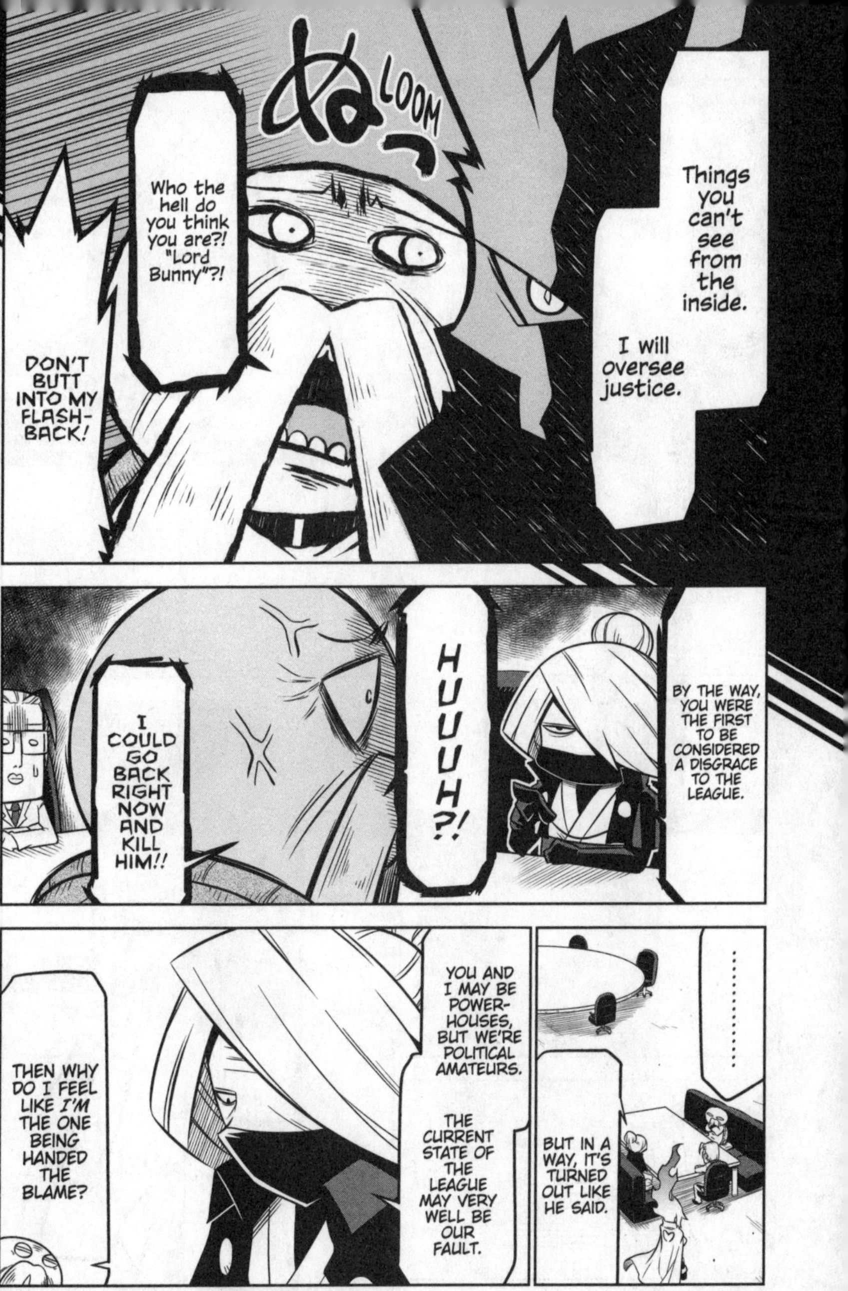
Things you can't see from the inside.
I will oversee justice.
ぬLOOMっ
Who the hell do you think you are?! "Lord Bunny"?!
DON'T BUTT INTO MY FLASHBACK!
BY THE WAY, YOU WERE THE FIRST TO BE CONSIDERED A DISGRACE TO THE LEAGUE.
HUUUUH?!
I COULD GO BACK RIGHT NOW AND KILL HIM!!
......
BUT IN A WAY, IT'S TURNED OUT LIKE HE SAID.
YOU AND I MAY BE POWERHOUSES, BUT WE'RE POLITICAL AMATEURS.
THE CURRENT STATE OF THE LEAGUE MAY VERY WELL BE OUR FAULT.
THEN WHY DO I FEEL LIKE *I'M* THE ONE BEING HANDED THE BLAME?

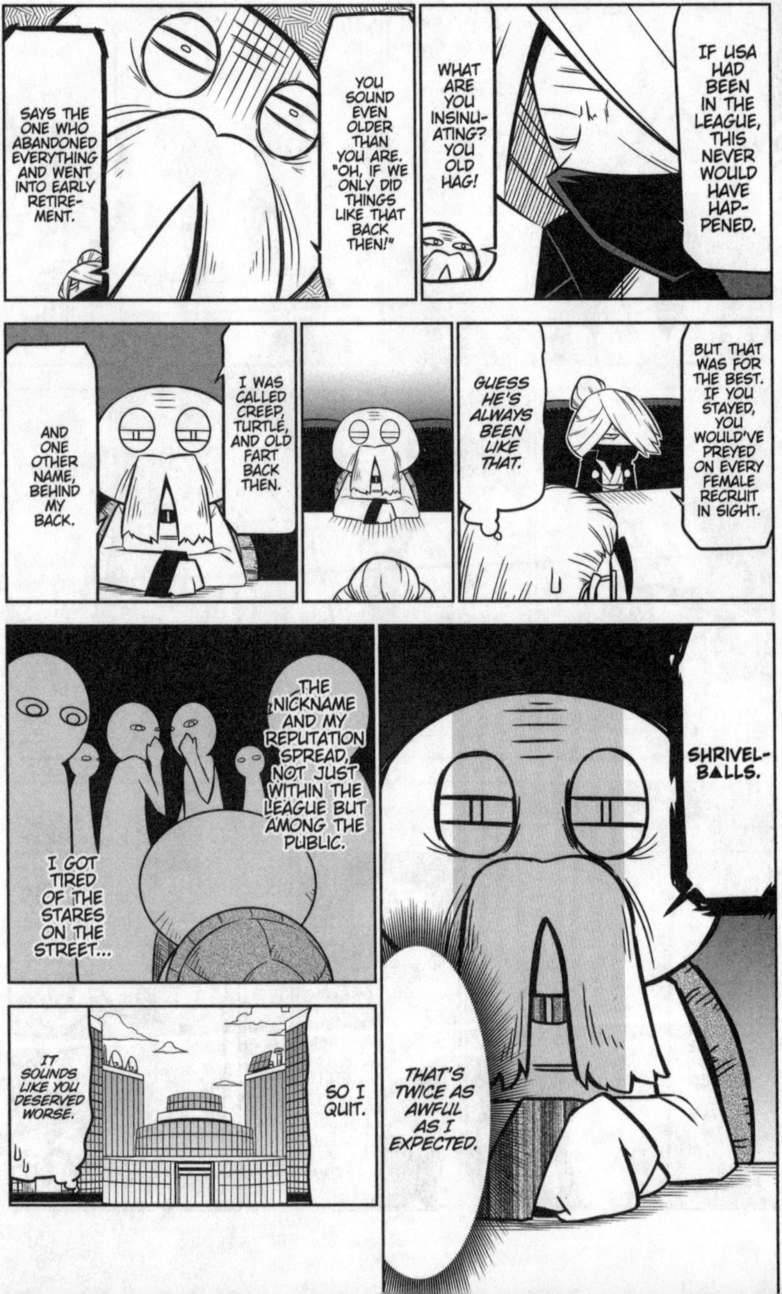
IF USA HAD BEEN IN THE LEAGUE, THIS NEVER WOULD HAVE HAPPENED.
WHAT ARE YOU INSINUATING? YOU OLD HAG!
YOU SOUND EVEN OLDER THAN YOU ARE. "OH, IF WE ONLY DID THINGS LIKE THAT BACK THEN!"
SAYS THE ONE WHO ABANDONED EVERYTHING AND WENT INTO EARLY RETIREMENT.
BUT THAT WAS FOR THE BEST. IF YOU STAYED, YOU WOULD'VE PREYED ON EVERY FEMALE RECRUIT IN SIGHT.
GUESS HE'S ALWAYS BEEN LIKE THAT.
I WAS CALLED CREEP, TURTLE, AND OLD FART BACK THEN.
AND ONE OTHER NAME, BEHIND MY BACK.
SHRIVEL-B▲LLS.
THAT'S TWICE AS AWFUL AS I EXPECTED.
THE NICKNAME AND MY REPUTATION SPREAD, NOT JUST WITHIN THE LEAGUE BUT AMONG THE PUBLIC.
I GOT TIRED OF THE STARES ON THE STREET...
SO I QUIT.
IT SOUNDS LIKE YOU DESERVED WORSE.

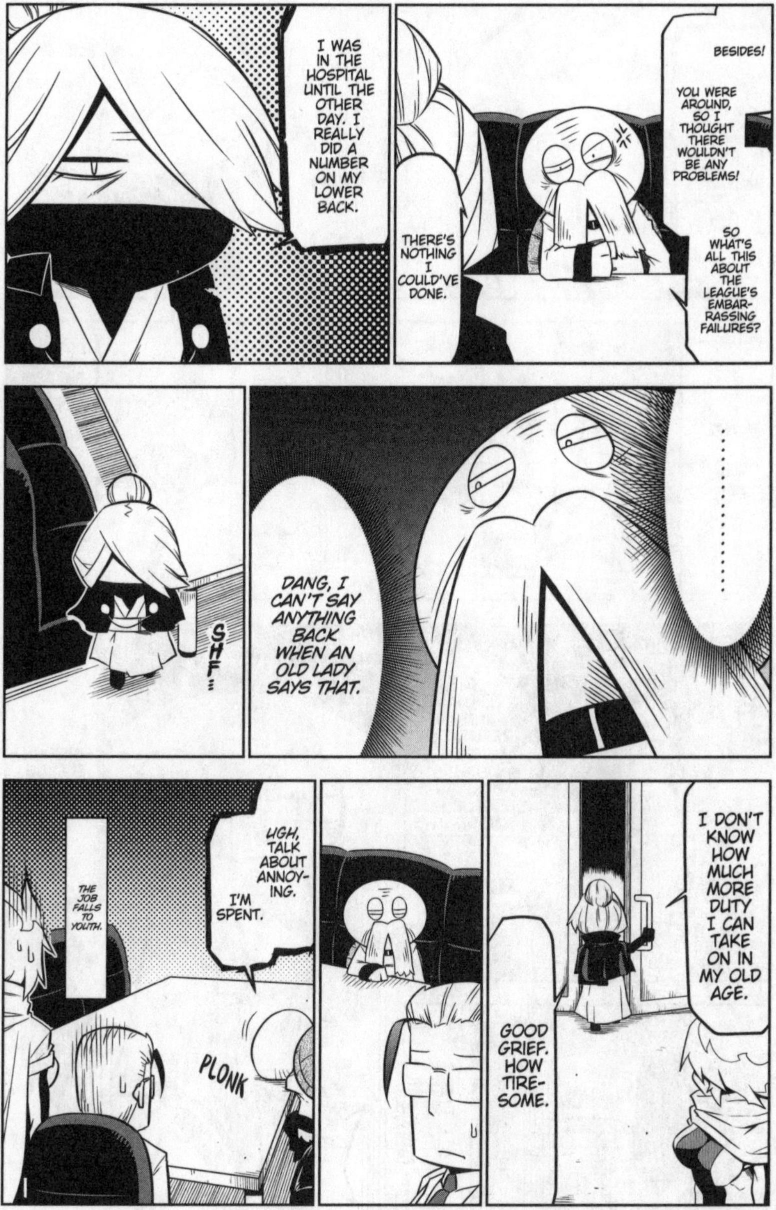
BESIDES!
YOU WERE AROUND, SO I THOUGHT THERE WOULDN'T BE ANY PROBLEMS!
SO WHAT'S ALL THIS ABOUT THE LEAGUE'S EMBARRASSING FAILURES?
THERE'S NOTHING I COULD'VE DONE.
I WAS IN THE HOSPITAL UNTIL THE OTHER DAY. I REALLY DID A NUMBER ON MY LOWER BACK.
......
DANG, I CAN'T SAY ANYTHING BACK WHEN AN OLD LADY SAYS THAT.
SHF...
I DON'T KNOW HOW MUCH MORE DUTY I CAN TAKE ON IN MY OLD AGE.
GOOD GRIEF. HOW TIRESOME.
UGH, TALK ABOUT ANNOYING.
I'M SPENT.
THE JOB FALLS TO YOUTH.
PLONK

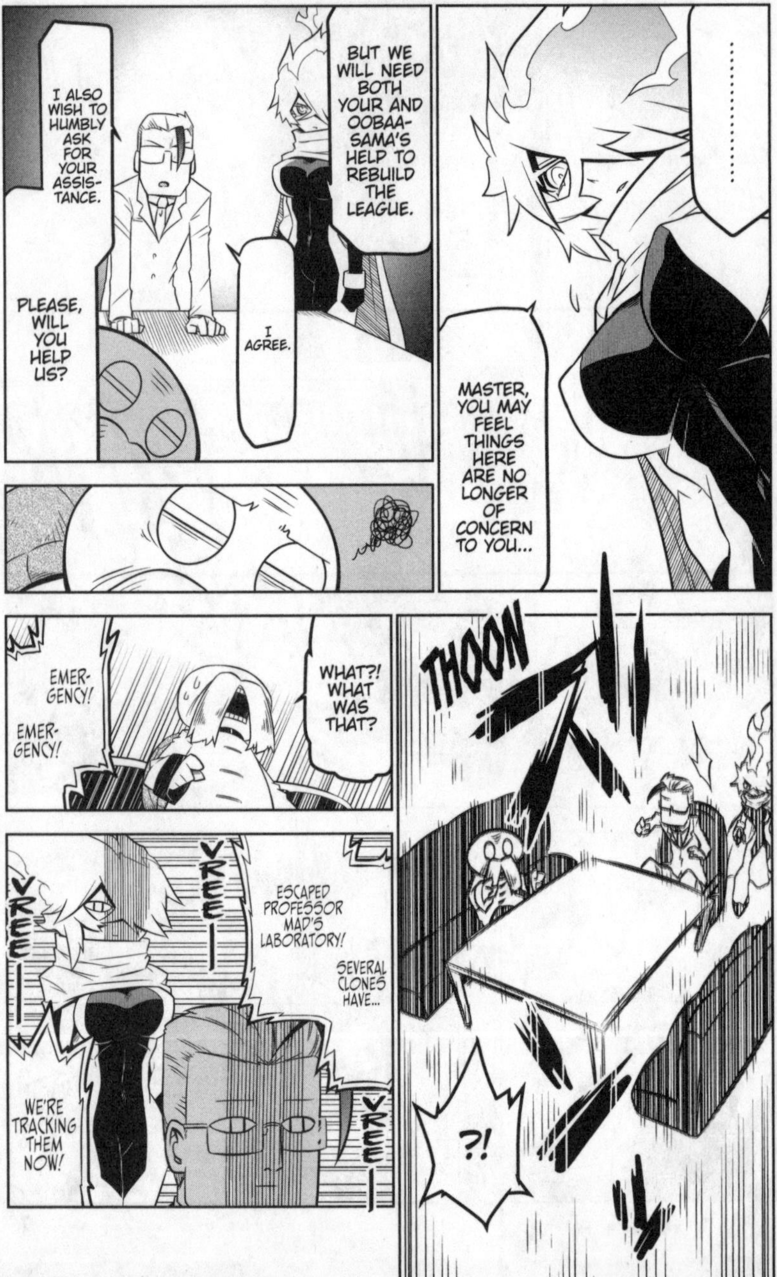
......
MASTER, YOU MAY FEEL THINGS HERE ARE NO LONGER OF CONCERN TO YOU...
BUT WE WILL NEED BOTH YOUR AND OOBAA-SAMA'S HELP TO REBUILD THE LEAGUE.
I AGREE.
I ALSO WISH TO HUMBLY ASK FOR YOUR ASSISTANCE.
PLEASE, WILL YOU HELP US?
THOON
?!
WHAT?! WHAT WAS THAT?
EMERGENCY!
EMERGENCY!
VREE
ESCAPED PROFESSOR MAD'S LABORATORY!
SEVERAL CLONES HAVE...
VREE
WE'RE TRACKING THEM NOW!
VREE

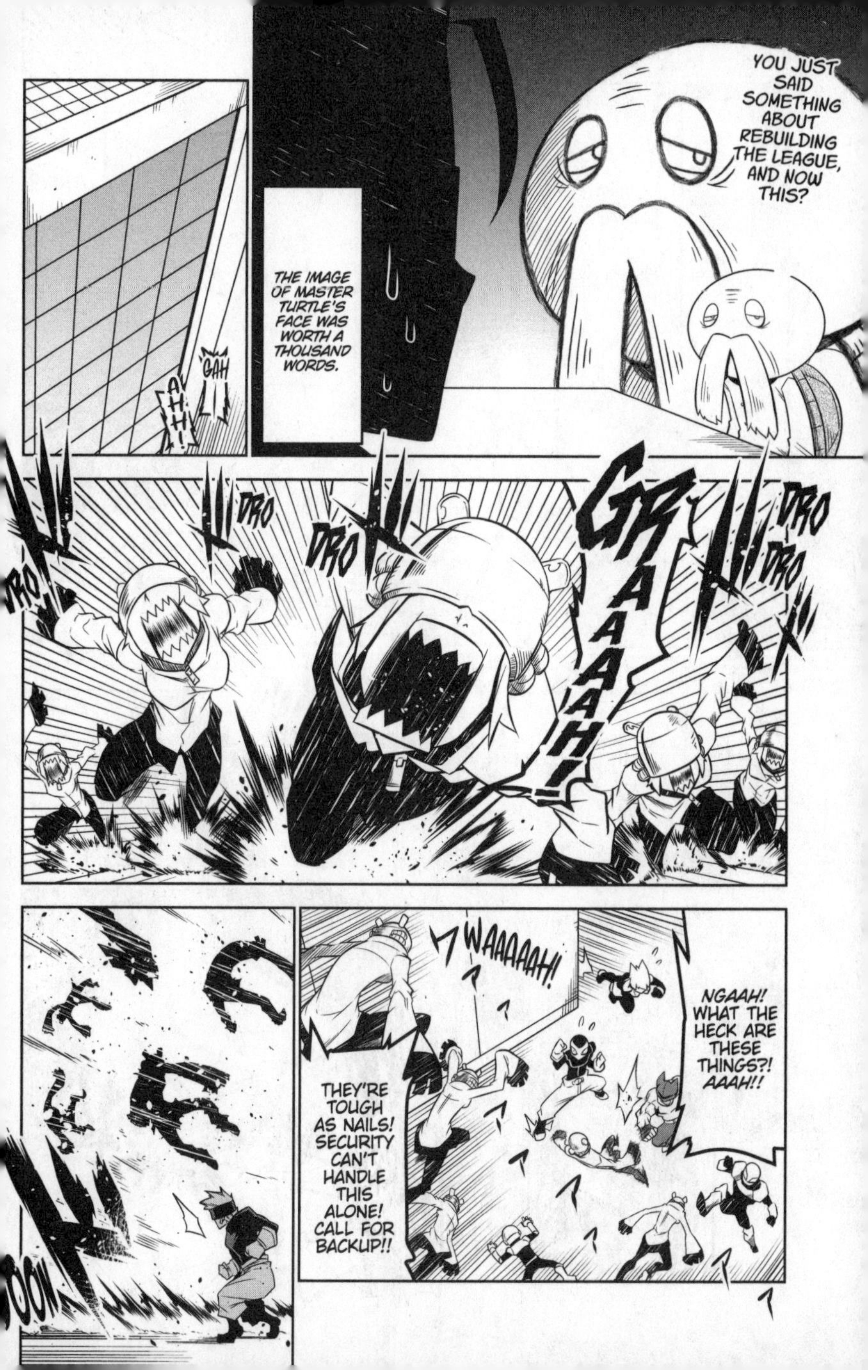

YOU JUST SAID SOMETHING ABOUT REBUILDING THE LEAGUE, AND NOW THIS?
THE IMAGE OF MASTER TURTLE'S FACE WAS WORTH A THOUSAND WORDS.
GAH
AHH!
DRO
DRO
GRAAAAAH!!
DRO
DRO
DRO
NGAAH! WHAT THE HECK ARE THESE THINGS?! AAAH!!
WAAAAAH!
THEY'RE TOUGH AS NAILS! SECURITY CAN'T HANDLE THIS ALONE! CALL FOR BACKUP!!

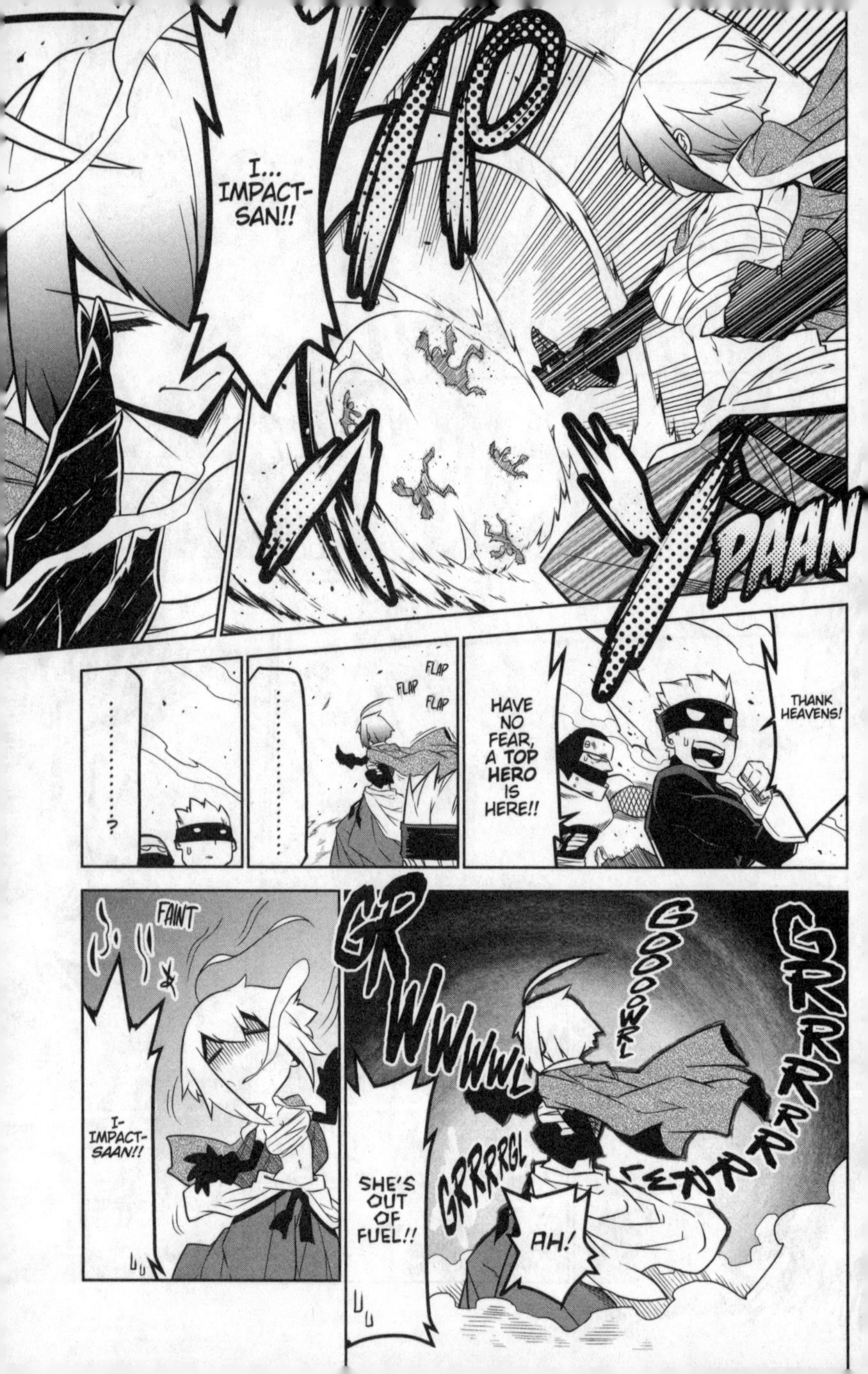
I... IMPACT-SAN!!
PAAN
THANK HEAVENS!
HAVE NO FEAR, A TOP HERO IS HERE!!
FLAP
FLAP
FLAP
......
......?
GRRRRRRR
GOOOOOWRL
GRWWWWL
GRRRRGL
AH!
SHE'S OUT OF FUEL!!
FAINT
I- IMPACT-SAAN!!

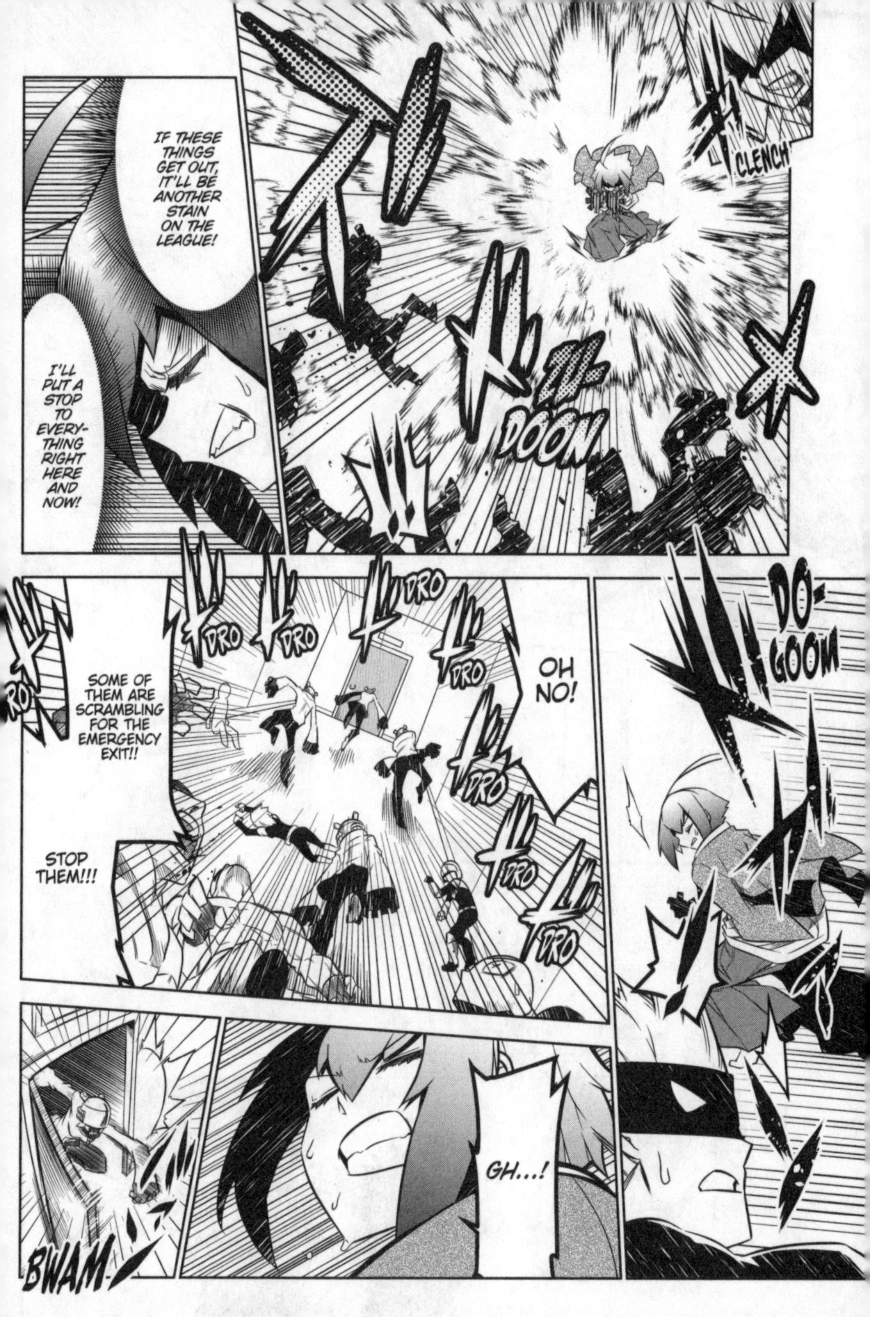
CLENCH
DOOM
IF THESE THINGS GET OUT, IT'LL BE ANOTHER STAIN ON THE LEAGUE!
I'LL PUT A STOP TO EVERYTHING RIGHT HERE AND NOW!
DO-GOOM
DRO
DRO
DRO
DRO
DRO
DRO
DRO
OH NO!
SOME OF THEM ARE SCRAMBLING FOR THE EMERGENCY EXIT!!
STOP THEM!!!
GH...!
BWAM

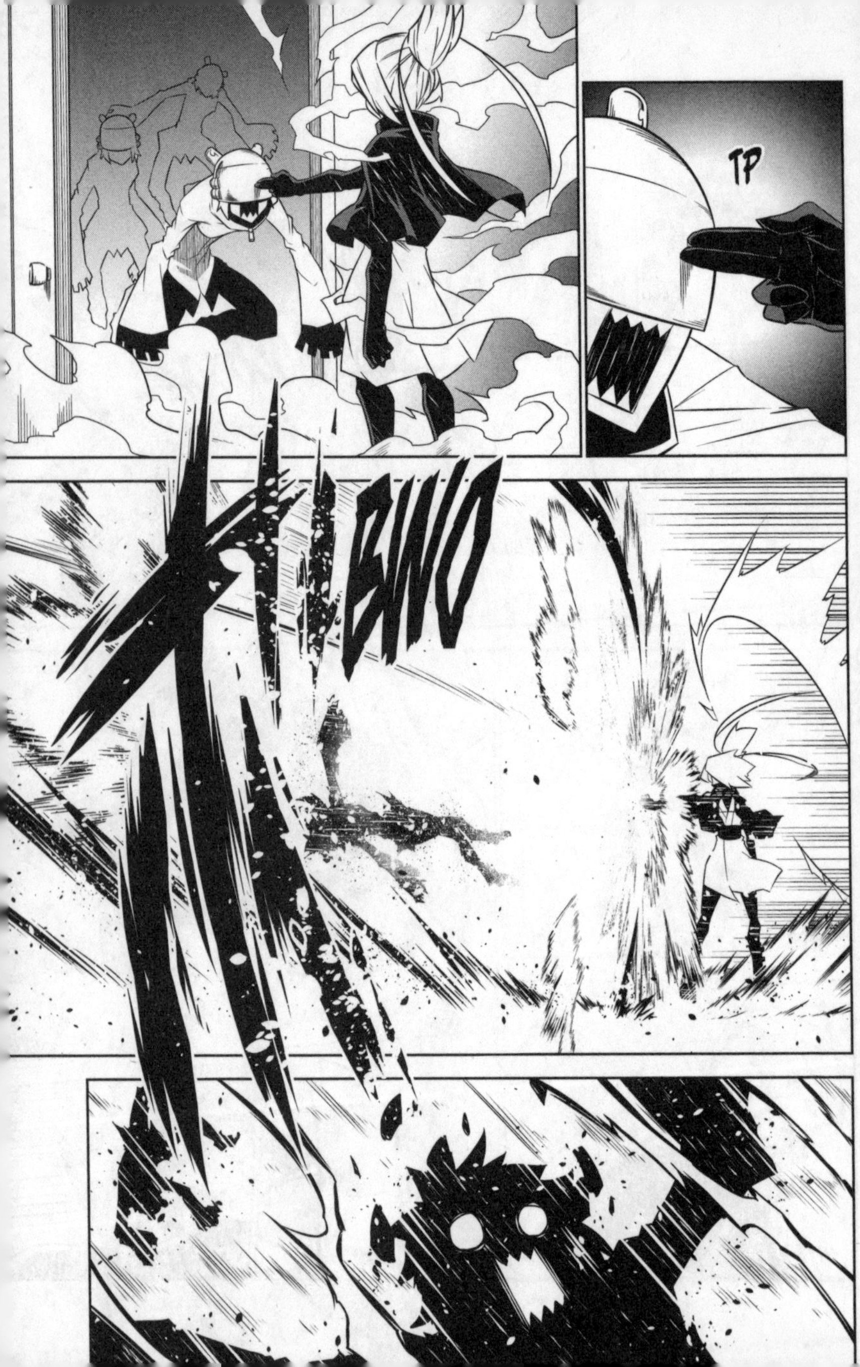
TP
BWO

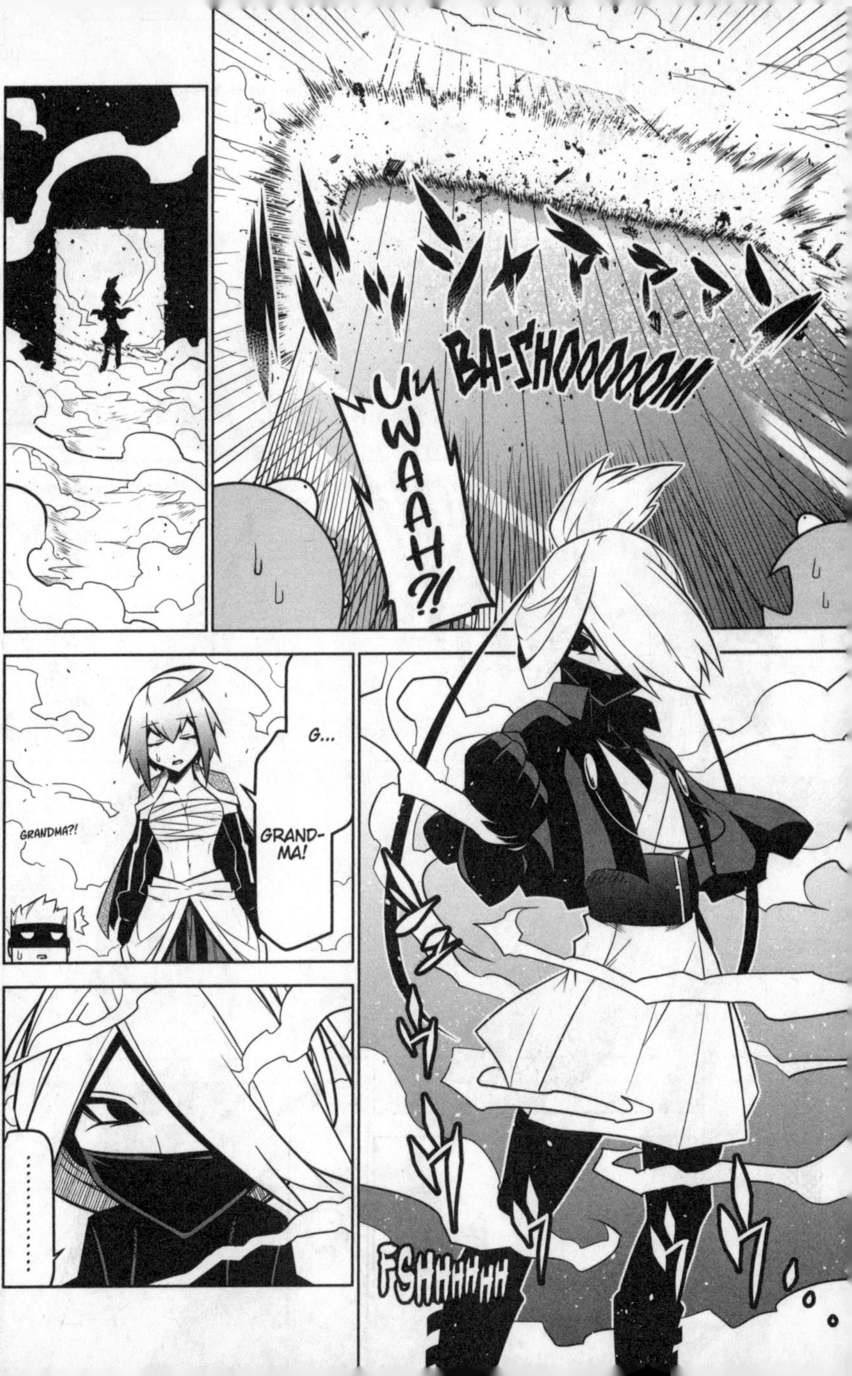

BA-SHOOOOOM
UWAAH?!
FSHHHHHH
G... GRAND-MA!
GRANDMA?!
......

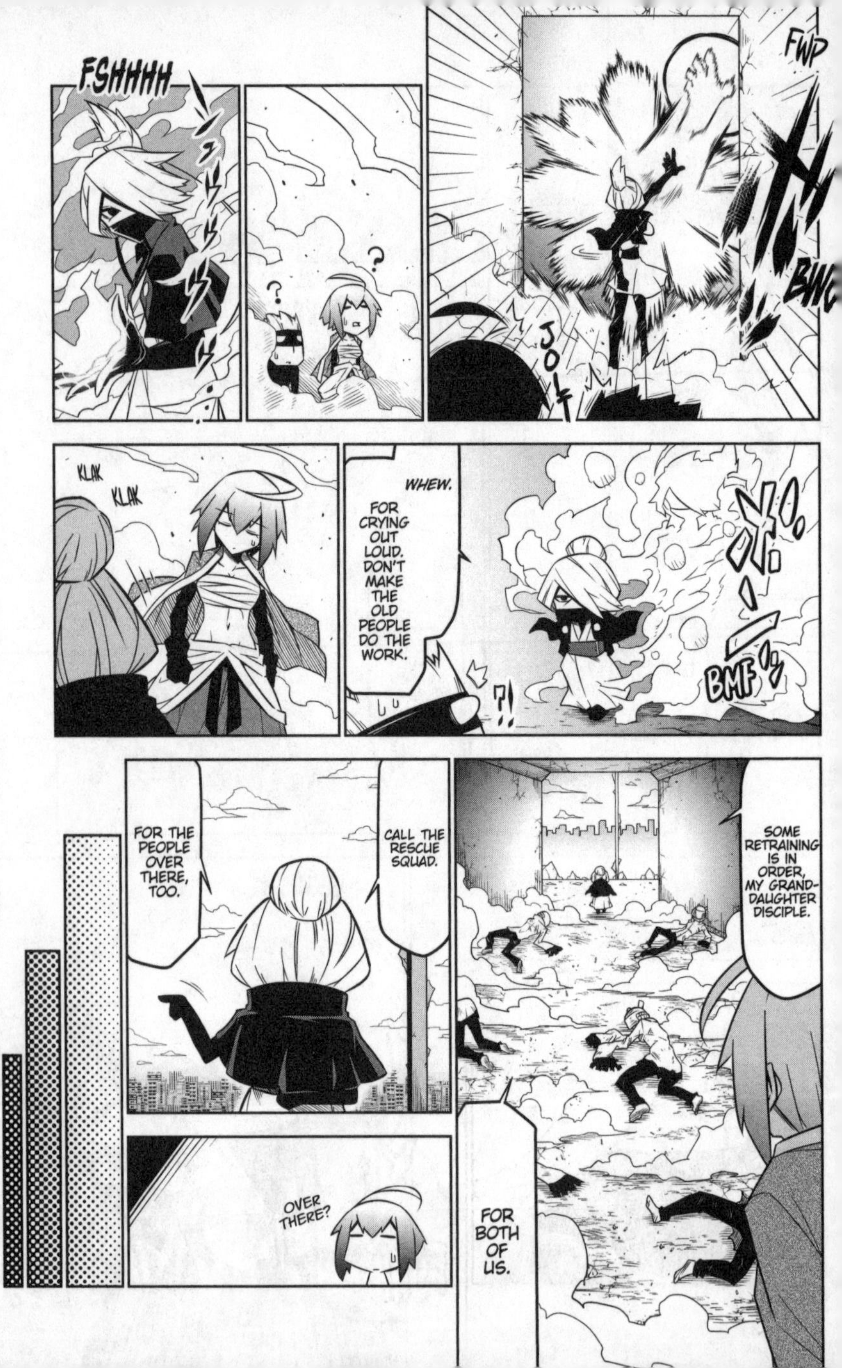
FWP
BWG
JOLT
F.SHHHH
WHEW.
FOR CRYING OUT LOUD. DON'T MAKE THE OLD PEOPLE DO THE WORK.
?!
BMF
KLAK
KLAK
SOME RETRAINING IS IN ORDER, MY GRAND-DAUGHTER DISCIPLE.
FOR BOTH OF US.
CALL THE RESCUE SQUAD.
FOR THE PEOPLE OVER THERE, TOO.
OVER THERE?

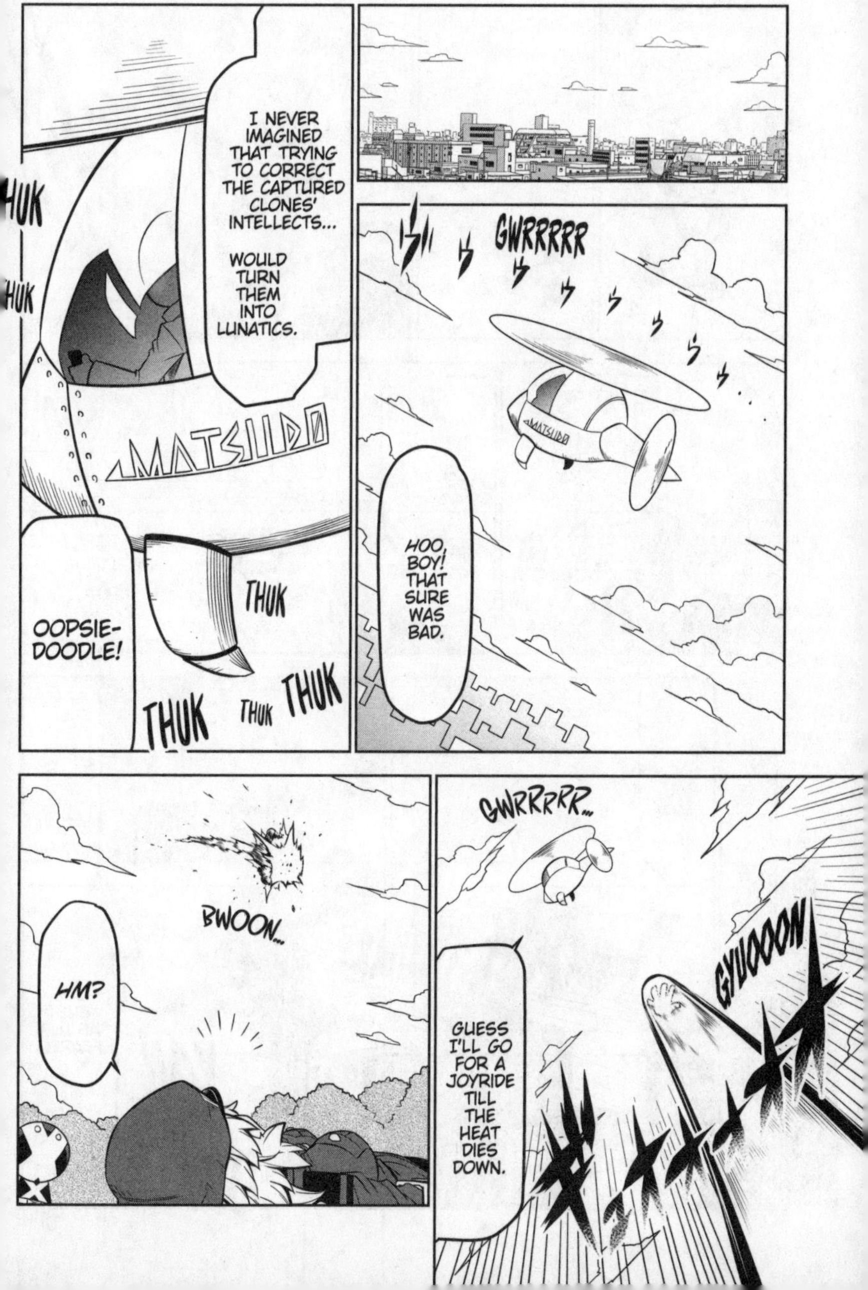
GWRRRR
HOO, BOY! THAT SURE WAS BAD.
I NEVER IMAGINED THAT TRYING TO CORRECT THE CAPTURED CLONES' INTELLECTS...
WOULD TURN THEM INTO LUNATICS.
THUK
THUK
OOPSIE-DOODLE!
THUK
THUK
THUK
THUK
GWRRRR...
GYUOOON
GUESS I'LL GO FOR A JOYRIDE TILL THE HEAT DIES DOWN.
BWOON...
HM?

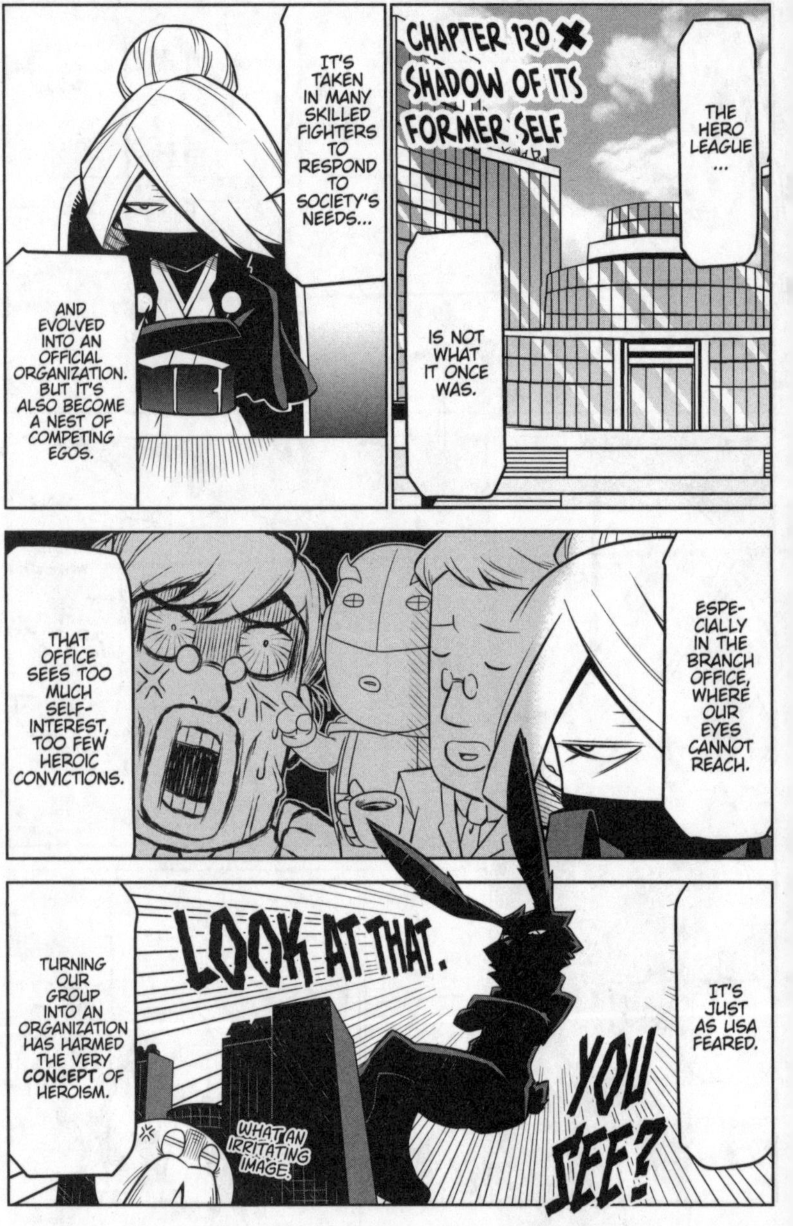
CHAPTER 120 ✖ SHADOW OF ITS FORMER SELF
THE HERO LEAGUE ...
IS NOT WHAT IT ONCE WAS.
IT'S TAKEN IN MANY SKILLED FIGHTERS TO RESPOND TO SOCIETY'S NEEDS...
AND EVOLVED INTO AN OFFICIAL ORGANIZATION. BUT IT'S ALSO BECOME A NEST OF COMPETING EGOS.
ESPE-CIALLY IN THE BRANCH OFFICE, WHERE OUR EYES CANNOT REACH.
THAT OFFICE SEES TOO MUCH SELF-INTEREST, TOO FEW HEROIC CONVICTIONS.
IT'S JUST AS USA FEARED.
LOOK AT THAT.
YOU SEE?
WHAT AN IRRITATING IMAGE.
TURNING OUR GROUP INTO AN ORGANIZATION HAS HARMED THE VERY CONCEPT OF HEROISM.

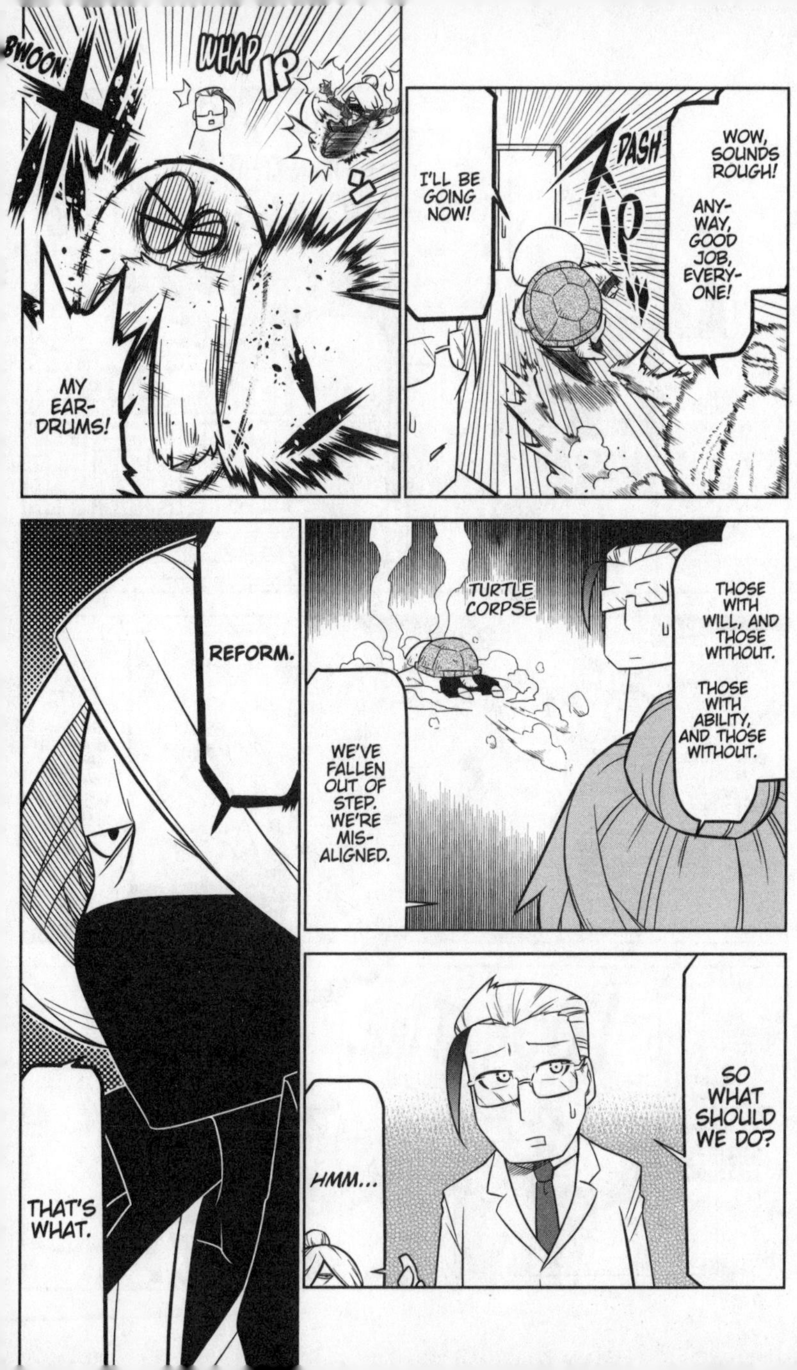
WOW, SOUNDS ROUGH!
ANY-WAY, GOOD JOB, EVERY-ONE!
DASH
I'LL BE GOING NOW!
WHAP
BWOON
MY EAR-DRUMS!
THOSE WITH WILL, AND THOSE WITHOUT.
THOSE WITH ABILITY, AND THOSE WITHOUT.
TURTLE CORPSE
WE'VE FALLEN OUT OF STEP. WE'RE MIS-ALIGNED.
SO WHAT SHOULD WE DO?
HMM...
REFORM.
THAT'S WHAT.

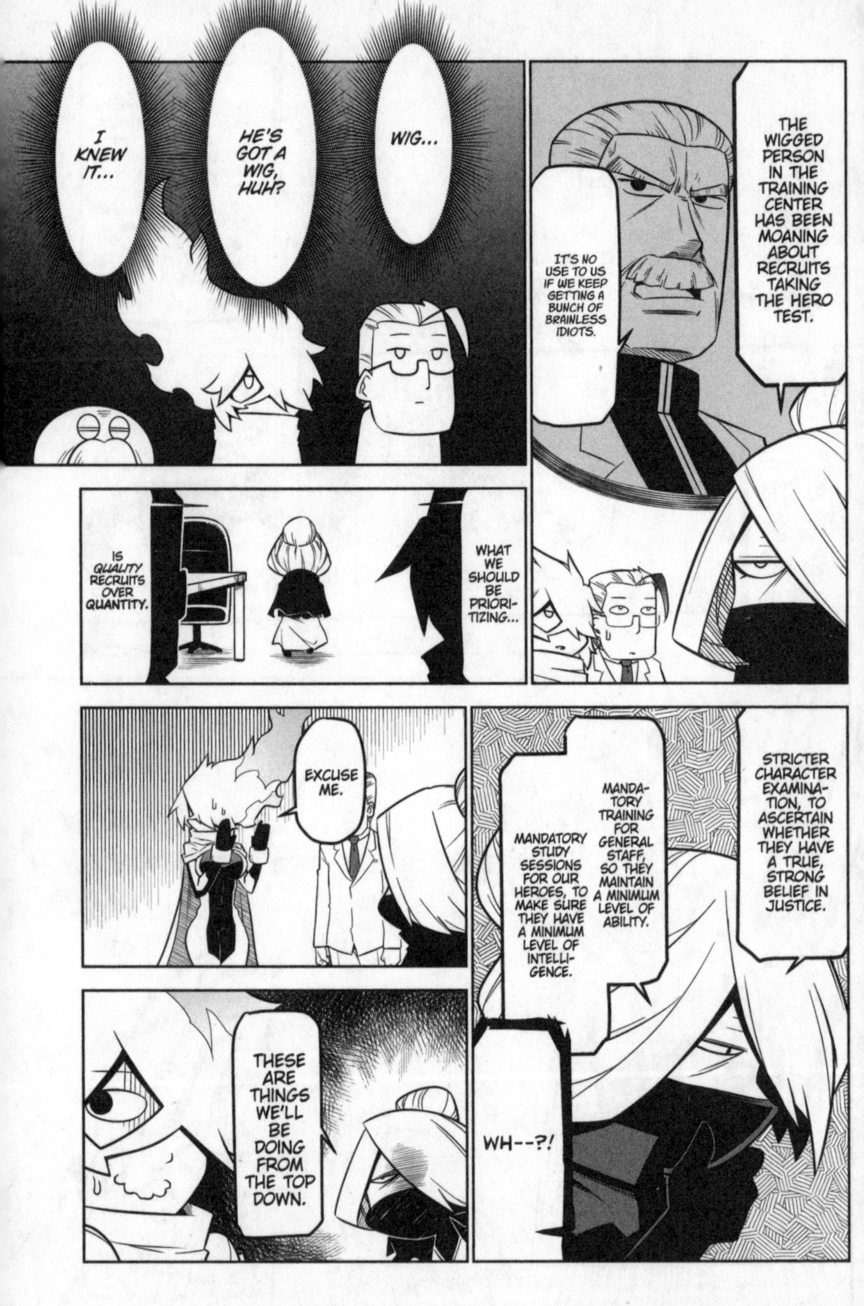
THE WIGGED PERSON IN THE TRAINING CENTER HAS BEEN MOANING ABOUT RECRUITS TAKING THE HERO TEST.
IT'S NO USE TO US IF WE KEEP GETTING A BUNCH OF BRAINLESS IDIOTS.
WIG...
HE'S GOT A WIG, HUH?
I KNEW IT...
WHAT WE SHOULD BE PRIORI-TIZING...
IS QUALITY RECRUITS OVER QUANTITY.
STRICTER CHARACTER EXAMINA-TION, TO ASCERTAIN WHETHER THEY HAVE A TRUE, STRONG BELIEF IN JUSTICE.
MANDA-TORY TRAINING FOR GENERAL STAFF, SO THEY MAINTAIN A MINIMUM LEVEL OF ABILITY.
MANDATORY STUDY SESSIONS FOR OUR HEROES, TO MAKE SURE THEY HAVE A MINIMUM LEVEL OF INTELLI-GENCE.
WH--?!
EXCUSE ME.
THESE ARE THINGS WE'LL BE DOING FROM THE TOP DOWN.

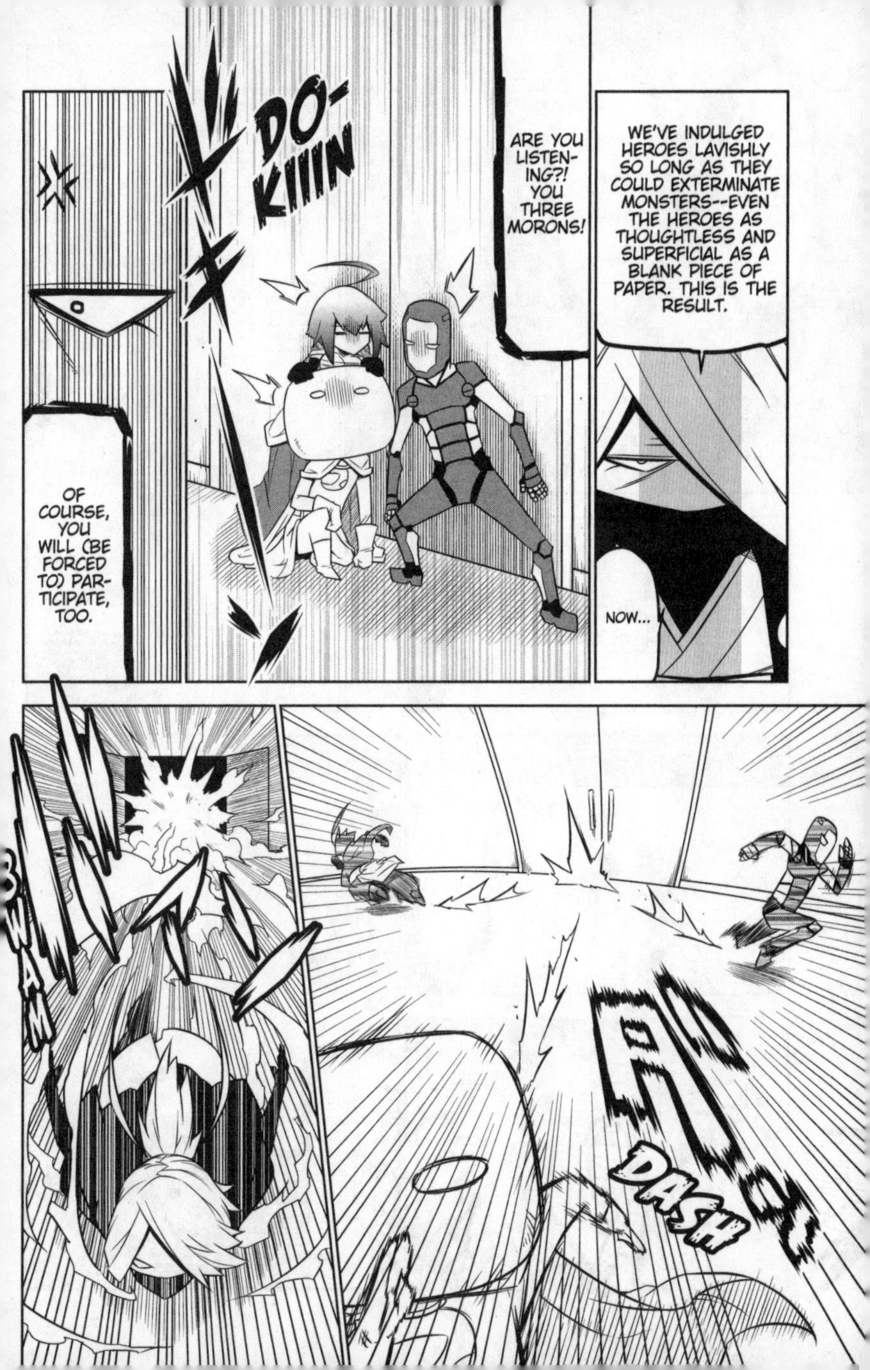
WE'VE INDULGED HEROES LAVISHLY SO LONG AS THEY COULD EXTERMINATE MONSTERS--EVEN THE HEROES AS THOUGHTLESS AND SUPERFICIAL AS A BLANK PIECE OF PAPER. THIS IS THE RESULT.
NOW...
ARE YOU LISTENING?! YOU THREE MORONS!
DO-KIIIN
OF COURSE, YOU WILL (BE FORCED TO) PARTICIPATE, TOO.
DASH
BWAM

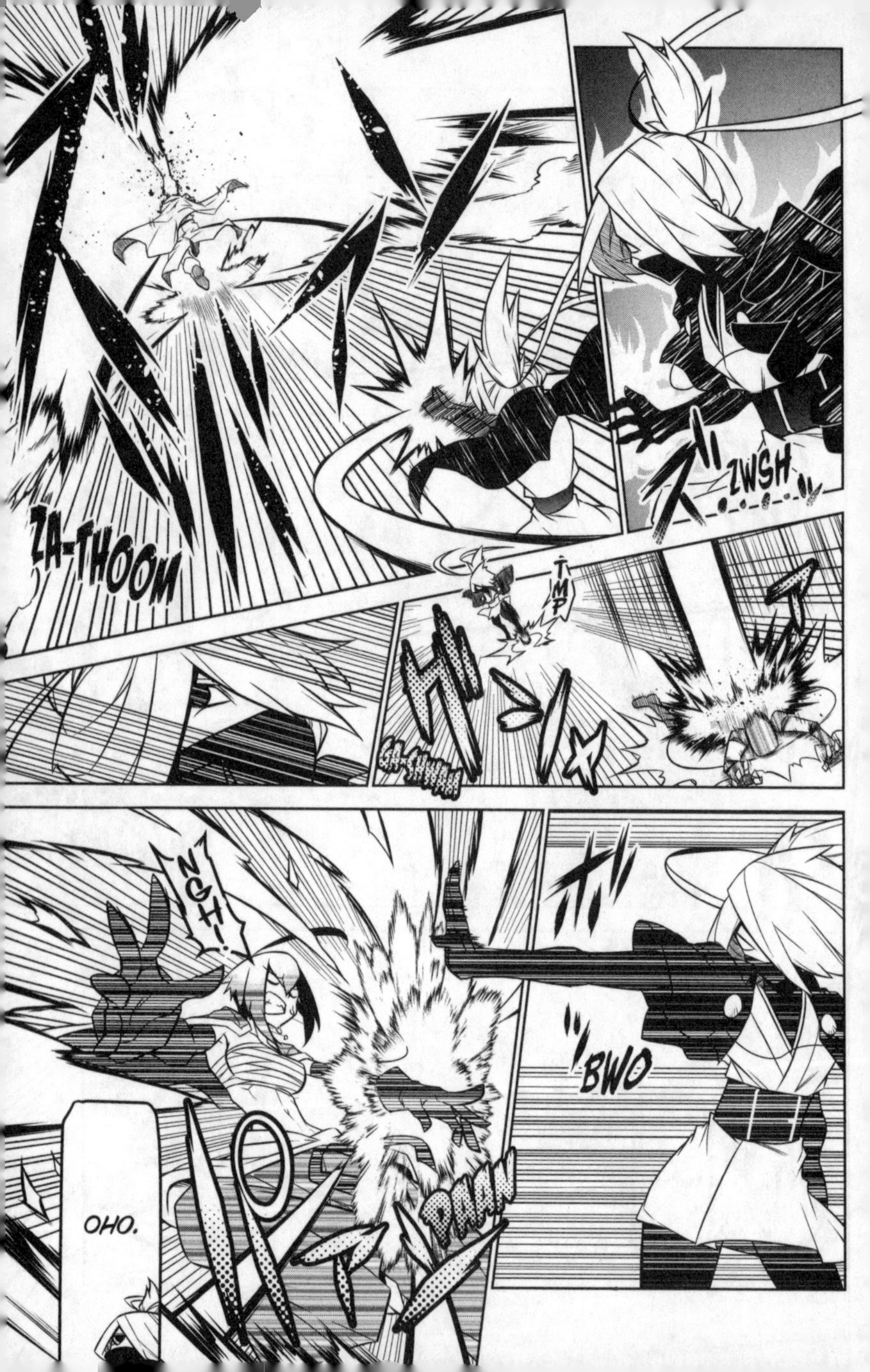
ZWSH
ZA-THOOM
TMP
BWO
NGH!
DHAN
OHO.

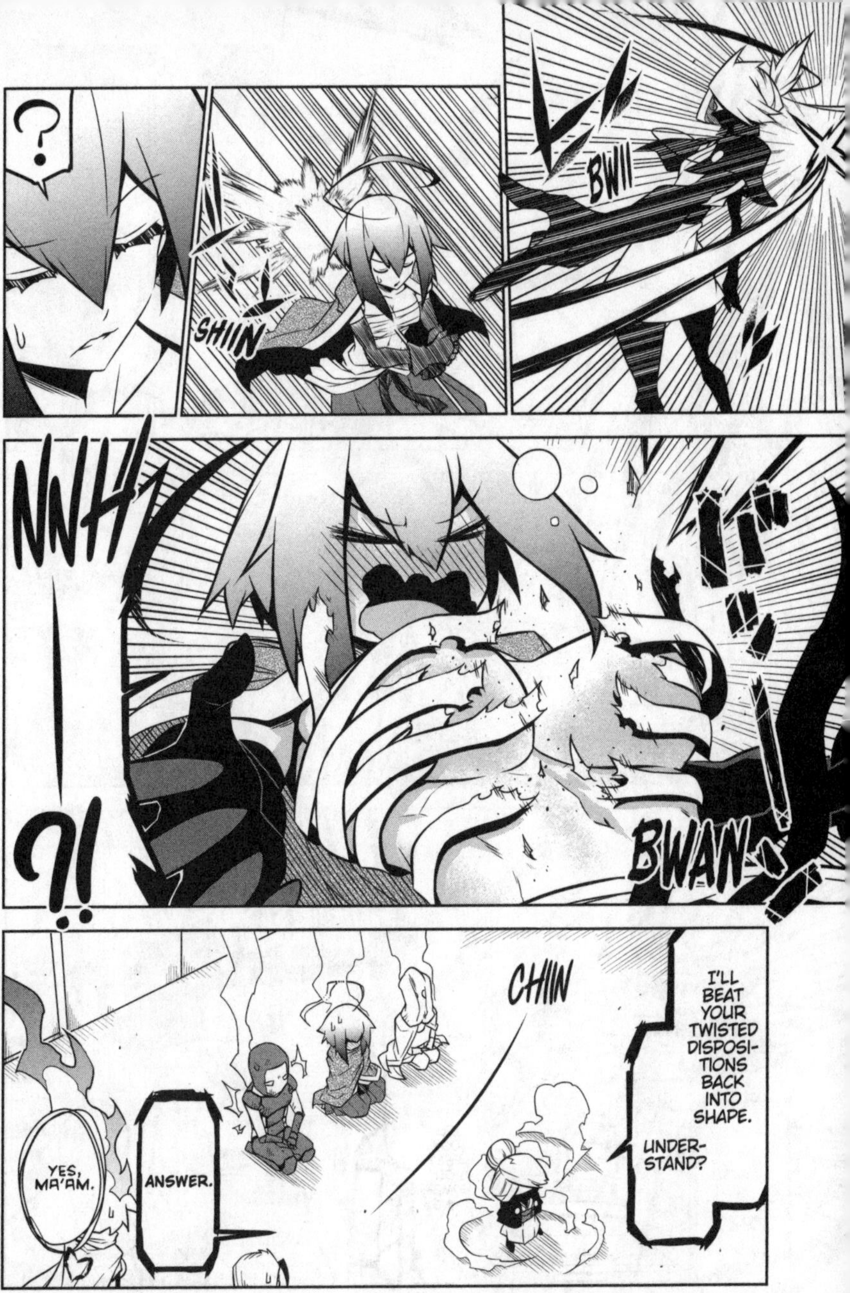
BWII
SHIIN
?
NNH—?!
BWAN
I'LL BEAT YOUR TWISTED DISPOSITIONS BACK INTO SHAPE.
UNDERSTAND?
CHIIN
ANSWER.
YES, MA'AM.

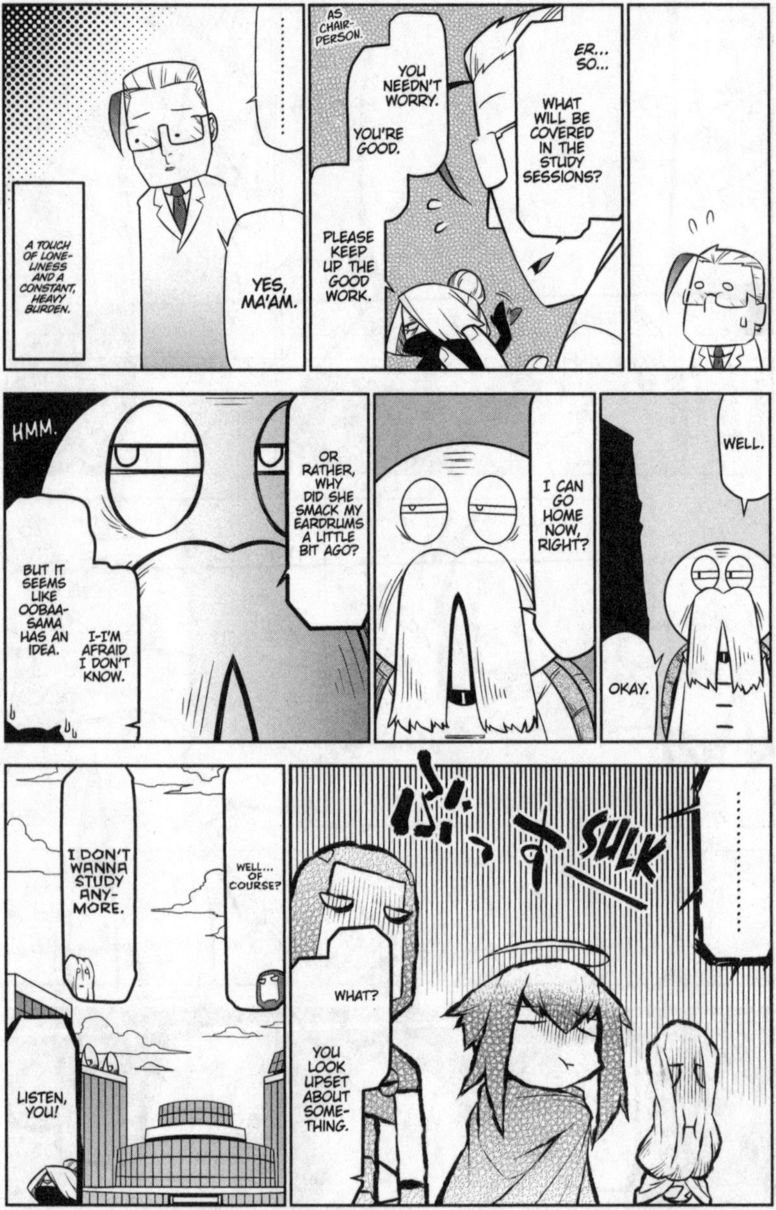
ER... SO...
WHAT WILL BE COVERED IN THE STUDY SESSIONS?
AS CHAIR-PERSON.
YOU NEEDN'T WORRY.
YOU'RE GOOD.
PLEASE KEEP UP THE GOOD WORK.
......
YES, MA'AM.
A TOUCH OF LONE-LINESS AND A CONSTANT, HEAVY BURDEN.
WELL.
OKAY.
I CAN GO HOME NOW, RIGHT?
OR RATHER, WHY DID SHE SMACK MY EARDRUMS A LITTLE BIT AGO?
HMM.
I-I'M AFRAID I DON'T KNOW.
BUT IT SEEMS LIKE OOBAA-SAMA HAS AN IDEA.
......
SULK
WHAT?
YOU LOOK UPSET ABOUT SOME-THING.
WELL... OF COURSE?
I DON'T WANNA STUDY ANY-MORE.
LISTEN, YOU!

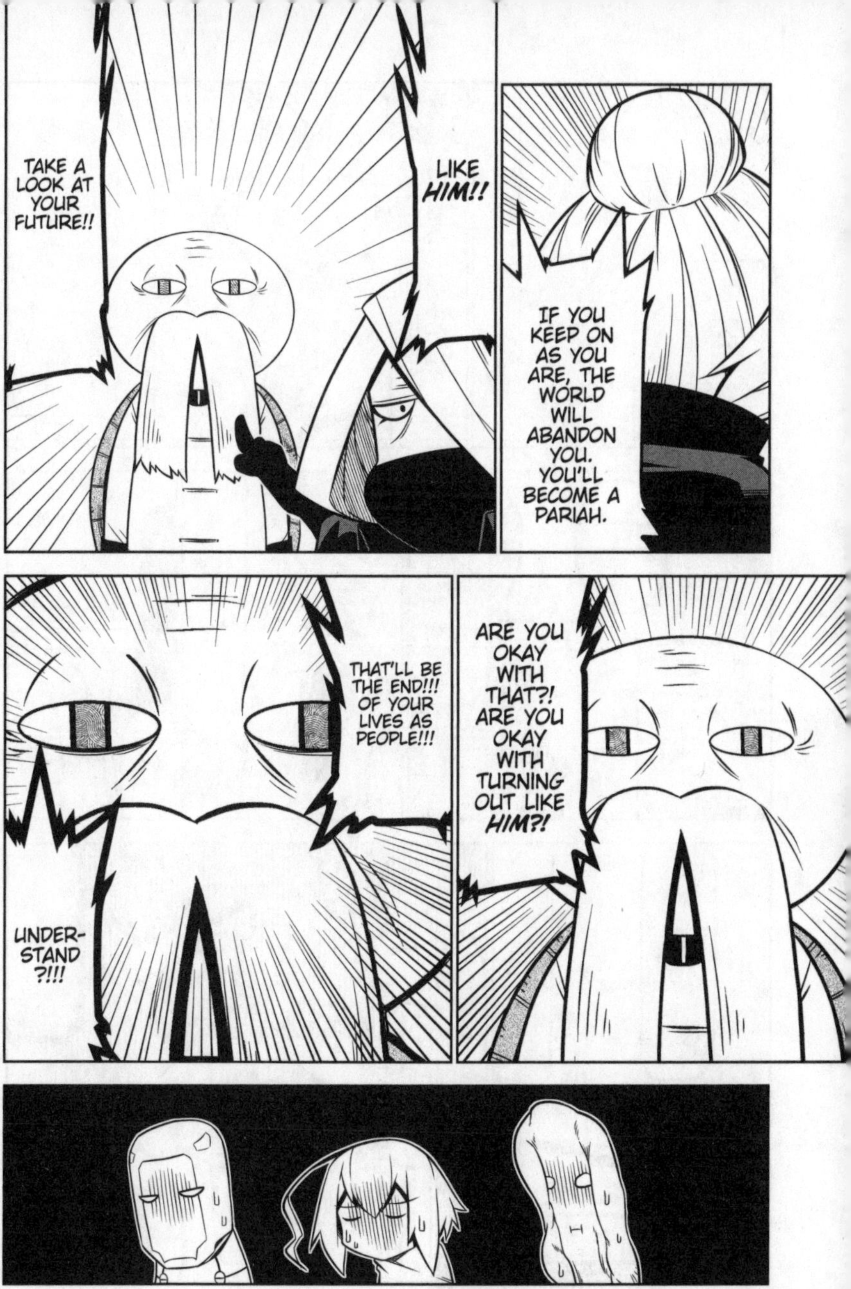
IF YOU KEEP ON AS YOU ARE, THE WORLD WILL ABANDON YOU. YOU'LL BECOME A PARIAH.
LIKE *HIM!!*
TAKE A LOOK AT YOUR FUTURE!!
ARE YOU OKAY WITH THAT?! ARE YOU OKAY WITH TURNING OUT LIKE *HIM?!*
THAT'LL BE THE END!!! OF YOUR LIVES AS PEOPLE!!!
UNDER-STAND ?!!!

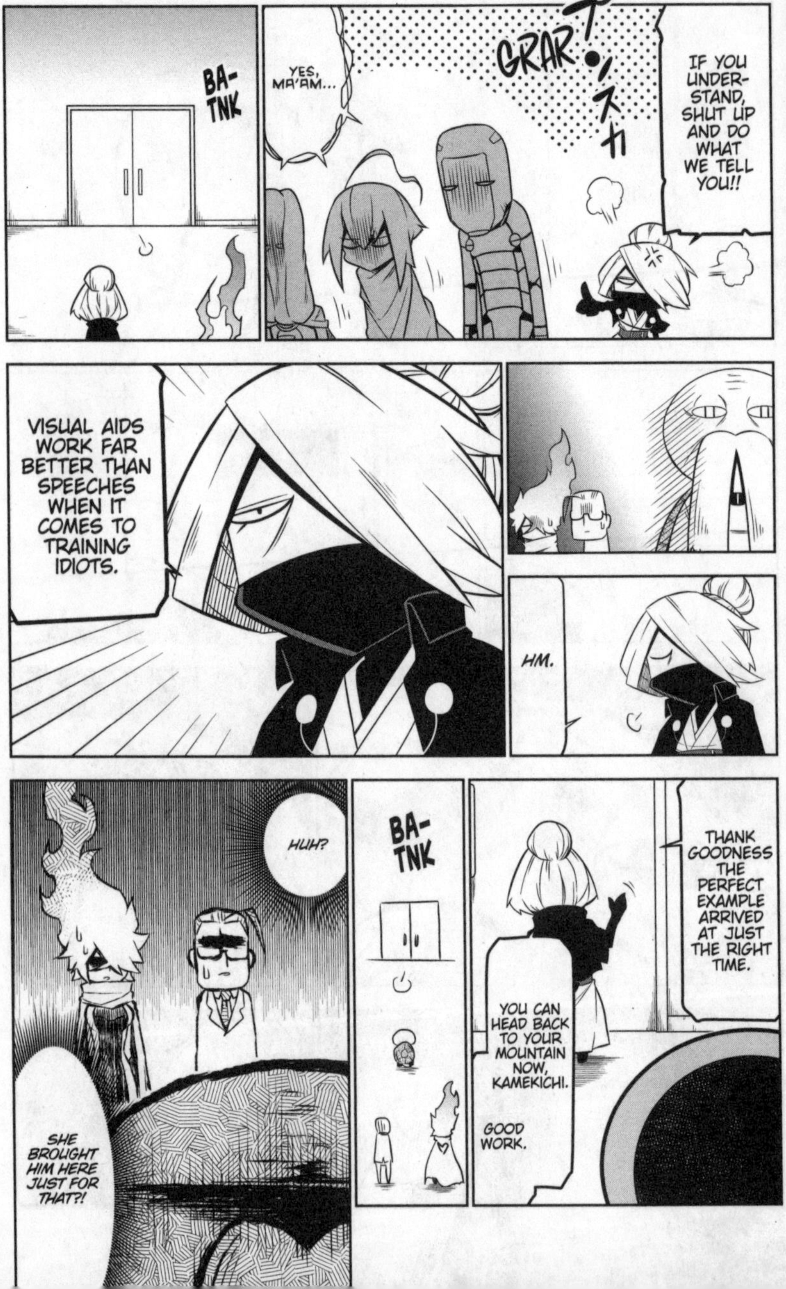
IF YOU UNDERSTAND, SHUT UP AND DO WHAT WE TELL YOU!!
GRAR
YES, MA'AM...
BA-TNK
HM.
VISUAL AIDS WORK FAR BETTER THAN SPEECHES WHEN IT COMES TO TRAINING IDIOTS.
THANK GOODNESS THE PERFECT EXAMPLE ARRIVED AT JUST THE RIGHT TIME.
YOU CAN HEAD BACK TO YOUR MOUNTAIN NOW, KAMEKICHI.
GOOD WORK.
BA-TNK
HUH?
SHE BROUGHT HIM HERE JUST FOR THAT?!

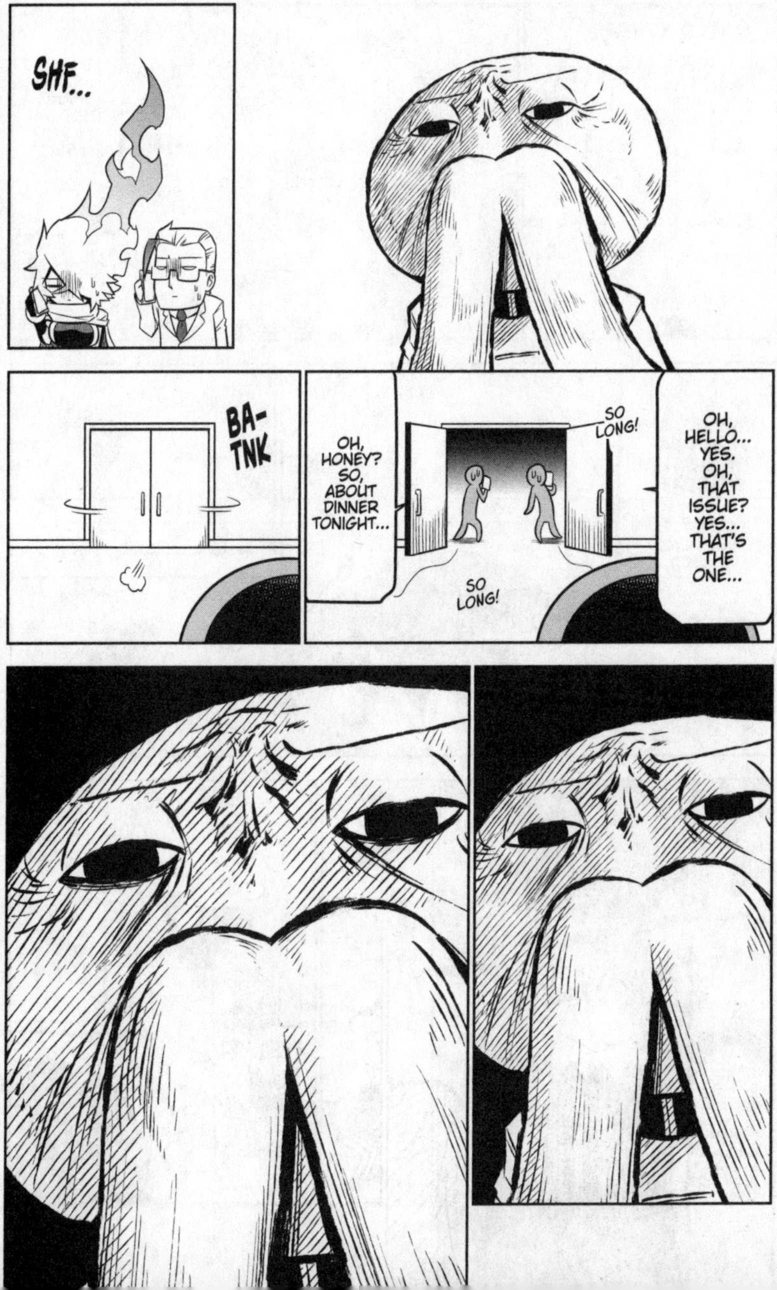
SHF...
OH, HELLO... YES. OH, THAT ISSUE? YES... THAT'S THE ONE...
SO LONG!
OH, HONEY? SO, ABOUT DINNER TONIGHT...
SO LONG!
BA-TNK

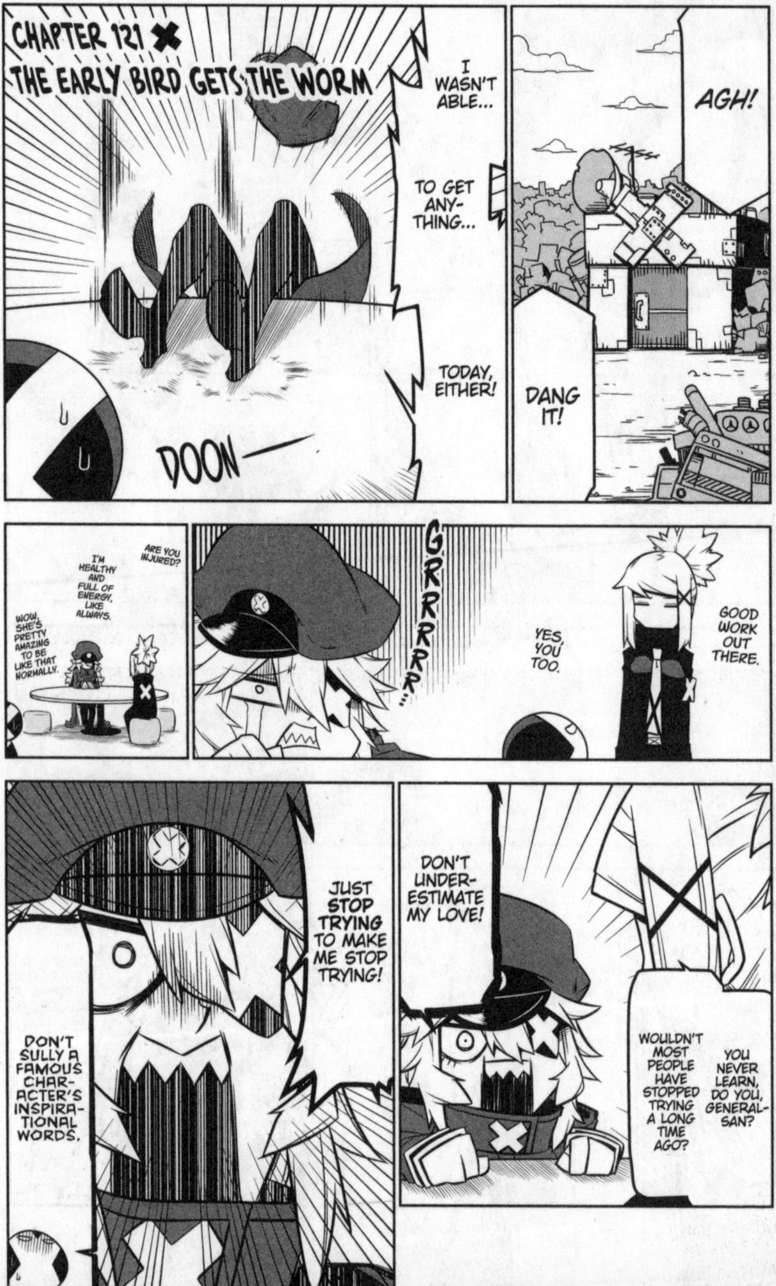
AGH!
DANG IT!
I WASN'T ABLE...
TO GET ANYTHING...
TODAY, EITHER!
CHAPTER 121 ✖ THE EARLY BIRD GETS THE WORM
DOON
GOOD WORK OUT THERE.
YES, YOU TOO.
GRRRRRR...
ARE YOU INJURED?
I'M HEALTHY AND FULL OF ENERGY, LIKE ALWAYS.
WOW, SHE'S PRETTY AMAZING TO BE LIKE THAT NORMALLY.
YOU NEVER LEARN, DO YOU, GENERAL-SAN?
WOULDN'T MOST PEOPLE HAVE STOPPED TRYING A LONG TIME AGO?
DON'T UNDERESTIMATE MY LOVE!
JUST STOP TRYING TO MAKE ME STOP TRYING!
DON'T SULLY A FAMOUS CHARACTER'S INSPIRATIONAL WORDS.

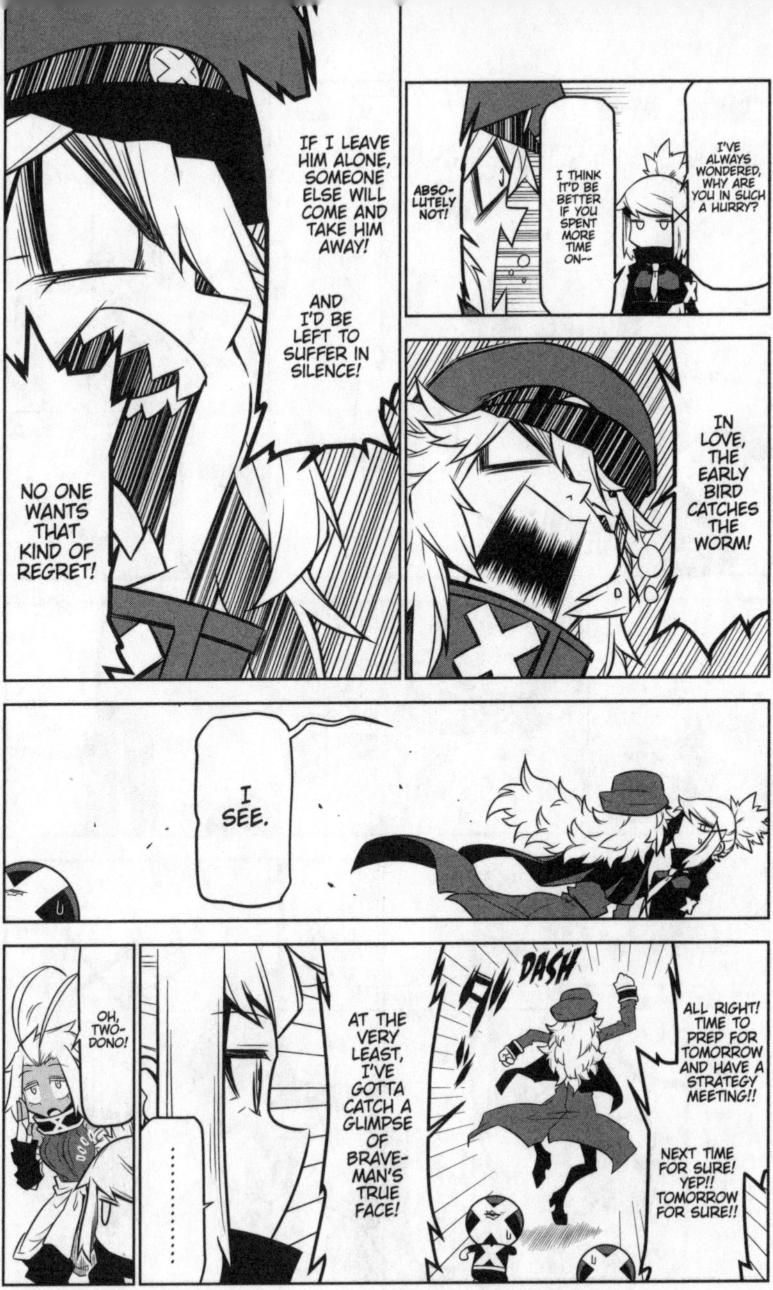
I'VE ALWAYS WONDERED, WHY ARE YOU IN SUCH A HURRY?
I THINK IT'D BE BETTER IF YOU SPENT MORE TIME ON--
ABSOLUTELY NOT!
IN LOVE, THE EARLY BIRD CATCHES THE WORM!
IF I LEAVE HIM ALONE, SOMEONE ELSE WILL COME AND TAKE HIM AWAY!
AND I'D BE LEFT TO SUFFER IN SILENCE!
NO ONE WANTS THAT KIND OF REGRET!
I SEE.
ALL RIGHT! TIME TO PREP FOR TOMORROW AND HAVE A STRATEGY MEETING!!
NEXT TIME FOR SURE! YEP!! TOMORROW FOR SURE!!
DASH
AT THE VERY LEAST, I'VE GOTTA CATCH A GLIMPSE OF BRAVE-MAN'S TRUE FACE!
......
OH, TWO-DONO!

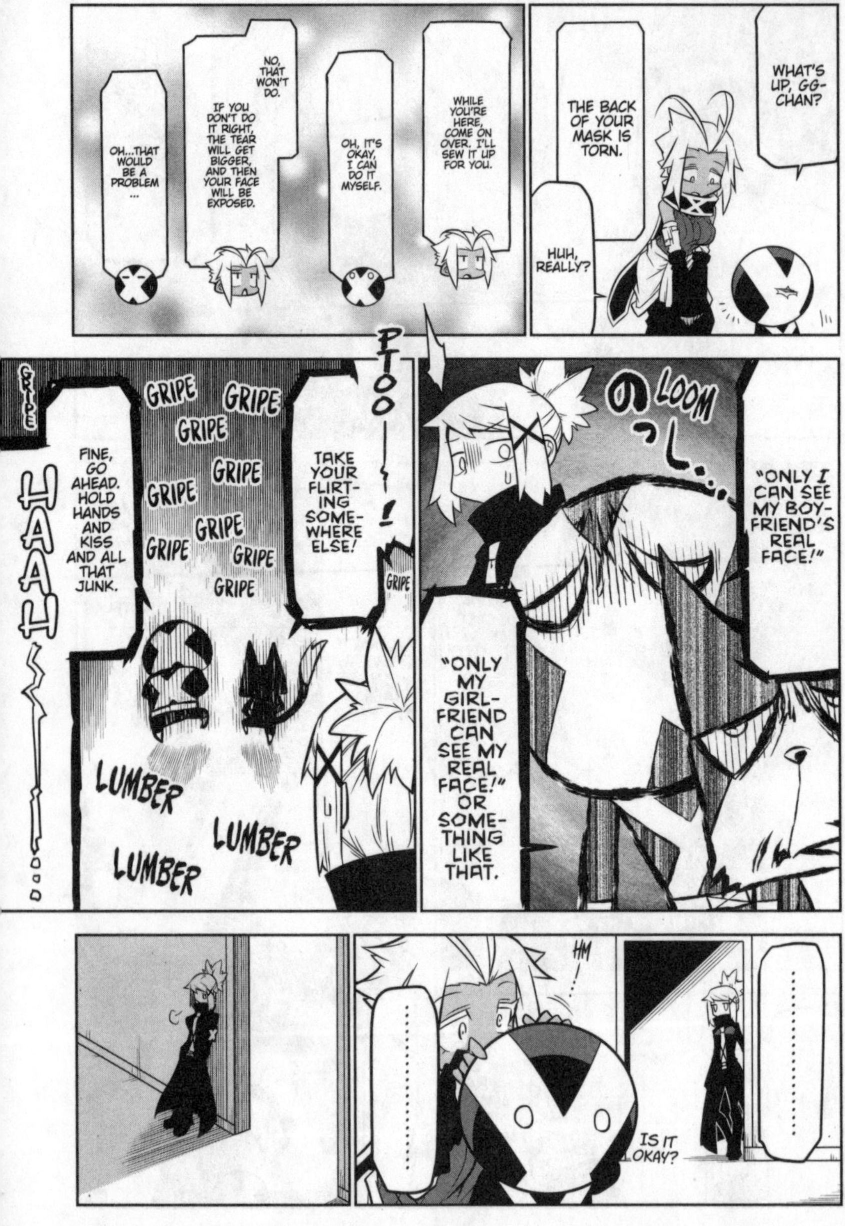
WHAT'S UP, GG-CHAN?
THE BACK OF YOUR MASK IS TORN.
HUH, REALLY?
WHILE YOU'RE HERE, COME ON OVER. I'LL SEW IT UP FOR YOU.
OH, IT'S OKAY, I CAN DO IT MYSELF.
NO, THAT WON'T DO.
IF YOU DON'T DO IT RIGHT, THE TEAR WILL GET BIGGER, AND THEN YOUR FACE WILL BE EXPOSED.
OH...THAT WOULD BE A PROBLEM ...
"ONLY I CAN SEE MY BOY-FRIEND'S REAL FACE!"
LOOM
のっし...
"ONLY MY GIRL-FRIEND CAN SEE MY REAL FACE!" OR SOME-THING LIKE THAT.
PTOO—!
TAKE YOUR FLIRT-ING SOME-WHERE ELSE!
GRIPE
GRIPE GRIPE GRIPE GRIPE GRIPE GRIPE GRIPE GRIPE GRIPE
GRIPE
FINE, GO AHEAD. HOLD HANDS AND KISS AND ALL THAT JUNK.
HAAAH—
LUMBER
LUMBER
LUMBER
......
HM...!
IS IT OKAY?
......

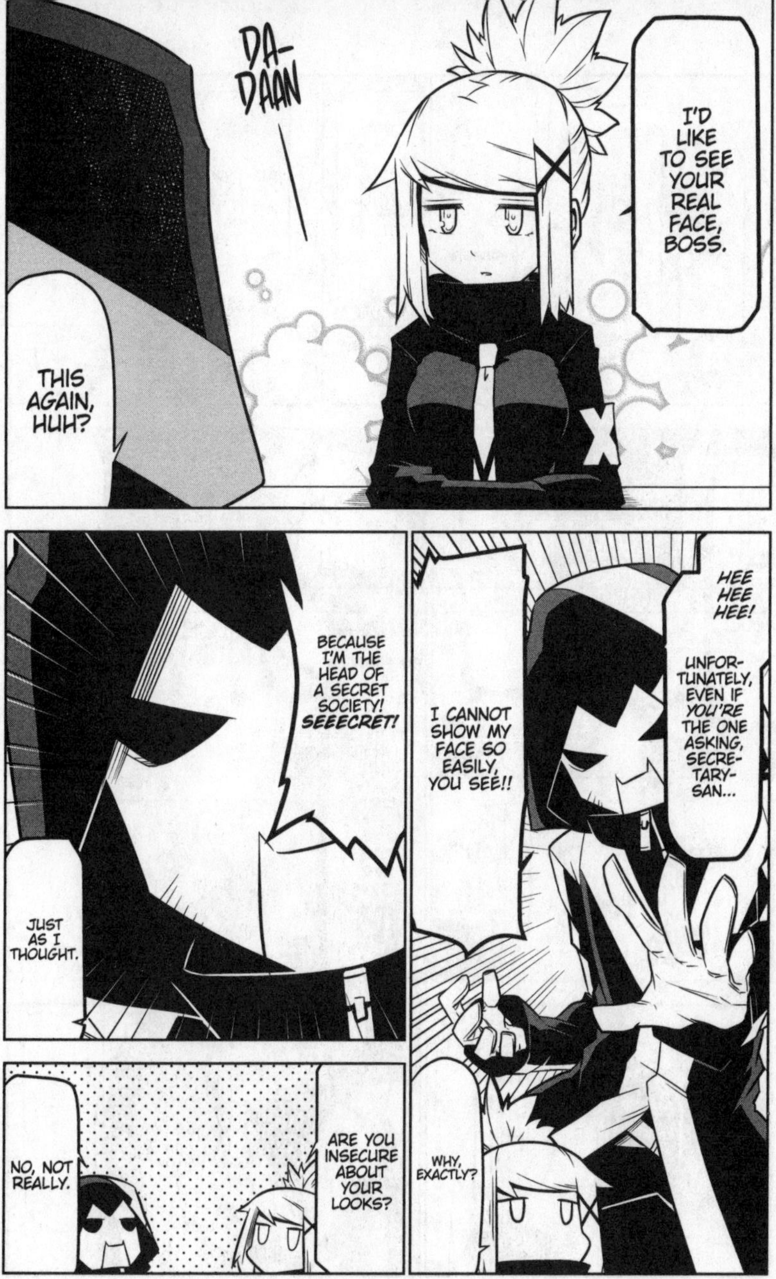
I'D LIKE TO SEE YOUR REAL FACE, BOSS.
DA-DAAN
THIS AGAIN, HUH?
HEE HEE HEE!
UNFORTUNATELY, EVEN IF *YOU'RE* THE ONE ASKING, SECRETARY-SAN...
I CANNOT SHOW MY FACE SO EASILY, YOU SEE!!
WHY, EXACTLY?
BECAUSE I'M THE HEAD OF A SECRET SOCIETY! ***SEEECRET!***
JUST AS I THOUGHT.
ARE YOU INSECURE ABOUT YOUR LOOKS?
NO, NOT REALLY.

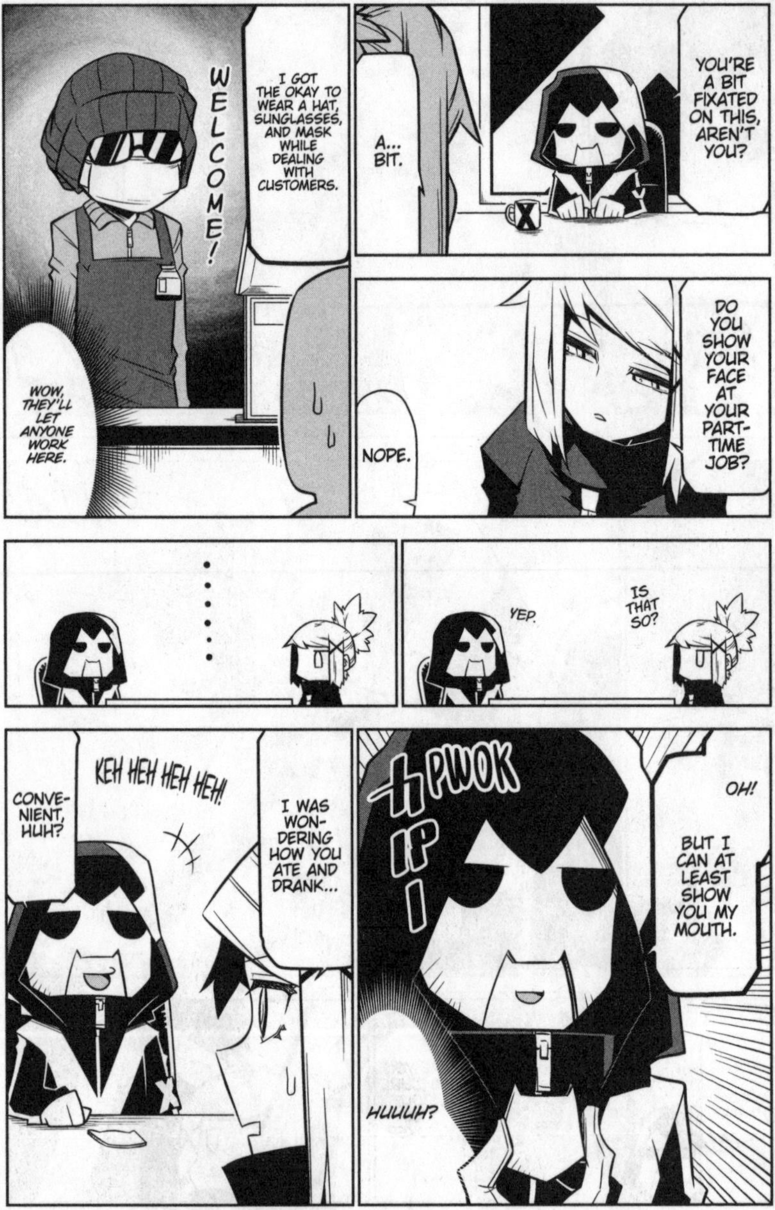
YOU'RE A BIT FIXATED ON THIS, AREN'T YOU?
A... BIT.
DO YOU SHOW YOUR FACE AT YOUR PART-TIME JOB?
NOPE.
I GOT THE OKAY TO WEAR A HAT, SUNGLASSES, AND MASK WHILE DEALING WITH CUSTOMERS.
WELCOME!
WOW, THEY'LL LET ANYONE WORK HERE.
IS THAT SO?
YEP.
......
OH!
BUT I CAN AT LEAST SHOW YOU MY MOUTH.
PWOK
HUUUH?
I WAS WONDERING HOW YOU ATE AND DRANK...
KEH HEH HEH HEH!
CONVENIENT, HUH?

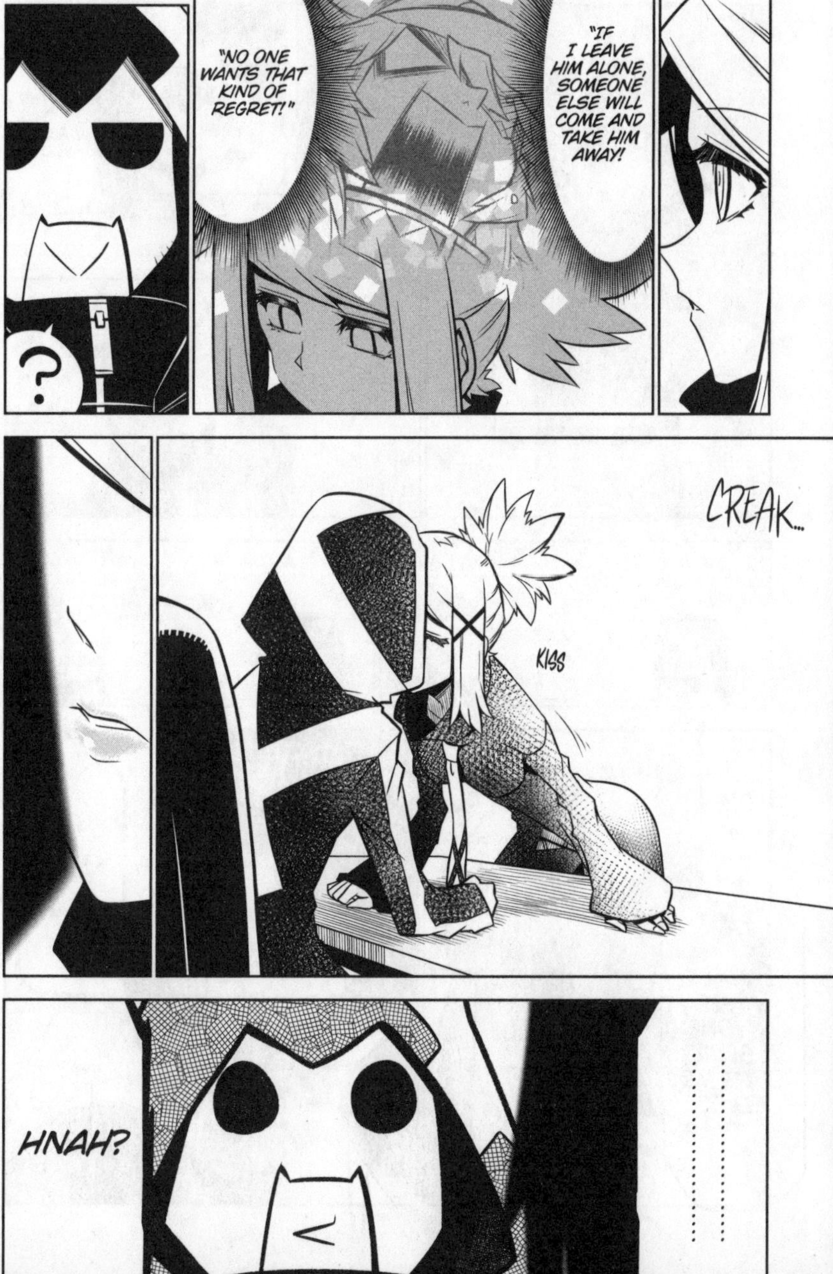
"IF I LEAVE HIM ALONE, SOMEONE ELSE WILL COME AND TAKE HIM AWAY!
"NO ONE WANTS THAT KIND OF REGRET!"
?
CREAK...
KISS
......
HNAH?

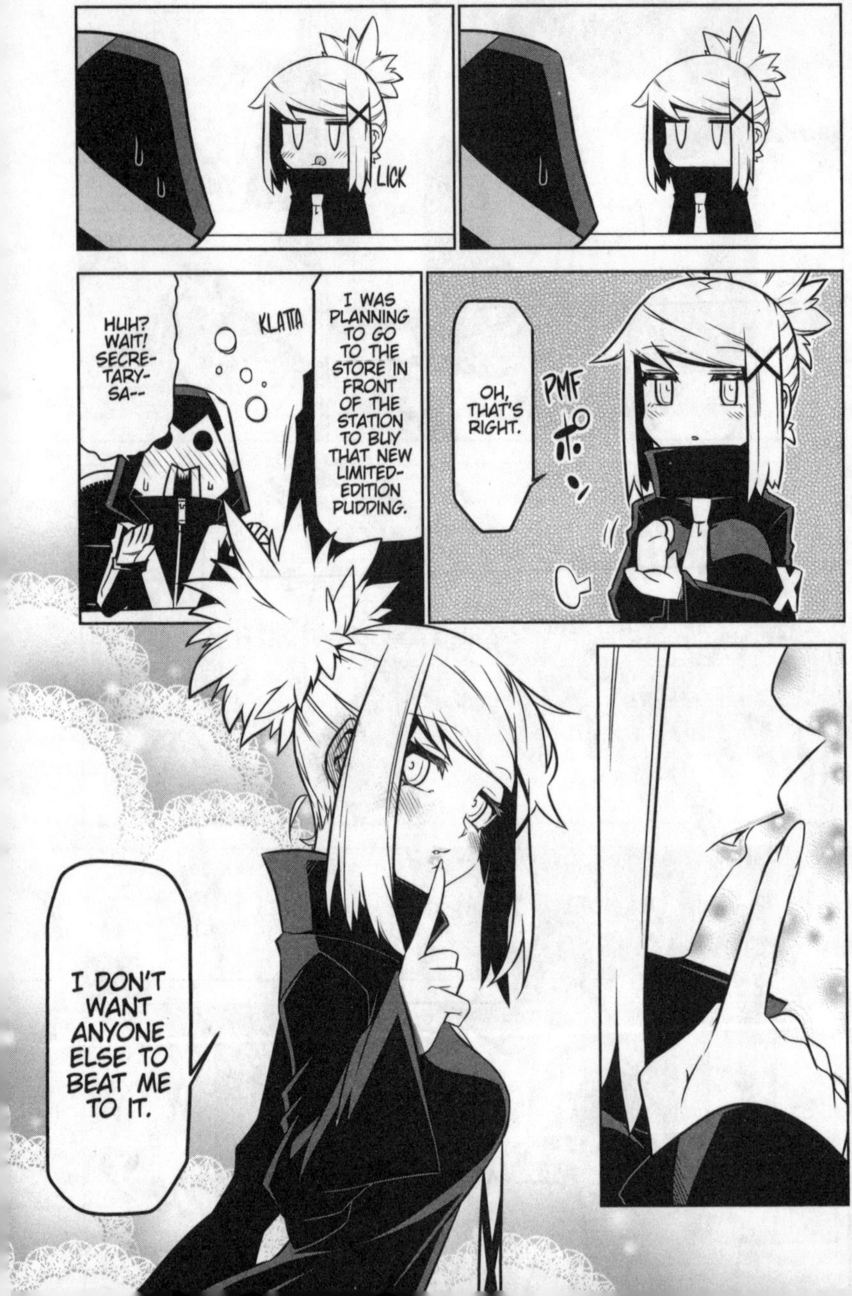
LICK
PMF
OH, THAT'S RIGHT.
I WAS PLANNING TO GO TO THE STORE IN FRONT OF THE STATION TO BUY THAT NEW LIMITED-EDITION PUDDING.
KLATTA
HUH? WAIT! SECRETARY-SA--
I DON'T WANT ANYONE ELSE TO BEAT ME TO IT.

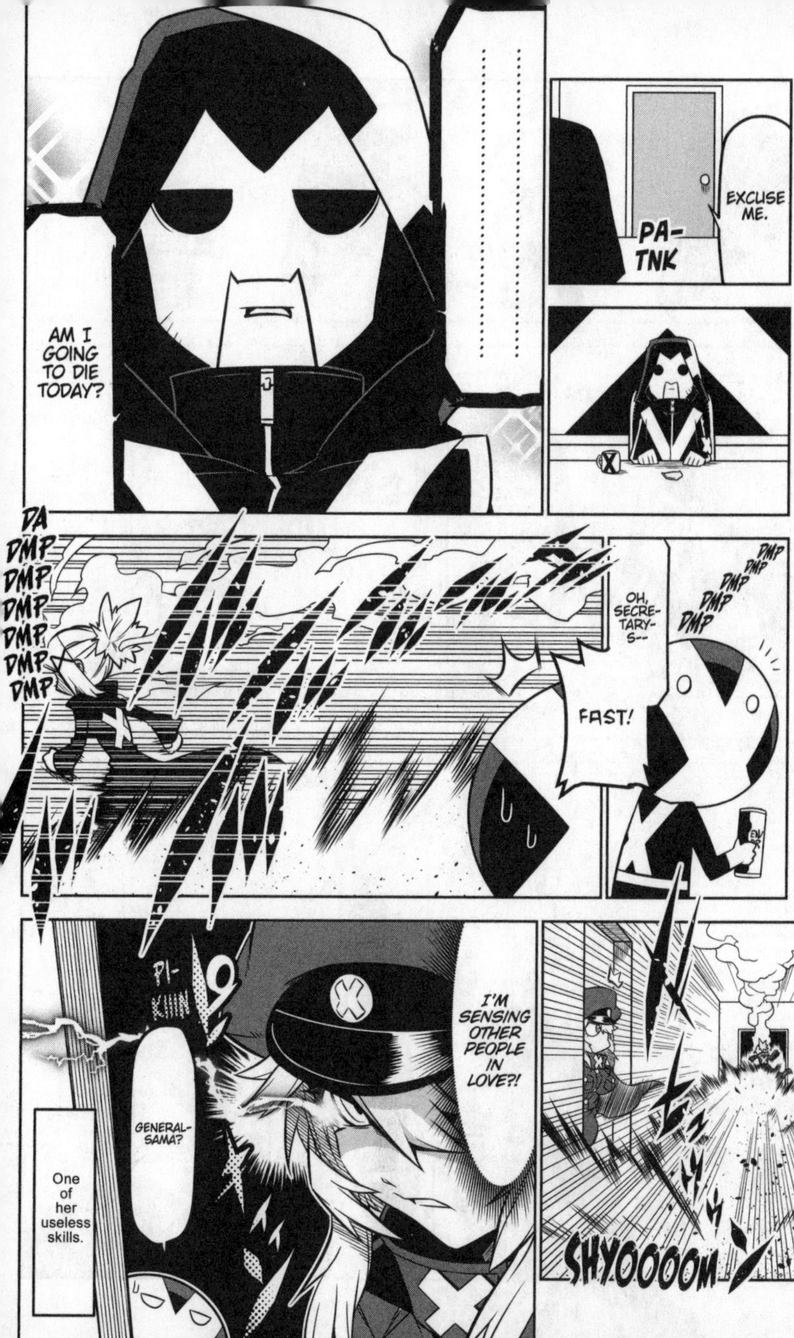
EXCUSE ME.
PA-TNK
......
AM I GOING TO DIE TODAY?
DMP DMP DMP DMP DMP
OH, SECRETARY-S--
FAST!
DA DMP DMP DMP DMP DMP DMP
SHYOOOOM
I'M SENSING OTHER PEOPLE IN LOVE?!
PI-KIIIN
GENERAL-SAMA?
One of her useless skills.

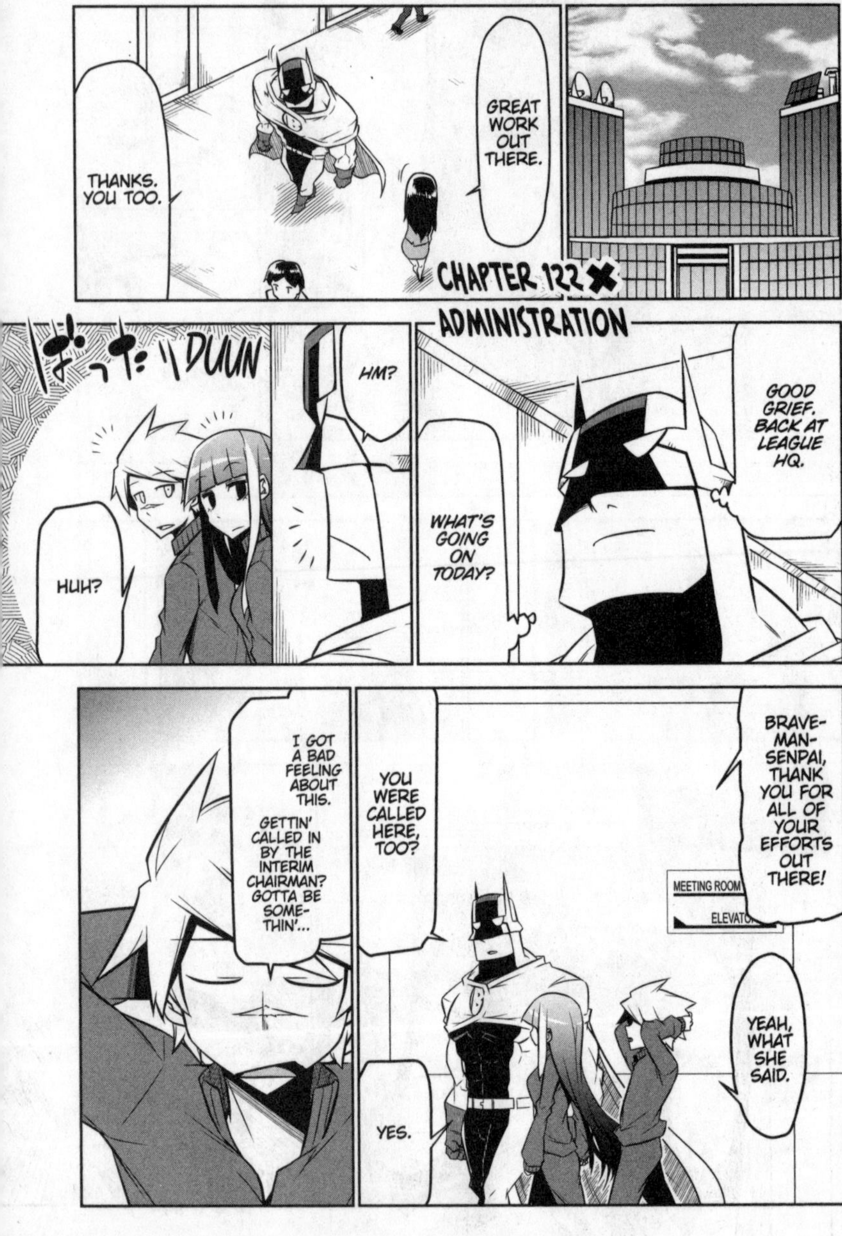
CHAPTER 122 ✖
ADMINISTRATION
GREAT WORK OUT THERE.
THANKS. YOU TOO.
GOOD GRIEF. BACK AT LEAGUE HQ.
WHAT'S GOING ON TODAY?
HM?
DUUN
HUH?
BRAVE-MAN-SENPAI, THANK YOU FOR ALL OF YOUR EFFORTS OUT THERE!
MEETING ROOM
YEAH, WHAT SHE SAID.
YOU WERE CALLED HERE, TOO?
YES.
I GOT A BAD FEELING ABOUT THIS.
GETTIN' CALLED IN BY THE INTERIM CHAIRMAN? GOTTA BE SOME-THIN'...

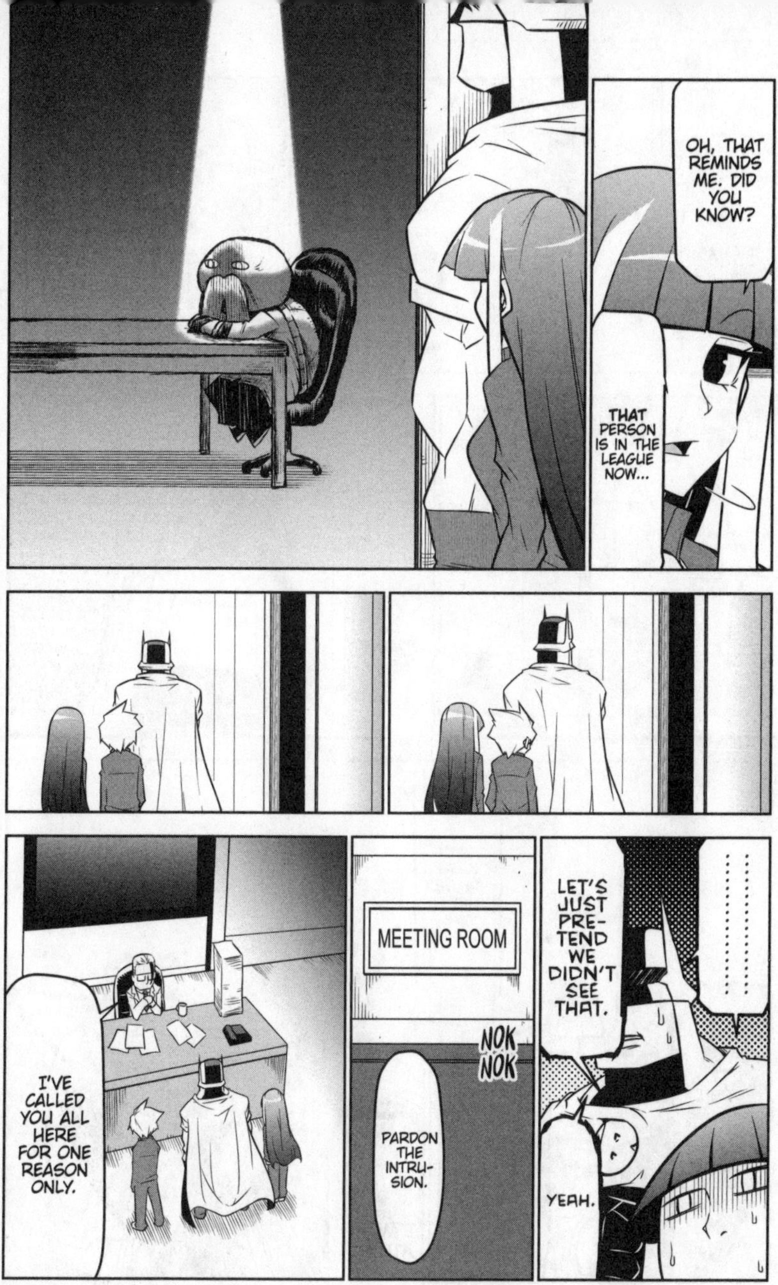

OH, THAT REMINDS ME. DID YOU KNOW?
THAT PERSON IS IN THE LEAGUE NOW...
......
LET'S JUST PRETEND WE DIDN'T SEE THAT.
YEAH.
MEETING ROOM
NOK NOK
PARDON THE INTRUSION.
I'VE CALLED YOU ALL HERE FOR ONE REASON ONLY.

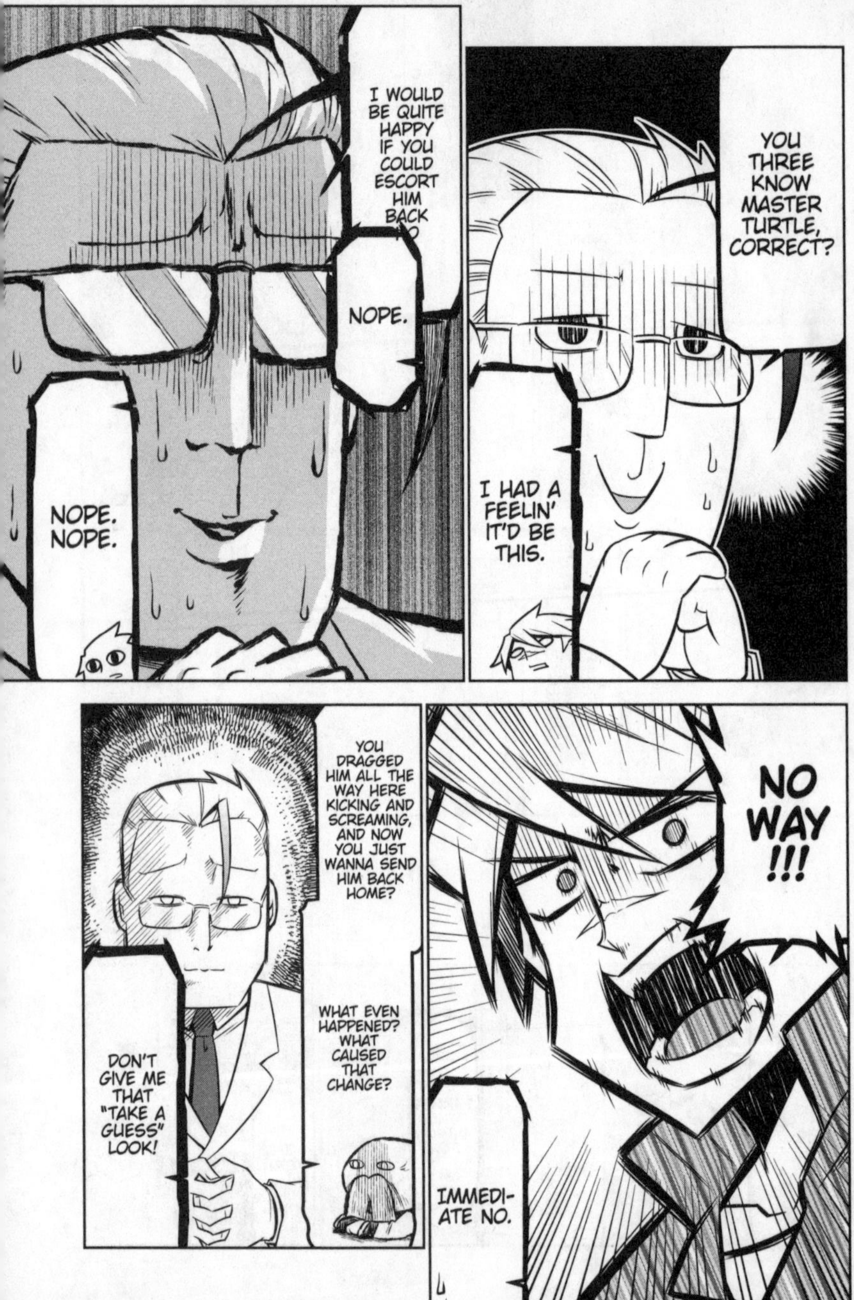
YOU THREE KNOW MASTER TURTLE, CORRECT?
I HAD A FEELIN' IT'D BE THIS.
I WOULD BE QUITE HAPPY IF YOU COULD ESCORT HIM BACK
NOPE.
NOPE. NOPE.
NO WAY!!!
IMMEDI- ATE NO.
YOU DRAGGED HIM ALL THE WAY HERE KICKING AND SCREAMING, AND NOW YOU JUST WANNA SEND HIM BACK HOME?
WHAT EVEN HAPPENED? WHAT CAUSED THAT CHANGE?
DON'T GIVE ME THAT "TAKE A GUESS" LOOK!

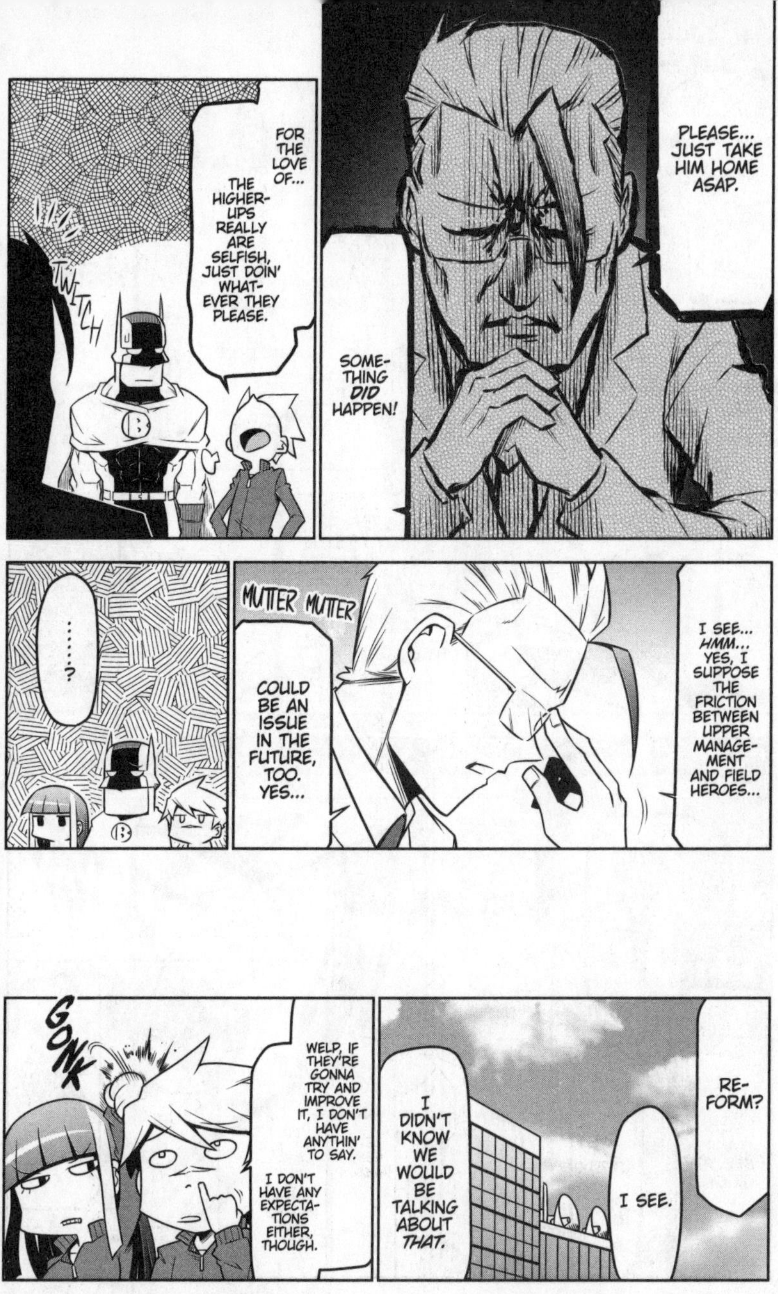
PLEASE... JUST TAKE HIM HOME ASAP.
SOMETHING *DID* HAPPEN!
FOR THE LOVE OF...
THE HIGHER-UPS REALLY ARE SELFISH, JUST DOIN' WHATEVER THEY PLEASE.
TWITCH
I SEE... *HMM*... YES, I SUPPOSE THE FRICTION BETWEEN UPPER MANAGEMENT AND FIELD HEROES...
MUTTER MUTTER
COULD BE AN ISSUE IN THE FUTURE, TOO. YES...
......?
REFORM?
I SEE.
I DIDN'T KNOW WE WOULD BE TALKING ABOUT *THAT*.
WELP, IF THEY'RE GONNA TRY AND IMPROVE IT, I DON'T HAVE ANYTHIN' TO SAY.
I DON'T HAVE ANY EXPECTATIONS EITHER, THOUGH.
GONK

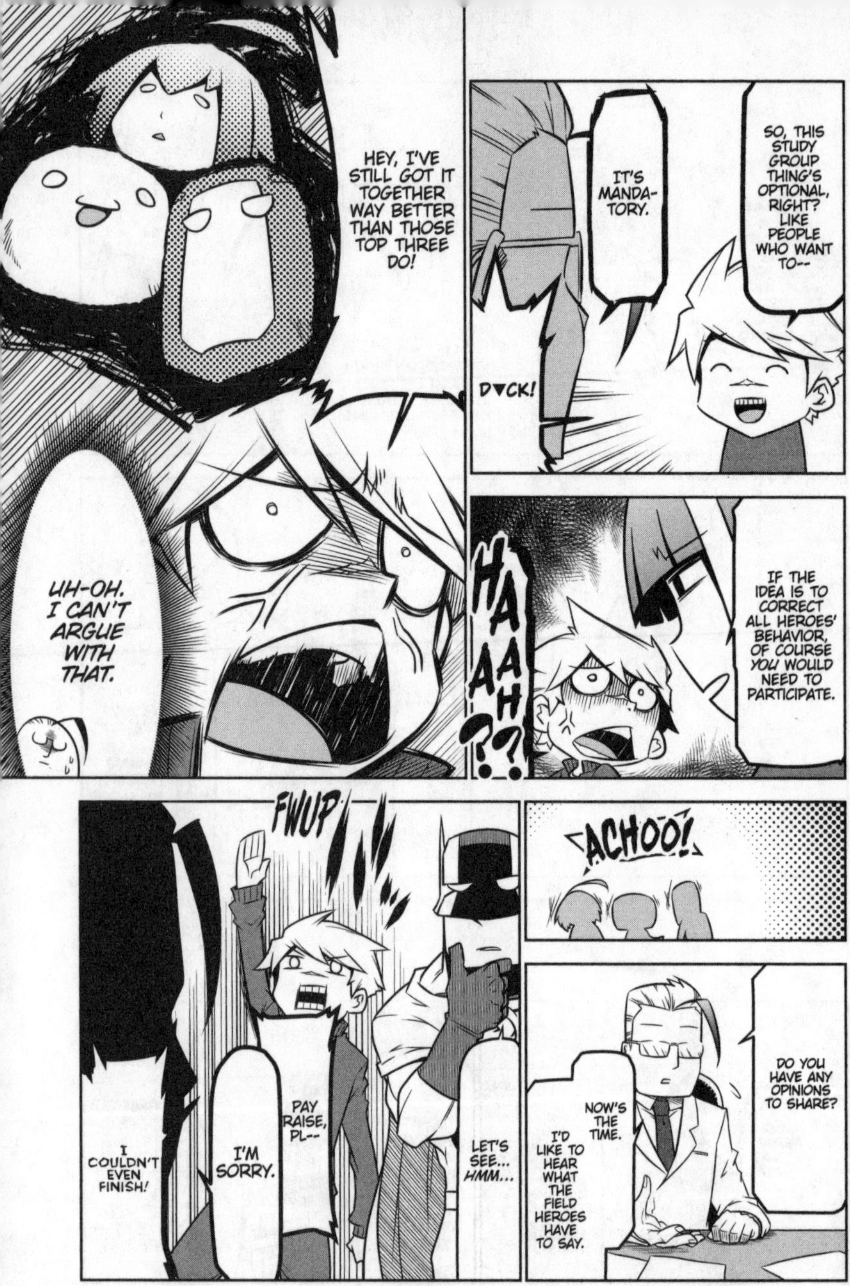
SO, THIS STUDY GROUP THING'S OPTIONAL, RIGHT? LIKE PEOPLE WHO WANT TO--
IT'S MANDA-TORY.
D▼CK!
IF THE IDEA IS TO CORRECT ALL HEROES' BEHAVIOR, OF COURSE *YOU* WOULD NEED TO PARTICIPATE.
HAAAH?!?!
HEY, I'VE STILL GOT IT TOGETHER WAY BETTER THAN THOSE TOP THREE DO!
UH-OH. I CAN'T ARGUE WITH THAT.
ACHOO!
DO YOU HAVE ANY OPINIONS TO SHARE?
NOW'S THE TIME.
I'D LIKE TO HEAR WHAT THE FIELD HEROES HAVE TO SAY.
FWUP
LET'S SEE... *HMM*...
PAY RAISE, PL--
I'M SORRY.
I COULDN'T EVEN FINISH!

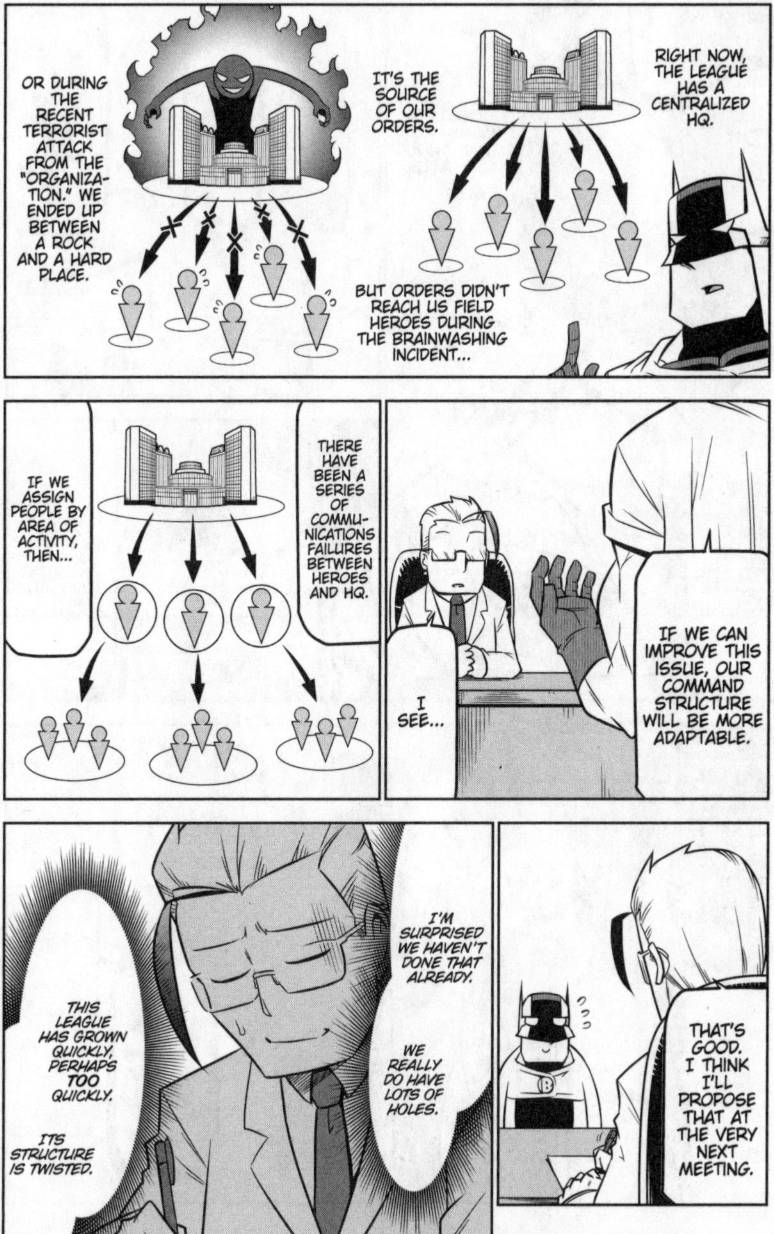
RIGHT NOW, THE LEAGUE HAS A CENTRALIZED HQ.
IT'S THE SOURCE OF OUR ORDERS.
BUT ORDERS DIDN'T REACH US FIELD HEROES DURING THE BRAINWASHING INCIDENT...
OR DURING THE RECENT TERRORIST ATTACK FROM THE "ORGANIZATION." WE ENDED UP BETWEEN A ROCK AND A HARD PLACE.
IF WE CAN IMPROVE THIS ISSUE, OUR COMMAND STRUCTURE WILL BE MORE ADAPTABLE.
I SEE...
THERE HAVE BEEN A SERIES OF COMMUNICATIONS FAILURES BETWEEN HEROES AND HQ.
IF WE ASSIGN PEOPLE BY AREA OF ACTIVITY, THEN...
THAT'S GOOD. I THINK I'LL PROPOSE THAT AT THE VERY NEXT MEETING.
I'M SURPRISED WE HAVEN'T DONE THAT ALREADY.
WE REALLY DO HAVE LOTS OF HOLES.
THIS LEAGUE HAS GROWN QUICKLY, PERHAPS TOO QUICKLY.
ITS STRUCTURE IS TWISTED.

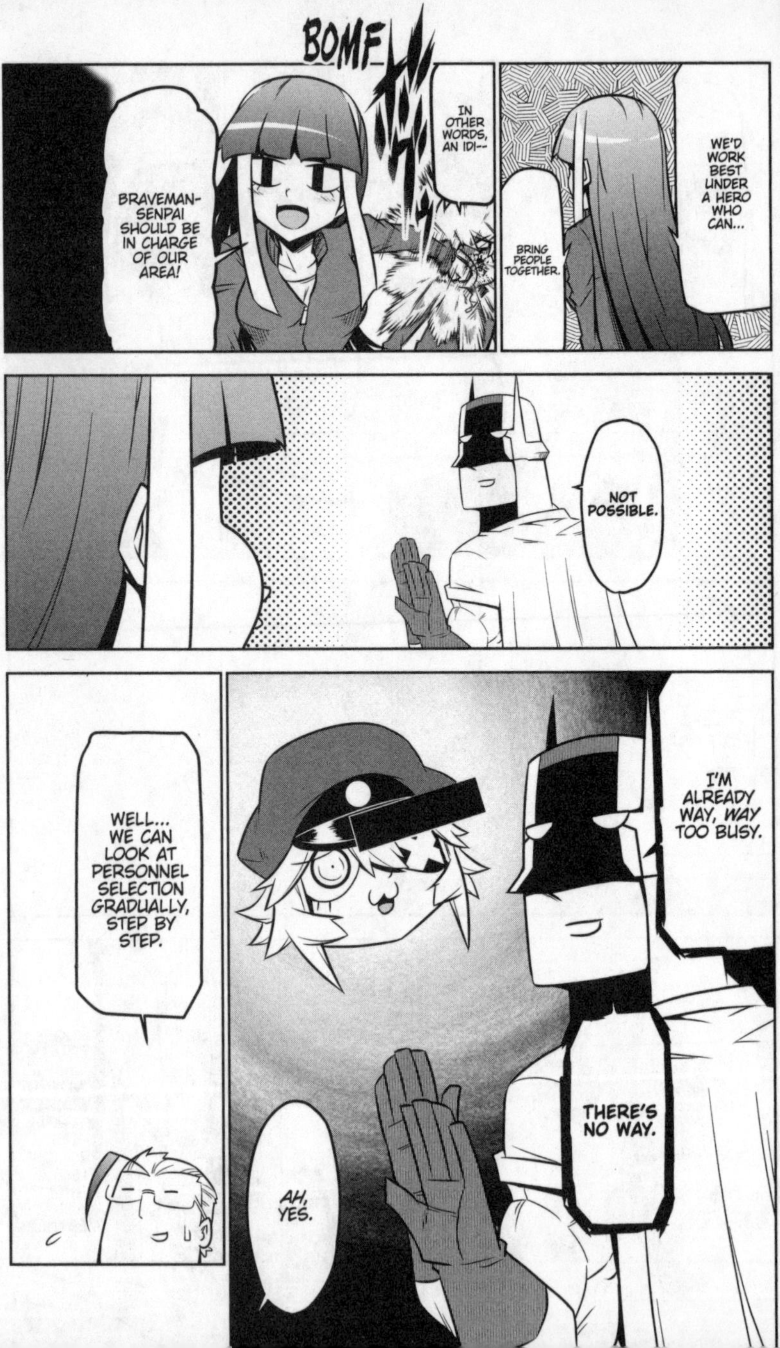
WE'D WORK BEST UNDER A HERO WHO CAN...
BRING PEOPLE TOGETHER.
IN OTHER WORDS, AN IDI--
BOMF
BRAVEMAN-SENPAI SHOULD BE IN CHARGE OF OUR AREA!
NOT POSSIBLE.
I'M ALREADY WAY, WAY TOO BUSY.
THERE'S NO WAY.
AH, YES.
WELL... WE CAN LOOK AT PERSONNEL SELECTION GRADUALLY, STEP BY STEP.

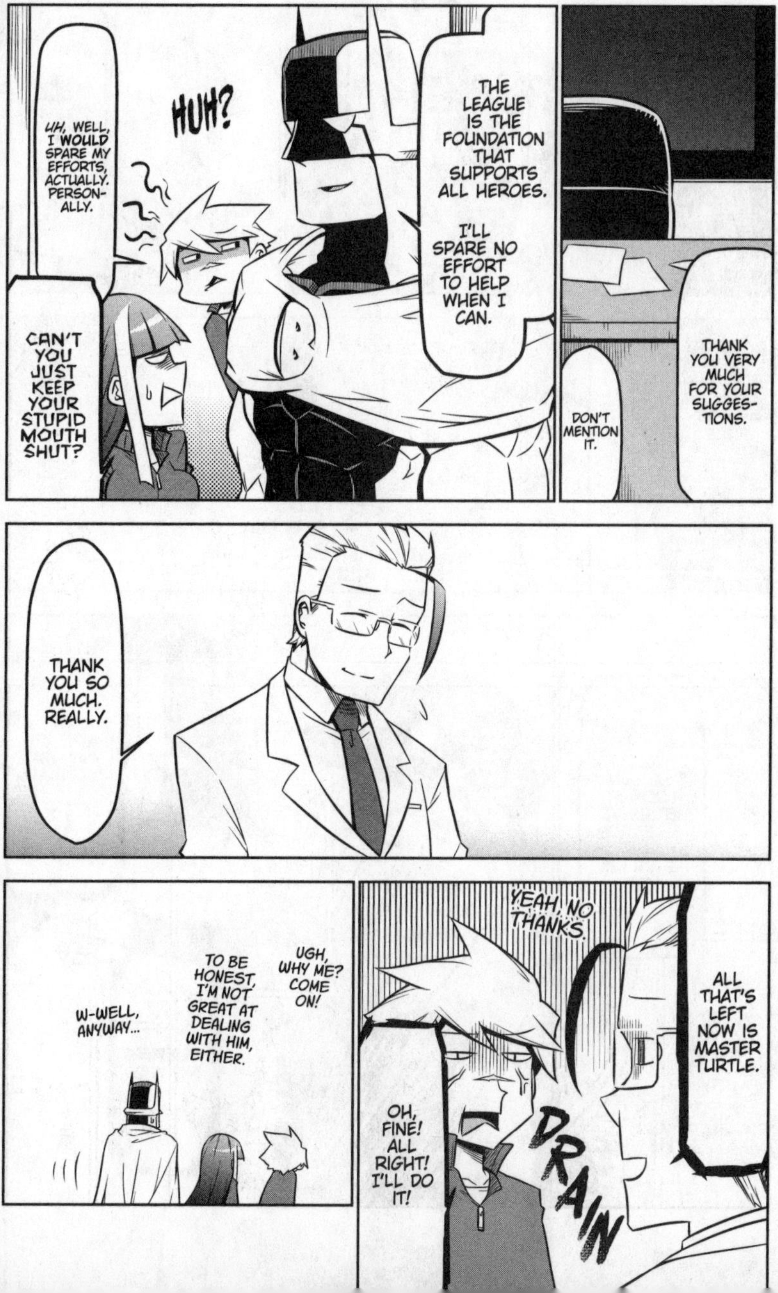
THANK YOU VERY MUCH FOR YOUR SUGGES-TIONS.
DON'T MENTION IT.
THE LEAGUE IS THE FOUNDATION THAT SUPPORTS ALL HEROES.
I'LL SPARE NO EFFORT TO HELP WHEN I CAN.
HUH?
UH, WELL, I WOULD SPARE MY EFFORTS, ACTUALLY. PERSON-ALLY.
CAN'T YOU JUST KEEP YOUR STUPID MOUTH SHUT?
THANK YOU SO MUCH. REALLY.
ALL THAT'S LEFT NOW IS MASTER TURTLE.
YEAH, NO THANKS.
DRAIN
OH, FINE! ALL RIGHT! I'LL DO IT!
UGH, WHY ME? COME ON!
TO BE HONEST, I'M NOT GREAT AT DEALING WITH HIM, EITHER.
W-WELL, ANYWAY...

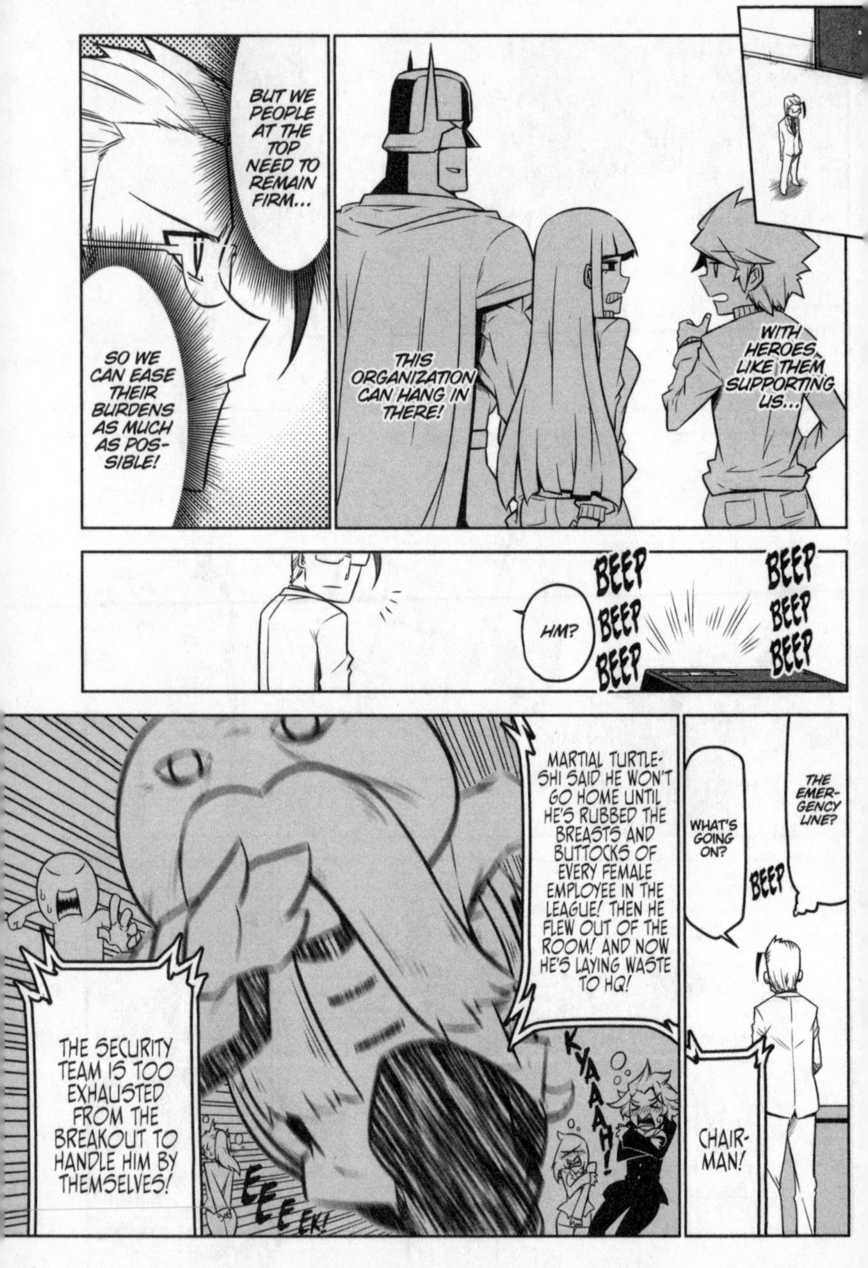
WITH HEROES LIKE THEM SUPPORTING US...
THIS ORGANIZATION CAN HANG IN THERE!
BUT WE PEOPLE AT THE TOP NEED TO REMAIN FIRM...
SO WE CAN EASE THEIR BURDENS AS MUCH AS POS-SIBLE!
BEEP BEEP BEEP
HM?
BEEP BEEP BEEP
THE EMERGENCY LINE?
BEEP
WHAT'S GOING ON?
CHAIRMAN!
MARTIAL TURTLE-SHI SAID HE WON'T GO HOME UNTIL HE'S RUBBED THE BREASTS AND BUTTOCKS OF EVERY FEMALE EMPLOYEE IN THE LEAGUE! THEN HE FLEW OUT OF THE ROOM! AND NOW HE'S LAYING WASTE TO HQ!
KYAAAAH!
THE SECURITY TEAM IS TOO EXHAUSTED FROM THE BREAKOUT TO HANDLE HIM BY THEMSELVES!
EEEEEK!

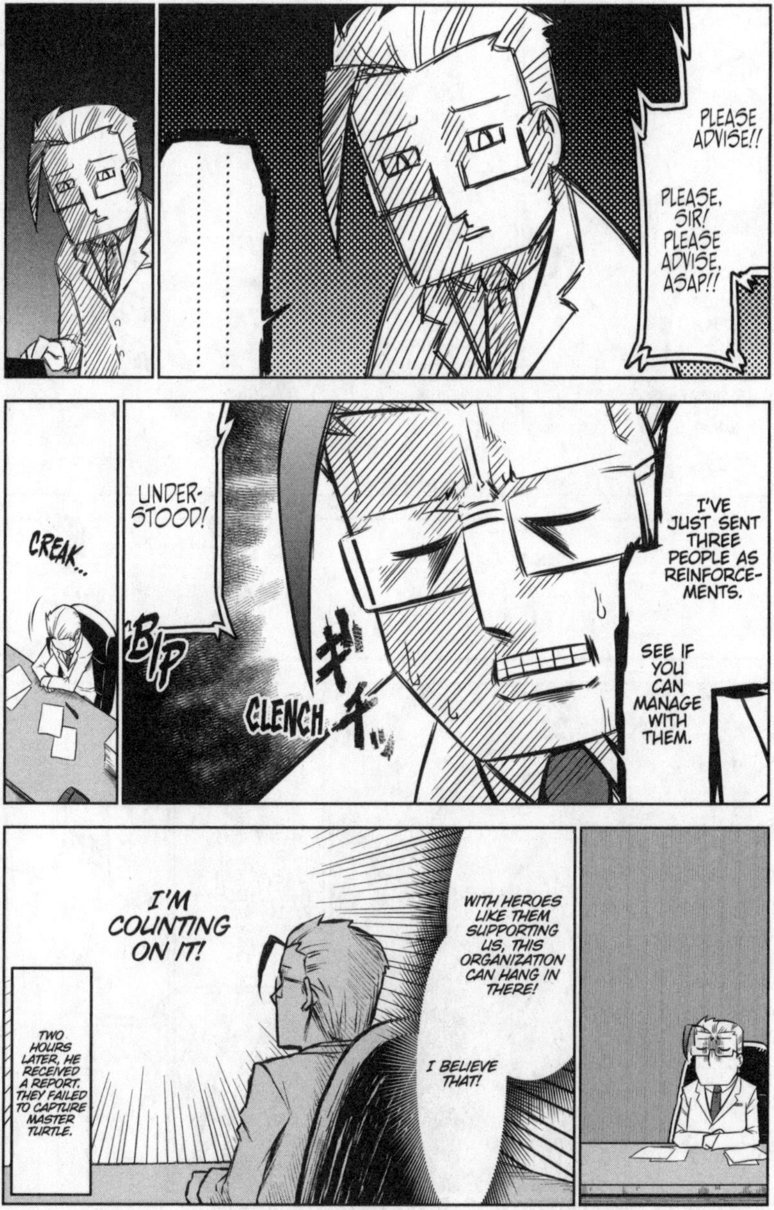
PLEASE ADVISE!!
PLEASE, SIR! PLEASE ADVISE, ASAP!!
I'VE JUST SENT THREE PEOPLE AS REINFORCEMENTS.
SEE IF YOU CAN MANAGE WITH THEM.
CLENCH
UNDER-STOOD!
BIP
CREAK...
WITH HEROES LIKE THEM SUPPORTING US, THIS ORGANIZATION CAN HANG IN THERE!
I BELIEVE THAT!
I'M COUNTING ON IT!
TWO HOURS LATER, HE RECEIVED A REPORT. THEY FAILED TO CAPTURE MASTER TURTLE.

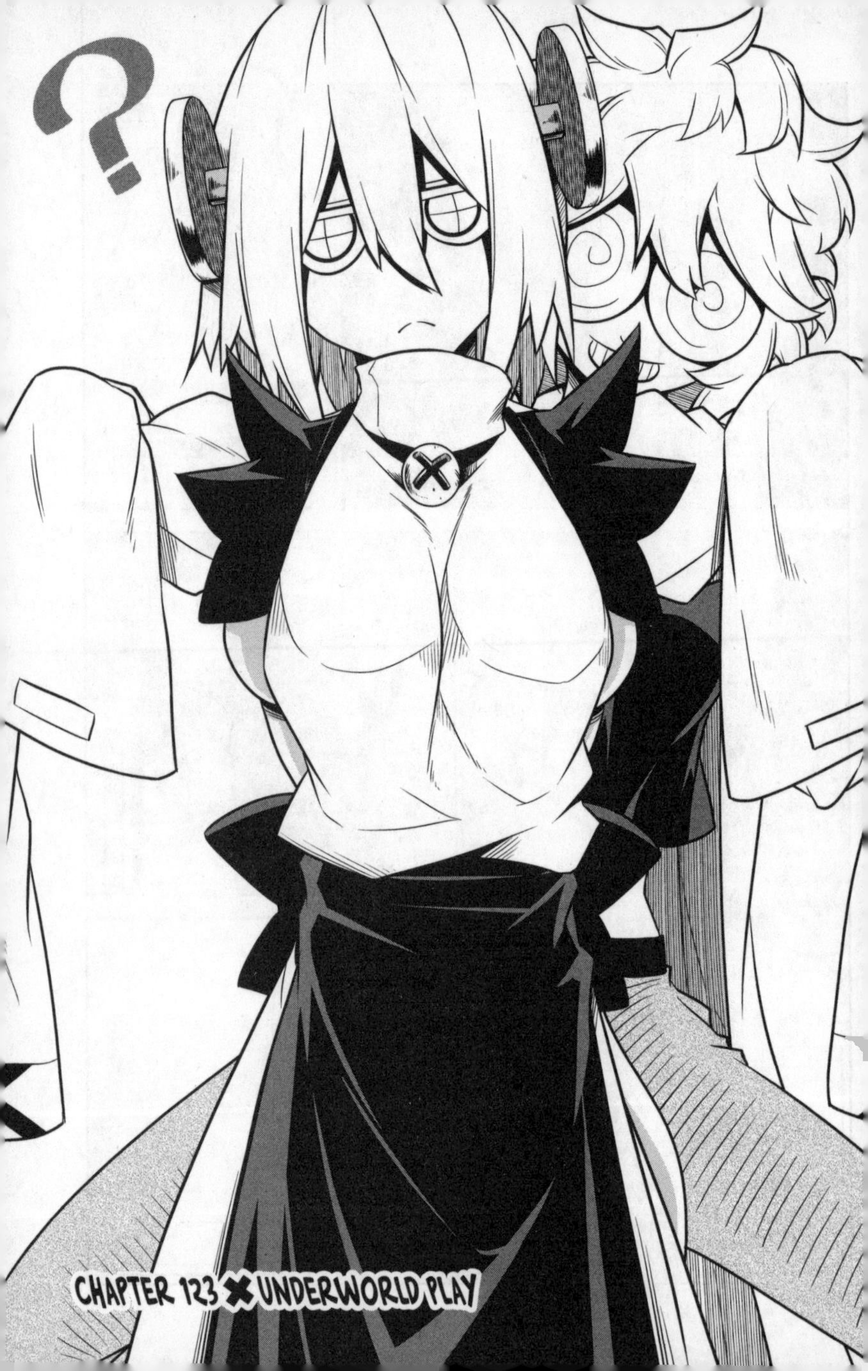
?
CHAPTER 123 ✖ UNDERWORLD PLAY

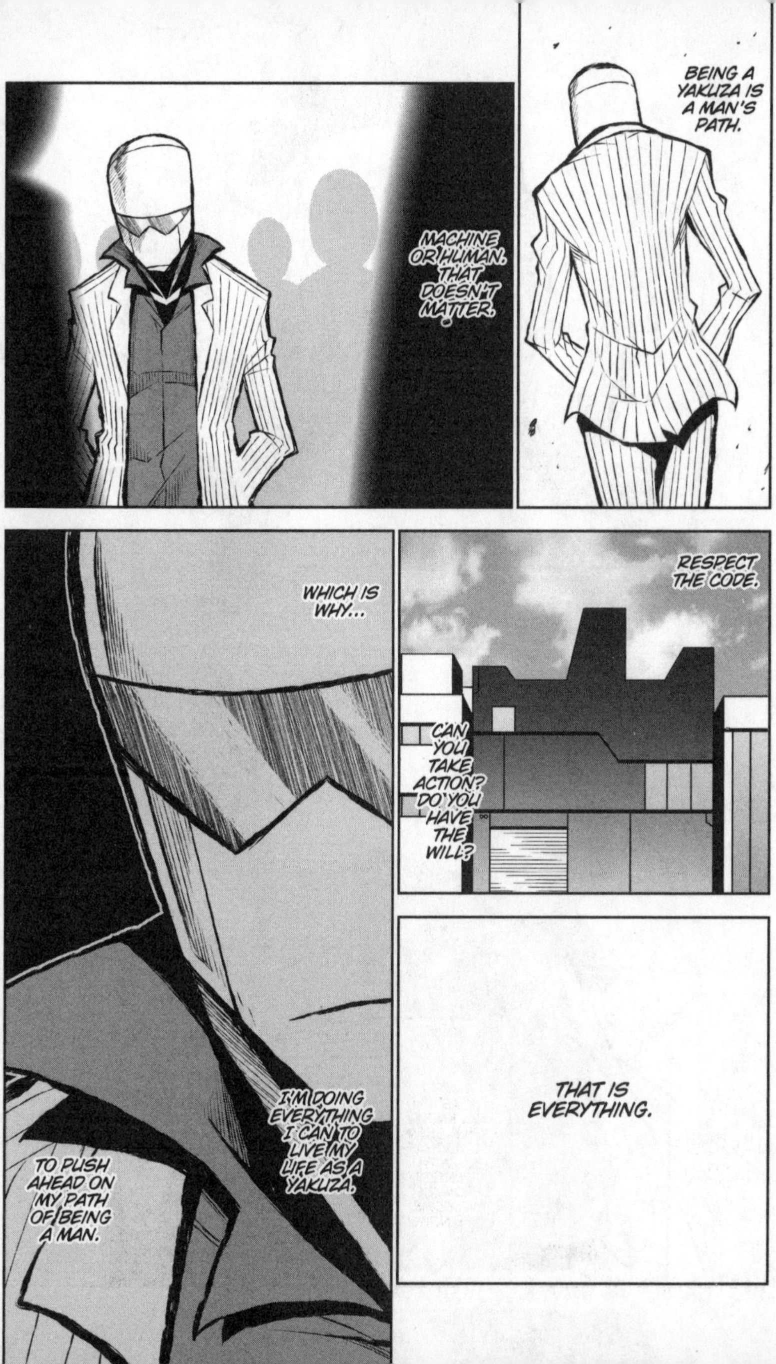
BEING A YAKUZA IS A MAN'S PATH.
MACHINE OR HUMAN. THAT DOESN'T MATTER.
RESPECT THE CODE.
CAN YOU TAKE ACTION? DO YOU HAVE THE WILL?
THAT IS EVERYTHING.
WHICH IS WHY...
I'M DOING EVERYTHING I CAN TO LIVE MY LIFE AS A YAKUZA.
TO PUSH AHEAD ON MY PATH OF BEING A MAN.

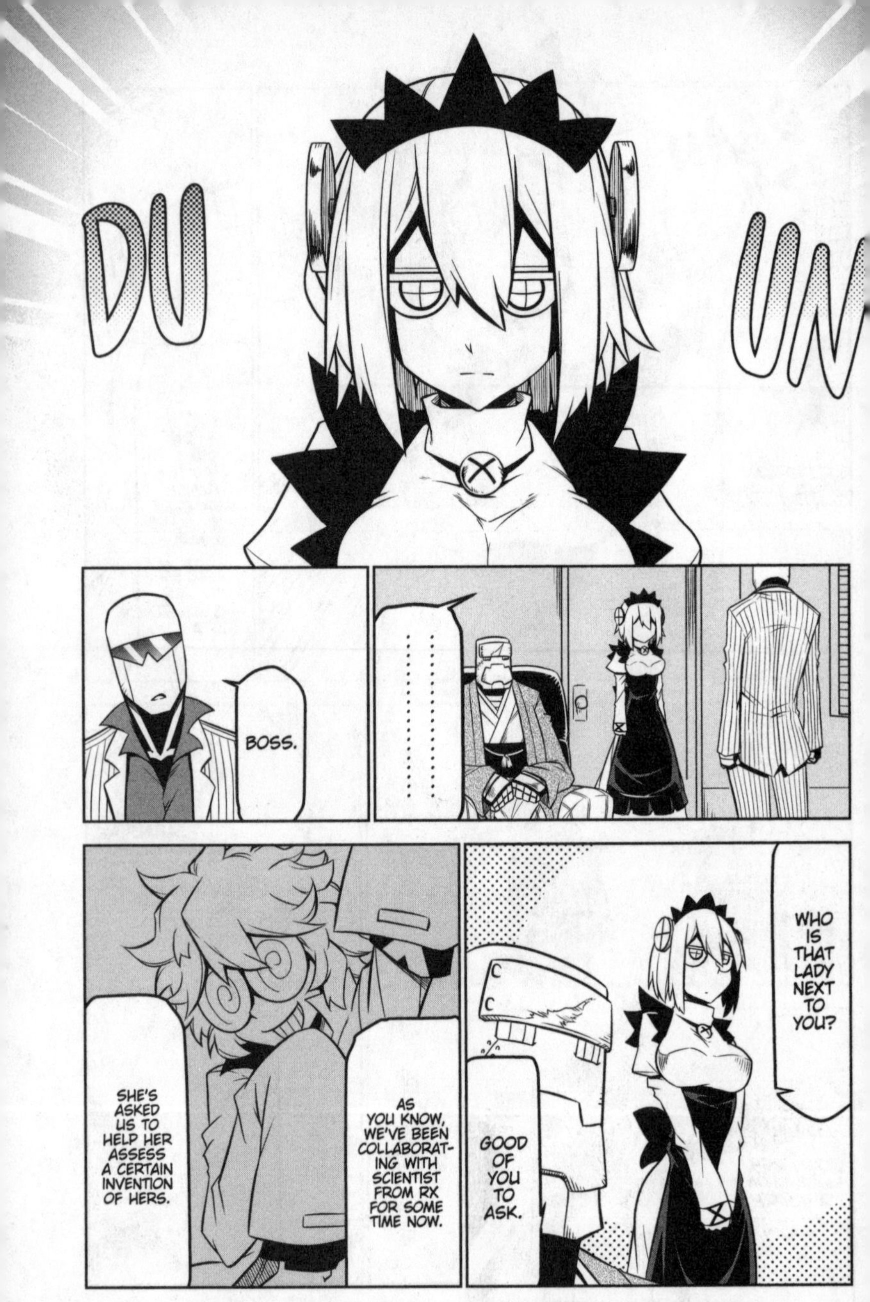
DU UN
......
BOSS.
WHO IS THAT LADY NEXT TO YOU?
GOOD OF YOU TO ASK.
AS YOU KNOW, WE'VE BEEN COLLABORATING WITH SCIENTIST FROM RX FOR SOME TIME NOW.
SHE'S ASKED US TO HELP HER ASSESS A CERTAIN INVENTION OF HERS.

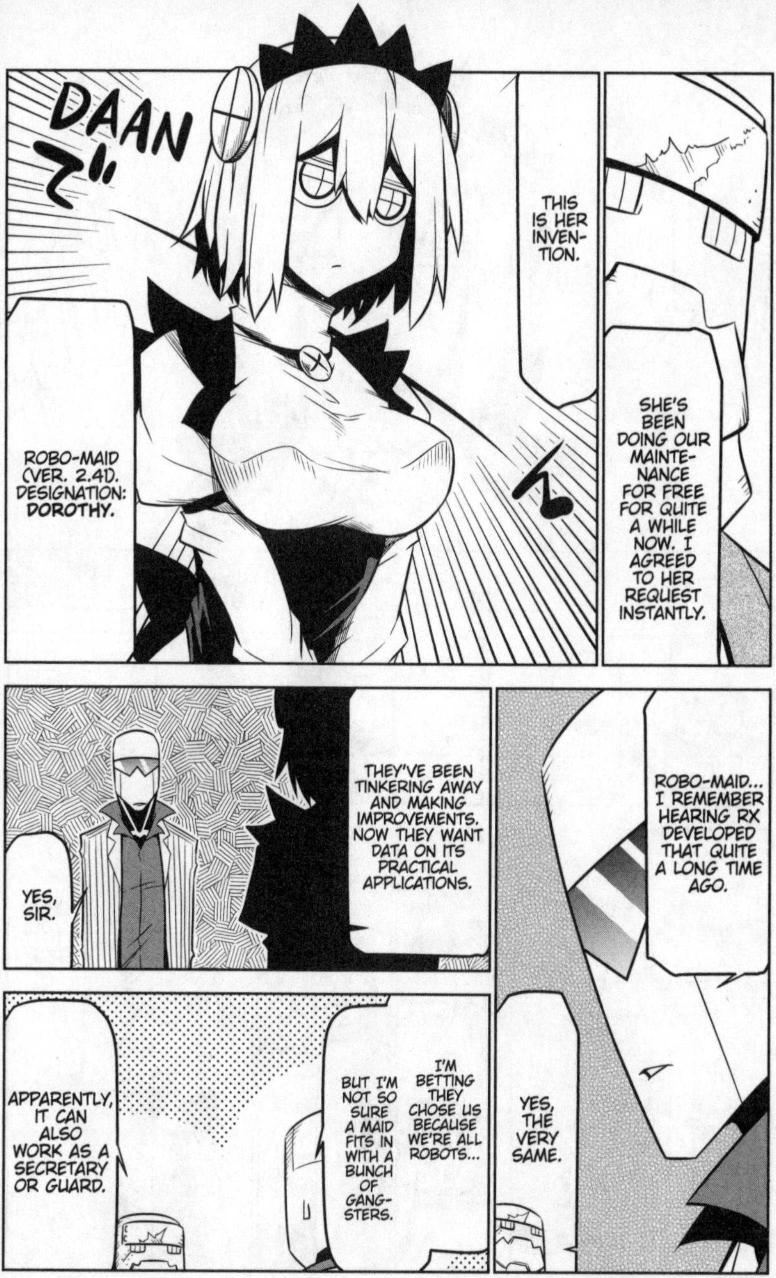
SHE'S BEEN DOING OUR MAINTENANCE FOR FREE FOR QUITE A WHILE NOW. I AGREED TO HER REQUEST INSTANTLY.
THIS IS HER INVENTION.
DAAN
ROBO-MAID (VER. 2.4). DESIGNATION: DOROTHY.
ROBO-MAID... I REMEMBER HEARING RX DEVELOPED THAT QUITE A LONG TIME AGO.
YES, THE VERY SAME.
THEY'VE BEEN TINKERING AWAY AND MAKING IMPROVEMENTS. NOW THEY WANT DATA ON ITS PRACTICAL APPLICATIONS.
YES, SIR.
I'M BETTING THEY CHOSE US BECAUSE WE'RE ALL ROBOTS...
BUT I'M NOT SO SURE A MAID FITS IN WITH A BUNCH OF GANGSTERS.
APPARENTLY, IT CAN ALSO WORK AS A SECRETARY OR GUARD.

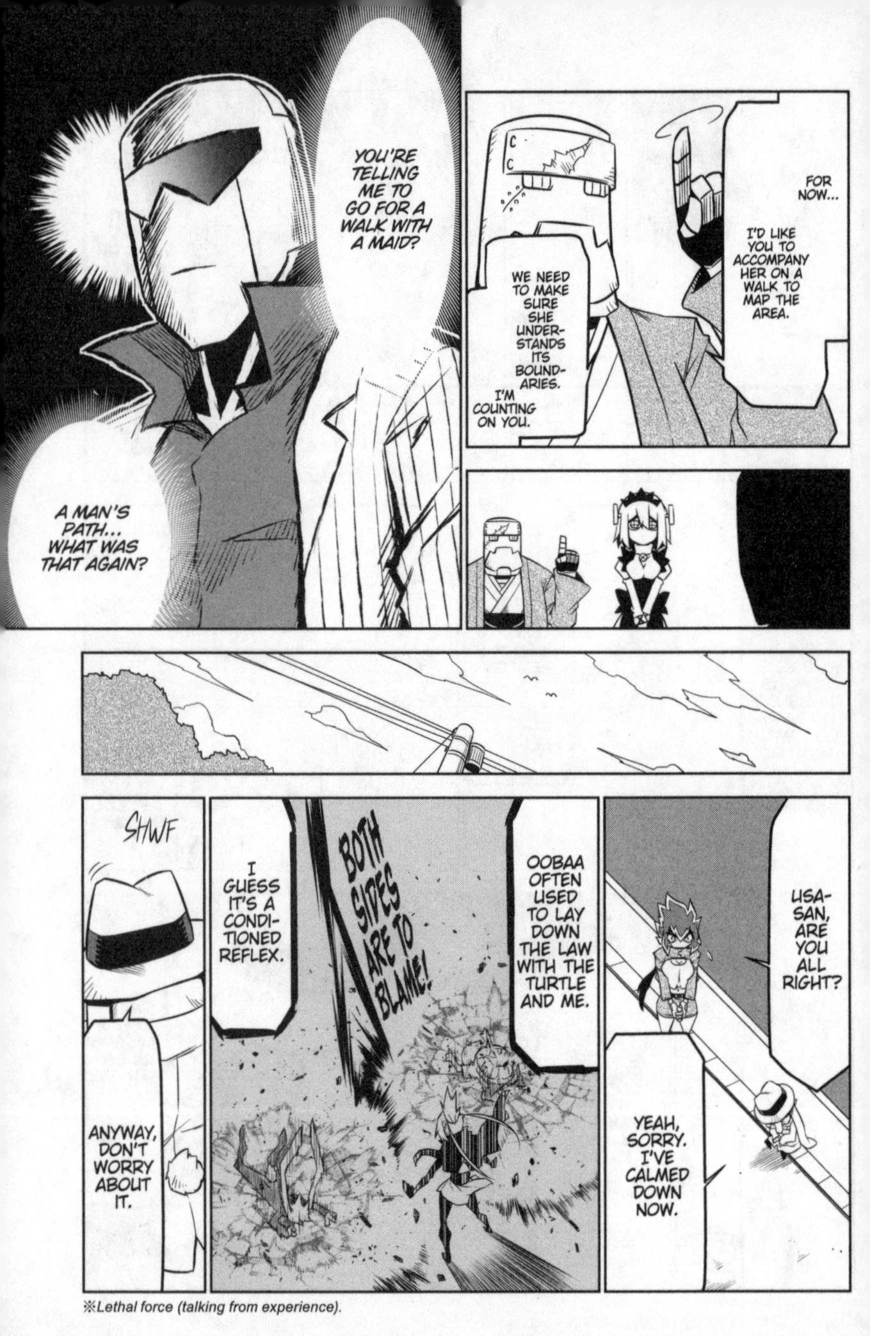
FOR NOW...
I'D LIKE YOU TO ACCOMPANY HER ON A WALK TO MAP THE AREA.
WE NEED TO MAKE SURE SHE UNDERSTANDS ITS BOUNDARIES.
I'M COUNTING ON YOU.
YOU'RE TELLING ME TO GO FOR A WALK WITH A MAID?
A MAN'S PATH... WHAT WAS THAT AGAIN?
USA-SAN, ARE YOU ALL RIGHT?
YEAH, SORRY. I'VE CALMED DOWN NOW.
OOBAA OFTEN USED TO LAY DOWN THE LAW WITH THE TURTLE AND ME.
BOTH SIDES ARE TO BLAME!
I GUESS IT'S A CONDITIONED REFLEX.
SHWF
ANYWAY, DON'T WORRY ABOUT IT.

※*Lethal force (talking from experience).*

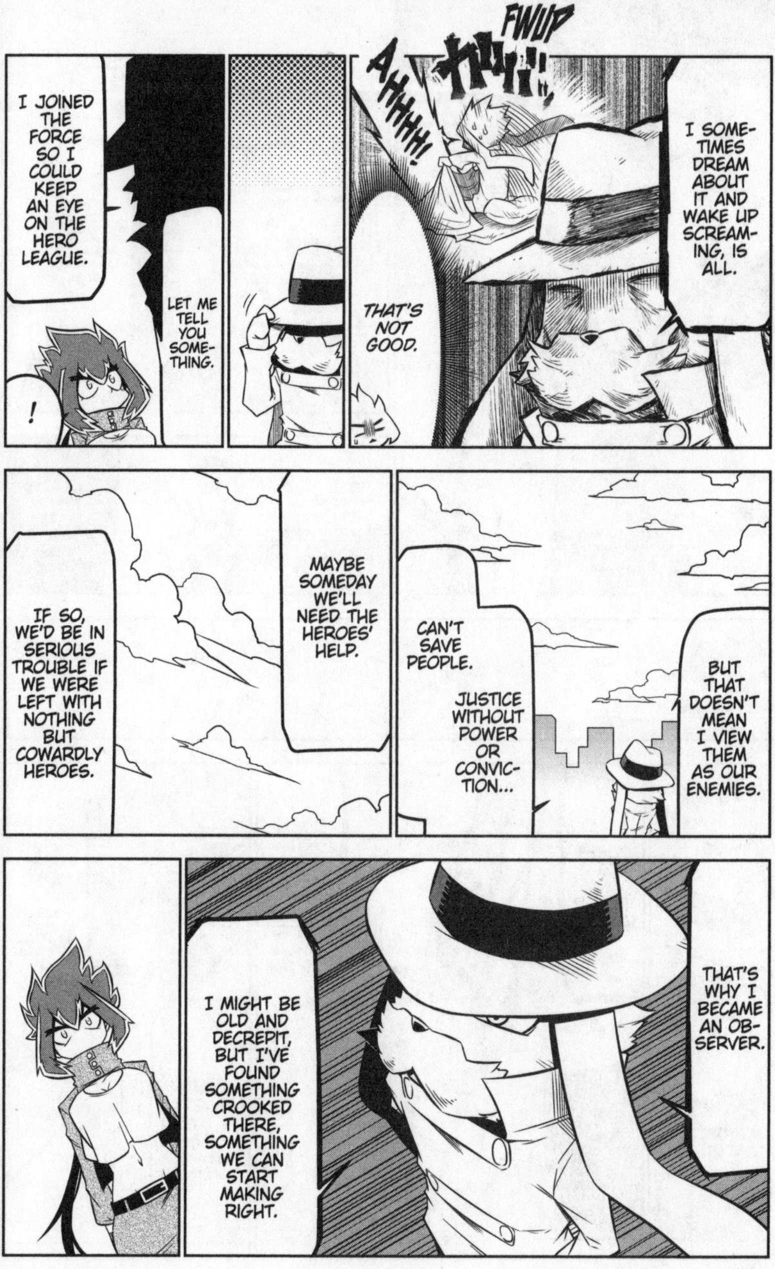
FWUP
AHHHH!
I SOME-TIMES DREAM ABOUT IT AND WAKE UP SCREAM-ING, IS ALL.
THAT'S NOT GOOD.
LET ME TELL YOU SOME-THING.
I JOINED THE FORCE SO I COULD KEEP AN EYE ON THE HERO LEAGUE.
!
BUT THAT DOESN'T MEAN I VIEW THEM AS OUR ENEMIES.
JUSTICE WITHOUT POWER OR CONVIC-TION...
CAN'T SAVE PEOPLE.
MAYBE SOMEDAY WE'LL NEED THE HEROES' HELP.
IF SO, WE'D BE IN SERIOUS TROUBLE IF WE WERE LEFT WITH NOTHING BUT COWARDLY HEROES.
THAT'S WHY I BECAME AN OB-SERVER.
I MIGHT BE OLD AND DECREPIT, BUT I'VE FOUND SOMETHING CROOKED THERE, SOMETHING WE CAN START MAKING RIGHT.

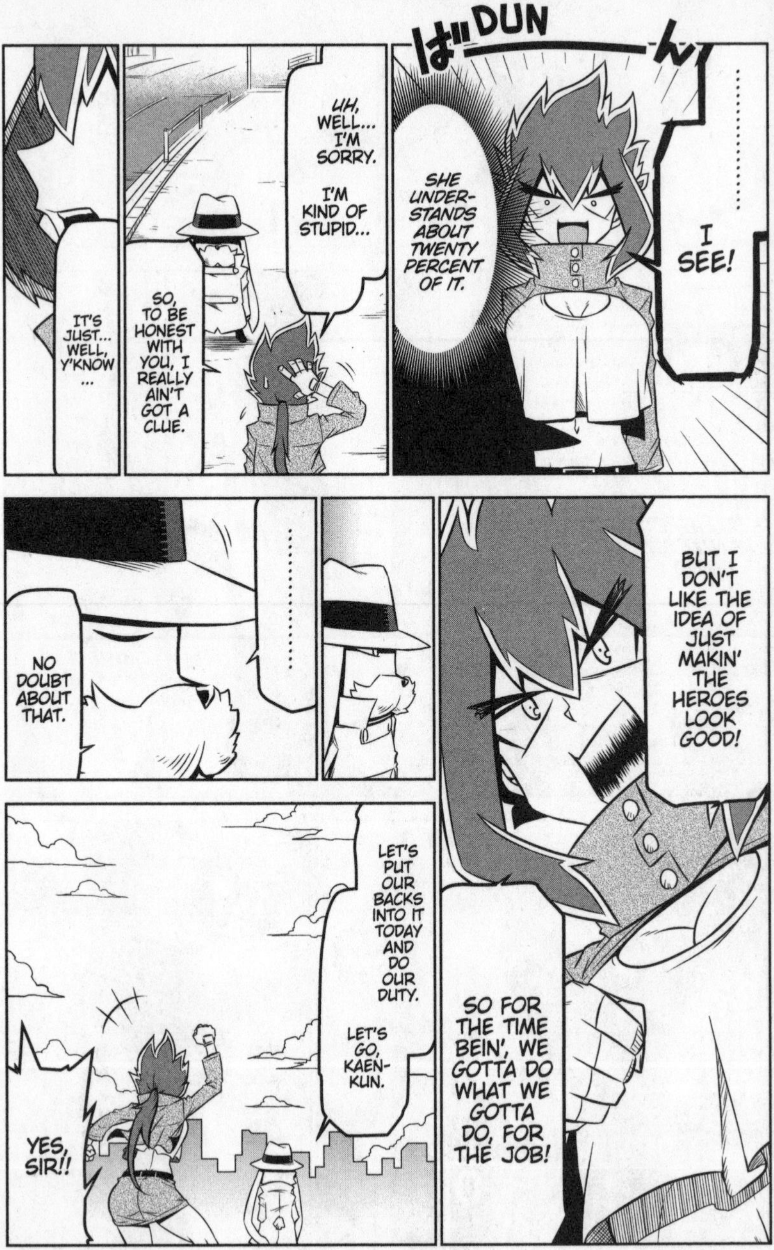

ばDUN———ん
....
I SEE!
SHE UNDERSTANDS ABOUT TWENTY PERCENT OF IT.
UH, WELL... I'M SORRY.
I'M KIND OF STUPID...
SO, TO BE HONEST WITH YOU, I REALLY AIN'T GOT A CLUE.
IT'S JUST... WELL, Y'KNOW ...
BUT I DON'T LIKE THE IDEA OF JUST MAKIN' THE HEROES LOOK GOOD!
SO FOR THE TIME BEIN', WE GOTTA DO WHAT WE GOTTA DO, FOR THE JOB!
....
NO DOUBT ABOUT THAT.
LET'S PUT OUR BACKS INTO IT TODAY AND DO OUR DUTY.
LET'S GO, KAEN-KUN.
YES, SIR!!

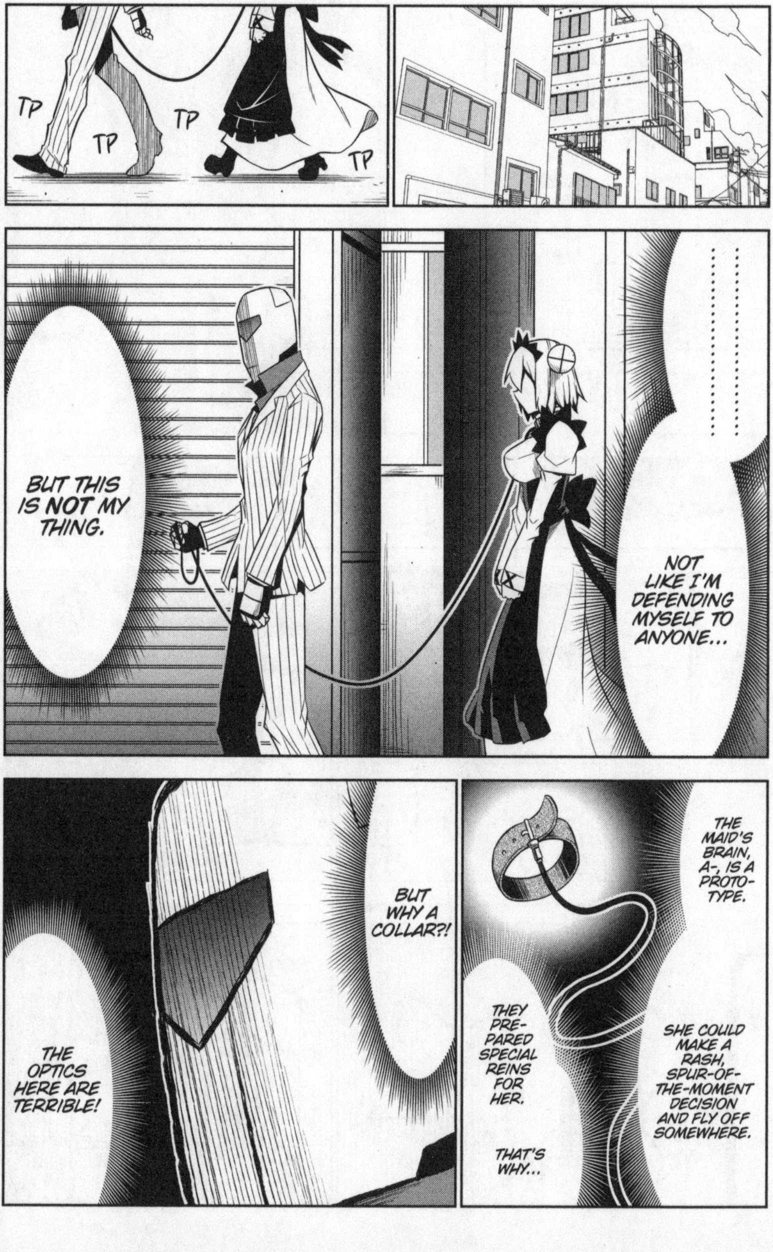
TP
TP
TP
TP
......
NOT LIKE I'M DEFENDING MYSELF TO ANYONE...
BUT THIS IS NOT MY THING.
THE MAID'S BRAIN, A-, IS A PROTOTYPE.
SHE COULD MAKE A RASH, SPUR-OF-THE-MOMENT DECISION AND FLY OFF SOMEWHERE.
THEY PREPARED SPECIAL REINS FOR HER.
THAT'S WHY...
BUT WHY A COLLAR?!
THE OPTICS HERE ARE TERRIBLE!

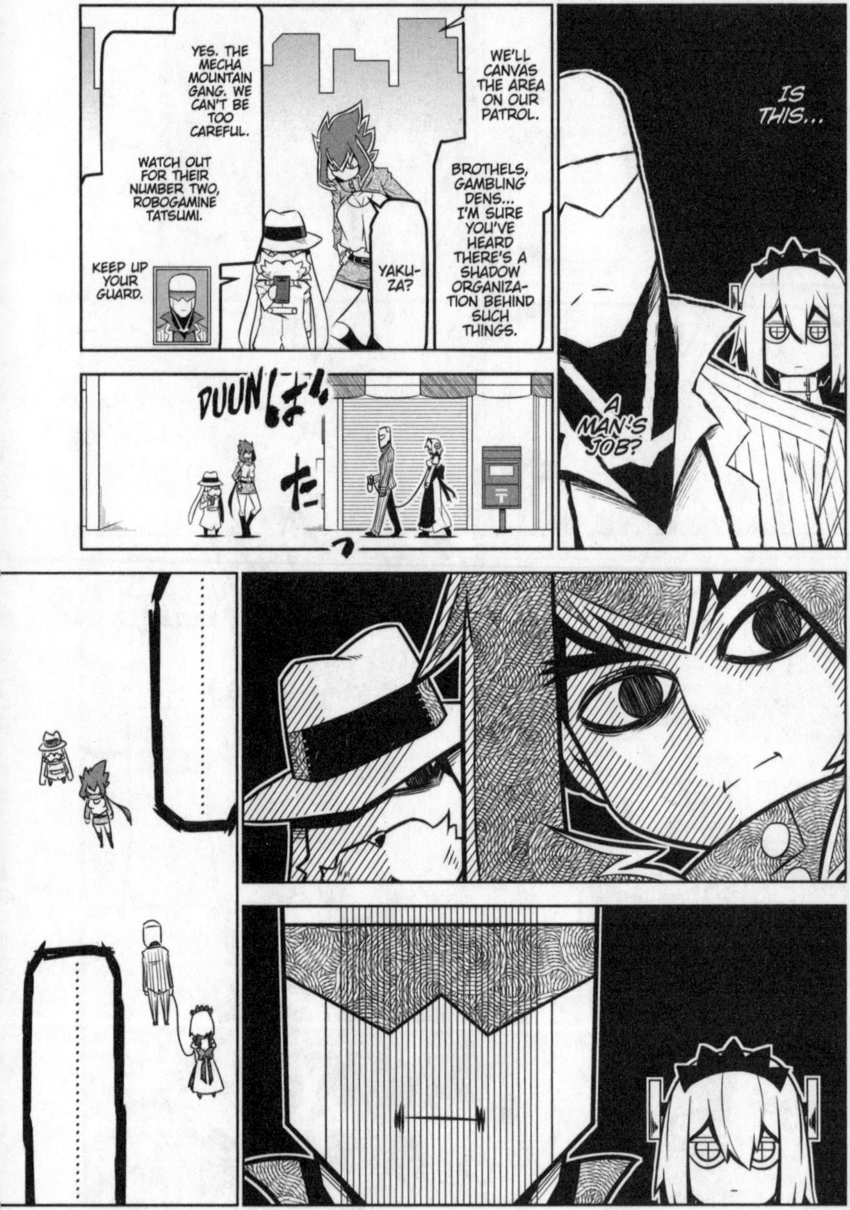
IS THIS...
A MAN'S JOB?
WE'LL CANVAS THE AREA ON OUR PATROL.
BROTHELS, GAMBLING DENS... I'M SURE YOU'VE HEARD THERE'S A SHADOW ORGANIZATION BEHIND SUCH THINGS.
YAKU-ZA?
YES. THE MECHA MOUNTAIN GANG. WE CAN'T BE TOO CAREFUL.
WATCH OUT FOR THEIR NUMBER TWO, ROBOGAMINE TATSUMI.
KEEP UP YOUR GUARD.
DUUN

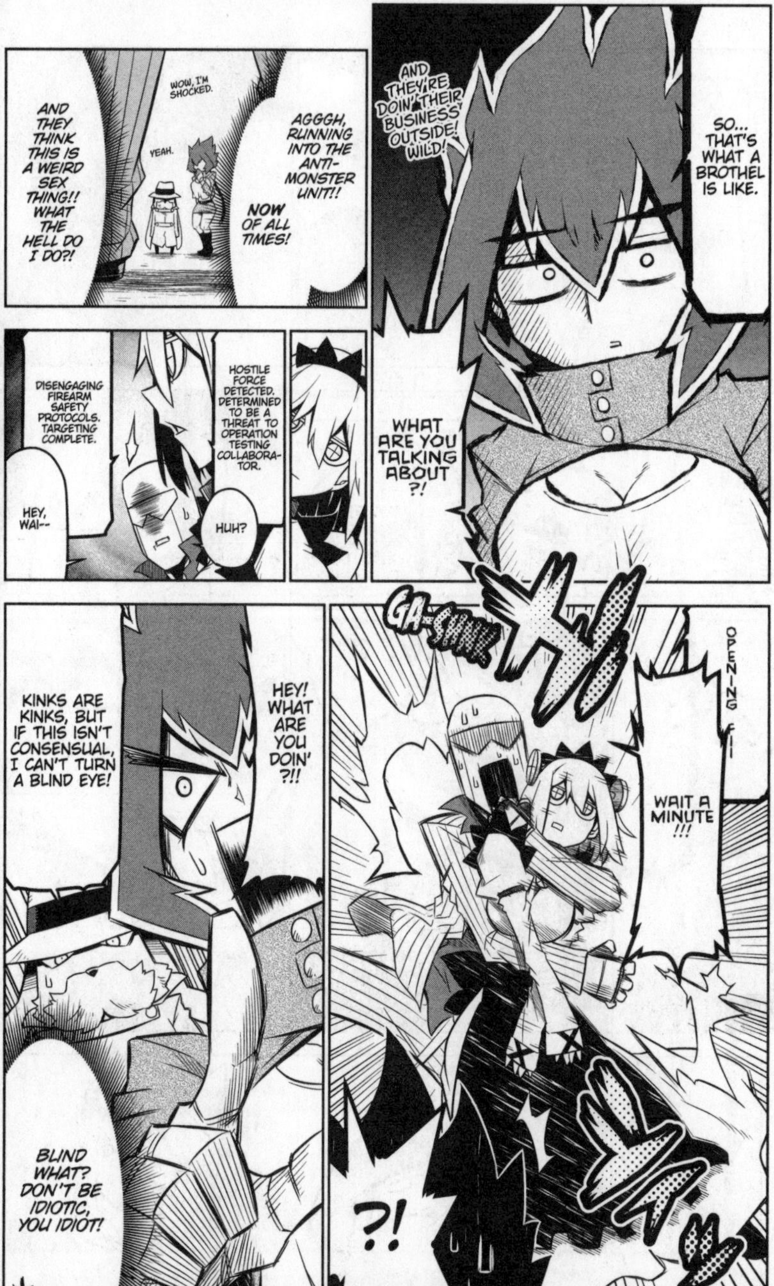
SO... THAT'S WHAT A BROTHEL IS LIKE.
AND THEY'RE DOIN' THEIR BUSINESS OUTSIDE! WILD!
WHAT ARE YOU TALKING ABOUT?!
WOW, I'M SHOCKED.
YEAH.
AGGGH, RUNNING INTO THE ANTI-MONSTER UNIT!!
NOW OF ALL TIMES!
AND THEY THINK THIS IS A WEIRD SEX THING!! WHAT THE HELL DO I DO?!
HOSTILE FORCE DETECTED. DETERMINED TO BE A THREAT TO OPERATION TESTING COLLABORATOR.
HUH?
DISENGAGING FIREARM SAFETY PROTOCOLS. TARGETING COMPLETE.
HEY, WAI--
GA-SHAK
OPENING FI
WAIT A MINUTE!!!
?!
HEY! WHAT ARE YOU DOIN'?!!
KINKS ARE KINKS, BUT IF THIS ISN'T CONSENSUAL, I CAN'T TURN A BLIND EYE!
BLIND WHAT? DON'T BE IDIOTIC, YOU IDIOT!

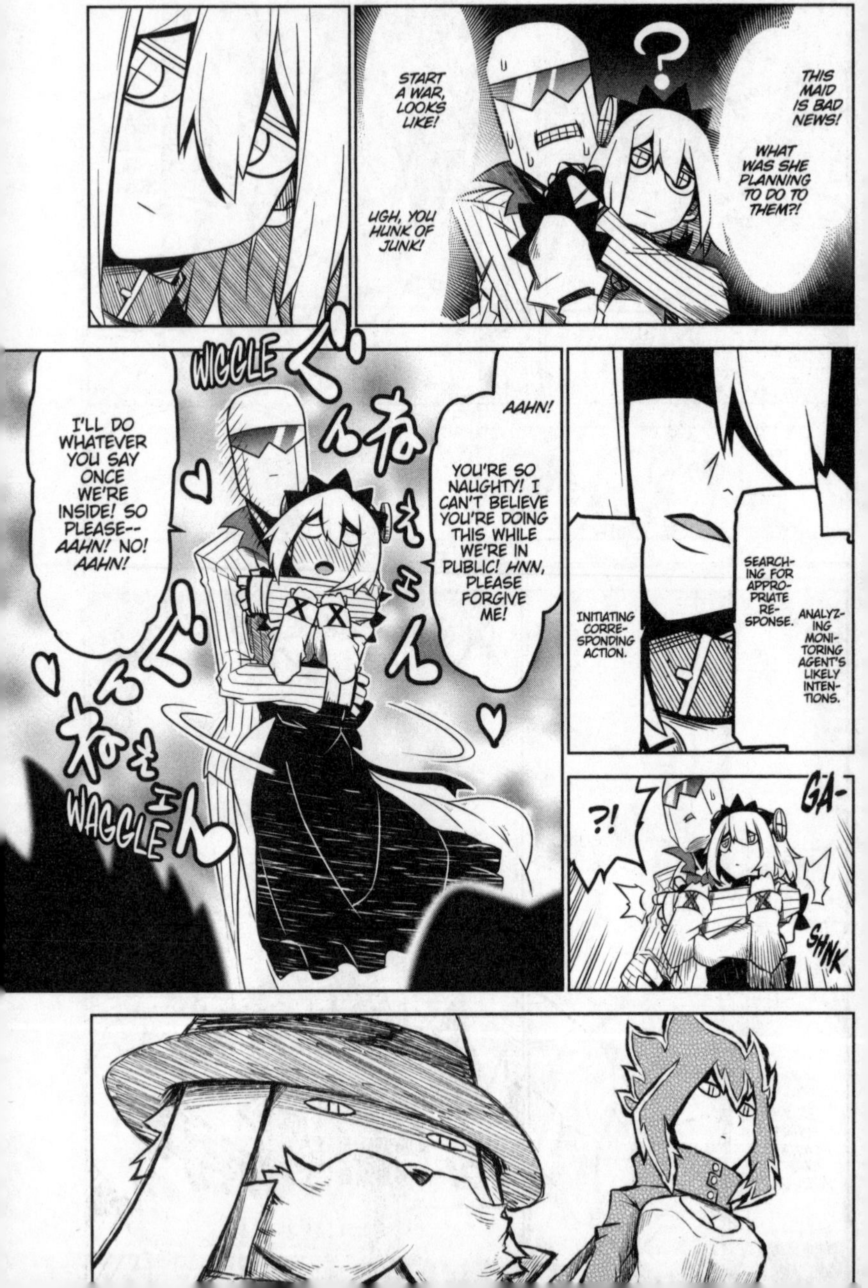

THIS MAID IS BAD NEWS!
WHAT WAS SHE PLANNING TO DO TO THEM?!
START A WAR, LOOKS LIKE!
UGH, YOU HUNK OF JUNK!
ANALYZING MONITORING AGENT'S LIKELY INTENTIONS.
SEARCHING FOR APPROPRIATE RESPONSE.
INITIATING CORRESPONDING ACTION.
GA-
?!
SHNK
AAHN!
YOU'RE SO NAUGHTY! I CAN'T BELIEVE YOU'RE DOING THIS WHILE WE'RE IN PUBLIC! HNN, PLEASE FORGIVE ME!
WIGGLE
ぐんねそェん
I'LL DO WHATEVER YOU SAY ONCE WE'RE INSIDE! SO PLEASE-- AAHN! NO! AAHN!
ぐんねそェん
WAGGLE

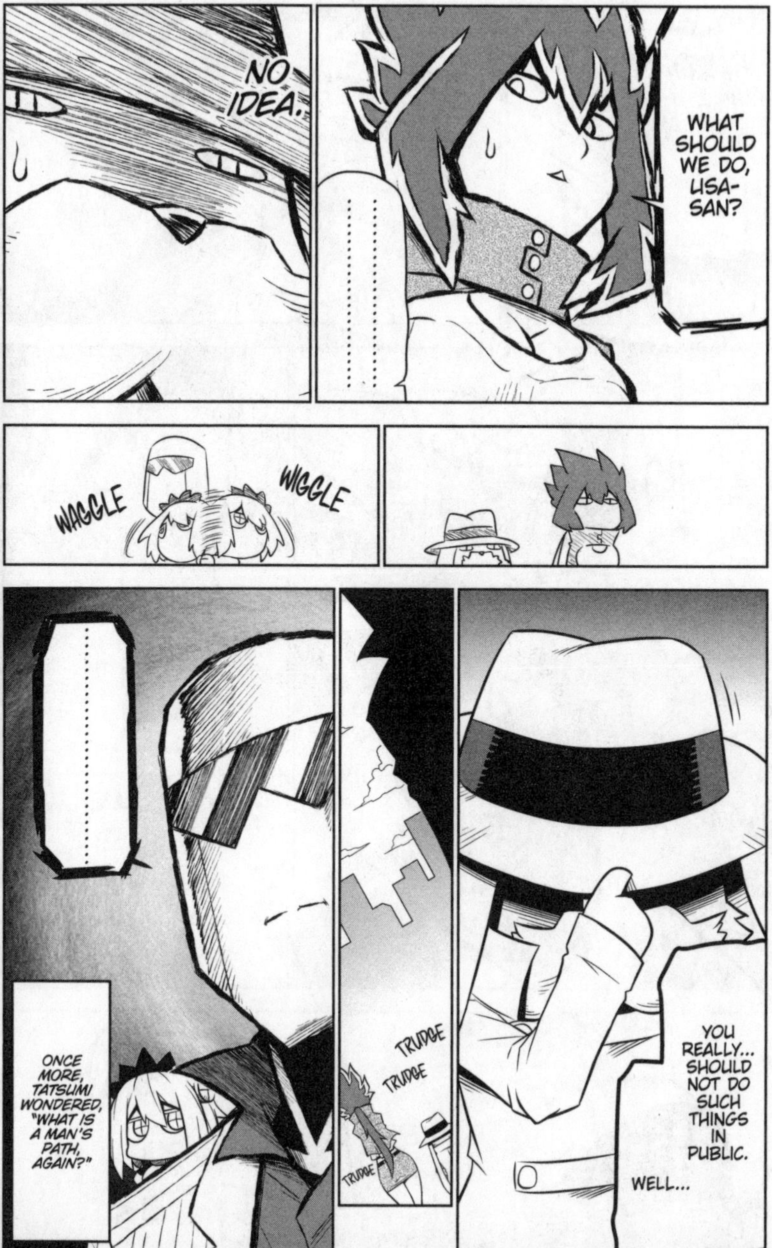
WHAT SHOULD WE DO, USA-SAN?
NO IDEA.
WIGGLE
WAGGLE
YOU REALLY... SHOULD NOT DO SUCH THINGS IN PUBLIC.
WELL...
TRUDGE
TRUDGE
TRUDGE
ONCE MORE, TATSUMI WONDERED, "WHAT IS A MAN'S PATH, AGAIN?"

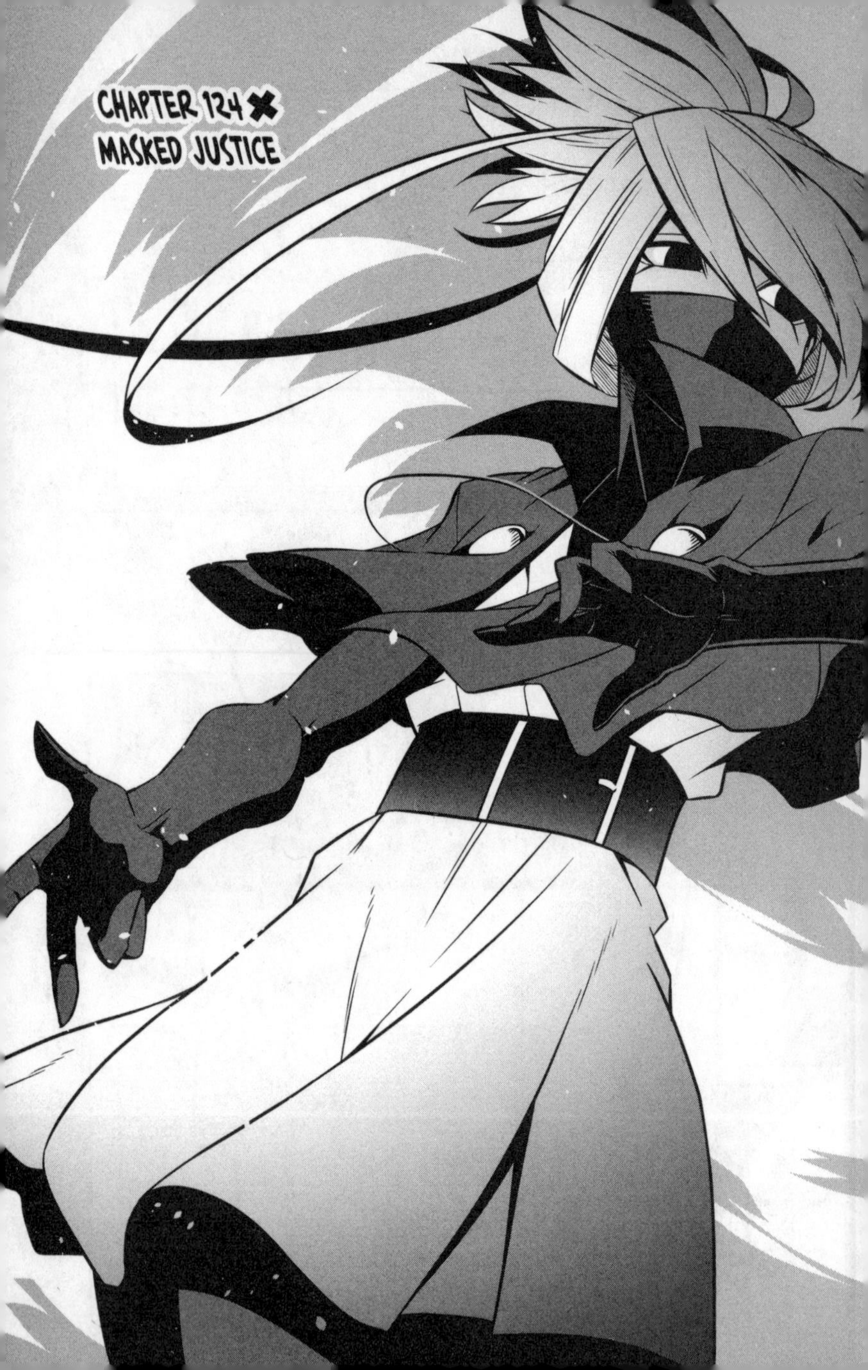
CHAPTER 124 ✖
MASKED JUSTICE

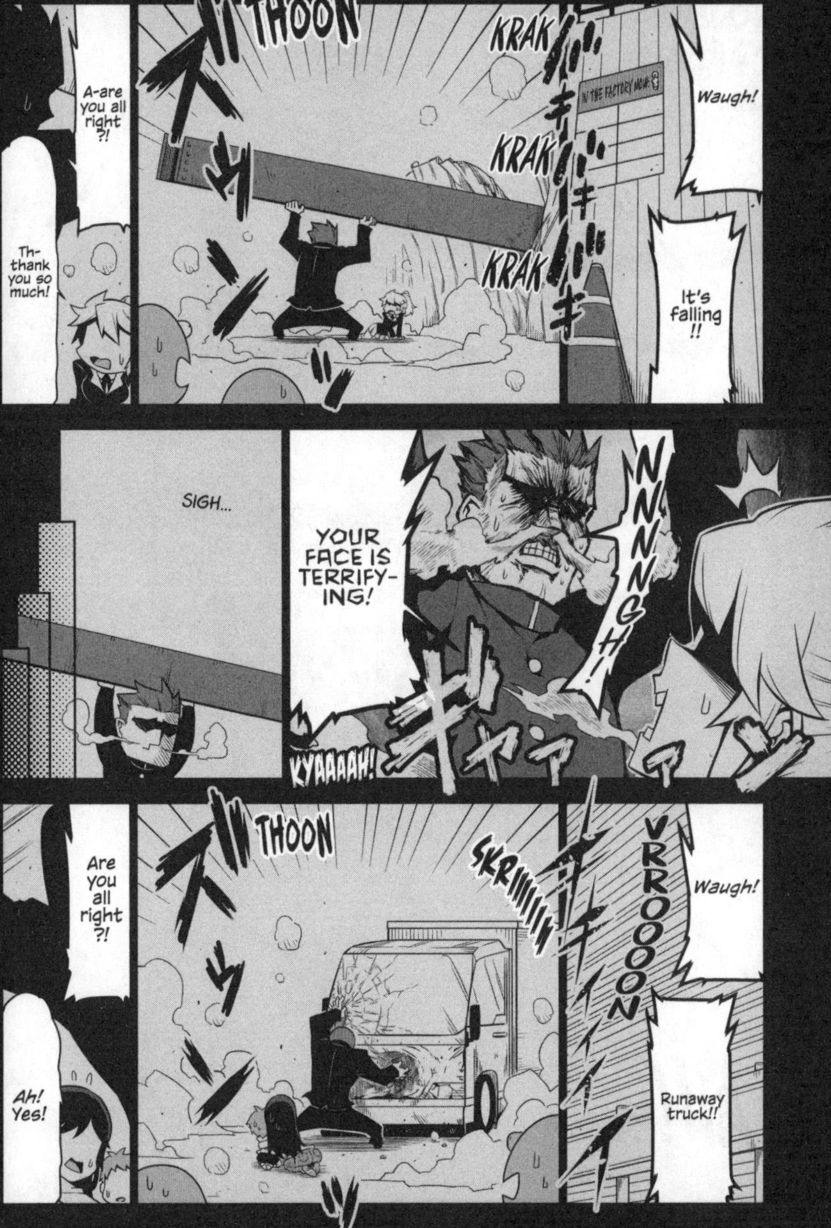
Waugh!
It's falling!!
IN THE FACTORY NOW
KRAK
KRAK
KRAK
THOON
A-are you all right?!
Th-thank you so much!
NNNNNGH!
YOUR FACE IS TERRIFYING!
KYAAAAH!
SIGH...
Waugh!
Runaway truck!!
VRROOOOOON
SKRIIIIIIII
THOON
Are you all right?!
Ah! Yes!

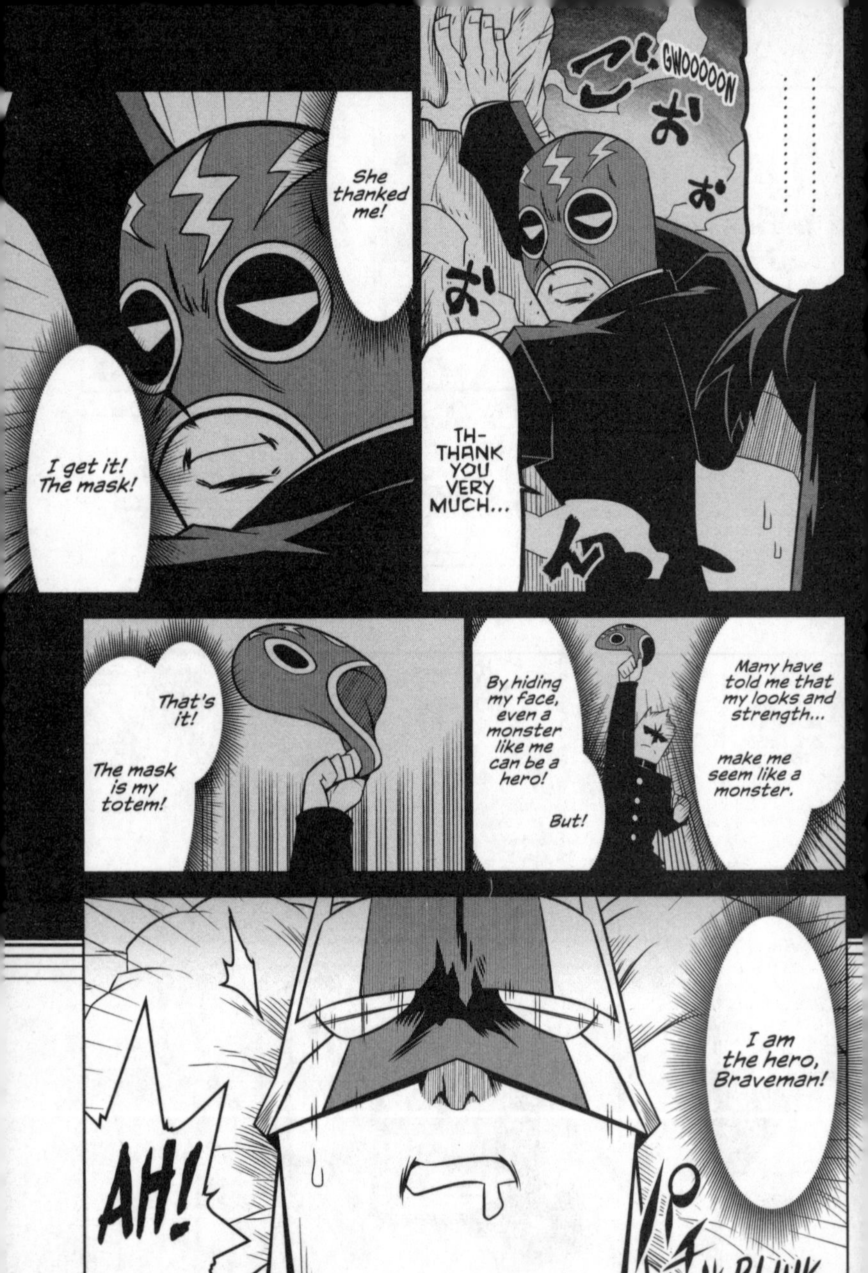

GWOOOOON
......
TH-THANK YOU VERY MUCH...
She thanked me!
I get it! The mask!
Many have told me that my looks and strength...
make me seem like a monster.
By hiding my face, even a monster like me can be a hero!
But!
That's it!
The mask is my totem!
I am the hero, Braveman!
BLINK
AH!

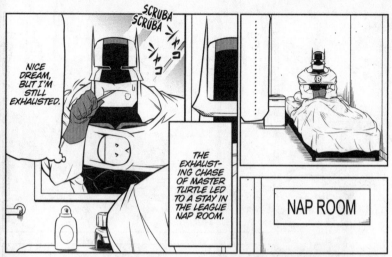

NAP ROOM
SCRUBA SCRUBA
THE EXHAUSTING CHASE OF MASTER TURTLE LED TO A STAY IN THE LEAGUE NAP ROOM.
NICE DREAM, BUT I'M STILL EXHAUSTED.
IT WAS RIGHT TO LET THOSE TWO HEAD BACK FIRST.
AHHHHH!
I NEVER IMAGINED HOW MUCH CHASING I'D HAVE TO DO.
AND I STILL DIDN'T CATCH HIM.
I DIDN'T EVEN COME CLOSE.
SCRUBA
SCRUBA
I GUESS HE'S ALWAYS BEEN VERY FIXATED.
BA-TNK
I'LL BE RUNNING ALL OVER TODAY, TOO.

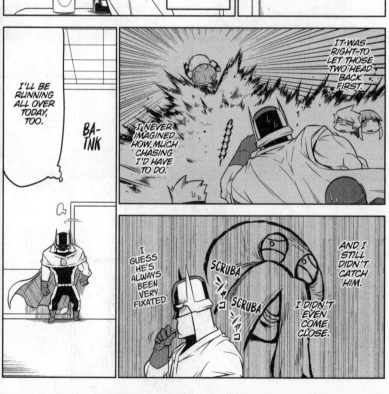

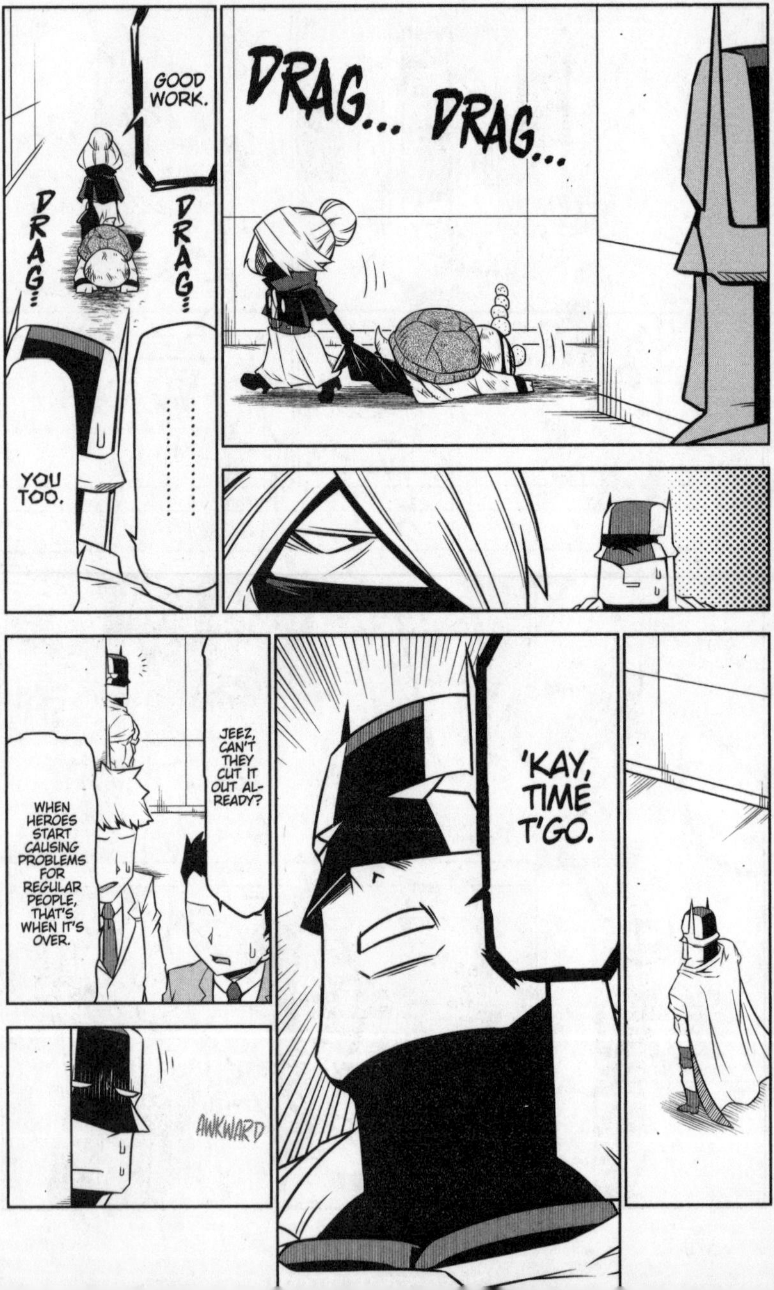
DRAG... DRAG...
DRAG... DRAG...
GOOD WORK.
......
YOU TOO.
'KAY, TIME T'GO.
JEEZ, CAN'T THEY CUT IT OUT AL-READY?
WHEN HEROES START CAUSING PROBLEMS FOR REGULAR PEOPLE, THAT'S WHEN IT'S OVER.
AWKWARD

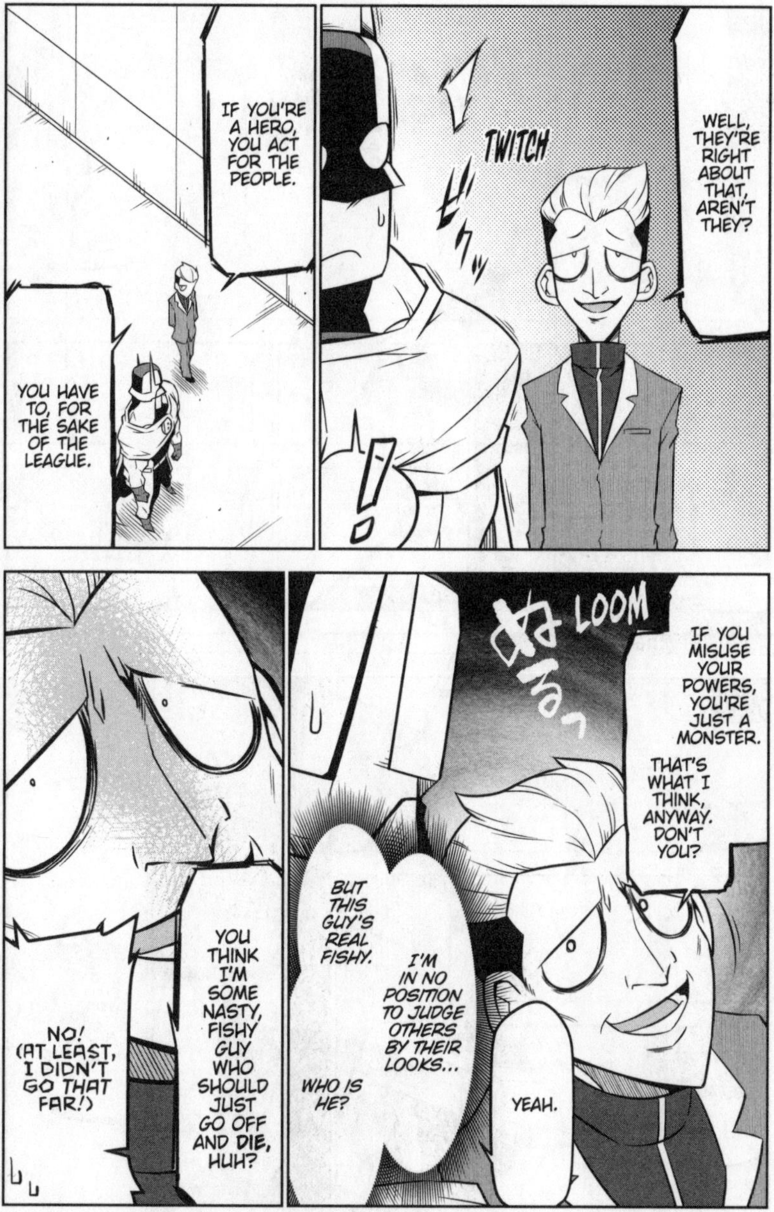
WELL, THEY'RE RIGHT ABOUT THAT, AREN'T THEY?
TWITCH
!
IF YOU'RE A HERO, YOU ACT FOR THE PEOPLE.
YOU HAVE TO, FOR THE SAKE OF THE LEAGUE.
LOOM
ぬるっ
IF YOU MISUSE YOUR POWERS, YOU'RE JUST A MONSTER.
THAT'S WHAT I THINK, ANYWAY. DON'T YOU?
YEAH.
I'M IN NO POSITION TO JUDGE OTHERS BY THEIR LOOKS...
BUT THIS GUY'S REAL FISHY.
WHO IS HE?
YOU THINK I'M SOME NASTY, FISHY GUY WHO SHOULD JUST GO OFF AND DIE, HUH?
NO! (AT LEAST, I DIDN'T GO THAT FAR!)

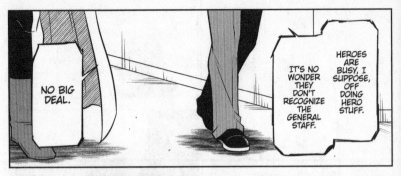

HEROES ARE BUSY, I SUPPOSE, OFF DOING HERO STUFF.
IT'S NO WONDER THEY DON'T RECOGNIZE THE GENERAL STAFF.
NO BIG DEAL.
DON'T WORRY ABOUT IT.
KLAK KLAK
......
SIGH...
WHAT KEEPS THE LEAGUE GOING IS...
US, THE POWERLESS GENERAL STAFF. WE'RE INDISPENS-ABLE.
SO ALL THIS REFORM TALK...
IS TROU-BLING.
PA-TNK
HE WAS TALKING SO LOUDLY, I THINK I WAS MEANT TO OVER-HEAR...

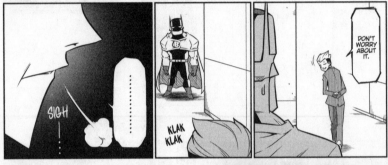

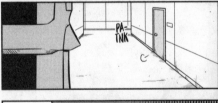

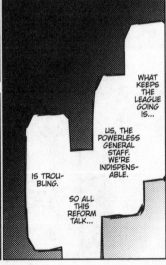

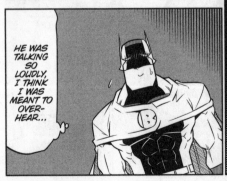

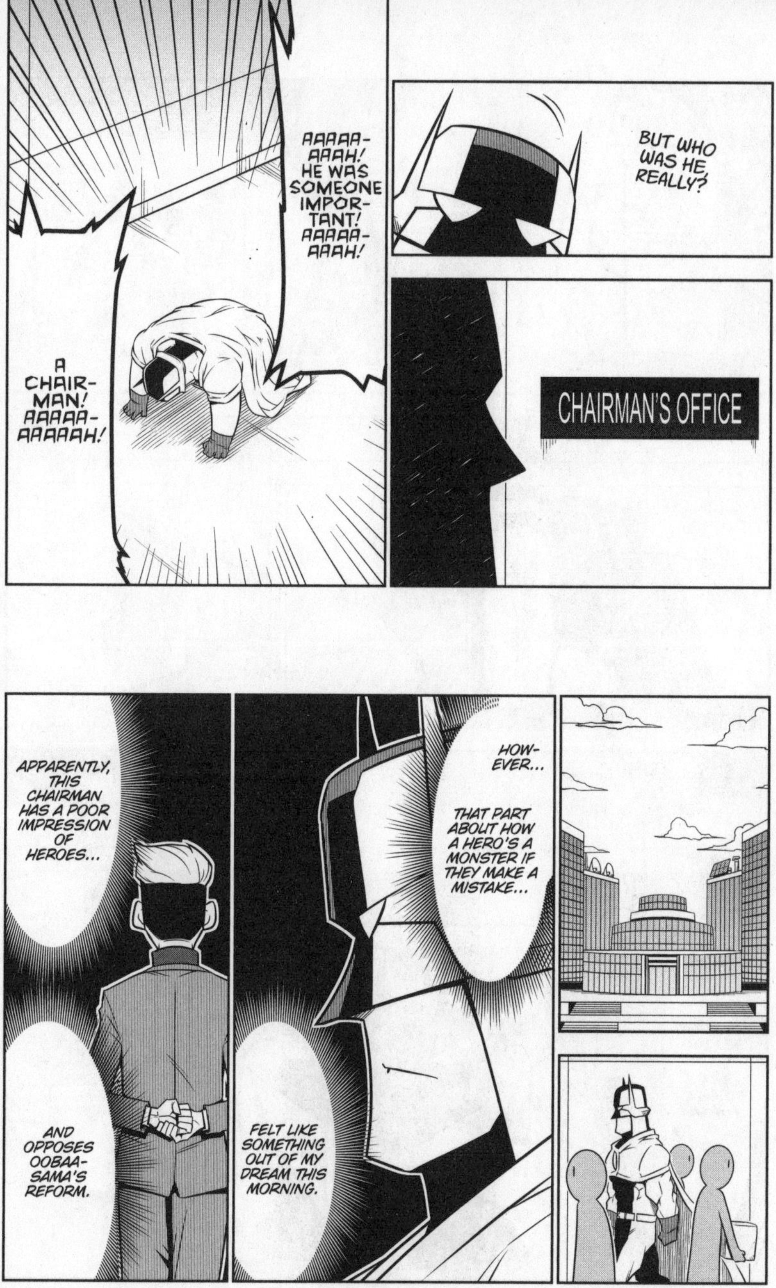
BUT WHO WAS HE REALLY?
CHAIRMAN'S OFFICE
AAAAA-AAAAH! HE WAS SOMEONE IMPORTANT! AAAAA-AAAAH!
A CHAIRMAN! AAAAA-AAAAAH!
HOW-EVER...
THAT PART ABOUT HOW A HERO'S A MONSTER IF THEY MAKE A MISTAKE...
FELT LIKE SOMETHING OUT OF MY DREAM THIS MORNING.
APPARENTLY, THIS CHAIRMAN HAS A POOR IMPRESSION OF HEROES...
AND OPPOSES OOBAA-SAMA'S REFORM.

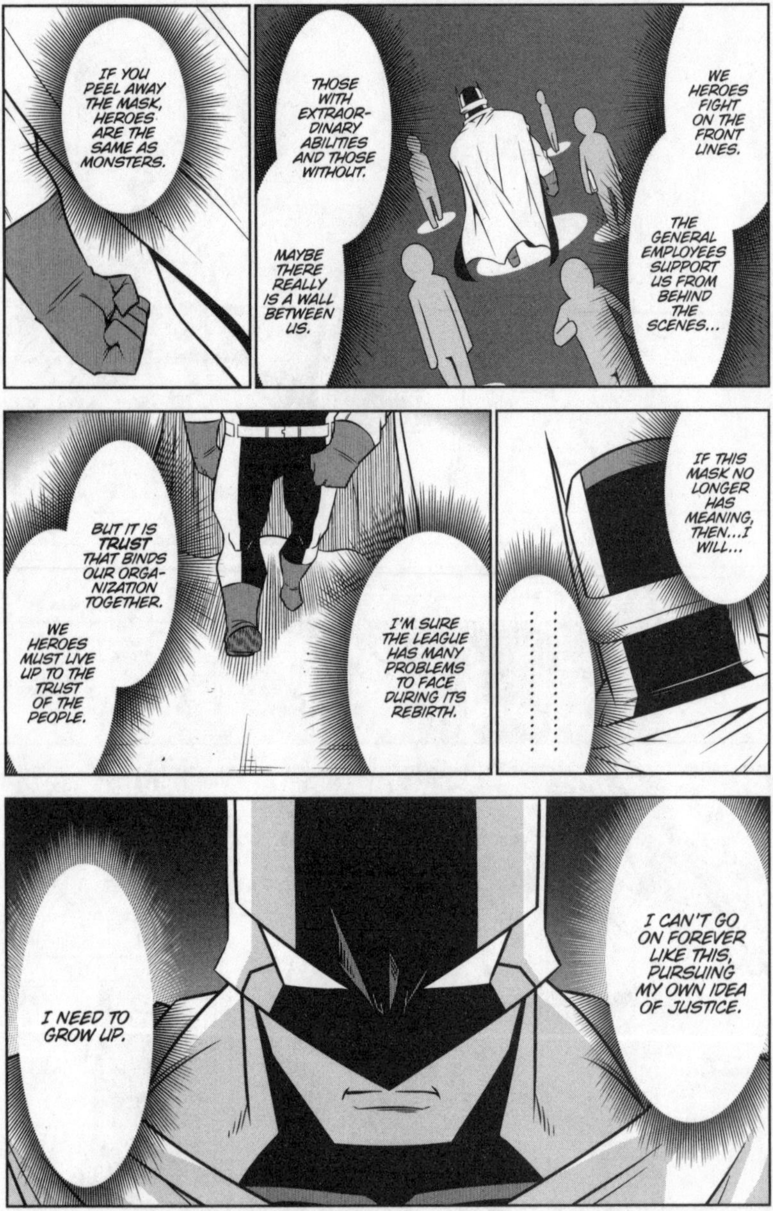
WE HEROES FIGHT ON THE FRONT LINES.
THE GENERAL EMPLOYEES SUPPORT US FROM BEHIND THE SCENES...
THOSE WITH EXTRAOR-DINARY ABILITIES AND THOSE WITHOUT.
MAYBE THERE REALLY IS A WALL BETWEEN US.
IF YOU PEEL AWAY THE MASK, HEROES ARE THE SAME AS MONSTERS.
IF THIS MASK NO LONGER HAS MEANING, THEN...I WILL...
......
I'M SURE THE LEAGUE HAS MANY PROBLEMS TO FACE DURING ITS REBIRTH.
BUT IT IS **TRUST** THAT BINDS OUR ORGA-NIZATION TOGETHER.
WE HEROES MUST LIVE UP TO THE TRUST OF THE PEOPLE.
I CAN'T GO ON FOREVER LIKE THIS, PURSUING MY OWN IDEA OF JUSTICE.
I NEED TO GROW UP.

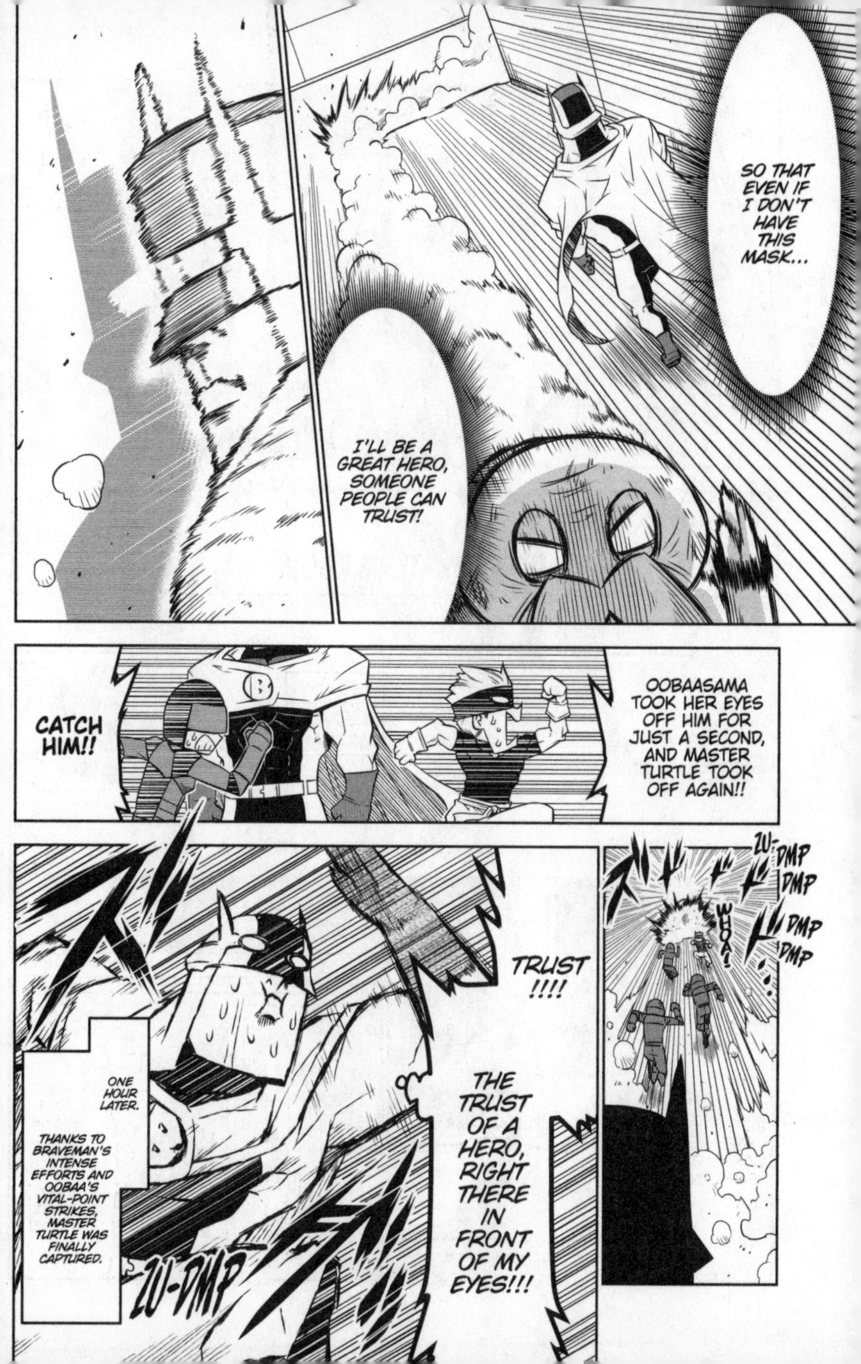
SO THAT EVEN IF I DON'T HAVE THIS MASK...
I'LL BE A GREAT HERO, SOMEONE PEOPLE CAN TRUST!
OOBAASAMA TOOK HER EYES OFF HIM FOR JUST A SECOND, AND MASTER TURTLE TOOK OFF AGAIN!!
CATCH HIM!!
ZU-DMP
DMP
DMP
DMP
WHOA!
TRUST!!!!
THE TRUST OF A HERO, RIGHT THERE IN FRONT OF MY EYES!!!
ONE HOUR LATER.
THANKS TO BRAVEMAN'S INTENSE EFFORTS AND OOBAA'S VITAL-POINT STRIKES, MASTER TURTLE WAS FINALLY CAPTURED.
ZU-DMP

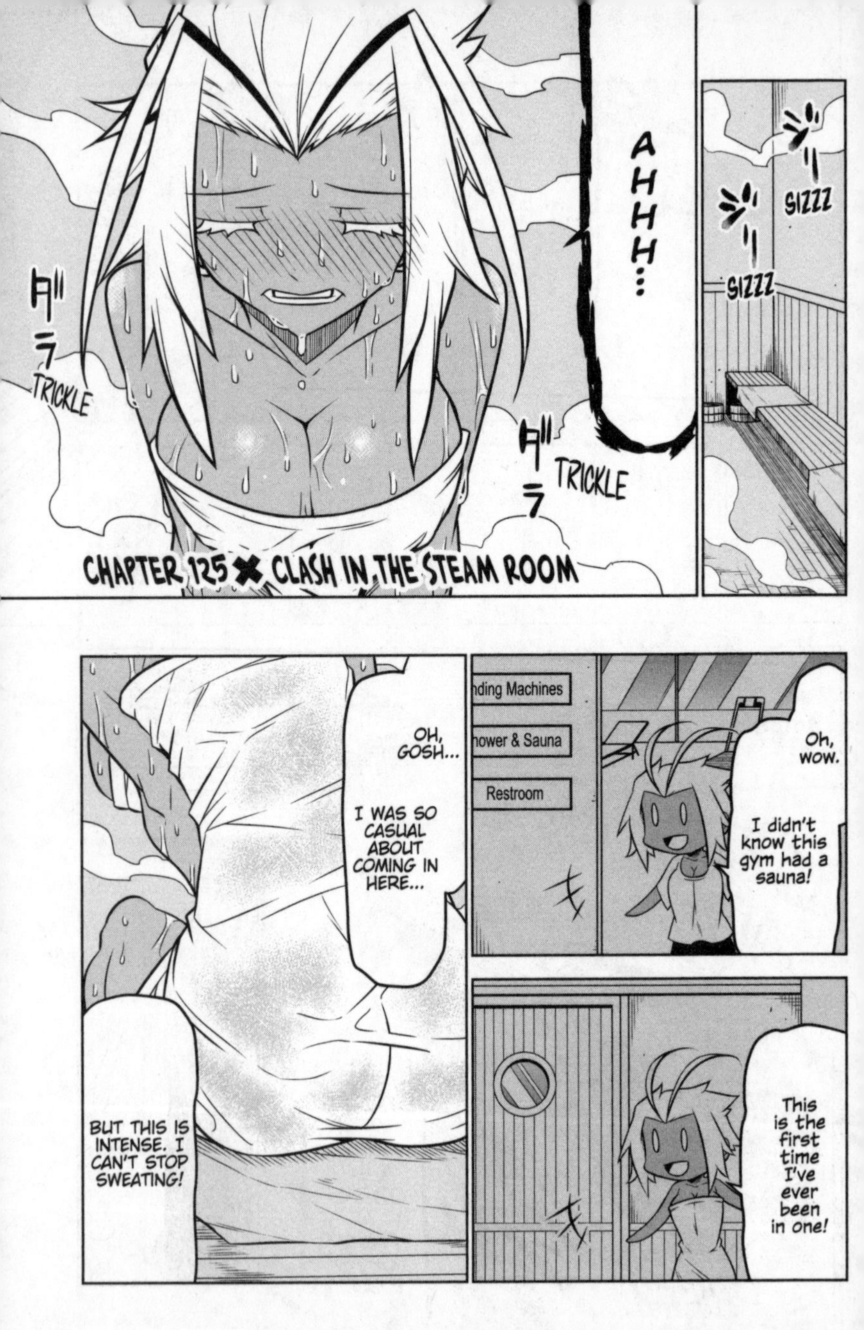
SIZZZ
SIZZZ
AHHH...
TRICKLE
TRICKLE
CHAPTER 125 ✖ CLASH IN THE STEAM ROOM
nding Machines
hower & Sauna
Restroom
Oh, wow.
I didn't know this gym had a sauna!
This is the first time I've ever been in one!
OH, GOSH...
I WAS SO CASUAL ABOUT COMING IN HERE...
BUT THIS IS INTENSE. I CAN'T STOP SWEATING!

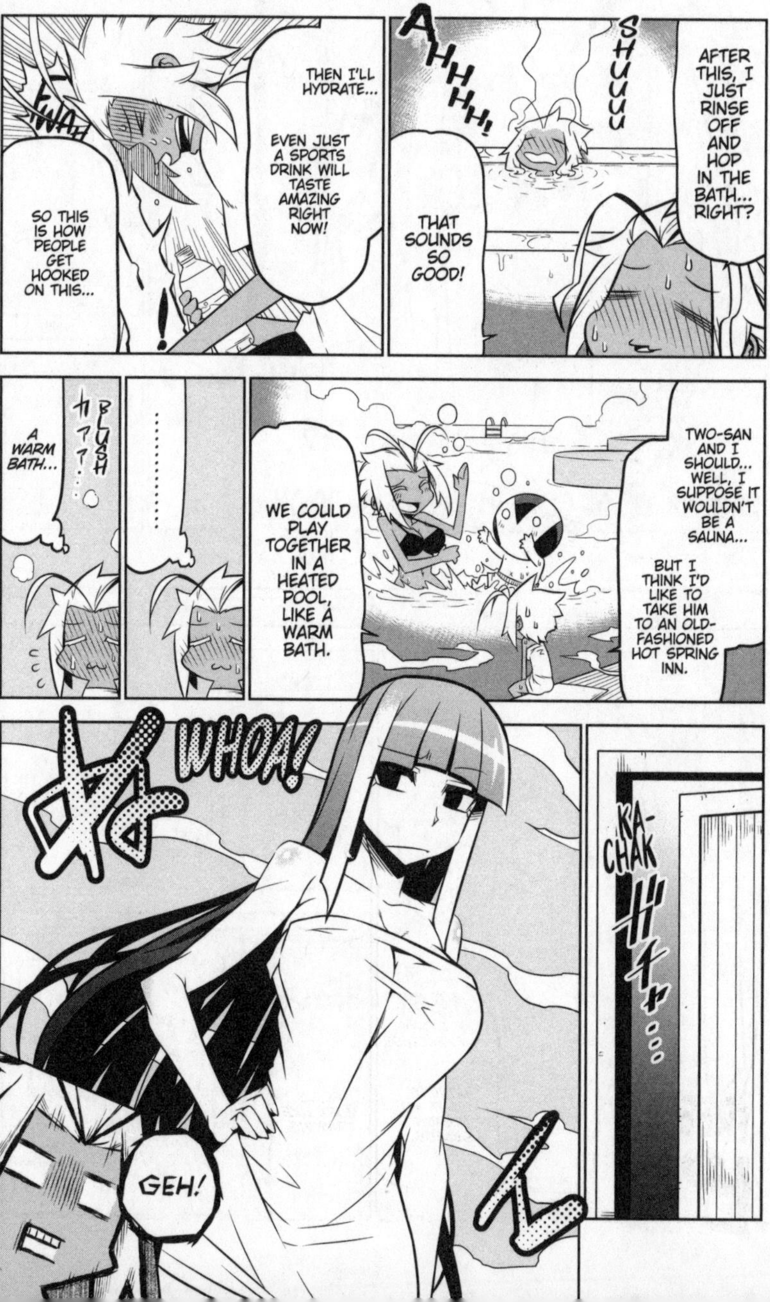
AFTER THIS, I JUST RINSE OFF AND HOP IN THE BATH... RIGHT?
SHUUUUU
AHHHHH!
THAT SOUNDS SO GOOD!
THEN I'LL HYDRATE...
EVEN JUST A SPORTS DRINK WILL TASTE AMAZING RIGHT NOW!
KWAH
SO THIS IS HOW PEOPLE GET HOOKED ON THIS...
!
TWO-SAN AND I SHOULD... WELL, I SUPPOSE IT WOULDN'T BE A SAUNA...
BUT I THINK I'D LIKE TO TAKE HIM TO AN OLD-FASHIONED HOT SPRING INN.
WE COULD PLAY TOGETHER IN A HEATED POOL, LIKE A WARM BATH.
......
BLUSH
A WARM BATH...
KA-CHAK
WHOA!
GEH!

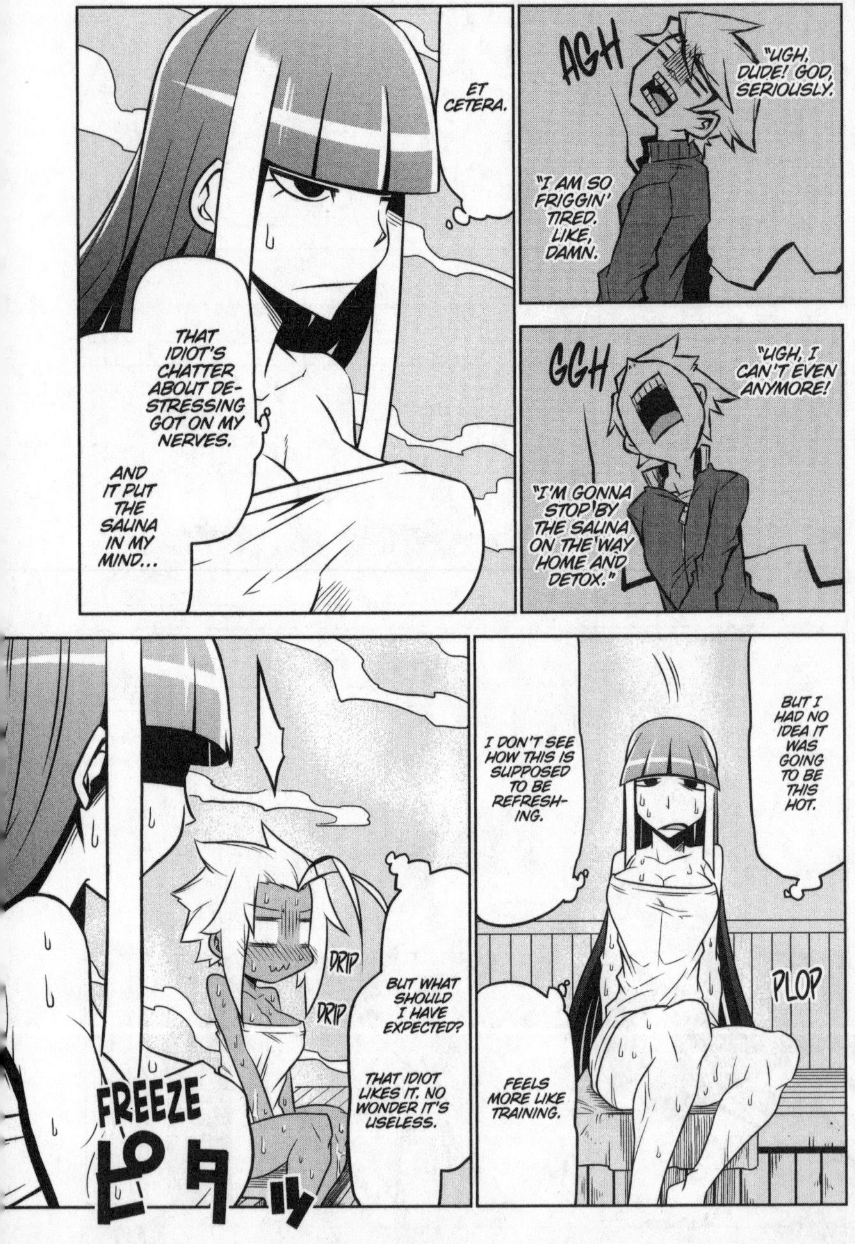
AGH
"UGH, DUDE! GOD, SERIOUSLY.
"I AM SO FRIGGIN' TIRED. LIKE, DAMN.
GGH
"UGH, I CAN'T EVEN ANYMORE!
"I'M GONNA STOP BY THE SAUNA ON THE WAY HOME AND DETOX."
ET CETERA.
THAT IDIOT'S CHATTER ABOUT DE-STRESSING GOT ON MY NERVES.
AND IT PUT THE SAUNA IN MY MIND...
BUT I HAD NO IDEA IT WAS GOING TO BE THIS HOT.
I DON'T SEE HOW THIS IS SUPPOSED TO BE REFRESH-ING.
PLOP
FEELS MORE LIKE TRAINING.
BUT WHAT SHOULD I HAVE EXPECTED?
DRIP
DRIP
THAT IDIOT LIKES IT. NO WONDER IT'S USELESS.
FREEZE

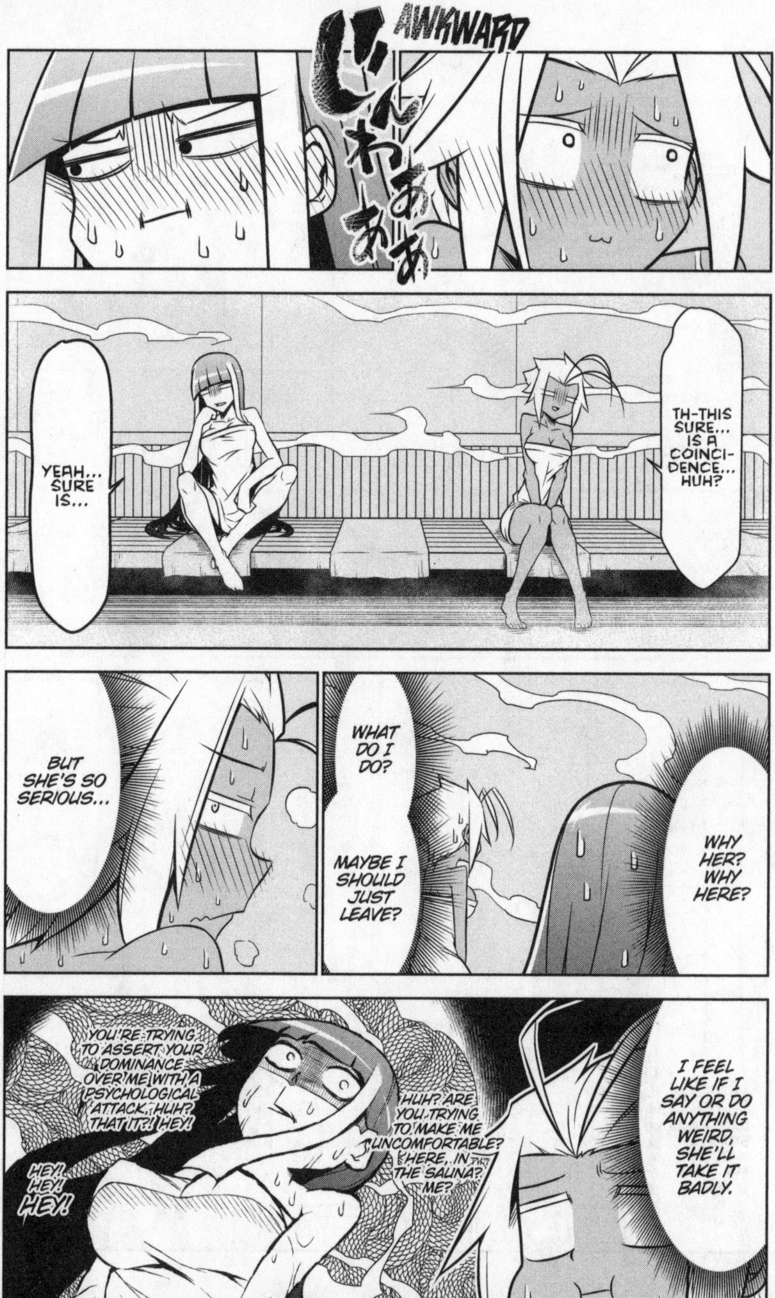
AWKWARD
TH-THIS SURE... IS A COINCIDENCE... HUH?
YEAH... SURE IS...
WHY HER? WHY HERE?
WHAT DO I DO?
MAYBE I SHOULD JUST LEAVE?
BUT SHE'S SO SERIOUS...
I FEEL LIKE IF I SAY OR DO ANYTHING WEIRD, SHE'LL TAKE IT BADLY.
HUH? ARE YOU TRYING TO MAKE ME UNCOMFORTABLE? HERE, IN THE SAUNA? ME?
YOU'RE TRYING TO ASSERT YOUR DOMINANCE OVER ME WITH A PSYCHOLOGICAL ATTACK, HUH? THAT IT?! HEY!
HEY! HEY! HEY!

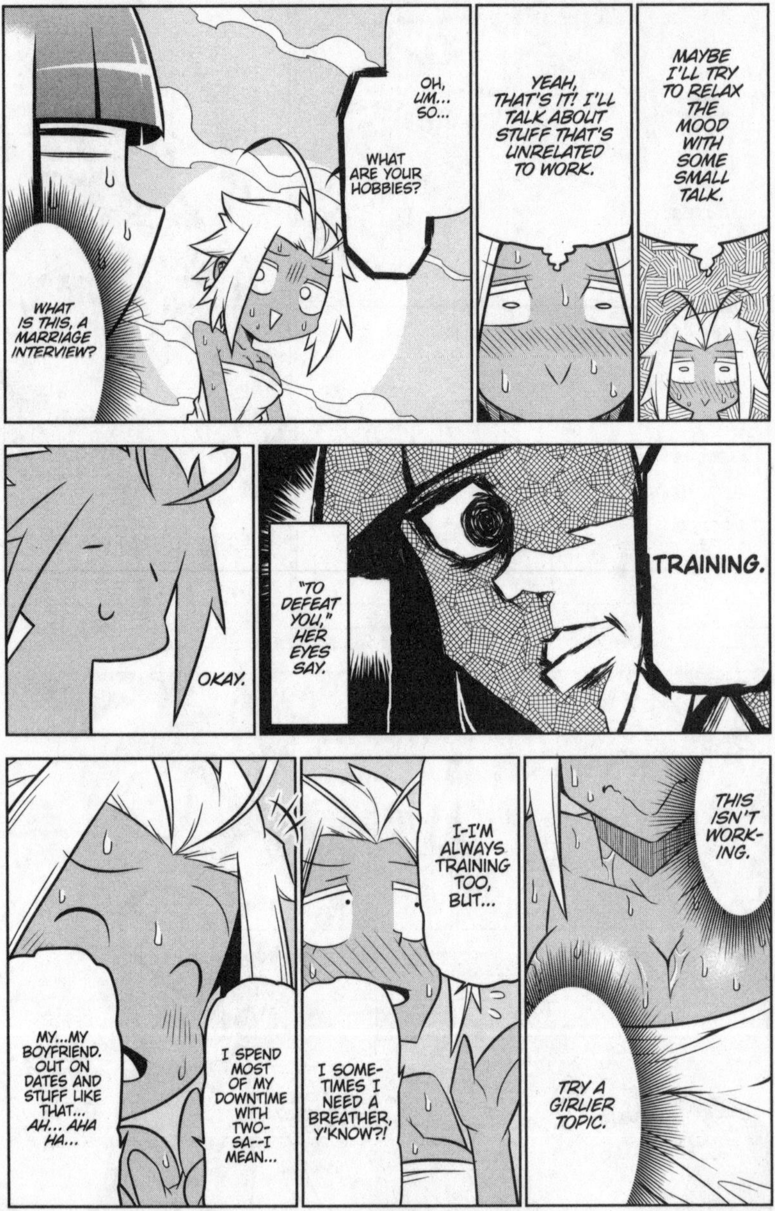
MAYBE I'LL TRY TO RELAX THE MOOD WITH SOME SMALL TALK.
YEAH, THAT'S IT! I'LL TALK ABOUT STUFF THAT'S UNRELATED TO WORK.
OH, UM... SO...
WHAT ARE YOUR HOBBIES?
WHAT IS THIS, A MARRIAGE INTERVIEW?
TRAINING.
"TO DEFEAT YOU," HER EYES SAY.
OKAY.
THIS ISN'T WORKING.
TRY A GIRLIER TOPIC.
I-I'M ALWAYS TRAINING TOO, BUT...
I SOMETIMES I NEED A BREATHER, Y'KNOW?!
I SPEND MOST OF MY DOWNTIME WITH TWO-SA--I MEAN...
MY...MY BOYFRIEND. OUT ON DATES AND STUFF LIKE THAT... AH... AHA HA...

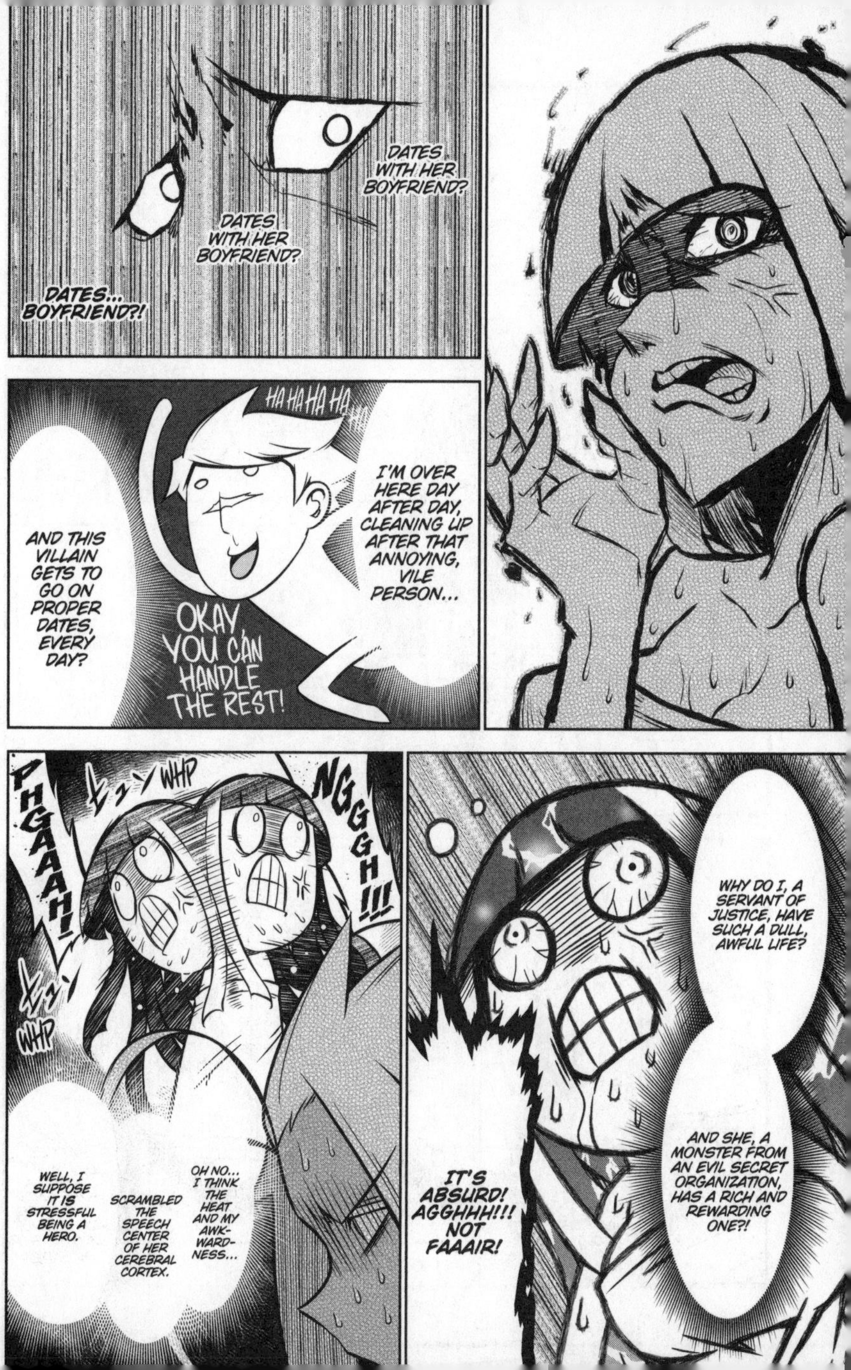
DATES WITH HER BOYFRIEND?
DATES WITH HER BOYFRIEND?
DATES... BOYFRIEND?!
HA HA HA HA HA
I'M OVER HERE DAY AFTER DAY, CLEANING UP AFTER THAT ANNOYING, VILE PERSON...
AND THIS VILLAIN GETS TO GO ON PROPER DATES, EVERY DAY?
OKAY YOU CAN HANDLE THE REST!
WHY DO I, A SERVANT OF JUSTICE, HAVE SUCH A DULL, AWFUL LIFE?
AND SHE, A MONSTER FROM AN EVIL SECRET ORGANIZATION, HAS A RICH AND REWARDING ONE?!
IT'S ABSURD! AGGHHH!!! NOT FAAAIR!
NGGGH!!!
ヒュッ WHP
PHGAAAAH!
ヒュッ WHP
OH NO... I THINK THE HEAT AND MY AWK-WARDNESS...
SCRAMBLED THE SPEECH CENTER OF HER CEREBRAL CORTEX.
WELL, I SUPPOSE IT IS STRESSFUL BEING A HERO.

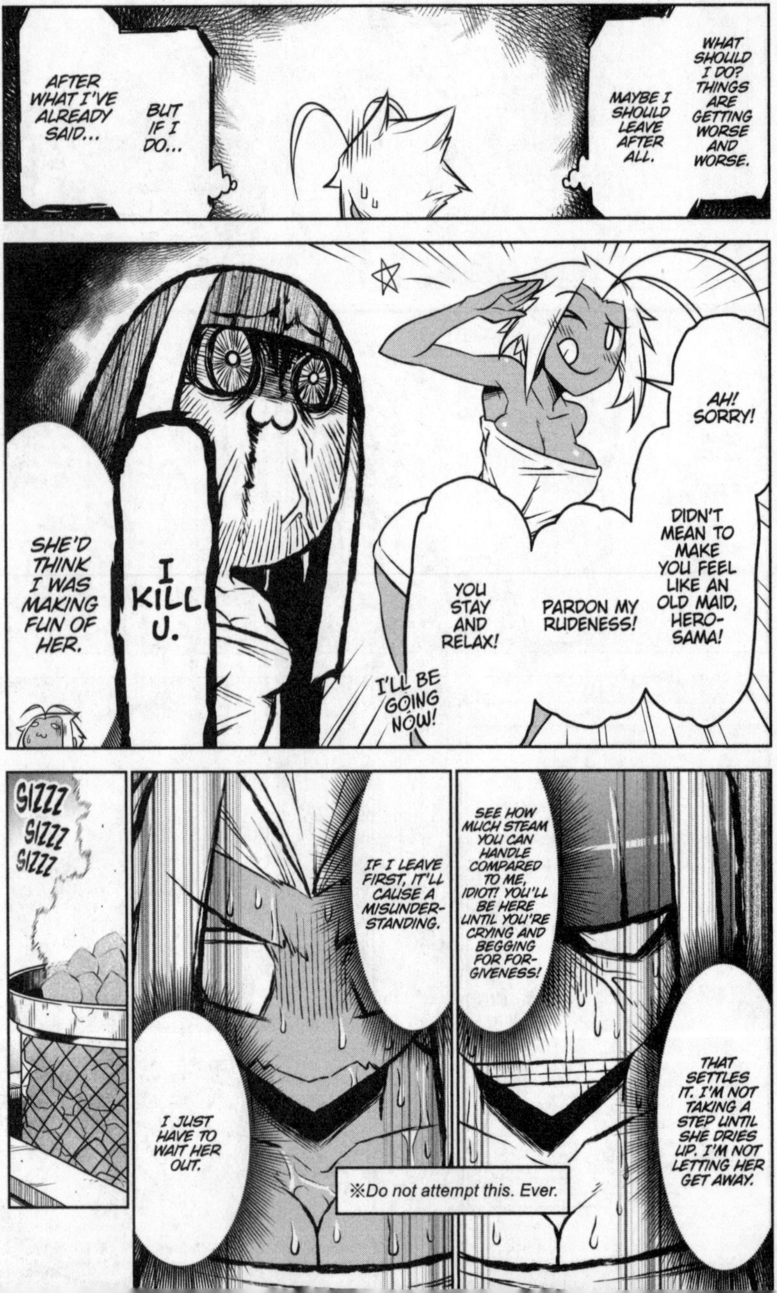
WHAT SHOULD I DO? THINGS ARE GETTING WORSE AND WORSE.
MAYBE I SHOULD LEAVE AFTER ALL.
BUT IF I DO...
AFTER WHAT I'VE ALREADY SAID...
AH! SORRY!
DIDN'T MEAN TO MAKE YOU FEEL LIKE AN OLD MAID, HERO-SAMA!
PARDON MY RUDENESS!
YOU STAY AND RELAX!
I'LL BE GOING NOW!
I KILL U.
SHE'D THINK I WAS MAKING FUN OF HER.
SEE HOW MUCH STEAM YOU CAN HANDLE COMPARED TO ME, IDIOT! YOU'LL BE HERE UNTIL YOU'RE CRYING AND BEGGING FOR FORGIVENESS!
THAT SETTLES IT. I'M NOT TAKING A STEP UNTIL SHE DRIES UP. I'M NOT LETTING HER GET AWAY.
IF I LEAVE FIRST, IT'LL CAUSE A MISUNDERSTANDING.
I JUST HAVE TO WAIT HER OUT.
※Do not attempt this. Ever.
SIZZZ SIZZZ SIZZZ

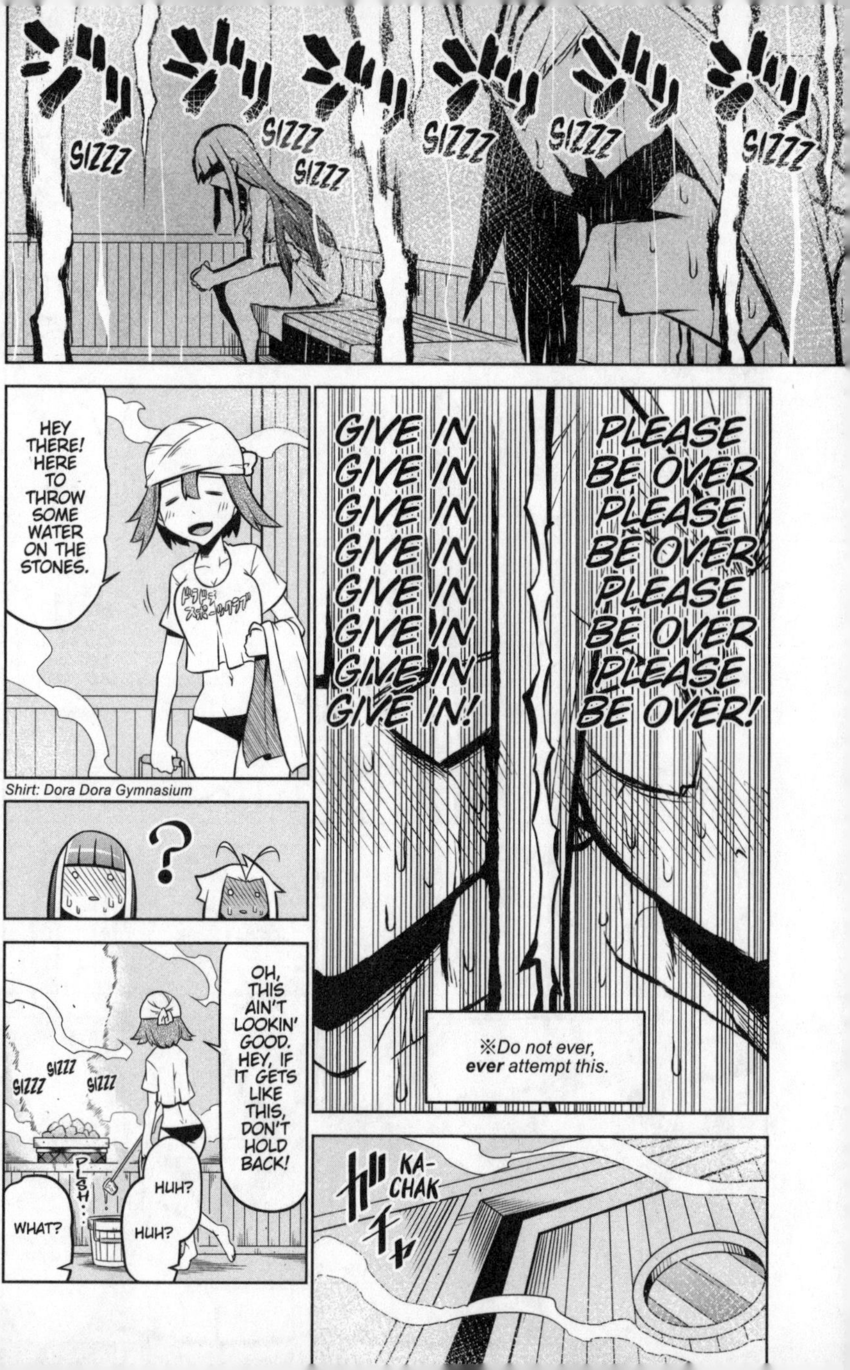
SIZZZ
SIZZZ
SIZZZ
SIZZZ
SIZZZ
SIZZZ
PLEASE BE OVER PLEASE BE OVER PLEASE BE OVER PLEASE BE OVER!
GIVE IN GIVE IN GIVE IN GIVE IN GIVE IN GIVE IN GIVE IN GIVE IN!
※Do not ever, **ever** attempt this.
KA-CHAK
HEY THERE! HERE TO THROW SOME WATER ON THE STONES.
Shirt: Dora Dora Gymnasium
?
OH, THIS AIN'T LOOKIN' GOOD. HEY, IF IT GETS LIKE THIS, DON'T HOLD BACK!
SIZZZ
SIZZZ
SIZZZ
PLSH...
HUH?
HUH?
WHAT?

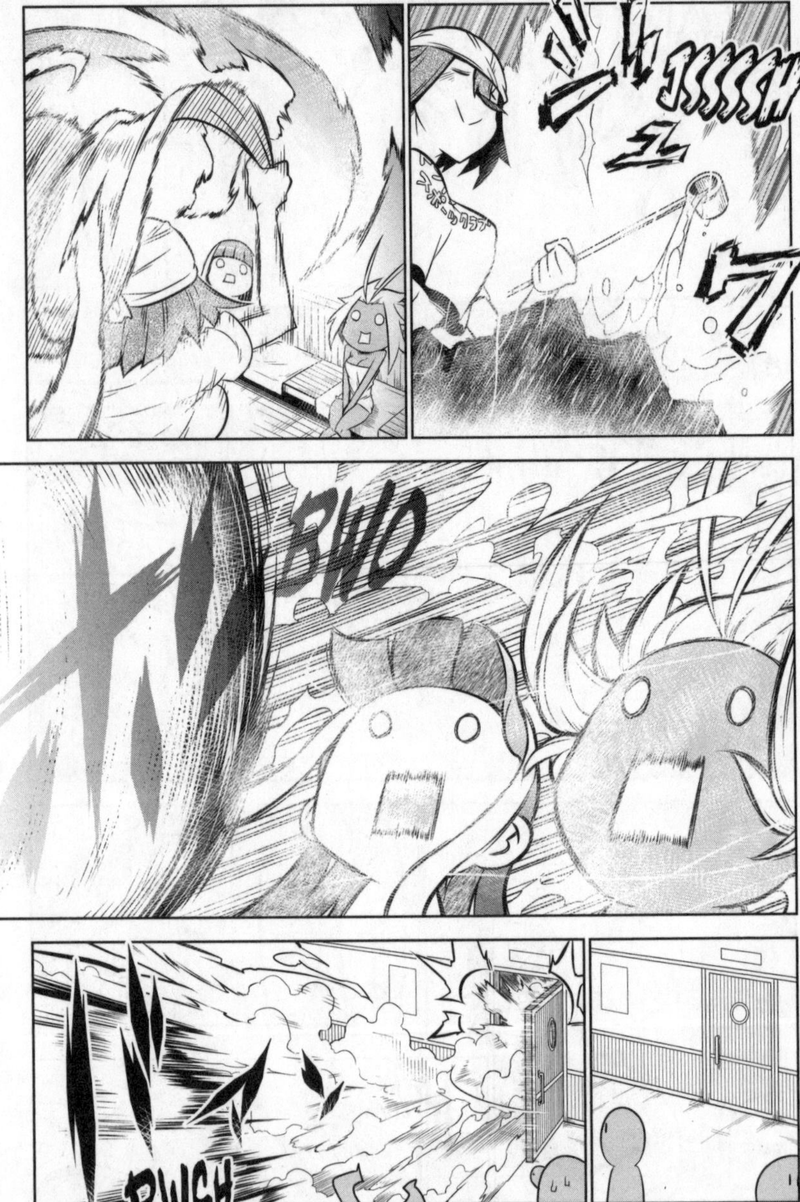
JSSSH
BWO
BWSH

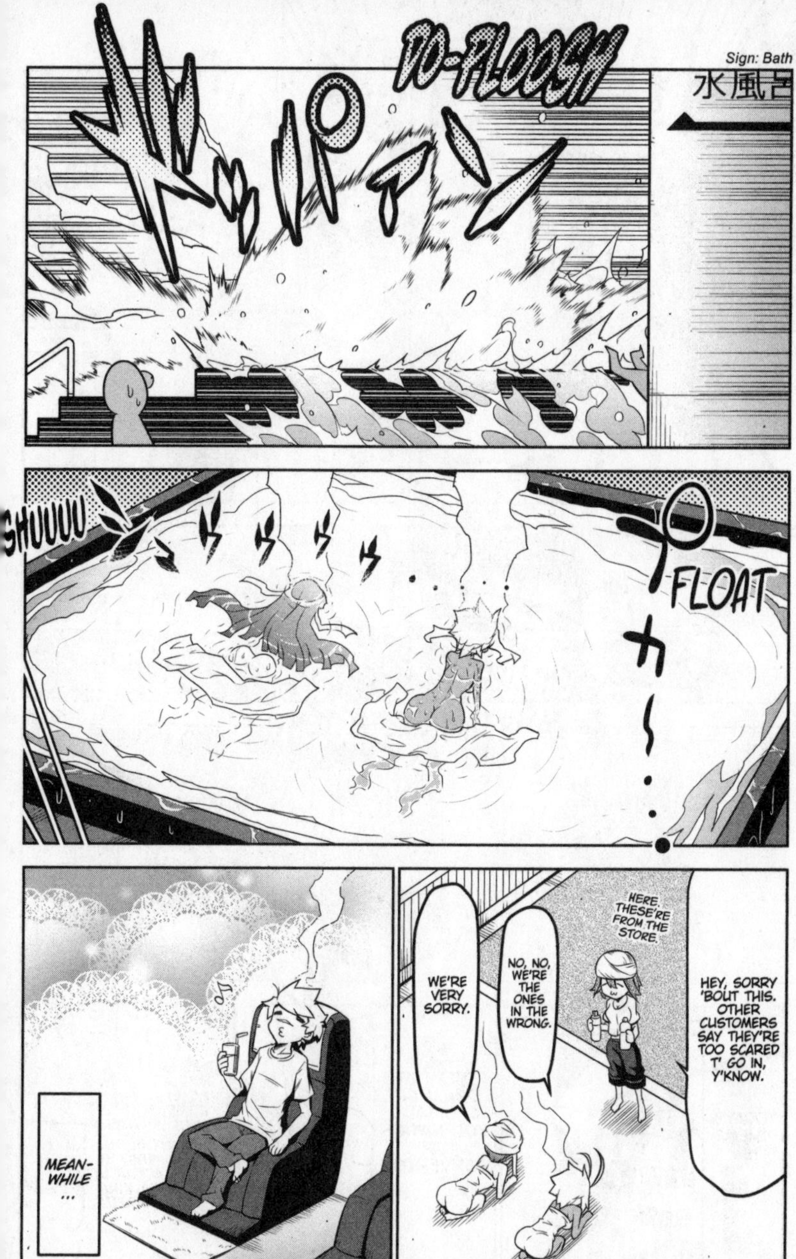
TO-FLOOSH
Sign: Bath
水風呂
SHUUUU
FLOAT
HEY, SORRY 'BOUT THIS. OTHER CUSTOMERS SAY THEY'RE TOO SCARED T' GO IN, Y'KNOW.
HERE. THESE'RE FROM THE STORE.
NO, NO, WE'RE THE ONES IN THE WRONG.
WE'RE VERY SORRY.
MEAN-WHILE ...

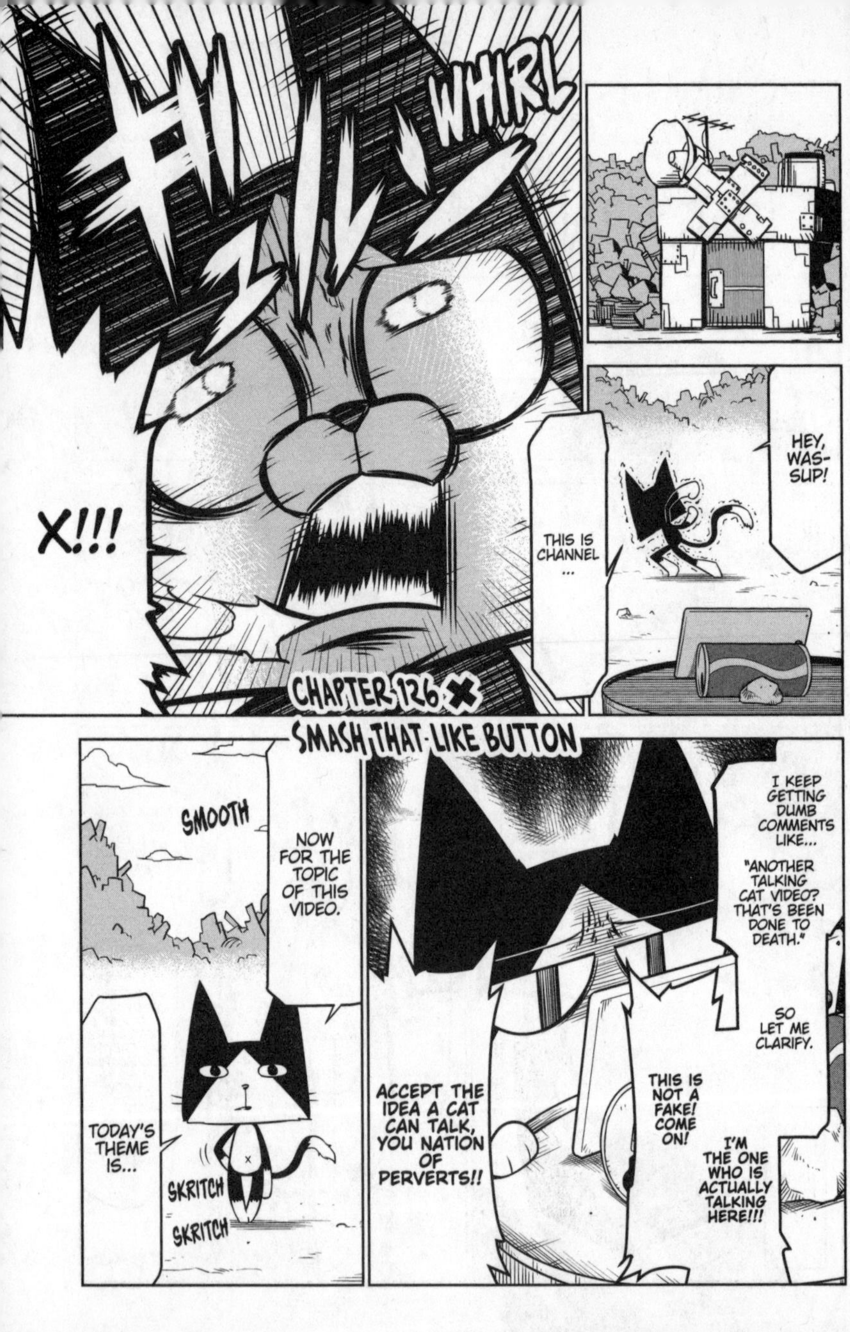
HEY, WAS-SUP!
THIS IS CHANNEL ...
WHIRL
X!!!
CHAPTER 126 ×
SMASH THAT-LIKE BUTTON
I KEEP GETTING DUMB COMMENTS LIKE...
"ANOTHER TALKING CAT VIDEO? THAT'S BEEN DONE TO DEATH."
SO LET ME CLARIFY.
I'M THE ONE WHO IS ACTUALLY TALKING HERE!!!
THIS IS NOT A FAKE! COME ON!
ACCEPT THE IDEA A CAT CAN TALK, YOU NATION OF PERVERTS!!
NOW FOR THE TOPIC OF THIS VIDEO.
SMOOTH
TODAY'S THEME IS...
SKRITCH
SKRITCH

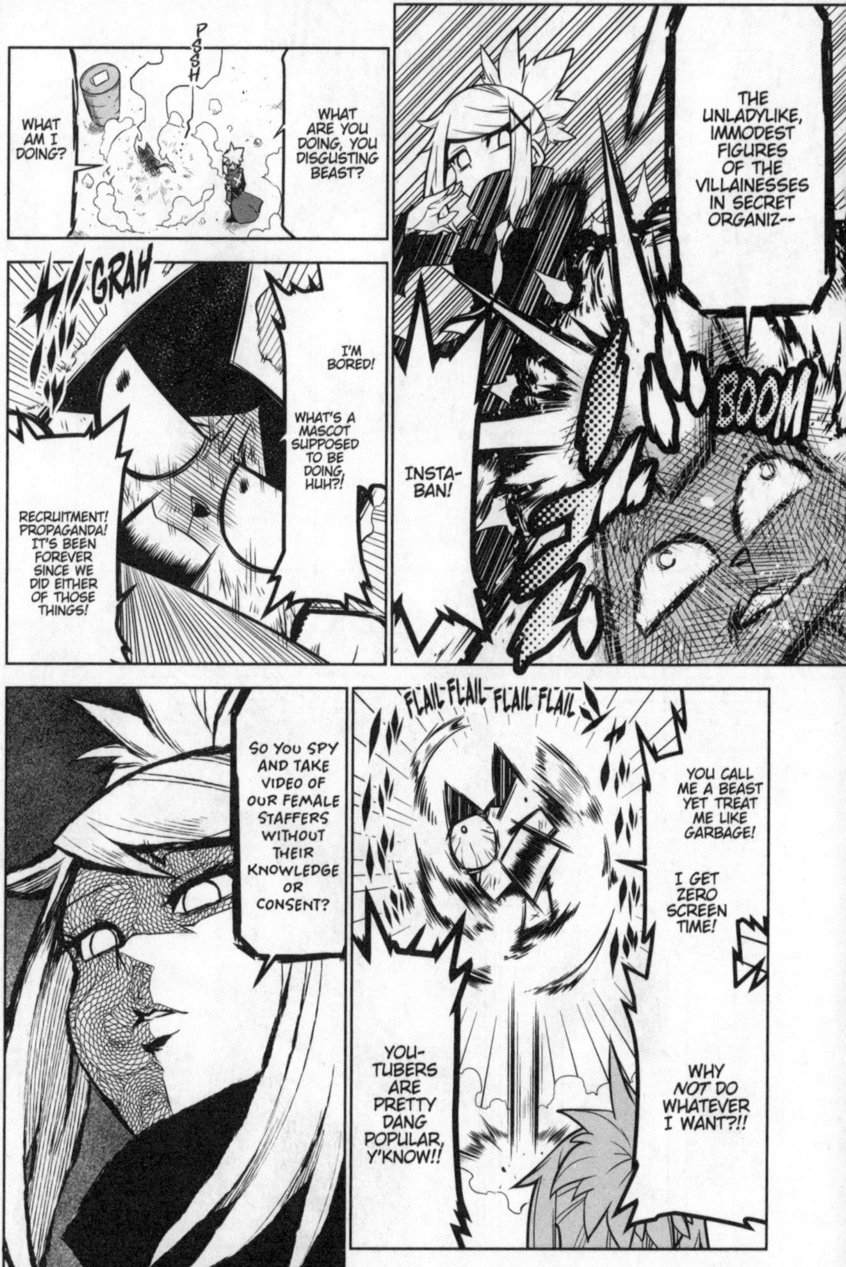
THE UNLADYLIKE, IMMODEST FIGURES OF THE VILLAINESSES IN SECRET ORGANIZ--
BOOM
INSTA-BAN!
PSSH
WHAT ARE YOU DOING, YOU DISGUSTING BEAST?
WHAT AM I DOING?
GRAH
I'M BORED!
WHAT'S A MASCOT SUPPOSED TO BE DOING, HUH?!
RECRUITMENT! PROPAGANDA! IT'S BEEN FOREVER SINCE WE DID EITHER OF THOSE THINGS!
FLAIL FLAIL FLAIL FLAIL
YOU CALL ME A BEAST YET TREAT ME LIKE GARBAGE!
I GET ZERO SCREEN TIME!
WHY *NOT* DO WHATEVER I WANT?!!
YOU-TUBERS ARE PRETTY DANG POPULAR, Y'KNOW!!
So YOU SPY AND TAKE VIDEO OF OUR FEMALE STAFFERS WITHOUT THEIR KNOWLEDGE OR CONSENT?

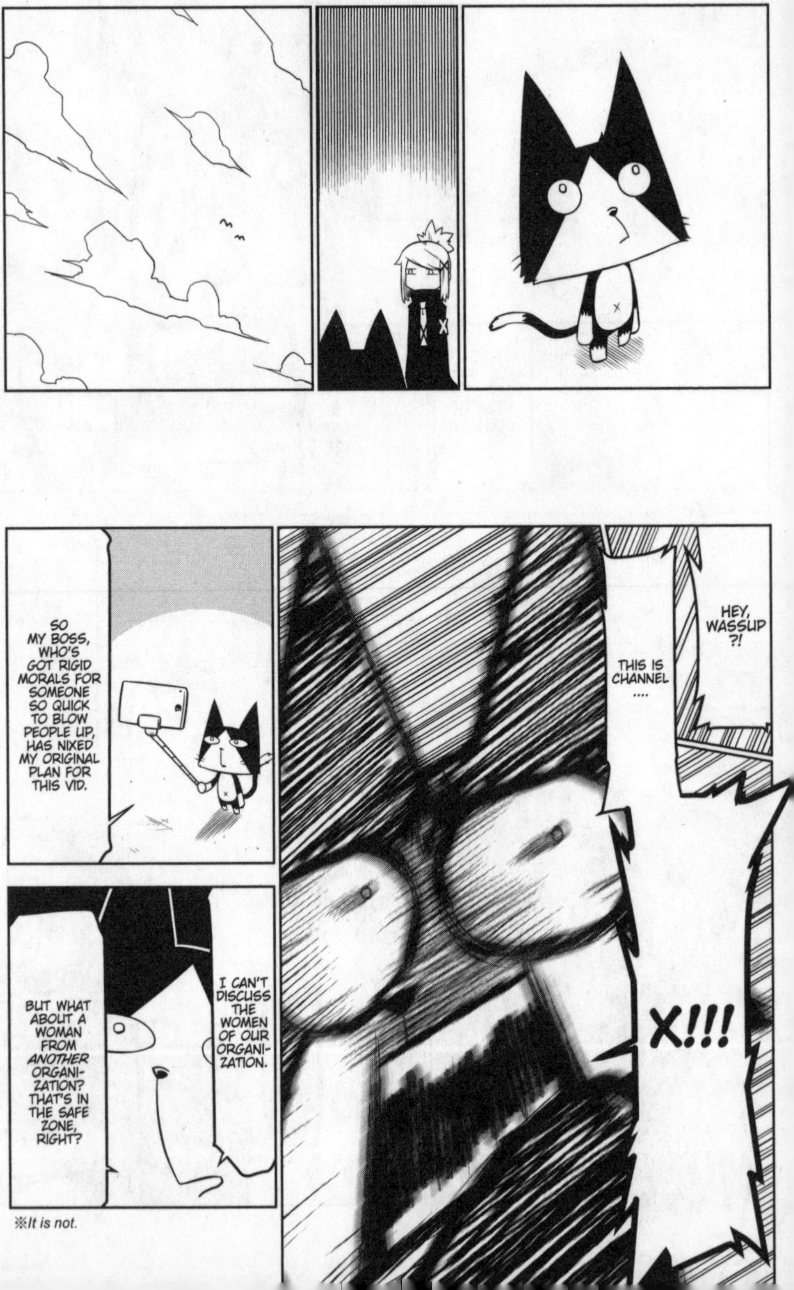
HEY, WASSUP?!
THIS IS CHANNEL....
X!!!
SO MY BOSS, WHO'S GOT RIGID MORALS FOR SOMEONE SO QUICK TO BLOW PEOPLE UP, HAS NIXED MY ORIGINAL PLAN FOR THIS VID.
I CAN'T DISCUSS THE WOMEN OF OUR ORGANI-ZATION.
BUT WHAT ABOUT A WOMAN FROM *ANOTHER* ORGANI-ZATION? THAT'S IN THE SAFE ZONE, RIGHT?

※*It is not.*

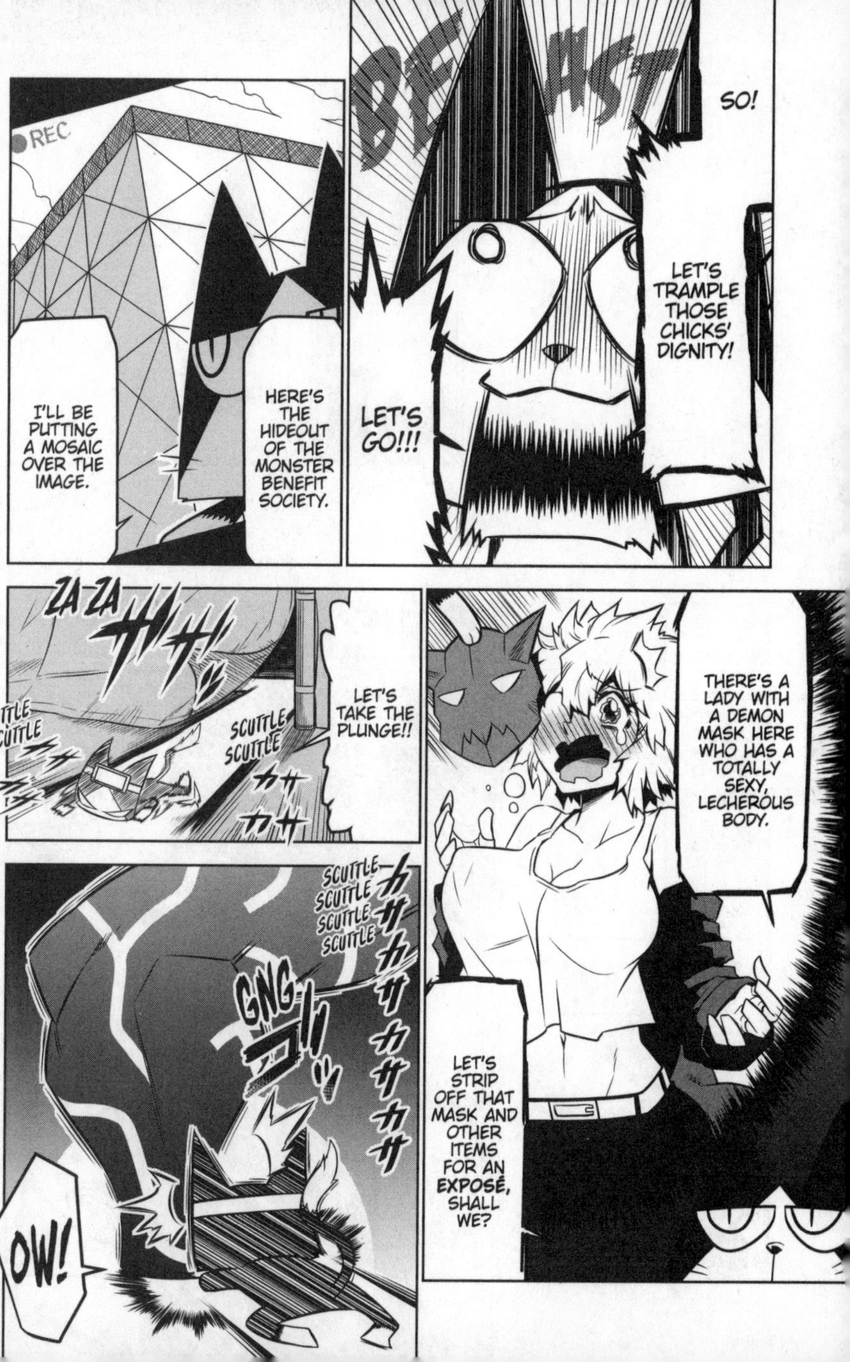
BEAST
SO!
LET'S TRAMPLE THOSE CHICKS' DIGNITY!
LET'S GO!!!
REC
HERE'S THE HIDEOUT OF THE MONSTER BENEFIT SOCIETY.
I'LL BE PUTTING A MOSAIC OVER THE IMAGE.
THERE'S A LADY WITH A DEMON MASK HERE WHO HAS A TOTALLY SEXY, LECHEROUS BODY.
LET'S STRIP OFF THAT MASK AND OTHER ITEMS FOR AN EXPOSÉ, SHALL WE?
ZA ZA
LET'S TAKE THE PLUNGE!!
SCUTTLE SCUTTLE
SCUTTLE SCUTTLE
SCUTTLE SCUTTLE SCUTTLE SCUTTLE
GNG
OW!

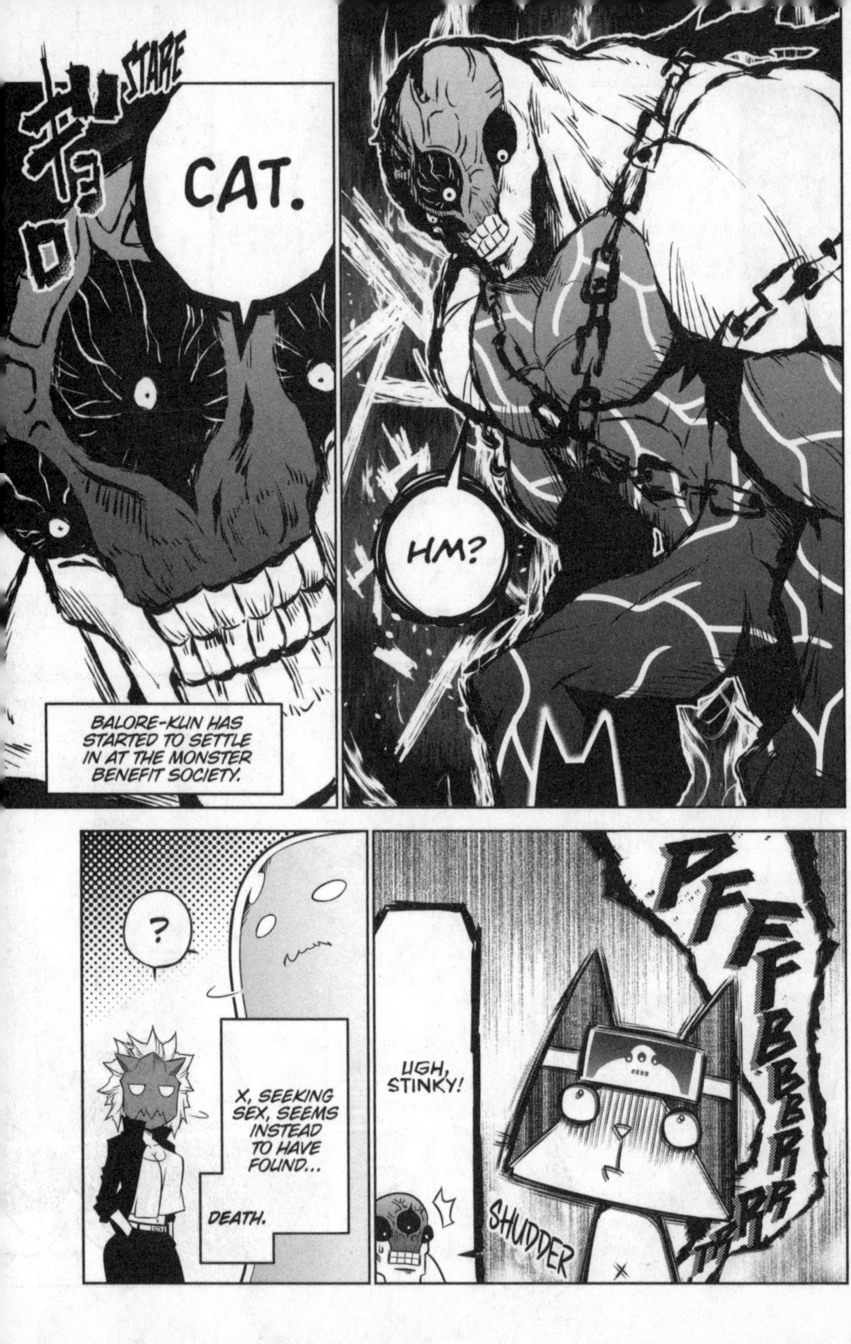
HM?
STARE
ギョロ
CAT.
BALORE-KUN HAS STARTED TO SETTLE IN AT THE MONSTER BENEFIT SOCIETY.
PFFFBBBRRR
UGH, STINKY!
SHUDDER
?
X, SEEKING SEX, SEEMS INSTEAD TO HAVE FOUND...
DEATH.

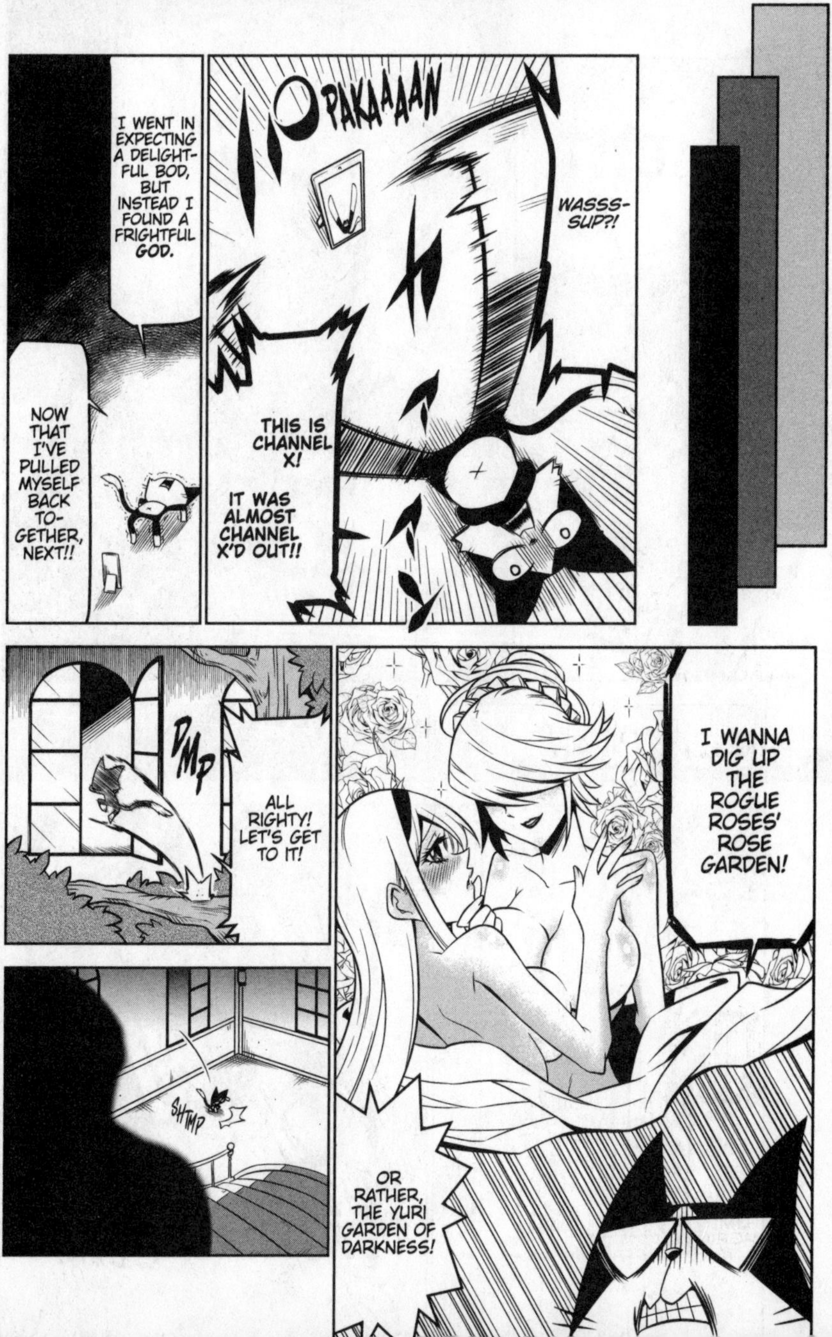
PAKAAAAN
WASSS-SUP?!
THIS IS CHANNEL X!
IT WAS ALMOST CHANNEL X'D OUT!!
I WENT IN EXPECTING A DELIGHTFUL BOD, BUT INSTEAD I FOUND A FRIGHTFUL GOD.
NOW THAT I'VE PULLED MYSELF BACK TOGETHER, NEXT!!
I WANNA DIG UP THE ROGUE ROSES' ROSE GARDEN!
OR RATHER, THE YURI GARDEN OF DARKNESS!
DMP
ALL RIGHTY! LET'S GET TO IT!
SHTMP

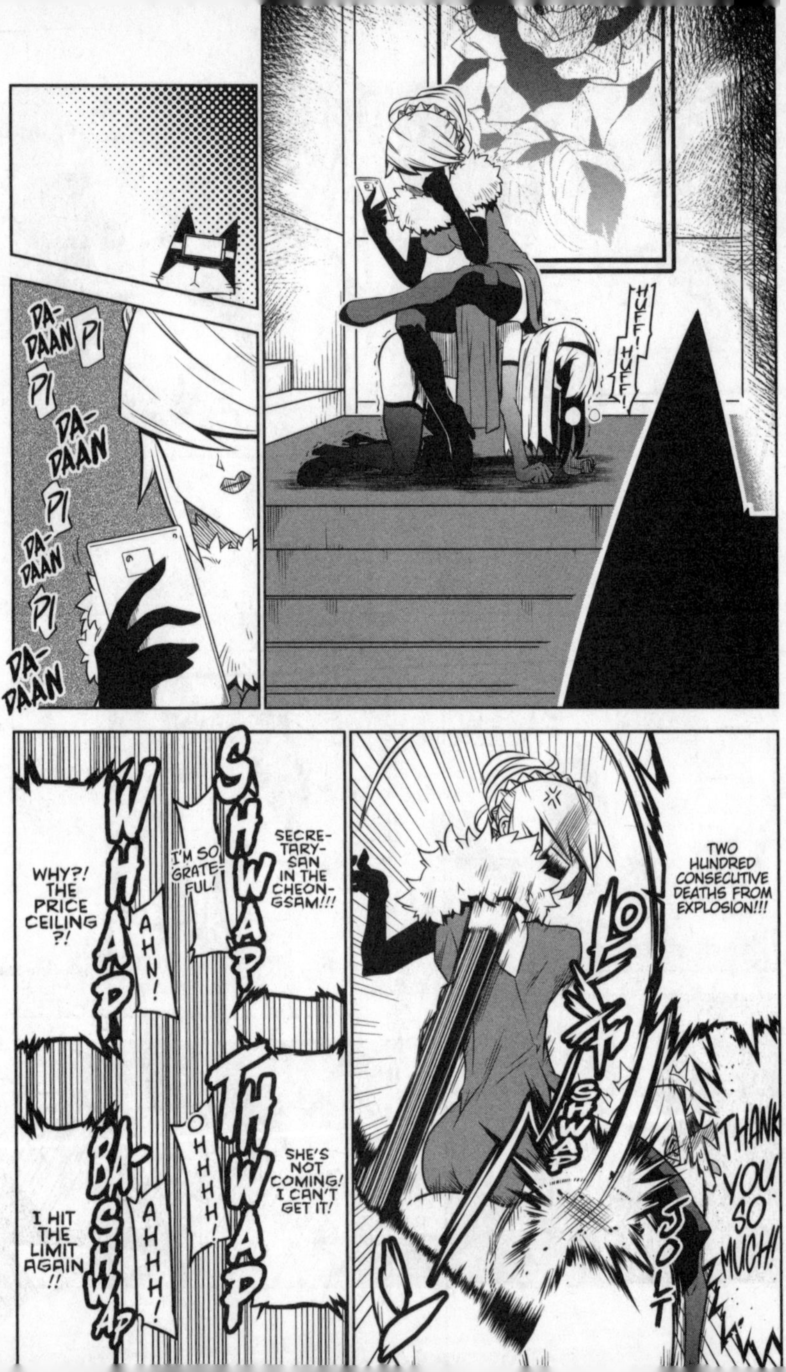
HUFF! HUFF! HUFF!
DA-DAAN
PI
PI
DA-DAAN
PI
DA-DAAN
PI
DA-DAAN
TWO HUNDRED CONSECUTIVE DEATHS FROM EXPLOSION!!!
SHWAP
THANK YOU SO MUCH!
JOLT
SECRETARY-SAN IN THE CHEONGSAM!!!
SHWAP
I'M SO GRATEFUL!
AHN!
WHY?! THE PRICE CEILING?!
WHAP
SHE'S NOT COMING! I CAN'T GET IT!
THWAP
OHHHH!
AHHH!
I HIT THE LIMIT AGAIN!!
BA-SHWAP

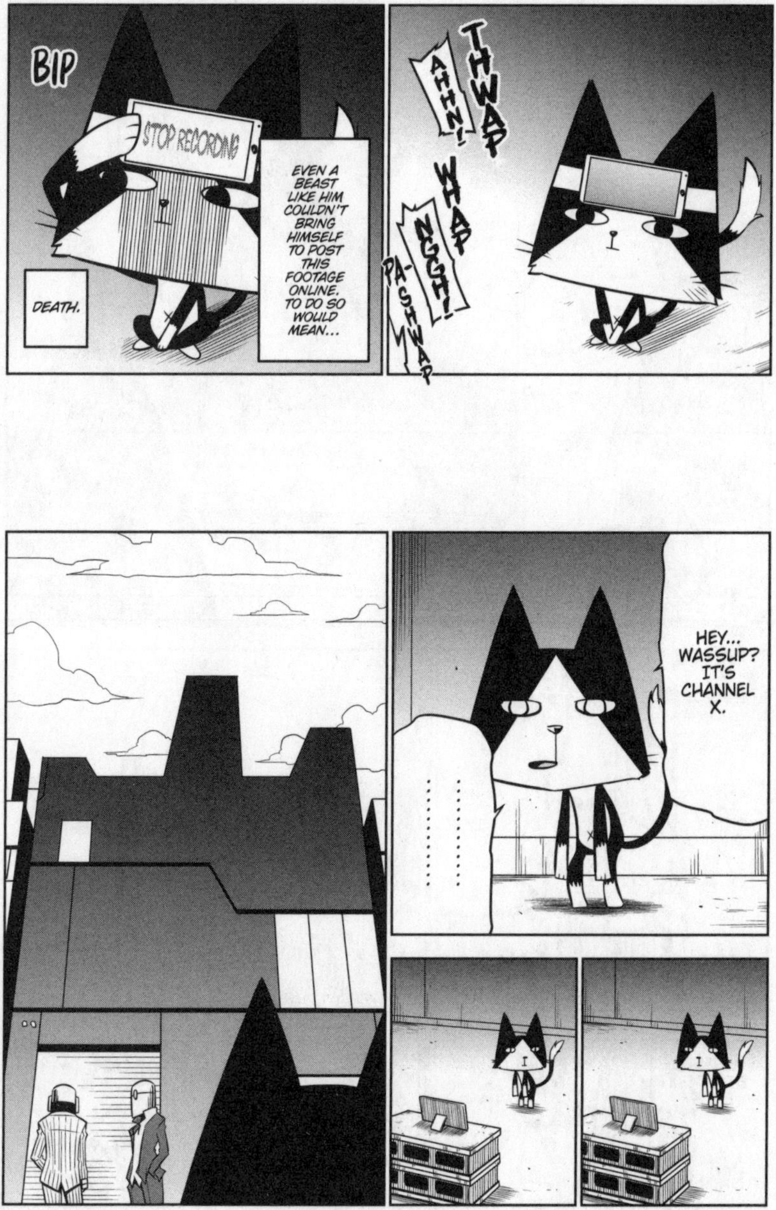
THWAP
AHHN!
WHAP
NGGH!
PA-SHWAP
BIP
STOP RECORDING
EVEN A BEAST LIKE HIM COULDN'T BRING HIMSELF TO POST THIS FOOTAGE ONLINE. TO DO SO WOULD MEAN...
DEATH.
HEY... WASSUP? IT'S CHANNEL X.

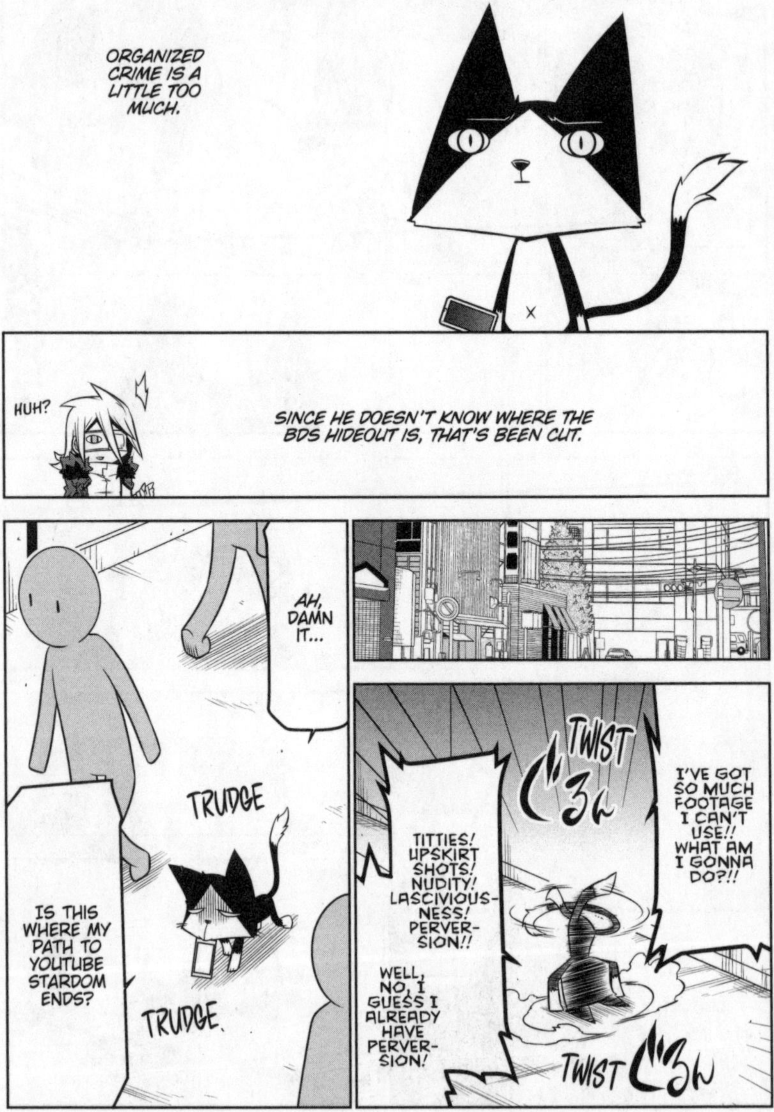
ORGANIZED CRIME IS A LITTLE TOO MUCH.
SINCE HE DOESN'T KNOW WHERE THE BDS HIDEOUT IS, THAT'S BEEN CUT.
HUH?
I'VE GOT SO MUCH FOOTAGE I CAN'T USE!! WHAT AM I GONNA DO?!!
TWIST
TITTIES! UPSKIRT SHOTS! NUDITY! LASCIVIOUSNESS! PERVERSION!!
WELL, NO, I GUESS I ALREADY HAVE PERVERSION!
TWIST
AH, DAMN IT...
TRUDGE
IS THIS WHERE MY PATH TO YOUTUBE STARDOM ENDS?
TRUDGE

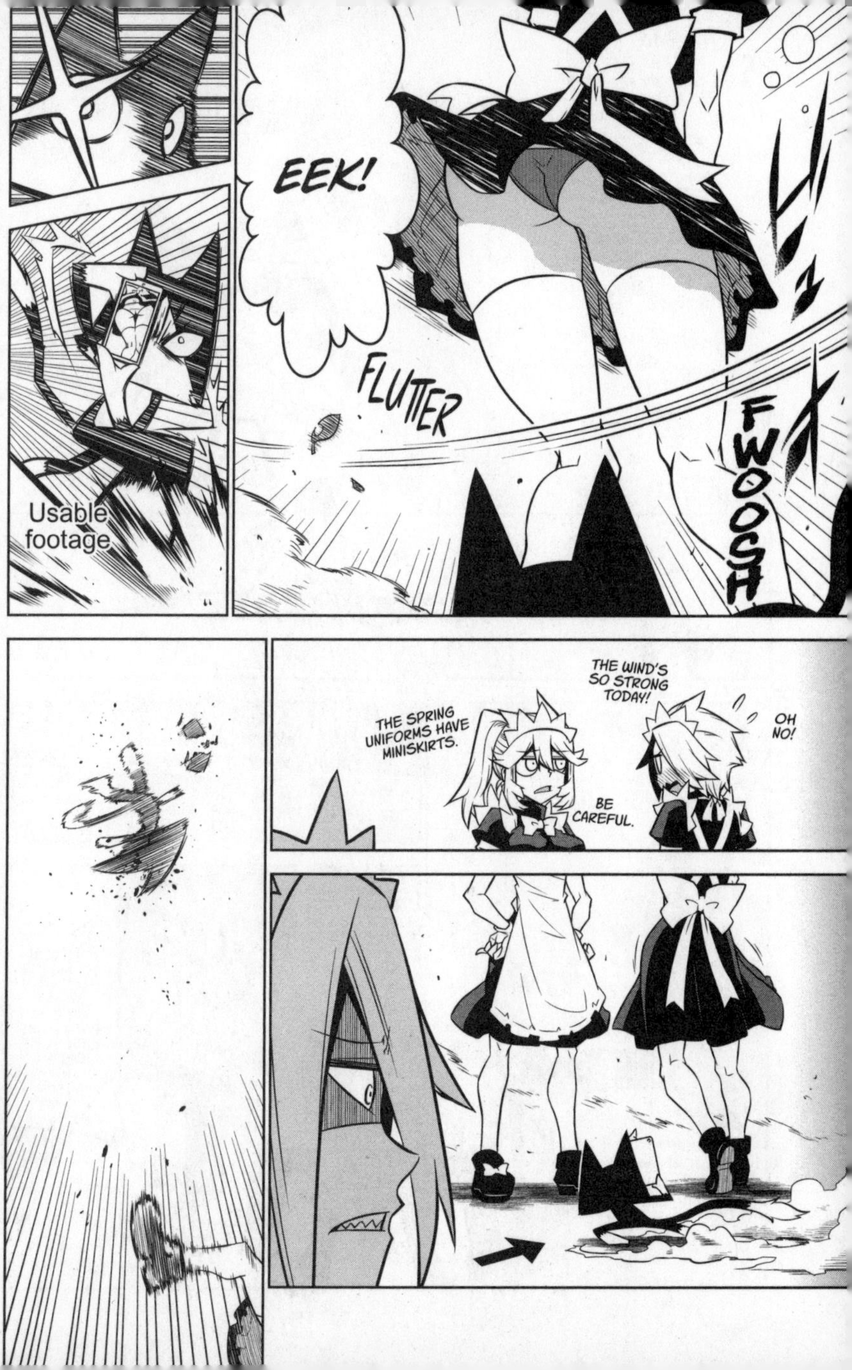
EEK!
FWOOSH
FLUTTER
Usable footage
OH NO!
THE WIND'S SO STRONG TODAY!
THE SPRING UNIFORMS HAVE MINISKIRTS.
BE CAREFUL.

CHAPTER 127 ✖ THE DAY HER HEART WAS SE

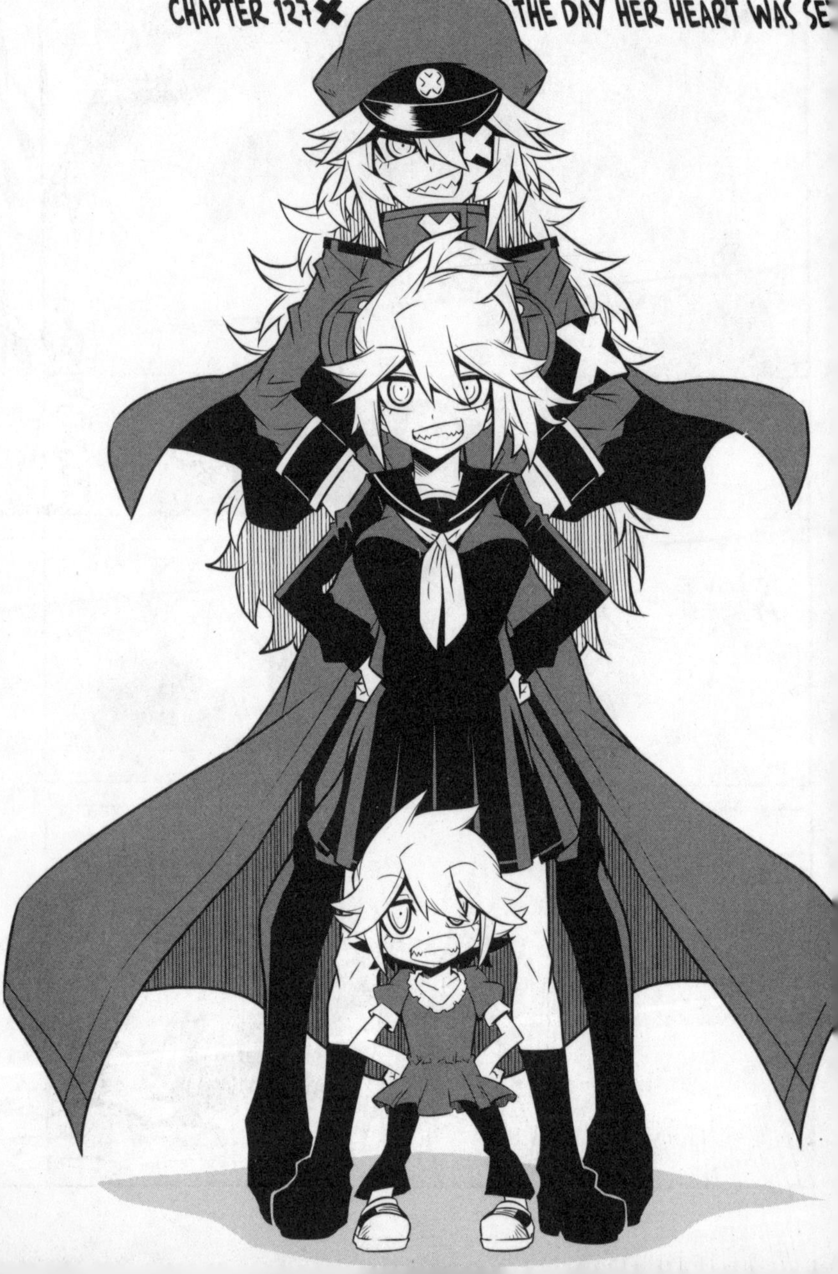

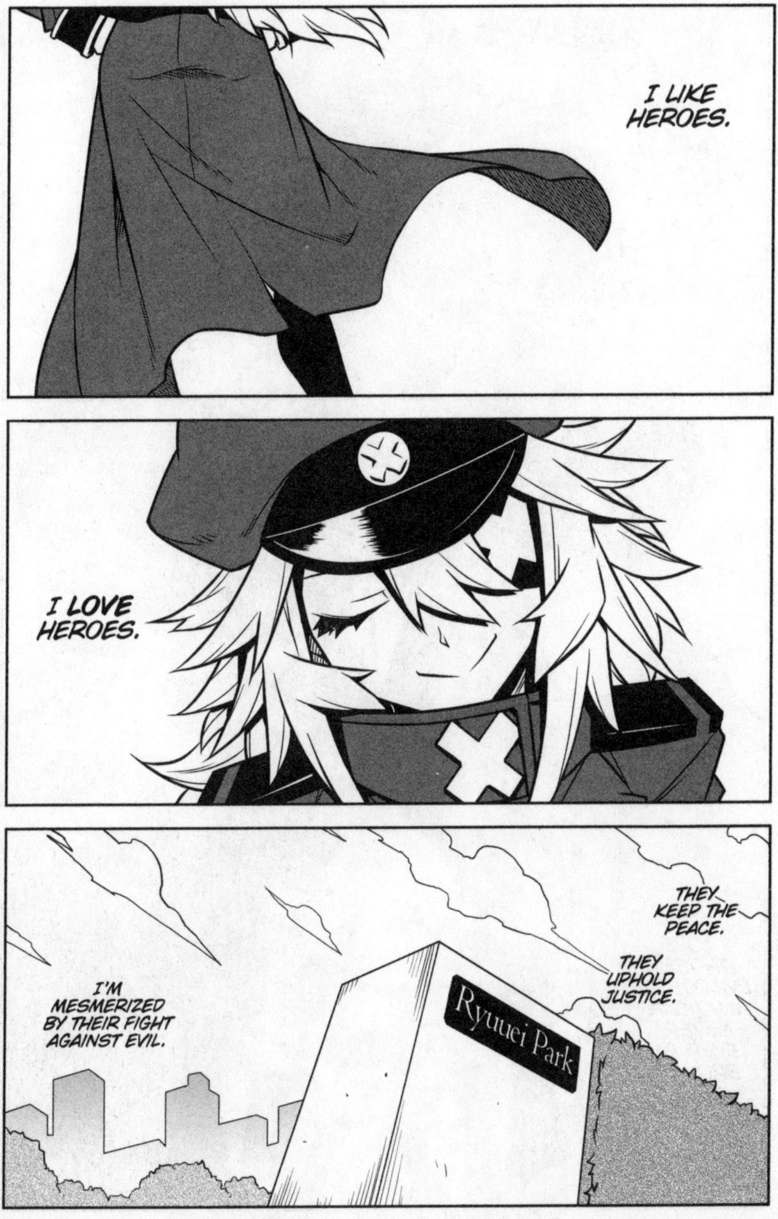
I LIKE HEROES.
I LOVE HEROES.
THEY KEEP THE PEACE.
THEY UPHOLD JUSTICE.
Ryuuei Park
I'M MESMERIZED BY THEIR FIGHT AGAINST EVIL.

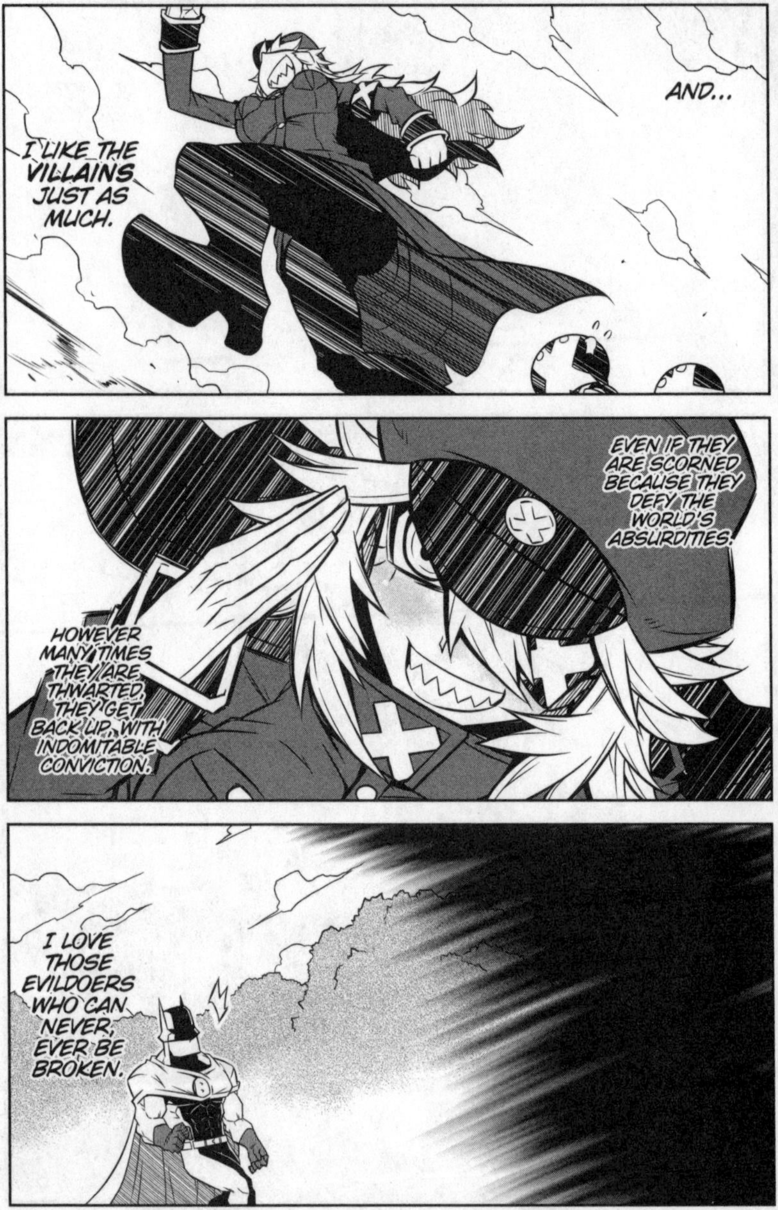
AND...
I LIKE THE VILLAINS JUST AS MUCH.
EVEN IF THEY ARE SCORNED BECAUSE THEY DEFY THE WORLD'S ABSURDITIES.
HOWEVER MANY TIMES THEY ARE THWARTED, THEY GET BACK UP, WITH INDOMITABLE CONVICTION.
I LOVE THOSE EVILDOERS WHO CAN NEVER, EVER BE BROKEN.

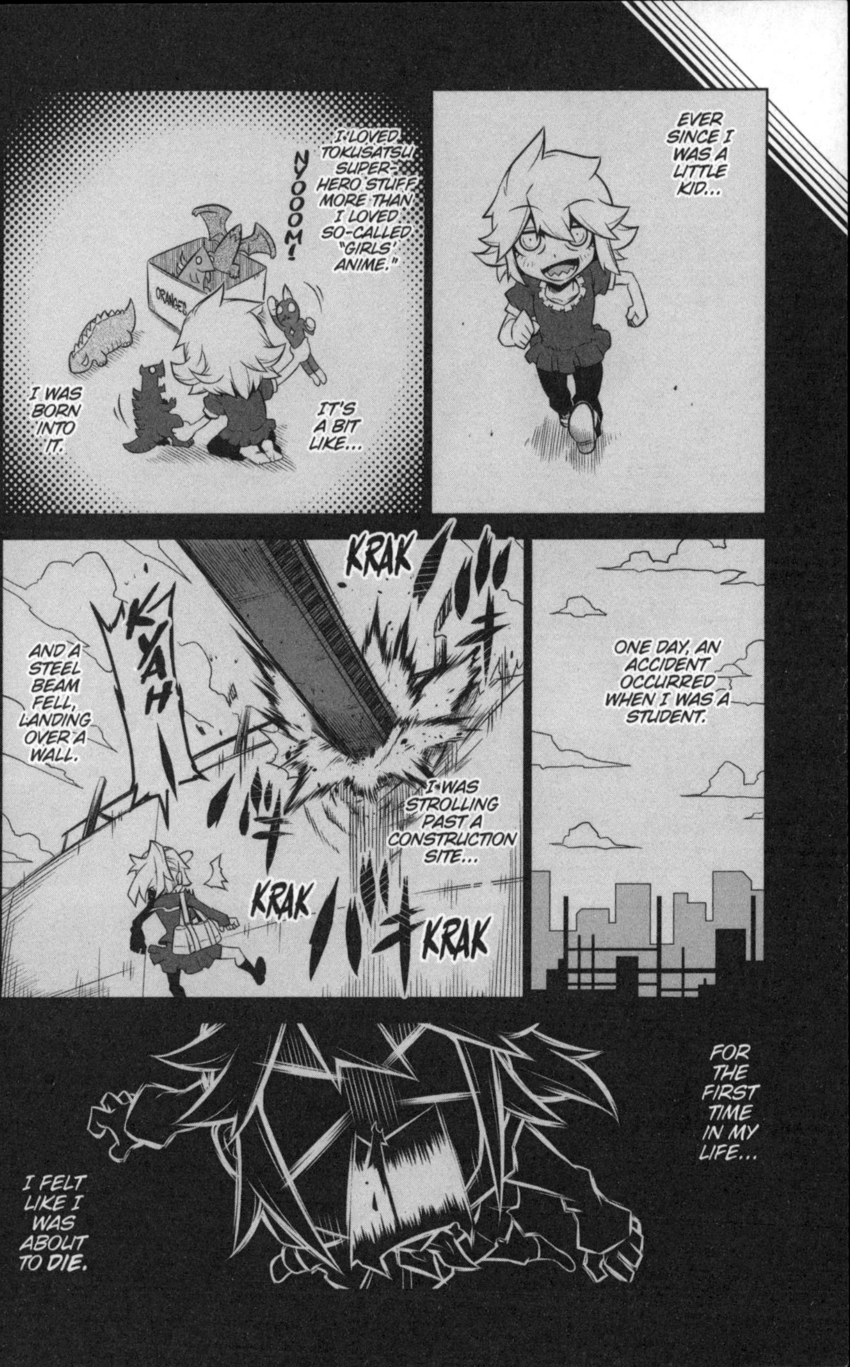
EVER SINCE I WAS A LITTLE KID...
I LOVED TOKUSATSU SUPER-HERO STUFF MORE THAN I LOVED SO-CALLED "GIRLS' ANIME."
NYOOOOM!
ORANGES
IT'S A BIT LIKE...
I WAS BORN INTO IT.
ONE DAY, AN ACCIDENT OCCURRED WHEN I WAS A STUDENT.
KRAK
KYAH
I WAS STROLLING PAST A CONSTRUCTION SITE...
AND A STEEL BEAM FELL, LANDING OVER A WALL.
KRAK
KRAK
FOR THE FIRST TIME IN MY LIFE...
I FELT LIKE I WAS ABOUT TO DIE.

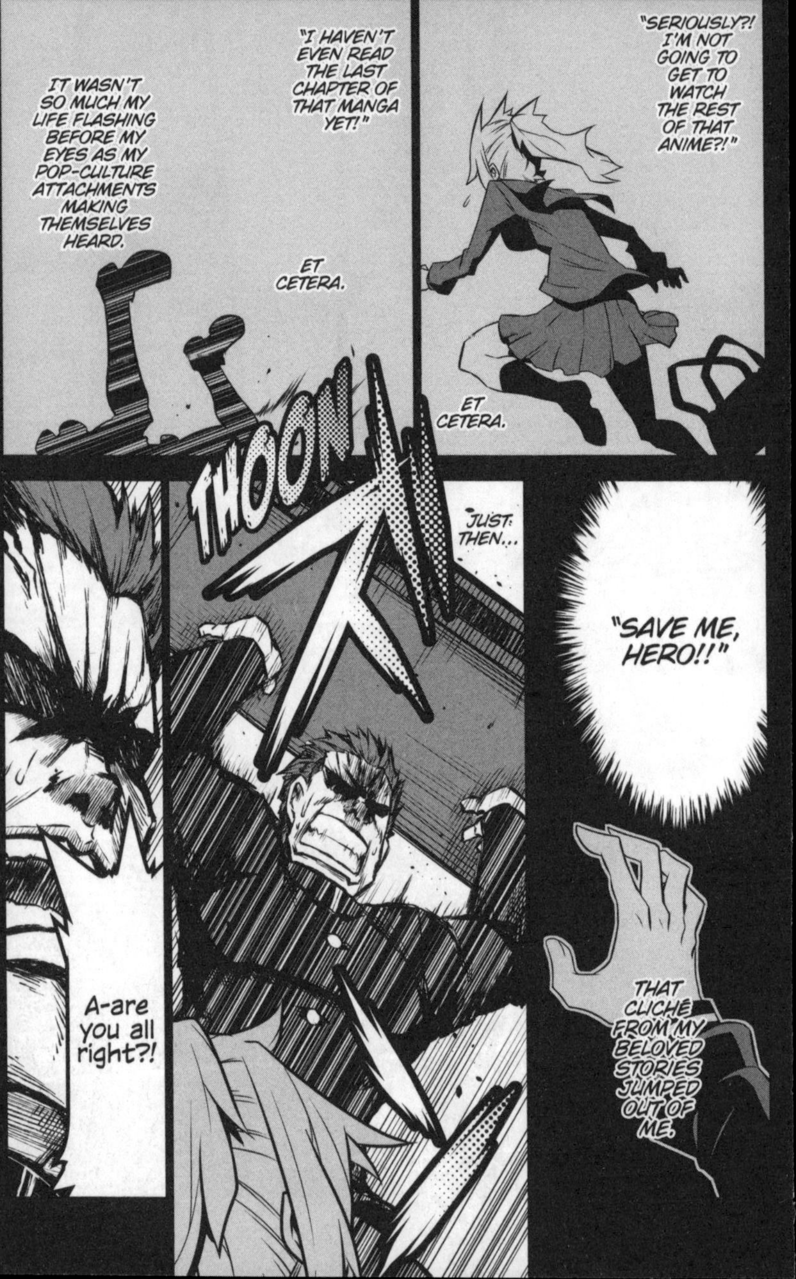
"SERIOUSLY?! I'M NOT GOING TO GET TO WATCH THE REST OF THAT ANIME?!"
ET CETERA.
"I HAVEN'T EVEN READ THE LAST CHAPTER OF THAT MANGA YET!"
IT WASN'T SO MUCH MY LIFE FLASHING BEFORE MY EYES AS MY POP-CULTURE ATTACHMENTS MAKING THEMSELVES HEARD.
ET CETERA.
"SAVE ME, HERO!!"
THAT CLICHE FROM MY BELOVED STORIES JUMPED OUT OF ME.
JUST THEN...
THOOM
A-are you all right?!

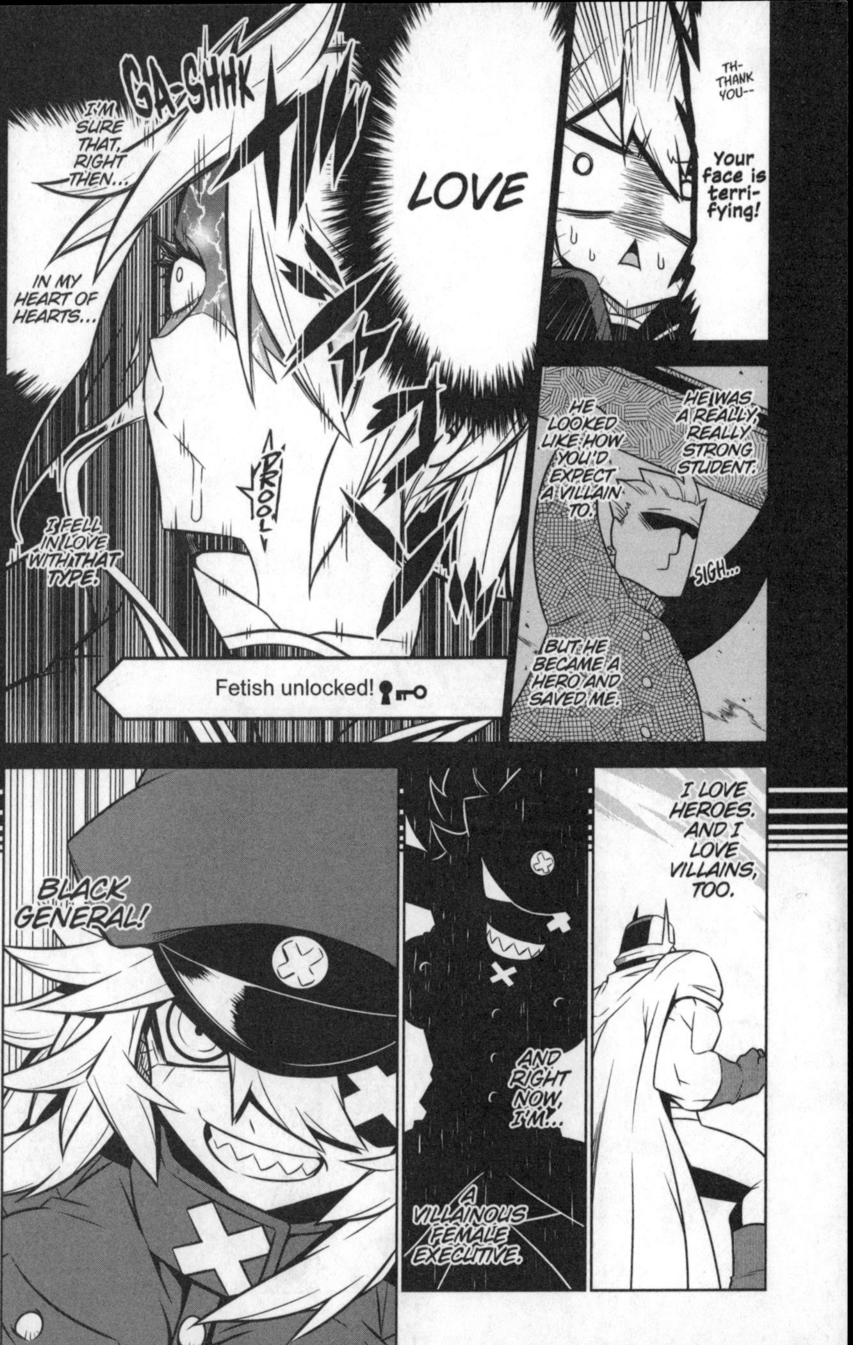
TH-THANK YOU--
Your face is terrifying!
HE WAS A REALLY, REALLY STRONG STUDENT.
HE LOOKED LIKE HOW YOU'D EXPECT A VILLAIN TO.
SIGH...
BUT HE BECAME A HERO AND SAVED ME.
GA-SHHK
I'M SURE THAT, RIGHT THEN...
IN MY HEART OF HEARTS...
LOVE
DROOL
I FELL IN LOVE WITH THAT TYPE.
Fetish unlocked!
I LOVE HEROES. AND I LOVE VILLAINS, TOO.
AND RIGHT NOW, I'M...
A VILLAINOUS FEMALE EXECUTIVE.
BLACK GENERAL!

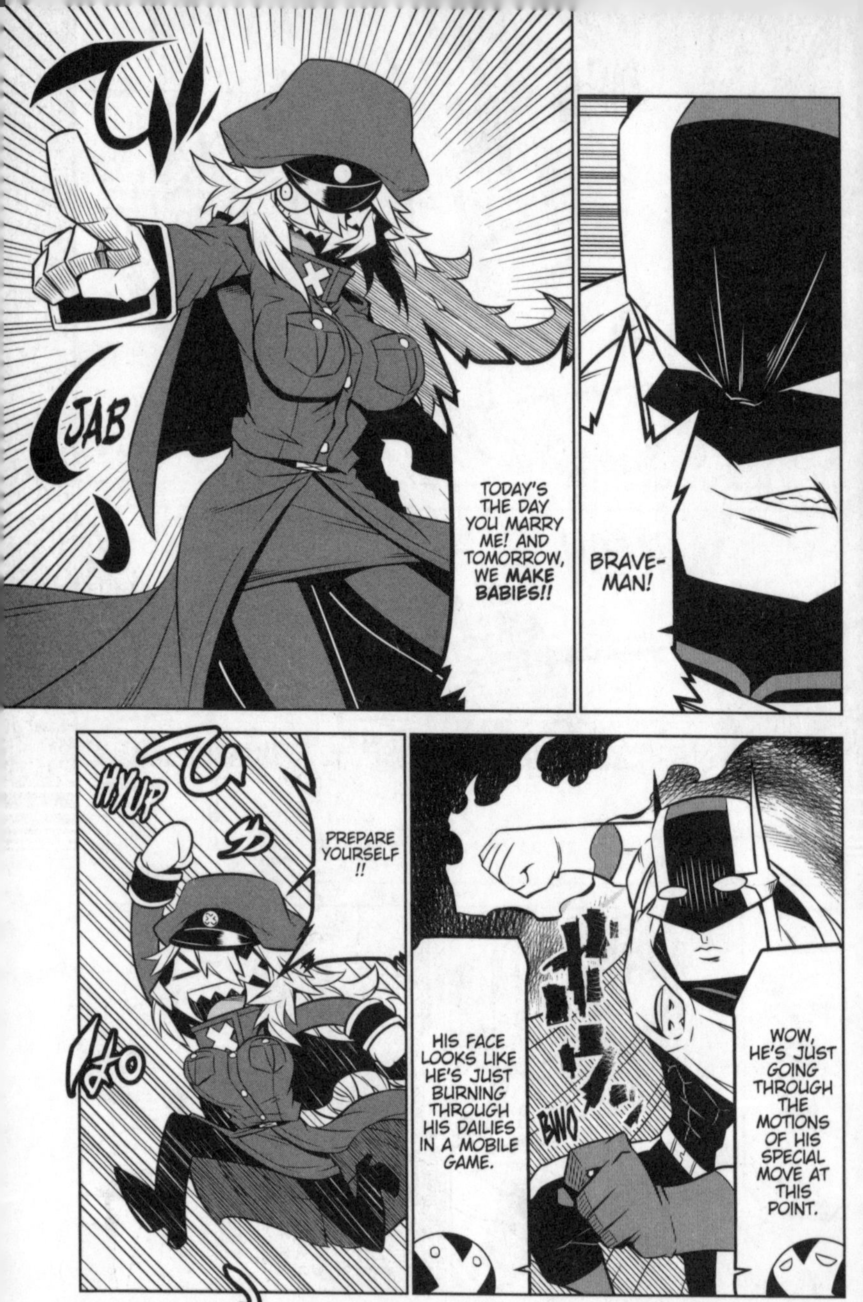
BRAVE-MAN!
TODAY'S THE DAY YOU MARRY ME! AND TOMORROW, WE MAKE BABIES!!
JAB
WOW, HE'S JUST GOING THROUGH THE MOTIONS OF HIS SPECIAL MOVE AT THIS POINT.
HIS FACE LOOKS LIKE HE'S JUST BURNING THROUGH HIS DAILIES IN A MOBILE GAME.
BWO
HYUP
PREPARE YOURSELF !!

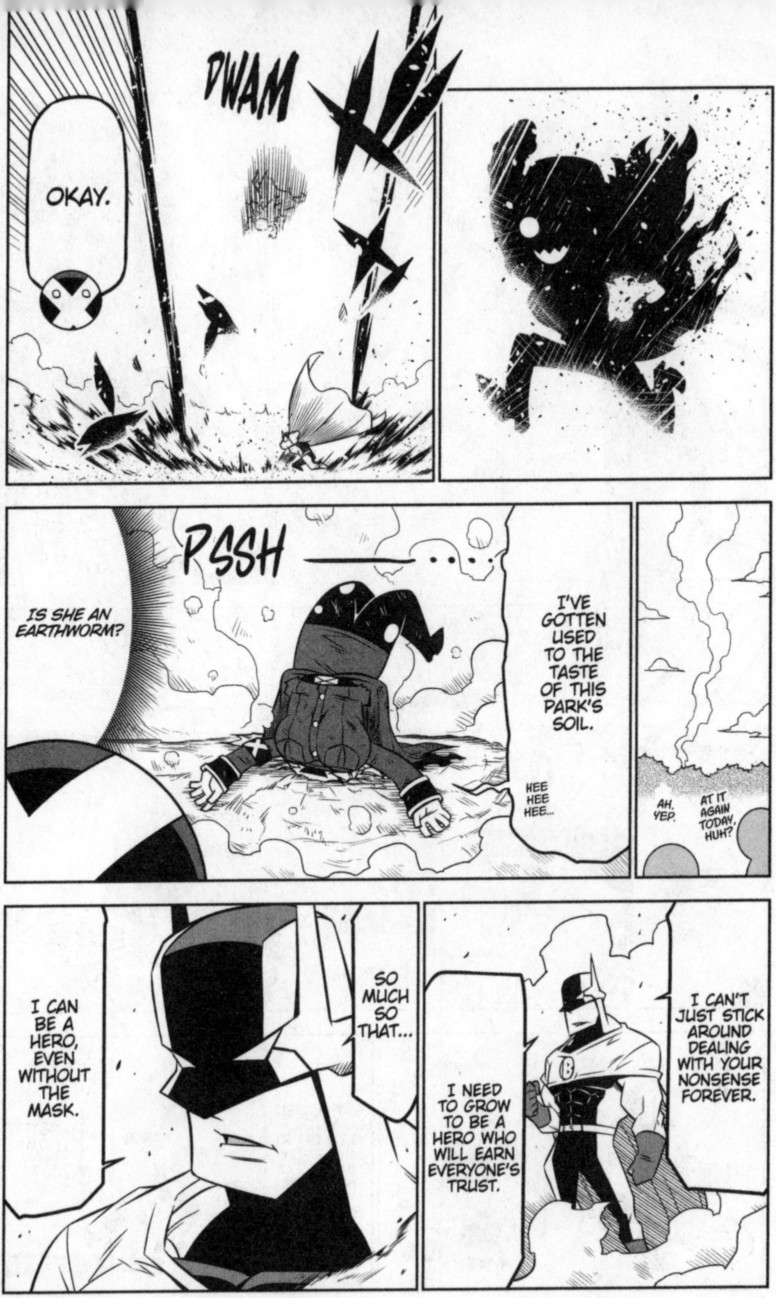
DWAM
OKAY.
AT IT AGAIN TODAY, HUH?
AH, YEP.
I'VE GOTTEN USED TO THE TASTE OF THIS PARK'S SOIL.
HEE HEE HEE...
——....
PSSH
IS SHE AN EARTHWORM?
I CAN'T JUST STICK AROUND DEALING WITH YOUR NONSENSE FOREVER.
I NEED TO GROW TO BE A HERO WHO WILL EARN EVERYONE'S TRUST.
SO MUCH SO THAT...
I CAN BE A HERO, EVEN WITHOUT THE MASK.

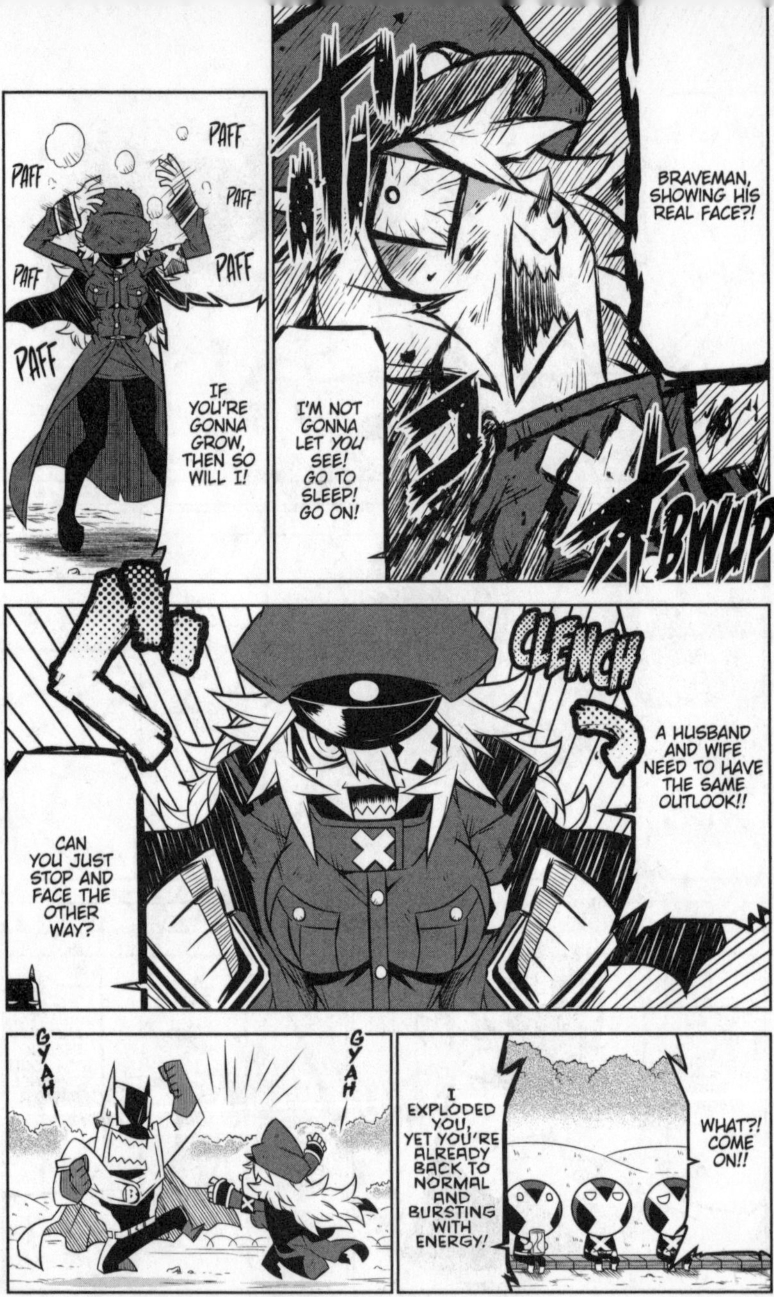
BRAVEMAN, SHOWING HIS REAL FACE?!
BWUP
I'M NOT GONNA LET YOU SEE! GO TO SLEEP! GO ON!
PAFF
PAFF
PAFF
PAFF
PAFF
PAFF
IF YOU'RE GONNA GROW, THEN SO WILL I!
CLENCH
A HUSBAND AND WIFE NEED TO HAVE THE SAME OUTLOOK!!
CAN YOU JUST STOP AND FACE THE OTHER WAY?
WHAT?! COME ON!!
I EXPLODED YOU, YET YOU'RE ALREADY BACK TO NORMAL AND BURSTING WITH ENERGY!
GYAH
GYAH

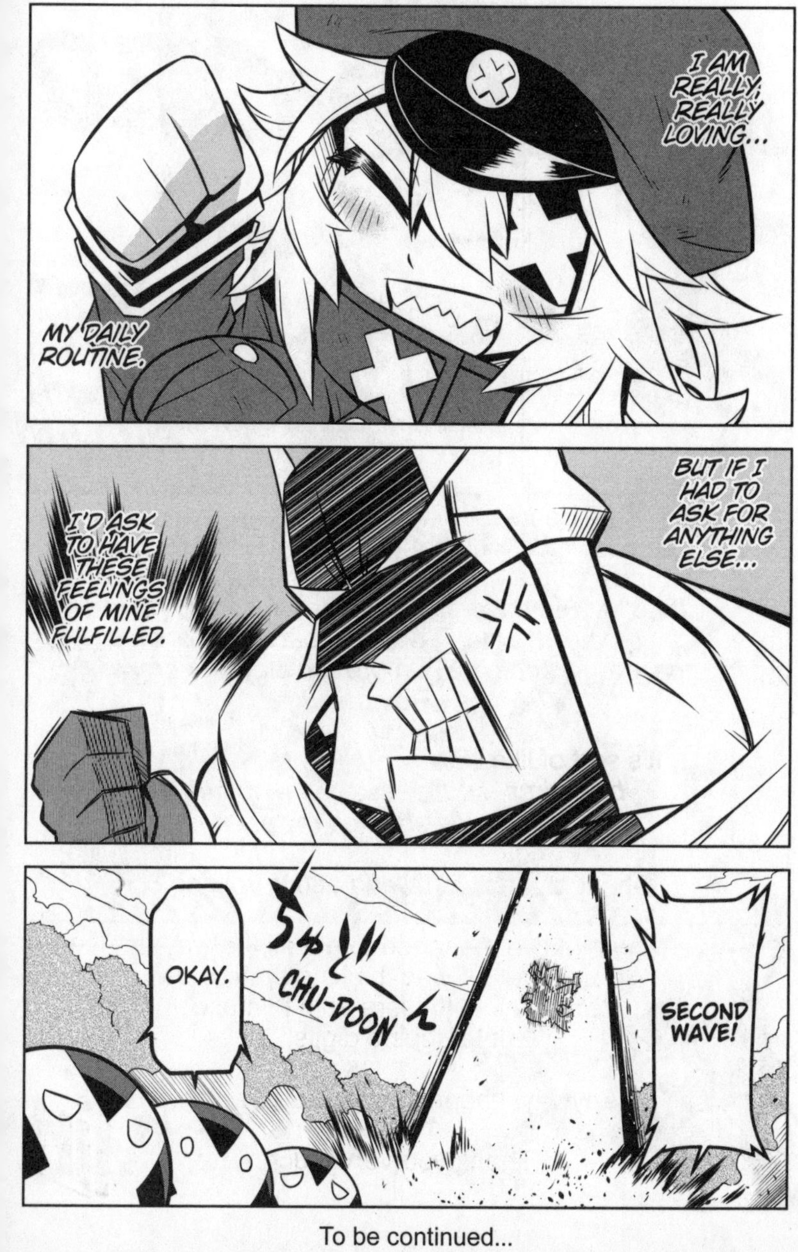
I AM REALLY, REALLY LOVING...
MY DAILY ROUTINE.
BUT IF I HAD TO ASK FOR ANYTHING ELSE...
I'D ASK TO HAVE THESE FEELINGS OF MINE FULFILLED.
SECOND WAVE!
ちゅど!!ーん
CHU-DOON
OKAY.

To be continued...

AFTERWORD

Thank you so much for purchasing Volume 8!

The world is being ravaged by a deadly disease, people are going about their lives wearing masks, and the words "tense situation" are repeatedly used in the news. Before, you'd only encounter something like this in a manga... I've been thinking about this a lot.

It's still depressing to deal with it every day, which is why I feel that entertainment really is a wonderful thing, especially now. I mean, think about it. You have thoughts like, *"I want to go to that movie theater. I want to read more of that manga. I want to have more fun playing games. I want to play gacha endlessly."*

It's sort of like, *"This is no time to be defeated by a virus. I'm busy over here. I need to earn my three stars on my phone."*

Oh, right, back to talking about Volume 8.

Now that I've managed to get all the way up to Volume 8, I was thinking that it'd be pretty nice if I were able to make it to double digits.

Anyway, I hope to see you all again.

Thank you very much.

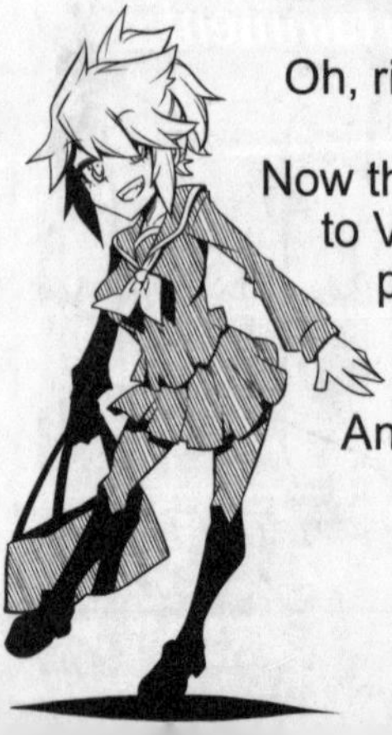

jin

SEVEN SEAS ENTERTAINMENT PRESENTS

PRECARIOUS WOMAN EXECUTIVE MISS BLACK GENERAL

story and art by **jin**

VOLUME 8

TRANSLATION
Timothy MacKenzie

ADAPTATION
T Campbell

LETTERING AND RETOUCH
Brandon Bovia

COVER DESIGN
Kris Aubin

PROOFREADER
Leighanna DeRouen

SENIOR EDITOR
Jenn Grunigen

PRINT MANAGER
Rhiannon Rasmussen-Silverstein

PRODUCTION DESIGNER
Christa Miesner

EDITOR-IN-CHIEF
Julie Davis

ASSOCIATE PUBLISHER
Adam Arnold

PUBLISHER
Jason DeAngelis

First published in Japan in 2021 by KADOKAWA CORPORATION, Tokyo.
English translation rights arranged with KADOKAWA CORPORATION, Tokyo.

Seven Seas press and purchase enquiries can be sent to Marketing Manager Lianne Sentar at press@gomanga.com. Information regarding the distribution and purchase of digital editions is available from Digital Manager CK Russell at digital@gomanga.com.

ISBN: 978-1-63858-331-8

Printed in Can

First Printing:

10 9 8 7 6

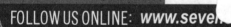

FOLLOW US ONLINE: ***www.seven***

READING DIRECTIONS

This book reads from ***right to left***, Japanese style. If this is your first time reading manga, you start reading from the top right panel on each page and take it from there. If you get lost, just follow the numbered diagram here. It may seem backwards at first, but you'll get the hang of it! Have fun!!

3
2
5
4
6
8
7
9

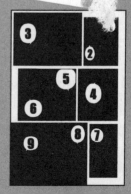

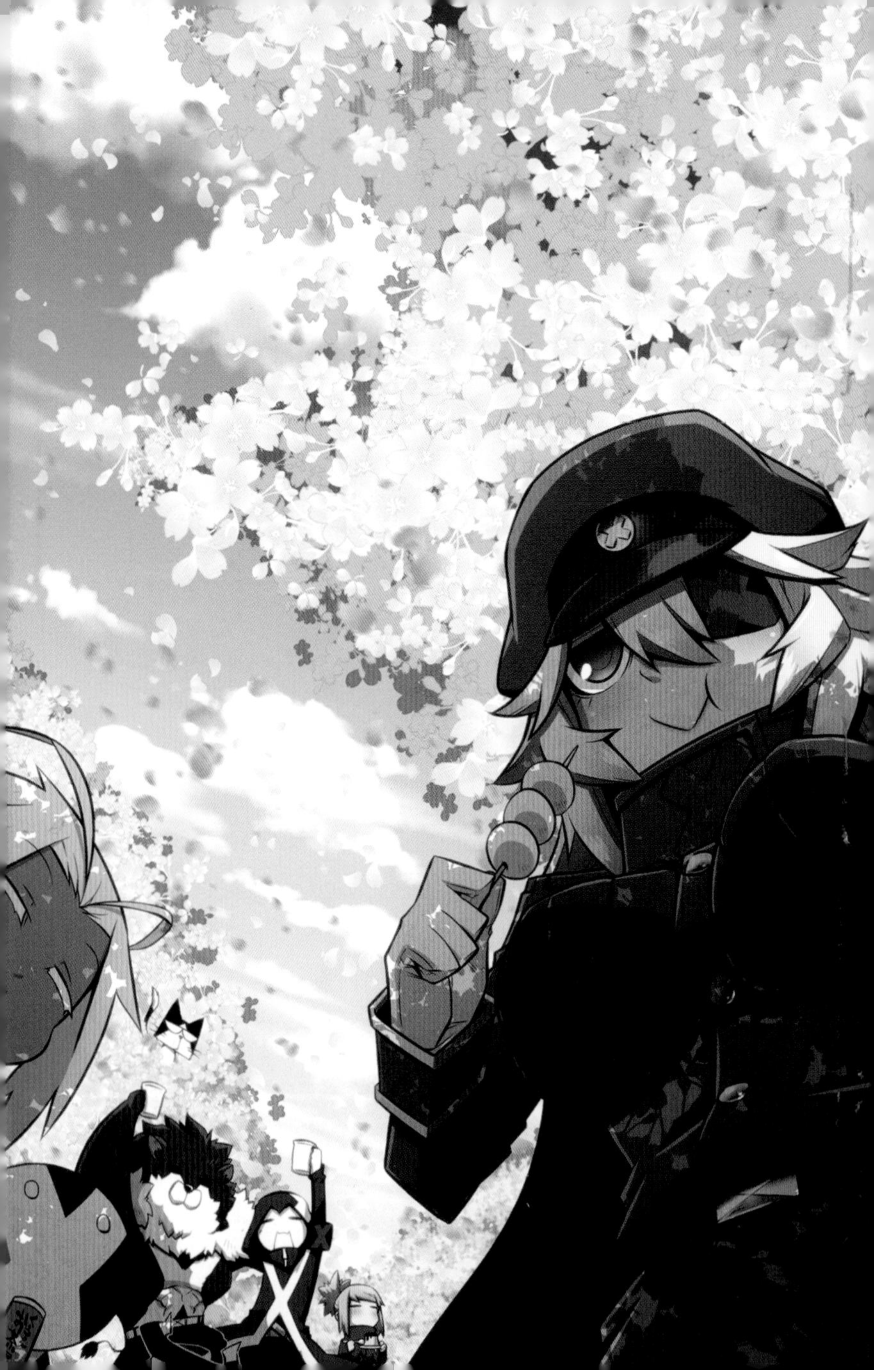

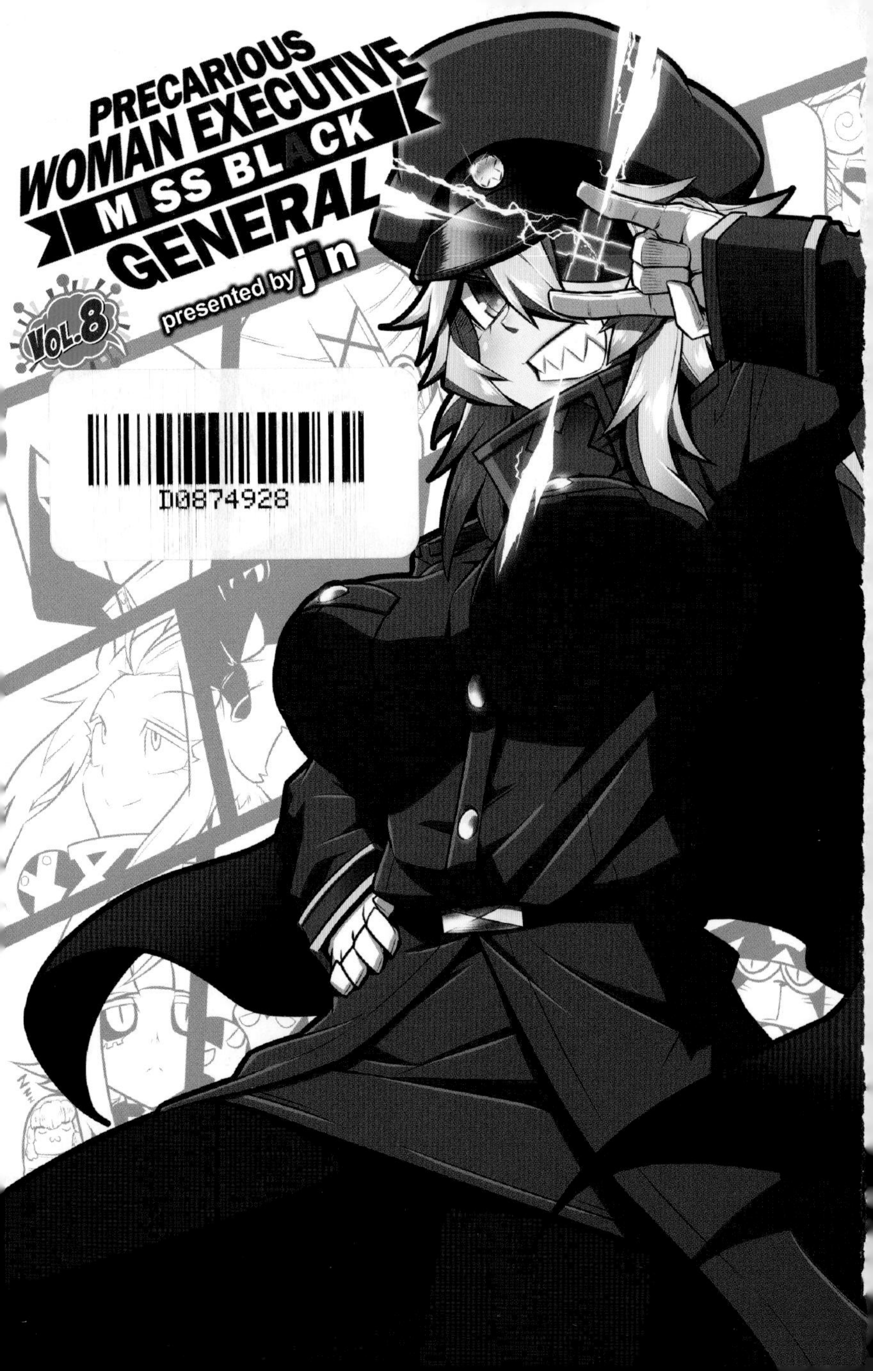
PRECARIOUS
WOMAN EXECUTIVE
MISS BLACK
GENERAL
presented by jin
VOL.8